MUSIC, MASTI, M
THE CINEMA OF N

AKSHAY MANWANI turned to freelance ⌐ ... 2009. He has since written on Indian cinema and popular culture for a variety of publications such as *The Caravan, The Indian Quarterly, Scroll.in, Mint, Business Standard* and *Mumbai Mirror.*

Akshay's first book, *Sahir Ludhianvi: The People's Poet,* was published in 2013 by HarperCollins. In 2014, Akshay won the RedInk award for Best Lifestyle and Entertainment Story, given by the Press Club, Mumbai, for his detailed feature on B.R. Chopra's television series *Mahabharat.* Akshay lives with his daughter and wife in Mumbai. He is a proud homemaker.

Courtesy: NH Films/Nuzhat Khan

MUSIC, MASTI, MODERNITY

The Cinema of Nasir Husain

Akshay Manwani

HarperCollins *Publishers* India

First published in India in 2016 by
HarperCollins *Publishers* India
Building No 10, Tower A, 4th Floor, DLF Cyber City, Phase II,
Gurugram – 122002
www.harpercollins.co.in

1 2 3 4 5 6 7 8 9 10

P-ISBN for PB edition: 978-93-5264-096-6
P-ISBN for HB edition: 978-93-5264-232-8
E-ISBN: 978-93-5264-097-3

Typeset in 12/15 Adobe Garamond Pro at
SŪRYA, New Delhi

To
Mom, Dad, Amma, Achchan,
Naina and Vidya

Nasir Husain Family Tree

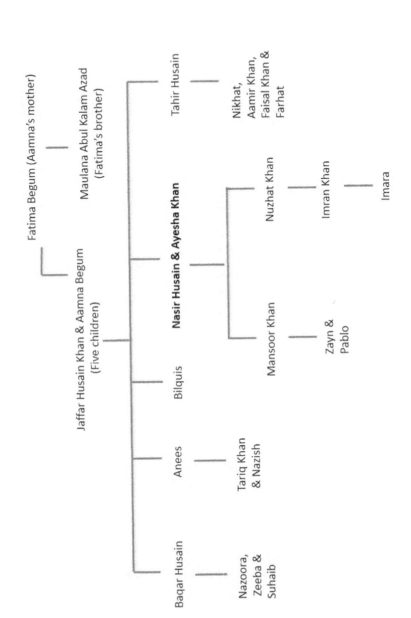

The screen turns to a dark, cloudy sky. There is thunder and lightning. A shimmering disk appears against this backdrop, accompanied by music that has a certain magical quality about it. As the background score gently works its way to a crescendo, finishing with a flourish of cymbals, a Greek column-like pedestal, bearing the 'NH Films' insignia, appears against a smoke-filled screen. Almost instantly, a booming voice recites a couplet, with a soft but distinct drum roll accompanying the oration. The couplet goes:

Kya ishq ne samjha hai, kya husn ne jaana hai?
Hum khaaq-nasheenon ki thokar mein zamaana hai

The voiceover ends with an emphatic drumbeat. The credits follow led by the opening credit, NASIR HUSAIN FILMS Presents...

CONTENTS

FOREWORD

Aamir Khan

One of my earliest memories of Chachajaan is him coming home from work and suddenly deciding, on the spur of the moment, to take all the kids to Khandala! So he bundled all the kids – Nuzhat, Mansoor, Nazish, Nikhat, Faisal and me – into the backseat of his car, Chachijaan sat in front with him, and off we went for a sudden adventure listening to the Beatles.

I think for me his films have this same quality. They are spontaneous, full of adventure, romance, fun, music and the outdoors … and highly entertaining … like a sudden freak holiday … and, there is always a journey in there somewhere.

The incident I described above probably happened around 1969-1970. You might be wondering how we listened to music in the car back then. At that time cars didn't have built-in music systems. This was before even cassette decks had come in. Well, Chachajaan had modified a turntable, and had got that fixed in his car. He had built his own music system for his car! It had a bouncy spring mechanism inside to keep the record steady, but on larger bumps it would skip. The records were the small 45 RPM types that were meant to be played at home on a regular turntable, but the centre of the record had to be cut into a larger hole to make them play in this gizmo. This should give you an idea just how much into music he was.

Chachajaan has always been like a father figure to me. My father, while very loving, caring and providing, was not around very often, and when he was, we were too scared of him to get too close. Chachajaan was different. He was always fun to be with. He was kind, gentle, caring, intelligent, with an amazing sense of humour. He was a natural storyteller. I was drawn to him. All the kids, his own, their friends, his nieces and nephews, were always happy to be around him. He was never strict, never giving us lectures, never boring, always exciting, always a naughty smile playing on his lips.

Half my childhood was spent at 'Pali', as the house was called. Since we lived right next door, at the slightest chance Nikhat and I would pop over. Both Chachajaan and Chachijaan were always welcoming. They were happy to see the house filled with kids. When I think about it now, it must have been quite a strain on them to have us around ALL the time. But never once did they make us feel unwanted or unwelcome. Such love and generosity! I truly feel privileged. Pali has been a very significant part of my growing-up years. A lot of what I am today is a result of those happy times I spent there, and all that I absorbed while growing up.

I feel very privileged for one more reason: I got to work under Chachajaan. I quit my formal education after completing junior college and started working with him as an assistant director. This brought me even closer to him. For four years I spent every waking moment with him. I sat in on all his meetings (creative and otherwise), music sessions with Pancham Uncle and Majrooh Sa'ab, business meetings with distributors and financiers. I travelled with him, ate with him, watched films with him, gave him his medicine, discussed everything under the sun with him.

Those four years were one of my biggest learnings ... my college! Working with him I got to see his professional side, and it was exactly the same as his personal side. He was very much the same person: jovial, full of fun, sharp sense of humour. His sets were like a picnic. Everyone working in good humour. The mood and atmosphere of any working space is created by the boss. And what a boss. Talented, kind, thoughtful, caring, intelligent, always cracking jokes. The only thing I discovered about him at work which I had not noticed at home was his leadership quality. Chachajaan was a natural leader, and everyone loved to follow him. He had a very quiet aggressive side to him, but which was never negative. It was a life force which propelled him.

Watching him work taught me many things about film-making, but more than that it taught me so many things which we never imagine to be a part of film-making but in fact are critical and essential to how a film turns out. One of the most important in that list is people management. How to handle stars, how to handle creative people, how to handle business people, when to be soft, when to put pressure, how to get out of a sticky situation, and the all-important: crisis management.

There was only one thing I was not able to learn from him, try as I might ... and that is, how to disconnect from my work. Chachajaan managed this beautiful balance between his professional responsibilities and his personal life. He always managed to finish his work by 6-6.30 p.m. and would be home by around 7 p.m. He spent a lot of time with family, at home. And when he was with family he was not distracted by thoughts of work. He was a man who believed in moderation, for example, two drinks every night, never more. I'm an obsessive personality, a person of extremes. Moderation is the one thing I was not able to imbibe from him.

Chachajaan is the person who gave me my first opportunity to act. I owe my career to him, and to Mansoor who directed my first film. Chachajaan was always so proud and happy to see me progress, grow from strength to strength. He saw me make mistakes, learn from my mistakes. He never told me what to do and what not to do. He let me be on my own. I always knew I could go to him for anything but he never imposed his thoughts on me. What a rare person.

My proudest moment was when I invited him and Chachijaan to the first day of shooting of the first film I produced, *Lagaan* (2001). My dad was there, my mother was there. These four people, Ammi, Abbajaan, Chachajaan and Chachijaan were the ones who had taught me a lot of what I have learnt in the journey of my life. I was so happy to show them the village set we had built in Kutch. I walked them around the location to show them all the production arrangements we had made. Their proud beaming faces brought tears to my eyes. They had held me in their hands when I was born, and now I had finally started my own company! I was a grown man now.

By and large, I am a happy man, with few regrets. One of my biggest regrets is that Chachijaan was not there when *Lagaan* released. She passed away a day after we completed the shoot. She never got to see the film.

Another big regret for me is that Chachajaan did not get to see *Taare Zameen Par* (2007), the first film I directed. I so, so wanted to show him what I had made. But he passed away soon after Chachijaan, in fact a year and a half later.

And my last regret is that both he and Chachijaan were not around to see their grandson become an actor. Imran, whom I launched in *Jaane Tu ... Ya Jaane Na* (2008). We all miss them so much.

I would like to thank Akshay Manwani for writing this book on Chachajaan, so that lovers of Indian cinema can read about him and his amazing work, and his films, which gave all of India so much joy. Chachajaan is one of the greatest film-makers we have had, and through this book we can cherish him and perhaps learn.

INTRODUCTION

It's hard to explain a book on Nasir Husain's cinema. He is not Mehboob Khan, V. Shantaram, Guru Dutt, Raj Kapoor or Bimal Roy, the high priests of Indian cinema, who merged social consciousness with box-office trappings. Neither is he Yash Chopra whose films have a certain seriousness, a certain intensity about them. Unlike Hrishikesh Mukherjee, his films do not celebrate the personal, intimate view. Nor does Husain have one genre-defining or groundbreaking film like K. Asif's *Mughal-E-Azam* (1960), Ramesh Sippy's *Sholay* (1975), Manmohan Desai's *Amar Akbar Anthony* (1977) or Ram Gopal Varma's *Satya* (1998). Two of Husain's best films are credited largely to the talents of other men. *Teesri Manzil* (1966), with its crisp editing and interesting cinematography, is testimony to Vijay Anand's terrific cinematic sensibilities. *Qayamat Se Qayamat Tak* (1988), which brought back a certain innocent romance amidst all the violent and garish films of the 1980s, is seen as Husain's son, Mansoor Khan's film.

But Husain is important. Making his directorial debut with *Tumsa Nahin Dekha* in 1957, Husain's films ushered in a new idiom. That he deliberately distanced himself from the nation-building narratives of the films of the post-independence era and perfected a certain kind of 'rom-com-musical' that was uniquely his, doesn't make his cinema any less meaningful. His cinema was entirely about entertainment. And he was unapologetic about it. 'I couldn't make the kind of films Mrinal Sen or Shyam Benegal makes. They are very good films, but it's not my style. I make entertainment films mainly for college kids, not for the elite.'[1]

Herein lies the problem. It is fashionable for a majority of those who write, critique or comment on Indian cinema to disregard anything frothy or fun. As Kaushik Bhaumik, associate professor at the School of Arts and Aesthetics, Jawaharlal Nehru University, New Delhi, said, 'It is the Gandhian guilt about fun. Nation-building was all very serious and everybody had to work very hard. No time for fun.' This is in complete contrast to the regard with which the Busby Berkeley and Vincente Minnelli musicals, or the films starring Fred Astaire and Gene Kelly, are held in the West. They are a very important part of American film tradition. 'In the Hollywood context, nobody is embarrassed about the big entertainment days. The late-1920s, early-1930s are considered heritage ... as part of American culture. The same attitude should be taken towards entertainment cinema made in India,' added Bhaumik.

Moreover, as film critic and author Jai Arjun Singh noted, 'Good cinema is not required to follow a specific, restricted model (say, the model of psychological realism as established by the European avant-garde or the American indie movement) ... In assessing a film, the far more relevant question is whether it has succeeded in realizing an integrated, internally consistent world – irrespective of whether that world is founded on hyper-drama or kitchen-sink realism or one of the many, many things in between.'[2]

This is precisely why Husain's work is significant. Within the contours of his own cinematic world, there is reflection on Indian

---

[1]Deepa Gahlot, 'It's the chase that is exciting', *Filmfare*, 01-15 November 1984, p. 77.

[2]Jai Arjun Singh, Jabberwock, 'Response to a column (and more thoughts on *Ship of Theseus*)', 27 July 2013, http://jaiarjun.blogspot.in/2013/07/response-to-column-and-more-thoughts-on.html

life and culture. His films place on record a cosmopolitanism and modernity in Indian society at a certain point in time – a largely untold story. Sure, his films have a distinct Western element, but how well they have been adapted to the Indian context. These are films laden with references and influences, from music to literature to the cinema of other directors and cultures. His song sequences speak of more than just an ear for good music; they are masterpieces of presentation and picturization. With every new movie, his dialogue-writing, yet another of his numerous talents, kept pace with changing times – moving from the Hindustani flavour of the 1950s and 1960s, to the 'Angry Young Man' cinema of the 1970s, to expressing the language of young, eternal love played out between Raj (Aamir Khan) and Rashmi (Juhi Chawla) in *Qayamat Se Qayamat Tak*. Through films like *Munimji* (1955), *Dil Deke Dekho* (1959), *Teesri Manzil* (1966), *Yaadon Ki Baaraat* (1973), *Hum Kisise Kum Naheen* (1977), *Qayamat Se Qayamat Tak* (1988) and *Jo Jeeta Wohi Sikandar* (1992), and over a career spanning forty-five years, Husain had a major impact in shaping Hindi cinema's legacy as it exists today.

Most importantly, he had, what the eminent film historian Nasreen Munni Kabir called, 'an individual voice, which was different from the others. You cannot say he was copying Bimal Roy, Mehboob sa'ab or Raj Kapoor or Kidar Sharma. He was not copying anyone.'

A few points need to be kept in mind while reading this book. This book is not a biography which looks at Husain's personal life in great detail. Instead, it focuses essentially on Husain's cinematic craft. If there are references to his life (as there are of his early life and his later years), these are merely to understand where he came from, the influences that shaped his sensibilities and the effect the withdrawal from films had on him. If one is looking for more sensational accounts of Husain's personal life or his life beyond films, this is not that book.

Secondly, this is not a strictly linear account of Husain's work. Instead, the endeavour is to examine the dominant themes, tropes, styles, sensibilities and impact of Husain's cinema by referring to his films across decades. However, a general linearity has been maintained, to understand Husain's evolution as a film-maker and how he adapted to the changing times. An attempt has, therefore, been made to discuss some of the broad developments and trends in Hindi cinema around Husain's time in the industry.

In the second season of Zee Classic's fine programme, *Classic Legends*, one of the episodes featured Nasir Husain. The show's host, the scriptwriter–lyricist Javed Akhtar, traced the many wonderful things Husain did over his career. At the end of the show, Akhtar remarked, 'It is time that someone spoke about Nasir Husain and told people what his legacy is. I feel that people don't realize how much Nasir Husain's direction, his writing, his films impacted mainstream cinema. But if we tell people, it would be good.'

This book is a modest attempt to address Akhtar's plea.

PROLOGUE

At the third edition of the Zee Cine Awards held at the Andheri Sports Complex in Mumbai in 2000, among the last awards given out on the night was the Lifetime Achievement Award. With a bevy of film personalities and stars, including Anil Kapoor, Sharmila Tagore, Rituparno Ghosh, Govinda, Boney Kapoor, Sridevi, Sanjay Leela Bhansali, Anupam Kher, Anand Bakshi and Sushmita Sen in attendance, the actor Shammi Kapoor, now at the cusp of seventy, took centre stage to hand out the award to writer–director–producer, Nasir Husain. Mike in hand, and dressed in an azure kurta and white pyjamas, with a rather large beaded mala strung around his neck, and a big, bold tilak on his forehead matching his enormous frame, Shammi launched into an extended soliloquy on the rich legacy of the man standing to his immediate right. From modulating his voice to produce the necessary inflection, to pausing to create the right effect, to taking great effort in enunciating clearly each of the superlatives to describe Husain's film career, Shammi's speech was filled with nostalgia, emotion, admiration and sincerity. This was, after all, about the man who had dramatically changed Shammi's destiny for the better, many, many years ago.

'Ladies and gentlemen, I feel very honoured today to give this very prestigious Lux Zee Cine award for lifetime achievement to a friend of mine I have great love and respect for, for a very distinguished career, for the lovely films he has given us, for the happy days we have spent together, watching him and his career make a graph which I don't think will ever be tenable by a lot of film-makers, who attempt to do so. Because he gave us very clean, happy, musical entertainers. We can never forget his great films, with great music, great heroes including Shammi Kapoor. I made *Tumsa Nahin Dekha* with him, his very first directorial picture [*sic*]. And that graph is something to be talked about and remembered. And the great musicals that he made, the great music he gave us, right from O.P. Nayyar's *Tumsa Nahin Dekha* and *Phir Wohi Dil Laya Hoon* to Shankar–Jaikishan in the great picture [*sic*] *Jab Pyar Kisise Hota Hai*. And the R.D. Burman movies, the great period of R.D. Burman music, right from *Teesri Manzil* and *Hum Kisise Kum Naheen, Caravan, Pyar Ka Mausam*, the great, great Nasir Husain, my friend and his wife, Asha.[1] I have pleasure, I have great pleasure in announcing this award and presenting it to them. Ladies and gentlemen, let's give them a standing ovation. Nasir Husain!'

As the audience rose to its feet in applause, and the night sky burst into a spectacle of fireworks, a fragile, seventy-four-year-old Husain, dressed in a tweed jacket, maroon shirt and black trousers for the evening, spoke up. With his wife, Ayesha Khan, draped in a white satin sari, standing coyly behind him, Husain, in complete contrast to Shammi Kapoor's 130-second-long tribute, offered a succinct, one-line assessment of his film career: 'Good evening! *Picturein banaayee nahin jaateen, aap hi bann jaati hain.* (Films are not made, they happen on their own.) Thank you.'

---

[1]Husain's wife. Her proper name after marriage was Ayesha Khan.

1

SHAREER LADKA TO ALMOST DIPLOMAT

'Badmaash? Gundaa? Lafangaa? Jee woh teeno yahaan nahin rehtey.
Kisi ne galat bata diya hoga. Aagey dekhiye.'
(Scoundrel? Rogue? Rascal? None of these people live here. You
have been misinformed. Go, look elsewhere.)
– Ramesh (Dev Anand) in *Paying Guest* (1957)

From his days at Alexandra High School, Bhopal, Nasir Husain recalled a classmate, Mansoor Ali Khan. 'Mansoor was the best at academics. He would come first class first.' Before their matriculation examinations, Mansoor asked the headmaster, one Mr Qureshi, in front of the entire class, how many students would pass the examination. Giving the question some thought, the headmaster surveyed all the students carefully. He cast his eyes on Husain. *'Agar Nasir pass ho gaya toh sab pass ho jaayenge* (If Nasir passes, everyone will),' said the headmaster. 'And that's exactly what happened. I passed with the bare minimum, 33 per cent marks, a third class. When I went to meet the headmaster, he said, "*Pata nahin kya dhool jhonki hai aur imtihaan pass kiya hai* (I don't know how you managed to pass)."'[1]

---

[1] Unless explicitly attributed to a different source, all quotes by Nasir Husain in this book are from his interview with Nasreen Munni Kabir on 18 August 2001.

1

It's a story Husain told Nasreen Munni Kabir with some delight, but the irony of the episode lies in the fact that Husain's father, Jaffar Husain Khan, was the first graduate from Shahabad, Uttar Pradesh, and a schoolteacher. Jaffar Husain was a Pathan and belonged to a family of zamindars, albeit of modest landholdings, settled in Shahabad. When Jaffar Husain married Aamna, he was told by the girl's family, 'Aap Bhopal mein hi rahiye (You have to live in Bhopal).' Aamna, Husain's mother, was of Arab ancestry. Her forefathers originally hailed from Jeddah before successive generations found their way to Calcutta, finally settling in Bhopal.

Jaffar Husain and Aamna were poles apart intellectually, as Husain's daughter, Nuzhat Khan, told me. Nuzhat is the younger of Husain's two children, the older being the film-maker–author–organic farm owner, Mansoor Khan. Nuzhat lives in 24 Pali Hill, the very same bungalow Husain bought in Mumbai's plush Bandra West area immediately after the spectacular success of his first home production, *Jab Pyar Kisise Hota Hai* (1961). Just outside the house, a beautiful white, three-storeyed structure ('We refer to the third floor as *Teesri Manzil*,' Nuzhat said), one can still find the words 'NASIR HUSAIN HOUSE' written in bold, capital letters.

Nuzhat is a practising psychoanalyst. She had her tryst with cinema when she co-wrote *Qayamat Se Qayamat Tak* (1988) with Husain. She is also the mother of the actor Imran Khan. The first time I interviewed Nuzhat was in Imran's study, an arc-shaped corner-office-like space cut off from the rest of Nasir Husain House, on the ground floor. The room is immaculately kept. Two large, colour posters of *Jab Pyar Kisise Hota Hai* and *Teesri Manzil* (1966) are framed on the left wall as you enter the room.

'My grandmother used to call herself "*middle-pass*", whatever that means. She was one of those ladies concerned with "*isne yeh kar diya, woh kar diya, arrey woh naukaron se jhagdaa kar raha hai* (household gossip, look he's picked a fight with the servants),'" Nuzhat said. At the other end was Husain's father, a history teacher at Alexandra High School, who liked to talk about life and give his views. 'I think the only graduate in Shahabad, a schoolteacher, would have had some kind of worldview.'

Nasir Husain Khan was born in Bhopal on 16 November 1926, the fourth of five children. The eldest of Husain's siblings was a brother, Baqar Husain. Then there were his two sisters, Anees and Bilquis. Husain's youngest sibling was Tahir Husain, the actor Aamir Khan's father.

But Husain's father wasn't the only man who would have a bearing on his life. His maternal grandmother, Fatima Begum, was a well-educated woman and was appointed the inspector of schools by the nawaab of Bhopal. This lady's brother was the well-known freedom fighter and scholar Maulana Abul Kalam Azad. At a later stage, it would be Maulana sa'ab who would play a pivotal role in clearing the way for Husain's foray into films.

The only earning member of his family, Jaffar Husain was a man of limited means. As Javed Akhtar noted wryly of Jaffar Husain's state despite his connection with Maulana, 'This harks back to a time when a minister's relatives could be poor as well.'[2] The young Husain, however, was a spendthrift. He described himself as quite a '*shaukeen* (extravagant) boy, a *paidaaeesh* [sic] *badmaash* (instinctively mischievous) – I used to spend all my time in coffee houses and picture houses. And I'd smoke. All expensive habits.'[3]

Husain's siblings echoed his sentiment. '*Nasir bahut shareer aur shaitaan bachcha thaa* (Nasir was a very impish and naughty

[2]Zee Classic's *Classic Legends: Season II*, featuring Nasir Husain.

[3]Resham Shaam, 'Little Big Man', *Super*, May 1978.

child),' said ninety-year-old Anees Bano, Husain's sister and Tariq Khan's (the youngest of the three brothers in *Yaadon Ki Baaraat*, 1973) mother. Tahir Husain wrote, '"Vagabond", "wayward" and similar epithets were used to describe Nasir, my elder brother during the early days of our childhood and youth. Not a day passed without someone or the other from the neighbourhood or school coming to lodge a complaint against him. For no rhyme or reason, he would often quarrel with a boy from a good family, or get into some scrape.'[4]

Anees elaborated. 'He would be out all day flying kites, playing gilli-danda, bringing home abandoned kittens and feeding them. He would get scolded a lot … During Ramzan, the cook in our house would start cooking only after breaking the roza. One day, she was waiting to break the roza. In those days, the breaking of the roza was signalled by three cannon shots being fired. This lady was a little hard of hearing. As she waited to hear the shots, Nasir found an empty water tank *aur dham dham teen baja diye* (and clanged it three times). The poor soul broke her roza.'

'He was the black sheep of the family,' Nuzhat confirmed. 'There was definitely the rebel in him right from the beginning because in every story he told me, he was not the good boy.' But such behaviour went hand-in-hand with his desperation to be loved and accepted by his father. He was constantly trying to win his father's approval, even if it meant biting the bitter pill, sometimes quite literally. 'Mealtime was the one time they could get the attention of their dad. Everybody else hated karela. Bitter. Dad would somehow get it down just to hear his dad say, "*Dekho, Nasir ko dekho, karela khaata hai* (Look at Nasir, he is the only one who eats bitter gourd)."'

Husain also tripped over himself in this process. 'Once, he was trotting along, smoking a cigarette. He saw his dad coming

---

[4]Tahir Husain, 'My brother Nasir', *Star & Style*, 1 October 1971, p. 39.

along the path and put the cigarette into his pocket. And smoke started coming out of it while he was talking because [his] dad called him,' said Nuzhat, chuckling, before adding a sobering note, 'He got quite a whacking for that apparently.'

These incidents from Husain's early years were perhaps what inspired such episodes and behaviour in the heroes of his films in later life. Think of the Dev Anand character from *Paying Guest* (1957) or any one of the Shammi Kapoor characters from Husain's three films with the actor, and words like 'shareer', 'shaitaan' can easily be associated with them. In *Paying Guest*, for which Husain wrote the screenplay and dialogue, when Ramesh (Dev Anand), a struggling lawyer, has managed to literally put a stick through the ceiling of his paying guest accommodation, an angry Shanti (Nutan) rushes down to confront him since the stick has found its way through the flooring of her first-floor home. Soon enough, Shanti is joined by her father, Babu Digambernath (Gyani).

> Babu Digambernath: *Main poochhta hoon, yeh kya harqat hai?* (What is this you have done?)
>
> Ramesh: *Harqat toh aap dekh hi rahe hain, poochhne ki kya zaroorat hai?* (You can see it for yourself, why ask?)
>
> Babu Digambernath: *Achha, ek toh chori, upar se seena zori.* (First you do something wrong and then you behave shamefully.)
>
> Ramesh: *Jee nahin, neechey se seena zori...* (I am quite shameless, you see.)[5]
>
> Babu Digambernath: *Badmaash, lafangey, thehar toh sahi* (You scoundrel, you rogue, I will teach you a lesson.)
>
> Shanti: *Babuji, babuji, aap gussa na kijiye, aapko khoon ka daura*

---

[5]The dialogue is a clever wordplay on the popular Hindi idiom, 'ek toh chori, upar se seena zori', and probably untranslatable. Husain plays upon the bit 'upar se' (on top of it) and inverts it to 'neechey se'.

pad jaayega. Aaiye, chalein. Iss badmaash ke moonh na lagey. Main isey dekh loongi. (Father, father, please don't get angry. You could have a stroke. Come, let's leave. Don't indulge this rascal any more. I will sort him out.)

Ramesh: *Mera khyaal hai yahi behtar hai.* (I would really enjoy that.)

Shanti: Shut up!

The impishness in Dev Anand's demeanour in this scene is identifiable with the adjectives used for Husain by his family in their telling of his early years. It is from those days that Husain developed his fascination for storytelling and drama as well. 'When he was young, he was interested in performing and showing off. He would play Sheikh Chilli.[6] He couldn't do it openly. So he would do it at the back of the house, where the servants lived, for all our friends from the neighbourhood, the kids. He would enact Sheikh Chilli's mannerisms. All the kids would clap,' remembered Anees. It was probably from the domestic help in the house that Husain learned of Sheikh Chilli and his stories.

Tahir Husain also wrote of Husain's drama endeavours. 'In the evenings, he [Husain] was often untraceable. Then one day, a close friend of the family informed us that Nasir spent his evenings in presenting some sort of skit in one locality or the other. The news was a great shock to the entire family because those days, all entertainers, including stage-actors and film personalities, were frowned upon by society.'[7]

Husain's only explanation was, 'Ours was an extremely orthodox family ... but I always wanted something different out

---

[6]A Sufi saint, famous for his follies and simplicity, who somehow morphed into a popular children's character in subcontinental literature.

[7]Tahir Husain, 'My brother Nasir', *Star & Style*, 1 October 1971, p. 39.

of life.'[8] Nuzhat concurred. 'In my dad's mind, he always thought himself to be special compared to his siblings.'

The other interest that Husain had from the very beginning was reading. 'P.G. Wodehouse was my favourite writer. Shafiq-ur-Rahman [Pakistani humourist and Urdu short-story writer] ... I used to read all kinds of books. I was a member of a library from where I used to borrow a book every week. That's how I managed to read so many books and this is how I started writing.' On the kind of stories he liked to read, Husain replied, 'Anything strange happening in them.' As late as 1978, well after *Hum Kisise Kum Naheen* (1977) had proved to be another of Husain's commercial blockbusters, Husain kept up with his reading habit. 'I read a lot. About eight-ten books a month. One has to keep growing, keep learning.'[9]

But so long as Jaffar Husain was around, Husain couldn't indulge his other love, films. This was after all an era when Hindi cinema was not for the educated. '*Yeh naachney gaaney waalon ka kaam hai* (It is for harlots and courtesans),' said Anees, elucidating the attitude towards films back then. Husain himself told Nasreen, 'When my father was alive, we weren't allowed to watch films. At most, we would see a couple of films a year.'

However, as things turned out, the man whose acceptance Husain sought the most, died early, when Husain was hardly fourteen or fifteen. 'He [Husain's father] was forty at the time of his death,' Anees recalled. While his father's loss must have certainly been devastating, it freed Husain from the guilt of watching films and seeking a career in Hindi cinema in later years without his father's blessings. 'After his death, I saw a couple of films every month. *Woh hotey toh film mein bhi na aata. Kaise aata?* (If my

---

[8]Resham Shaam, 'Little Big Man', *Super*, May 1978.
[9]Ibid.

father was alive, I would never have come into films. How could I?),' he told Nasreen.

Following his father's death, Husain moved to Lucknow for his BA. 'There was no college in Bhopal. We had to move out.' While Husain couldn't recall the name of the college, neither did Anees, it was from Lucknow that he completed his 'Inter' and graduation. 'I graduated with a second division. My subjects were English literature, Urdu and economics.'

At college, Husain's writing flourished. '*Un dinon bahut se afsaane likh daaley* (I wrote a lot of stories in those days),' he said.[10] Husain wrote short stories for magazines, plays for AIR (All India Radio) and occasionally participated in them as well. 'I was paid Rs. 20/- for a programme. Even if I did just two shows a month, I made enough money to live on.'[11] During this time, Husain also contributed a story to an Urdu magazine, *Aaj Kal*. The story went on to fetch him the first prize in a story-writing competition featuring students from Lucknow, Allahabad and Aligarh universities.

Husain admitted to Nasreen that he hadn't thought of entering films at that point. Having completed his graduation, the more important question on his mind was, 'Where can I get a job? I was just a BA pass. There are thousands of students who have done their BA. You don't get a job by doing a BA.' He would put this line into a film later. Based on the story for which Husain had won the first prize, the film was very close to Husain's heart and very different from his usual mould of cinema.

---

[10] Ambarish Mishra, 'I will always be a romantic at heart', *The Times of India*, 7 May 2000.

[11] Resham Shaam, 'Little Big Man', *Super*, May 1978.

In his quest for a job, Husain reached out to that familiar eminent person in the family, Maulana Azad. Husain had great respect for his maternal granduncle. 'He was a very nice man, a very educated person and very intelligent. He didn't say much to me, but whenever he spoke to the others, I would just sit quietly and listen to him,' Husain told Nasreen. Husain sent the Maulana a letter, to which Maulana sa'ab replied, asking him to come to Delhi. There was an opening for an assistant supervisor at the Imperial Archives.

Husain came to Delhi and even stayed with the Maulana. But Husain's move coincided with India's independence and there were riots in Delhi. Considering the tense situation, Maulana sa'ab told Husain to go back to Lucknow. Husain duly returned.

However, in his very brief stay with Maulana Azad, Husain's career was almost hijacked for supposedly more vital purposes. It so happened that while Husain was in Delhi, Vijaya Lakshmi Pandit, then Indian ambassador to the USSR and Jawaharlal Nehru's sister, offered to make Husain a diplomatic envoy. Maulana stymied the move. 'He didn't like the idea of his relatives occupying high posts in the government.'[12] It wouldn't be the last time Maulana had a say in Husain's profession.

On his return to Lucknow, Husain took up a job as a secretary in the Shahabad municipality. He worked there for about a year. 'Then I came to Bombay. I met a lot of people, including people from the film industry. I met Majrooh sa'ab [Majrooh Sultanpuri, the poet–songwriter]. He would come to meet my aunt's [Husain's mother's sister, with whom Husain stayed initially in Bombay] husband. Even he [Majrooh] was just starting out in films at that time.'

It is unclear what exactly triggered Husain's decision to start

---

[12]*Filmfare*, 'Behind the screen: Producer-Director, Nasir Husain', 1 May 1964, p. 39.

working in films. The only clue we have is from what he told Nasreen: 'You will only get a job if you have some talent, when you are capable of doing something. That's why I started writing.' Seen in the light of his interest in films, this remark probably offers an insight into what could have spurred him on to pursue a career in Hindi cinema.

When I suggested to Nuzhat that had Jaffar Husain been alive, Husain would possibly never have come into films, she replied, 'Very likely. For him, his dad's approval meant so much that I don't think he could have run away from home the way he did. It was way too rebellious.' On Husain's possible career as a diplomat, when I proposed that Husain's wit would have come handy in diffusing many a diplomatic crisis, Nuzhat laughed. As far as she is concerned, her father's appointment would have been an unmitigated disaster. 'He would have had to be good for far too long.'

2

FILMISTAN

Ratan: *Mujhe aap par rashk aata hai.* (I envy you.)

Raj: *Kyun?* (Why?)

Ratan: *Aapka jeevan ek behtey huey jharney ki tarah hai. Na koi fikra aur na koi dukh.* (Your life is like a free-flowing stream. You know no sorrow or grief.)

— Ratan (Pran) and Raj (Dev Anand) in *Munimji* (1955)

The Bombay film industry of the late 1940s was in a state of flux. The studio system, which emerged in the mid-1920s, predominantly as a result of infusion of large capital to equip the industry to handle the introduction of sound technology, was on its last legs. Under the studio system, actors, film-makers, composers and other technicians worked as employees of a studio and were paid salaries for their services. In this set-up, not only was it normal for actors, composers and writers to work on several films for the same studio, there was little or no opportunity for freelancing. Actors and technicians had to report to studios to work even if they weren't shooting. The producers or the owners of these studios such as Bombay Talkies, New Theatres, Ranjit Studios and Prabhat, and their founders like Himanshu Rai (Bombay Talkies) and Chandulal Shah (Ranjit), called the shots. The success of *Khazanchi* (1941), directed by Moti Gidwani,

11

made its composer, Ghulam Haider, something of a household name. For *Khazanchi*, Haider combined popular ragas with the zest of Punjabi folk music and revolutionized the Hindi film song. The songs of the film, including numbers such as '*Saawan ke nazaare hain*', became a hit. Haider's success shook the foundations of the studio system. Suddenly, the composer became a bigger entity than the studio that employed him. It created an opportunity for freelancing. In the period following the Second World War, as wartime profiteers looked for conduits to launder black money, 'they offered huge sums of money to actors to entice them away from the established studios and thus capture the audience'.[1] Consequently, by the late 1940s, several of the big-ticket studios were well past their heyday. A new system, the star system, emerged, and freelancing came into vogue.

Ironically enough, personalities groomed in the studio system enjoyed some of the longest or most distinguished careers in Hindi cinema. Stars like Ashok Kumar, Dilip Kumar and Dev Anand or film-makers such as Bimal Roy and Mehboob Khan, all started their film careers within the studio system.

One studio that came into being in the early 1940s, and largely continued in the tradition of the earlier studio era, was Filmistan. The man helming Filmistan, at least on the film-making side, was Shashadhar Mukerji or S. Mukerji, as he was more popularly known. Mukerji had been personally handpicked by Himanshu Rai in the 1930s and groomed in several aspects of film-making. In the years leading to Rai's untimely death in 1940 and after,

[1]Brian Shoesmith, 'From Monopoly to Commodity: The Bombay Studio in the 1930s', http://wwwmcc.murdoch.edu.au/ReadingRoom/hfilm/BOMBAY.html

Mukerji produced several spectacular hits for Bombay Talkies, including *Kangan* (1939), *Bandhan* (1940), *Jhoola* (1941) and *Kismet* (1943).

Following Rai's demise, and Devika Rani's (Rai's widow and prima donna star herself) unwillingness to cede control of Bombay Talkies, Mukerji established Filmistan in 1943-44. Partnering Mukerji in this enterprise were Rai Bahadur Chunilal, the composer Madan Mohan's father, and Ashok Kumar, Mukerji's brother-in-law. Filmistan's very first film *Chal Chal Re Naujawan* (1944), which starred Kumar, was a huge success. It set Filmistan on its way to producing some of the biggest hits of the late 1940s through the late 1950s. The success of films like *Safar* (1946), *Do Bhai* (1947), *Shehnai* (1947), *Shaheed* (1948), *Shabnam* (1949), *Sargam* (1950), *Shrimati Ji* (1952), *Jagriti* (1954), *Nagin* (1954), *Nastik* (1954) made Mukerji a power figure. Everything he touched turned gold or platinum. 'I made 100-weekers with complete ease,' Mukerji once said.[2]

Mukerji had a reputation for plucking raw talent out of nowhere and giving them the opportunity to prove their mettle. From directors (Bibhuti Mitra [*Safar*], P.L. Santoshi [*Shehnai*] and Ramesh Saigal [*Shaheed*]), to composers (S.D. Burman [*Shikari*, 1946, and *Do Bhai*] and Hemant Kumar [*Anand Math*, 1952, and *Nagin*]), to actors (Rehana [*Shehnai*], Pradeep Kumar [*Anand Math*] and Kamini Kaushal [*Do Bhai*]), Mukerji either gave these names their first big break or provided them the opportunity that catapulted them to fame. With *Love in Simla* (1960), he gave the actor Sadhana and the film director R.K. Nayyar their first big film. Mukerji's own son, Joy Mukerji, was also given the lead role in this film.

'Nearly 200 people in the film industry directly and

[2]Harish Kumar Mehra, 'The Story of Movie Moghul S. Mukerji', *Star & Style*, 28 June 1968, p. 9.

indirectly owe their careers to him. Even technicians – editors, cinematographers, writers, lyrics writers,' Neelam Mukerji, Joy Mukerji's wife and Mukerji's daughter-in-law, told me when I met her in December 2014. Javed Akhtar agreed, 'He was a grand personality. An institution by himself. He gave so many people a break ... The list is endless.'[3]

Husain met S. Mukerji after a year in Bombay. 'He asked me, "What do you do?" I told him I was a writer and I was looking for a job. He asked me to read out something that I had written. I showed him a novel, which I had written. The novel hadn't been published. It was a long story. I read out some portion of the novel to him. He said, "Ok, fine," and the matter hurriedly ended there.'

A few months later, Husain got a telephone call. Mukerji had called for him. The screenwriter Aghajani Kashmeri had been writing the dialogue for a film. He had fallen ill. 'I was asked to complete the dialogues along with Ali Raza.'[4]

This film for which Husain completed Aghajani Kashmeri's unfinished dialogues with Raza was *Chandni Raat* (1949). Unfortunately, all attempts to get a copy of the film have proved futile. Husain himself wasn't sure whether he was credited. One can only hazard a guess going by the number (10) and nature of songs (the words 'dil', 'saiyyan', 'bewafaa' and 'pyaar' feature prominently in the mukhdas) in the film[5] that it was some kind

---

[3]Zee Classic's *Classic Legends: Season II*, featuring Nasir Husain.

[4]Ali Raza: dialogue writer who worked with Mehboob Khan on films like *Aan* (1952) and *Mother India* (1957).

[5]Har Mandar Singh 'Humraaz', *Hindi Film Geetkosh, Volume II, 1941-1950*, p. 477.

of romantic tearjerker. The film was directed by M. Ehsan and starred Naseem Banu, actor Saira Banu's parents. Although the film wasn't a Filmistan production, it must have been Mukerji who referred Husain to the film-maker. Nonetheless, *Chandni Raat* did the trick for Husain. 'Mukerji sa'ab liked my work. After that he kept me at Filmistan. I worked at Filmistan for almost 10-11 years, as a writer.'

After *Chandni Raat*, Husain became a regular writer at Filmistan. Initially, he worked as an associate to the more established screenplay writer and lyricist, Qamar Jalalabadi. For *Shabnam*, which starred Dilip Kumar and Kamini Kaushal, and where Jalalabadi was credited for 'Lyrics and Dialogue', Husain was acknowledged as 'Associate'. Then came *Shabistan* (1951), which became famous for its hero Shyam falling off a horse during the shooting and dying young. Here, Husain was acknowledged as writer alongside Jalalabadi. For *Shart* (1954), starring Shyama and Dipak, Husain was given an equal writing credit with Jalalabadi and I.S. Johar, who, going against his established comic persona, also played a rather Machiavellian villain in the film. All three films were directed by Bibhuti Mitra and like his first hit film, *Safar*, were romantic dramas, filled with songs. They steered clear of any political statement. Even *Shabnam*, which was set in 1942 and began with Indians fleeing Burma following the Japanese invasion, used this historical event merely as a backdrop. The film, which had Kamini Kaushal in the guise of a young man at the beginning, was essentially a light-hearted romantic story.

Mitra's films were very much in keeping with the Filmistan philosophy. The objective was to entertain. Be it costume dramas (*Shabistan* or *Nagin*) or musical entertainers (*Shehnai* and *Sargam* [1950]), the idea was to have the protagonists fall in love before the villain or fate intervenes, give the audience a few laughs, make them listen to a number of good songs and send them home happy. Even a weepy, crime drama like *Shart* had no less than twelve songs and an extended three-minute silent comic sequence in the last forty minutes of the film, when the hero and the heroine unwittingly and inexplicably end up wearing each other's night suits. This when the heroine is on the run for allegedly having murdered her stepmother and is being blackmailed into committing another murder. Needless to say, the film had a happy ending.

The emphasis on entertainment at Filmistan stemmed from S. Mukerji's commitment to the theme. Mukerji put a premium on a lightness of touch and stayed away from subjects that explored concepts of nation-building or social reform, very much the flavour of cinema in independent India. This is not to disregard films like *Shaheed*, *Anand Math* or *Jagriti*, which had strong nationalistic sentiments, but were exceptions to the Filmistan school of film-making.

The Filmistan productions had a small canvas. They were generally restricted to indoor settings. When the protagonists ventured out, either travelling by car or train, there was complete reliance on back projection. The city skyline, like the streets, or the hero–heroine romancing against the backdrop of a moonlit night or a river or stream, or any exotic setting (the local space of *Nagin*), was shown through sets. At the most there would be an outdoor sequence at the climax, but even that would be bereft of spectacle. The cinematography was restricted to medium and close shots. As Nasreen told me, 'You look at the films, the sets are not lavish – what I remember about their films – two or three songs outdoor, everything is set. And even the camerawork is not as sophisticated as what was going on in Raj Kapoor's films.'

Subhash Mukerji, S. Mukerji's nephew and film-maker Subodh Mukerji's son, explained Mukerji's ideology through an interesting anecdote. Mukerji, Mehboob Khan and V. Shantaram were travelling by train to attend some film function. Shantaram and Mehboob teased Mukerji all through the journey. 'They kept asking him, "*Kya picture banaata hai tu? Hum logon ko dekh. Main bana raha hoon iss tarah ki picture, woh bana raha hai uss tarah ki picture* (What films do you make? Look at us, look at the kind of films we make)." Mukerji heard them patiently and then said, 'I have such a subject. Listen.' He narrated the story to both gentlemen. 'It was a story with social consciousness, grandeur of scale, the works.' Shantaram and Mehboob were elated. They told Mukerji excitedly, 'Now this is a subject. You should make this film.' Mukerji, as Subhash recalled, replied nonchalantly, 'You make it. It will take me five years to make this film. I don't have that kind of patience. I need to make a couple of films every year.'

But if Mukerji compromised on scale, spectacle and films dedicated to the idea of Nehruvian socialism, he made up on other fronts. No less a man than Dilip Kumar, who referred to Mukerji as a 'guru' and who made his debut with Bombay Talkies' *Jwar Bhata* (1944), said of him, that he 'found him [Mukerji] to be a man of considerable worth not only in terms of the technical knowledge he had painstakingly acquired by regular interactions with the foreign technicians and consistent reading of relevant literature but also in a personal sense as a friend one could trust and rely upon'.[6] Husain, too, remarked of Mukerji's involvement in his own sphere of work, 'Mr. Mukherjee [sic] devoted a lot of attention to the script. He would keep offering suggestions.'[7] In another article, Husain said of Mukerji's influence, 'S. Mukerji would always insist on one scene written in various ways, on many

---

[6]Dilip Kumar, *The Substance and the Shadow: An Autobiography*, Hay House India, 2014, pp. 124, 131.

[7]Ambarish Mishra, 'I will always be a romantic at heart', *The Times of India*, 7 May 2000.

tunes for a single situation, or various methods for shooting the same scene, and I followed this from day one of my career.'[8]

It must have been Mukerji's instinctive knack of backing a good story that made him produce *Anarkali* (1953). The film, starring Bina Rai in the title role and Pradeep Kumar as 'Prince Saleem', was credited to Husain for 'Story', but the roots of the film lay in Imtiaz Ali Taj's play *Anarkali*. Although the Filmistan production did not acknowledge this, at least four films borrow from the play, which Ali first wrote in 1922 and then rewrote in 1931. Besides the 1953 film, the other three films were *Anarkali* (1928, silent – also known as *Loves of a Moghul Prince*, directed by Prafulla Roy and Charu Roy), *Anarkali* (1935, directed by R.S. Choudhury) and *Mughal-E-Azam* (1960, directed by K. Asif).[9]

Unlike *Mughal-E-Azam*, which had a lavish canvas, and spoke of class conflict between 'the elite and the plebeian'[10] at its core, Husain's story was a cinematic retelling of Ali's play. It was a doomed love story where Anarkali is entombed for having dared to romance the heir apparent of the Mughal Empire. Where Asif's film gave a far more significant role to Emperor Akbar (the film is titled *Mughal-E-Azam*, meaning 'The Great Mughal', which refers to Akbar), in Husain's film, Akbar is a far more effete figure. The focus is on Anarkali.

Thematically, the difference between the films is also underscored in the manner Anarkali is asked to dance in the

---

[8]Rajiv Vijayakar, 'Adieu Nasir Husain', *Screen*, 22 March 2002.

[9]Alain Désoulières, http://www.urdustudies.com/pdf/22/08 DesoulieresAnarkali.pdf, accessed on 25 April 2016.

[10]Anil Zankar, 'On a Larger Canvas', *Mughal-E-Azam: Legend as Epic*, HarperCollins *Publishers* India, 2013, p. 172.

'Sheesh Mahal' in front of the emperor. In the 1953 film, when Bina Rai dances to '*Mohabbat mein aise kadam dagmagaaye*', she is not in her senses. She has been drugged. She is apologetic as she sings, '*Mujhe ilzaam na dena meri behoshi ka, meri majboor mohabbat ki yeh rusvaayee hai*' (Do not blame me for not being in my senses, this is the shaming of my helpless love). Contrastingly, in *Mughal-E-Azam*, Shakeel Badyauni's lyrics for Anarkali, as she is placed before Akbar, are defiant. '*Jab pyaar kiya toh darna kya*' (When in love, why be afraid), Anarkali tells an enraged Akbar.

Moreover, the canvas of Asif's film is Hindustan. The sets gave a certain spectacle to the film. The Filmistan production had a smaller canvas in comparison (even if bigger than most of their other films). The story was very much about the romance between Anarkali and Saleem and the characters who try to keep them apart. It may have had a poignant ending, but a tight screenplay, great music and good direction (the film was helmed by Nandlal Jashwantlal) ensured that the film was a box-office hit.

Anarkali's success established Husain's value at Filmistan but the film's significance must be seen in the context of the films of the 1950s and Husain's own oeuvre. The era of period films, very much in fashion in the 1930s and 1940s, was passé by then. Anil Zankar, freelance film-maker and author, explained the demise of the historical films in the 1950s by suggesting that patriotism and identity were always underlined in such films. 'This defiant patriotic agenda was not required in an independent India occupied with rebuilding itself.'[11]

Husain was never associated with any other period film thereafter. It is therefore difficult to suggest that he was being prescient in some manner, knowing what would work with the audiences at that time by writing a film like *Anarkali*. Instead, the film's success must have emphasized the Filmistan formula – the

---

[11]Ibid. p. 183.

value of romance, quality songs and a well-knit screenplay – on his film-making sensibilities.

But even as Husain's star was on the rise within Filmistan, there was still opposition to his career within the family. His older brother, his sisters, his mother in Lucknow, had all stopped writing to him. They even turned to Maulana Azad, hoping that a strong word from him would force Husain to seek a more honourable profession. 'Maulana sa'ab had come to Bombay. I went one morning to meet him. When I reached where he was staying, I found khala jaan,[12] with whom I initially stayed when I came to Bombay, her husband and all the other family members had also come to meet him. They complained, "*Nasir ko mana kariye. Bahut buri harqat ki hai isne. Isne film industry join kar li* (Please admonish Nasir. He has done a very bad thing. He has joined the film industry)."'

Husain must have feared the strongest possible rebuke from the Maulana. Instead, he heard the Maulana ask him calmly, '*Kya kartey ho*? (What do you do?)' Nasir replied that he wrote dialogues for films. On hearing Husain's reply, the Maulana said, '*Dialogue likhtey ho, toh kya bura kartey ho. Achha kartey ho* (What's wrong with writing dialogues? It's a good thing).' That one sentence from Maulana Azad and '*sab chup ho gaye*' (everyone was silenced), Husain recalled. After the meeting with Maulana, 'my aunt even wrote to my mother informing her of what Maulana had said'.

Family opposition out of the way, Husain concentrated on learning the art of film-making. Bombay gave him the opportunity to watch films from the West and he used them to hone his own craft. 'I used to see a lot of Hollywood films. And I saw each film

---

[12]Aunt: mother's sister.

seven or eight times. Once from a writer's point of view, once from a director's point of view and so on. Then I came home and reconstructed the film on paper shot by shot to see if I got it right. I rewrote the script according to the way I would like to make the film.' On whether he was influenced by any particular film-maker, Husain said, 'No ... I had my own style.'[13]

Filmistan offered Husain the opportunity to interact with technicians across the film spectrum. He made the most of it. 'Everything was new to me.' He would visit the sets of every director working for Filmistan and see how they were doing things. He even visited the sets of directors he never worked with. 'In those days, there were five or six directors [like] Bibhuti Mitra, P.L. Santoshi working at Filmistan on different stages. I used to take notes that if I had done it, how differently would I do it. I would go for editing as well. Sound editing used to happen. Scenes would get edited. I used to go and sit and watch. There was this old editor Mr. [D.N.] Pai. He told me that the day you learn editing, you will know direction.'

Another young director emerging at Filmistan around this time was Subodh Mukerji, S. Mukerji's younger brother. He had been working at Filmistan for some time in the capacity of a technician and writer. (In *Sargam* [1950], Subodh was credited for 'Scenario' along with the film's director, P.L. Santoshi.) 'He was P.L. Santoshi's man Friday,' Subhash Mukerji told me. It was at Filmistan that Husain met Subodh and the two hit it off.

Originally hailing from Jhansi, Subodh Mukerji had studied in Lucknow. This shared educational lineage got Subodh acquainted

---

[13]Deepa Gahlot, 'It's the chase that is exciting', *Filmfare*, 1-15 November 1984, p. 74.

with Husain. 'There was some familiarity, some things they could talk about together. Both had a sense of humour. It was a meeting of temperaments. So when he wanted to make his first movie, he wanted Nasir sa'ab as his dialogue writer,' said Subhash. This first film, which Subodh directed for Filmistan, was the 1955 Dev Anand–Nalini Jaywant–Pran starrer, *Munimji*.

Munimji's story idea came from the actor Ranjan, but its screenplay and dialogues were credited to Husain (dialogue credits were shared with Jalalabadi). *Munimji* is the story of a woman, Malti (Nirupa Roy), having a son, Ratan, out of a relationship with a man named Ramlal. Ramlal has another son, Amar, from his marriage, but his wife has passed away. When Malti goes to confront Ramlal about their relationship and giving their son his due rights, Ramlal refuses. Not one to give up, Malti switches the two children at Ramlal's house. Ramlal comes to know of this, courtesy the birthmark on Amar's chest. He threatens to kill Malti if she doesn't return his son, but succumbs to a snakebite.

Malti takes up a job as Ratan's nanny at the house of Ramlal's best friend, Captain Suresh (S.L. Puri). She passes off Amar as her own son, but is always on the lookout for Ratan, even to the extent of condoning his bad behaviour towards Amar. Amar (Dev Anand) grows up with a sense of being wronged and takes on a double-life. In one part, he is in disguise and is known to everyone as Captain Suresh's trusted munimji Amar, looking after the monetary affairs of Captain Suresh's timber factory in the jungle. In this guise, he is at the receiving end of Ratan's (Pran) violent temper and holds back out of respect for Malti, who he believes to be his mother. In the other part, Dev Anand is Raj, a smart, young man out to woo Captain Suresh's daughter, Roopa (Nalini Jaywant), and willing to take on Ratan. Ratan, meanwhile, also has another identity, that of Kala Ghoda, a feared dacoit, who frequently loots the rich and wealthy to finance his debauched ways. The climax of the film revolves around Malti admitting to having wronged Amar and telling Captain Suresh the truth about Ratan's and Amar's identities. She even shoots Ratan, her own son, for all his misdeeds. The film was a smash hit.

Although the film has a violent ending, *Munimji*, true to its opening sequence – which has a frothy musical tune playing as the credits roll – is a breezy entertainer for the most part. In the guise of the munim, who walks with a stick, bears a slight stoop, is bespectacled, sports a thick moustache and wears a black munim cap, Dev Anand's behaviour is affected and shackled. He bears his humiliation at the hands of Ratan only out of a sense of duty towards the woman he thinks is his mother. But as Raj, there is a complete makeover to his persona. Freed from the burden of anyone knowing who he is (except Malti), Raj is at his charismatic best. Whether he is wooing Roopa or standing up to Ratan, there is not only a distinct sense of flamboyance, but also the devil in him. He is gallant but doesn't mind using guile in order to win Roopa's affection. He is fearless in his dealings with Ratan, but also resorts to wit and humour to embarrass him in front of Roopa. In the lead up to the song, '*Dil ki umangey hai jawaan*', he enthusiastically strums a guitar and coaxes Ratan into laughing and singing with abandon to prove his love for Roopa, but has him riding a donkey by the end of the sequence. It is with Raj that Husain gave a glimpse into the kind of hero figure he would present in his own cinema. But the character was also important considering Dev Anand's own body of work up to that point.

Before *Munimji*, Anand's roles fitted into two categories. In films like *Vidya* (1948) or *Namoona* (1949) or *Milap* (1955) his character is weighed down by his indigent state and he is embarrassed to indulge in romance of any kind. In *Namoona*, his character is so passive that he has no role to play in the resolution of the film's climax. In other films like *Ziddi* (1948) or *Sazaa* (1951), where he is part of the elite social order, he is unable to rise above family opposition and depends on their change of heart to ultimately marry the woman he loves. In both films, Anand is shown losing control over his mental faculties, a victim who suffers as people around him stand on their notions of propriety and class structures. Madhulika Liddle, author and host of the popular blog 'Dusted Off', where she frequently writes about Hindi cinema of the pre-1970s, called Anand's characterization in these films, 'insipid'.

The other character that Anand played, and more successfully, was in the noir-oriented films like *Baazi* (1951), *Jaal* (1952), *Taxi Driver* (1954) and *House No. 44* (1955). In these films, one sees a certain brazenness about Anand, emanating from the amorality of the characters. He is a man of the streets, a survivor who is at home in the criminal underbelly. He hardly has time for romance and he spends most of his time undoing the Faustian exchange he has made with the villain. More importantly, as Madhulika noted, Dev Anand's character in such films can hardly be termed 'flamboyant or sophisticated'.

In *Munimji*, Anand as Raj is very much an urbane character. He rights the wrongs done to his alter ego, Amar, with élan, panache and style. This confidence and aggression on Raj's part are not linked to any moral decline in his character. In his dealings with Roopa, like while playing cards with her at the club, he is comfortable in this urban, upper-class space. When he pulls up one of Ratan's accomplices for cheating, and things are about to get violent, some British characters rush to his side, guns in hand, to show their support. 'What's the trouble, Raj?' one such gentleman asks, reaffirming Raj's status as an insider in this world.

A few scenes later, when Roopa begs Raj to save her from a tiger in the immediate vicinity where she is bathing in the jungle pond, '*Mujhe bachaaiye, mujhe bachaaiye*,' he quips, '*Par kaise*

bachaaoon? Sher mera koi sageywaalaa hai? (How can I save you?
Is the tiger a relative of mine?)' Elsewhere, he quotes the poet Faiz
Ahmad Faiz to her ('*Mujhse pehli si mohabbat mere mehboob na
maang...*' – My beloved, do not ask me for the love we shared
once ...). He is debonair, sophisticated and woos Roopa as an
equal, unembarrassed about his background (his mother works
in Roopa's house as a maid) or true identity. It is a subtle change
in Dev Anand's persona, but it is a change all right. As Akhtar
commented, '*Munimji* gave Dev Anand a new image, a dashing
romantic hero, who flirts with the heroine but with a certain class
and who sings with a certain style.'[14]

The 16 September 1955 edition of *Filmfare* wrote in its review,
'The picture is irresistibly entertaining deriving this quality
from the portrayals, the songs, the dances, the dialogue and the
action ... Dev Anand extracts the maximum from every scene
and every shot, displaying not only the charm and flair which
put him among the top romantic heroes of the screen today, but
also augmenting those enviable qualities with a debonair, gay
and gallant personality. It is certainly the best performance of
his career.'

After *Munimji*'s success, Subodh Mukerji and Nasir Husain made
Paying Guest (1957). The film marked Husain's first independent
writing assignment as he was credited for 'Screenplay and
Dialogues'. Subodh Mukerji was credited for 'Story and Scenario'.

Paying Guest is the story of a struggling advocate Ramesh Kumar
(Dev Anand), who has to change accommodation frequently either
because he fails to keep up with the rent or his waggish behaviour
lands him in trouble. In one such accommodation, Ramesh gets

---

[14]Zee Classic's *Classic Legends: Season II*, featuring Nasir Husain.

to know and immediately falls for Babu Digambernath's daughter
Shanti. Much of the film's first half deals with Ramesh wooing
Shanti. Both Shanti and her friend, Chanchal (Shubha Khote),
hold opposing views on marriage. Shanti believes in love while
Chanchal is pragmatic and holds that wealth is the key to a happy
marriage. To this end, Chanchal even marries the eminent but
elderly lawyer, Dayal (Gajanan Jagirdar).

Soon enough, Chanchal finds Dayal has no time for anything
but his work. Shanti, on the other hand, has to cope with her
father's declining health and a fiendish brother-in-law, Prakash
babu (Yakub), even as Chanchal attempts to seduce Ramesh.
Matters take a turn for the worse when Dayal dies and Shanti
is arrested for Prakash's murder. In the end, though, Ramesh
comes to Shanti's rescue as he is able to establish not only who
killed Prakash, but Dayal as well. *Paying Guest*, too, was a big hit.
'Mukerji sa'ab really enjoyed *Paying Guest*,' Husain told Nasreen.

Paying Guest foregrounded Husain's and Subodh Mukerji's
connection with Lucknow as the film was based in that city. The
film has a remarkable frothiness to it. Dev Anand as the struggling
advocate Ramesh leaves you in splits with his quick-wittedness.
His spirited defence of a man charged with running away with
a minor girl purely on the grounds of passion and sentiment
is hilarious. So confident is he of his argument, bereft of any
evidence, that he even walks up to congratulate his client before
the verdict and says, '*Milaao haath meri jaan, muqadamma jeet
liya hai ... Tumhaari mehbooba ka haath tumhaarey haath mein
hoga* (Congratulations, my friend, we have won the case ... You
will be holding your beloved's hand soon).' It's a line that comes to
haunt Ramesh as after the judge holds his client guilty, the man's
hand is shown being held by the hawaldar instead.

If *Munimji* saw Dev Anand as flamboyant and sophisticated,
Paying Guest has him play a happy-go-lucky character. Ramesh

laughs off his inability to pay the rent and is quite happy to go along with Shanti's ruse to help him pay off her father. Before that, in his disguise as the old and supposedly respectable Wajahat Mirza, he even cons Babu Digambernath into thinking of him as a most suitable paying guest. Totally floored, Digambernath even tells Shanti to carry Mirza sa'ab's luggage inside, to his room.

Ramesh (as Wajahat Mirza): *Digambernath ji, aapki khaatir dekh ke aisa lagta hai ki, main, main, main apne sasuraal mein aa gaya hoon.* (Mr Digambernath, your hospitality makes me feel like I am visiting my in-laws.)

Babu Digambernath [laughing heartily]: *Bade mazaakiyaa hain aap.* (You have a fine sense of humour.)

Ramesh [also laughing]: *Aji abhi toh aapney dekha kya hai.* (You haven't seen anything yet.)

Whether he is wooing Shanti in this guise, staging a fight between Mirza sa'ab and Ramesh to win Shanti's sympathy, or conning another hawaldar as he sits perched on a tree, enjoying ('*Shaabaash, ek meri taraf se bhi, zor se*' – Well done, land one on my behalf as well, hard) a free-for-all between Shanti and Chanchal, Ramesh is quite the delightful charlatan, without a care in the world. Even his floundering career as an advocate doesn't weigh him down. Equally, he doesn't shy away from or make any serious attempt to fight Chanchal's flirtatious behaviour towards him. He is at ease with her attention and straddles her world of coffee shops and bars ('Pride of Asia'), dressed in tux and bowtie, with complete flair.

The one film that comes close to Anand's characterizations in *Munimji* and *Paying Guest*, and which was sandwiched right between the two films, was *C.I.D.* With the film's storyline based in Bombay, *C.I.D.* saw Anand play an outright modern, sophisticated character. But there is a subtle difference between

Anand's character in *C.I.D.* and the two films written by Husain. In Raj Khosla's film, while Anand as Inspector Shekhar is urbane, he is hardly impish or mischievous. His romantic moments with Rekha (Shakila) are few and infrequent. For most of the film, Shekhar is more concerned with the murder he is investigating. He does not indulge in the kind of constant playfulness that defines Raj's and Ramesh's characters in *Munimji* and *Paying Guest*.

These two films gave Dev Anand a different persona. 'Before *Munimji* and *Paying Guest*, Dev Anand was there, but this Dev Anand was different,' explained Javed Akhtar. 'This hero was much more suave, sophisticated, westernized and modern. This hero was not laden or overburdened by what you call Indian emotions, that melodrama. He had more style.' It is this Dev Anand that we see in later films like *Jaali Note* (1960), *Hum Dono* (1961), *Tere Ghar Ke Samne* (1963), *Teen Devian* (1965) and *Jewel Thief* (1967).

Husain gave this new Dev Anand persona full rein when he presented him as the charming, sharp-witted, confidence trickster Sunder in his own film, *Jab Pyar Kisise Hota Hai* (1961). The actor Jeetendra, a twenty-year-old at the time of the film's release, gushed over Anand's portrayal, '*Aap Dev Anand ko dekhiye. Jab Pyar Kisise Hota Hai mein jaisa dikhey hain, aisa kabhi nahin dikhey. Arrey train top pe baithey huey hain. Aapney kabhi kisi ko dekha hai train top par baith ke gaaney gaa raha hain?* (Look at Dev Anand. The way he was presented in *Jab Pyar Kisise Hota Hai* was unique. He is sitting on top of the train. Have you seen anyone sitting atop a train and singing?)'

The song Jeetendra referred to is the frothy '*Jiya ho, jiya o jiya, kuchh bol do*', which has Dev Anand singing on the top of a car moving parallel to the train in which Asha Parekh, the film's heroine, is travelling. The larger point is that in all these three films, Dev Anand had one song which brought to the fore his buoyant character. In all three songs, he is irritating his female protagonist with his mischief. Like '*Jiya ho*', *Munimji's* '*Jeevan ke safar mein raahi*' and *Paying Guest's* '*Maana janaab ne pukaara nahin*' best epitomize Dev Anand's distinct character shift in these films.

While a lot of the credit for these portrayals goes to Subodh Mukerji, the man helming *Munimji* and *Paying Guest*, Husain's role as writer was the primary source of Anand's makeover. His dialogues and situations, created around the unfolding storyline, provided for Anand's sophisticated, flamboyant, modern and comic persona. Nasreen remarked on the importance of Husain's work in the larger context, 'The minute you get out of the silent era – how is the character of the hero or heroine defined? It is through speech. And if you don't have a certain kind of depth, whether it's irony, whether it is intelligence or compassion, all these emotions come through the choice of vocabulary. So if you don't have very strong dialogue writers, screenplay writers, you will never connect to the story. So both are important.'

Husain's last film with Subodh was after he himself had turned director. The film was the Dev Anand–Mala Sinha starrer, *Love Marriage* (1959). Although the film failed to work at the box office, it again presented Anand as a fun-loving, carefree, modern young man, Sunil, who comes to Bombay from Jhansi after his brother has set him up with a job. There he meets Geeta (Sinha), and the two share an instant chemistry. They fall in love and get married before they return to Jhansi where Sunil has to deal with his brother's extramarital affair that threatens to destroy their entire family.

Husain's dialogues give Geeta and Sunil a great deal of lightness, and produce many of the fun moments in the film. Geeta is an equal match for Sunil's wit and humour. When Sunil, having rented Geeta's paying guest accommodation,[15] enquires about

---

[15]It is interesting that both *Paying Guest* and *Love Marriage* involve accommodation, or finding your feet in the city.

the facilities he would be entitled to, her response is dripping with sarcasm:

> Sunil: *Yeh pachaas rupaye, sirf kamrey ke hain, ya iske saath khaana bhi milega?* (Are these fifty rupees only for the accommodation or does it include my meals as well?)
>
> Geeta: *Ji nahin. Pehanney ko kapdey bhi milengey, dhobi ki dhulaayee bhi, roz ki hajaamat bhi.* (No, no. You will get clothes to wear, your clothes will be laundered and you will get a shave as well.)[16]

Sunil, who is shown to be completely at ease in the city, whether he is being entertained at a club by his boss or in his sartorial choices, is similarly given a blithe demeanour. When his brother pulls him up for getting married without even informing them, he responds, '*Bhaiyya, phir nahin karoonga* (Brother, I won't do it again),' breaking the tension of the moment.

Subodh Mukerji and Husain remained lifelong friends. Beginning with *Jab Pyar Kisise Hota Hai*, Husain also named one character in each of the films that he directed 'Subodh Mukerji'. Subhash, who himself shared a good rapport with Husain, recalled Husain often dropping into their house unannounced to take his father's advice. 'I took my father to Nasir sa'ab's funeral. Nuzhat has seen how Baba cried. He was very close to Nasir sa'ab.'

Before we move ahead, we must also look back at the genealogy of the 'rom-com-musical' films that Husain championed with the success of his first four directorial ventures. While it is true that the 1930s and 1940s were essentially about historicals and

---

[16]The delightful pun lies in the fact that 'hajaamat' can be seen as a beating as well. So can 'dhulaayee'.

mythologicals, a film like *Khazanchi* (1941), directed by Moti B. Gidwani, had many of the same elements as Husain's cinema, including youthful romance, best highlighted in the opening sequence of the film through the memorable song, '*Saawan ke nazaare hain*'. The film had its moments of humour, dealt to some extent with the urban elite and also ventured into the club space briefly. The film's soundtrack marked a milestone in Indian cinema. But as *Khazanchi* veers towards the halfway mark, its focus shifts to the crime that has falsely implicated the hero's father and threatens to ruin his relationship with the heroine. Correspondingly, the last hour of the film is a weepy crime drama, devoid of the charm of the first half. National Award–winning film historian and documentary film-maker Sanjit Narwekar summarized it: '*Khazanchi* is not very strong on humour. It's strong on music and a little bit of nok-jhonk you can say.'

Khazanchi, however, is a very distant film from the time Husain appeared on Bombay's film landscape. Instead, it was the more immediate Filmistan grounding that shaped Husain's own sensibilities. The likes of P.L. Santoshi, I.S. Johar and Subodh Mukerji, who were very much a part of Filmistan during Husain's time at the studio, surely influenced and developed his own cinema.

I.S. Johar, tragically, is remembered (if at all) solely as a comedian but there were many facets to his cinematic contributions. He was one of the very first Hindi film actors to have acted – and excelled – in several Western films.[17] Johar also worked as writer and wrote

---

[17] *The New York Times* review of the Stewart Granger film *Harry Black and the Tiger* (1958) summed up the film thus: 'But a chirpy, bright-eyed little man named I.S. Johar, as Mr. Granger's faithful servant, has only to open his mouth to own the picture. Mr. Johar, that is – and the tiger.' (http://www.nytimes.com/movie/review?res=990CE6D71430E73BBC4152DFBF668383649EDE)

some of the producer–director R.K. Shorey's most successful comedy films such as *Ek Thee Ladki* (1949) and *Dholak* (1951). Johar then turned director and scripted two other noteworthy comedies – *Shrimati Ji* (1952) and *Hum Sab Chor Hain* (1956) – both of which were Filmistan productions.

The comic element in Johar's films largely originated from jokes about language, catchphrases, a general lampooning of English-speaking characters, plenty of situational comedy and a steady dose of disguise and impersonation – all of which were also quite conspicuous in Husain's films. He also had music organically integrated into his films. *Dholak*'s hero is a songwriter and much of the film's storyline revolves around its protagonists spending time first at the Modern School of Music and then at the Sangeet Maha Vidyalaya. Likewise, the protagonists in *Shrimati Ji* and *Hum Sab Chor Hain* find themselves in or are associated with the theatre space, which allowed for music to be part of the film's screenplay.

At the individual element level, too, *Dholak* gives us many clues of Husain's influences. Not only does the climax of the film hinge on a music competition, but there are moments in *Dholak* that Husain built upon and presented in a refreshing way in his own films. At the start of the film itself, the song '*Hulla gulla*' follows after the boys and girls have reminisced over their college years since '*Aaj college ka aakhri din hai*'.[18] Later, there is an exchange between Ajit and Manmohan Krishna in the film about '*Mohabbat ki manziley bhi hoti hain*' (There are various stages in love as well), a line that would recur in several of Husain's own films.

It's hard, therefore, to discount Johar's influence on Husain, more so given that *Shrimati Ji* and *Hum Sab Chor Hain* were produced by Filmistan. The two, as noted earlier, also worked on the dialogues of *Shart* (1954) with Qamar Jalalabadi. Veteran

---

[18]In *Qayamat Se Qayamat Tak*, '*Papa kehtey hain*' begins with Raj saying, '*Humaarey liye college ka yeh aakhri din hai…*'

FILMISTAN33

journalist and author Sidharth Bhatia said that Johar, basically, 'told the same story in all his films'. Husain has been accused of the same thing. Unlike Husain's films, however, the focus of Johar's films is on the heroine. In *Ek Thee Ladki*, *Shrimati Ji* and *Hum Sab Chor Hain*, the female protagonist walks away with the lion's share of screen time and the male clearly plays a secondary role. Further, the strength of these films lies in their comic element, but the music (perhaps with the exception of *Ek Thee Ladki* for which the heroine Meena Shorey came to be known as the '*Lara lapa*' girl) can hardly be termed memorable.

The one man, then, whose films seem to be the origin of the 'rom-com-musical', and whose cinema most certainly seems to have influenced Husain was the director Rajkumar Santoshi's father, P.L. Santoshi. Husain had clearly mentioned Santoshi's name from among the directors whose sets he visited while at Filmistan. Although Santoshi is most known for *Barsaat Ki Raat* (1960), he made some genuinely amusing comic-musical films in the initial years of his career. It was S. Mukerji who revived Santoshi's career, coaxing him into making something far more enjoyable than the serious fare he had dished out in his first film *Hum Ek Hain* (1946). Santoshi made the best of the opportunity with *Shehnai* (1947), following it up with *Sargam*, which proved to be another big hit.

Although Santoshi's *Shehnai* and *Sargam* are based in the rural hinterland for the most part, the parallels to Husain's films are strong. The music in his films, particularly *Shehnai*, which had the delightful '*Aana meri jaan, Sunday ke Sunday*', was very good. The comedy, too, had a lot of situational elements to it. There were jokes about English-speaking characters and the protagonists never bothered about playing fair to get ahead. Narwekar quoted the popular film magazine of the time, *Film India*, about Santoshi's films, comments which bore an uncanny similarity to Javed Akhtar's remarks about Husain's cinema, quoted later in the book. 'For Santoshi, the story has always been a necessary evil on which to base his more important structure of songs, dances and comedy.'[19]

One of Husain's biggest takeaways from Santoshi's cinema was the general buoyancy of the protagonists despite their tumultuous circumstances. In both *Shehnai* and *Sargam*, the emphasis is on a bunch of female protagonists, all sisters, who face their difficult situation head-on and spring into action rather than weeping over their sad state of affairs. The other, possibly, more significant influence was the manner in which Santoshi integrated music into his narratives. In all his films, Santoshi incorporated a musician character (or characters) – *Shehnai*'s female characters work with their father in his nautanki company; *Sargam*'s women are classical music exponents and *Barsaat Ki Raat* is about an Urdu poet. Such screenplays naturally gave Santoshi's characters the licence to break into song routines without the music obstructing the narrative of the film. Husain took forward Santoshi's legacy, but put his own stamp on it by scripting a bunch of films with a performative musician character and where music had a much larger role to play.

Working with Subodh Mukerji gave Husain the opportunity to familiarize himself with the practicalities of film-making. Although he was a writer on Subodh's films, Subodh used him as an assistant in every capacity. He would involve Husain in shot compositions before the stars arrived on the sets, honing Husain's own understanding of the craft. 'He used Nasir sa'ab in place of Dev Anand to compose his shots,' Subhash Mukerji said.

The Filmistan days had their lighter moments as well. Around

---

[19]Sanjit Narwekar, 'The Image Manipulators', *Eena Meena Deeka: The Story of Hindi Film Comedy*, Rupa & Co., 2005, p. 161.

the time Husain was working on *Munimji* and *Paying Guest*, he was romantically involved with a young Catholic girl, Margaret Francina Lewis, who worked as an assistant choreographer in films. After a brief courtship, spent mostly riding around town on Husain's motorcycle, Husain married Margaret (name later changed to Ayesha Khan). Subhash Mukerji remembered how his father played Cupid and worked the situation to his own advantage. 'For the romantic scenes, for the songs,[20] he would use Nasir sa'ab and Asha [Ayesha's pet name], to compose [the shot] instead of the hero and the heroine. Lighting used to take hours in those days. So in composing the romantic poses, they fell in love.'

The character artiste and television personality Tabassum worked as a child artiste on films like *Sargam* (1950) in Filmistan, and later in a couple of Husain's films (*Phir Wohi Dil Laya Hoon* [1963] and *Pyar Ka Mausam* [1969]). She recalled knowing Husain from the making of *Sargam*. '*Main 1950 se Nasir-bhai ko jaanti hoon* (I know Nasir since 1950). I was very young at that time, barely five-six years old. I was very fond of Nasir-bhai because he used to give me lots of chocolates. He used to play with me. He had a very jovial nature.' Tabassum shared another memory, laughing all through. 'At that time, we lived in Byculla Bridge. Nasir-bhai was staying somewhere in Mahim or Bandra. We used to come in our car, a Morris Eight, and when we would cross Bandra, Nasir-bhai would say, "*Main apni motorcycle ka switch off kar doonga aur aap ki motor pe haath rakh kar chaloonga, toh petrol bhi bachega* (I will switch off my motorbike engine and hold on to your car and be drawn along. This will save me petrol)."'

Husain spent about a decade at Filmistan as a writer. '*Dus-gyarah saal toh humney yeh sab hajaam-patti ki hai. Baad mein hum director banein* (I slogged for ten to eleven years doing all this.

---

[20]Ayesha Khan is also one of the junior artistes in the songs '*Shivji bihaane chaley*' and '*Nain khoye khoye*' in *Munimji*.

It was only later that I turned director).' These extended years, working as a salaried writer at the studio, helped him when he turned film-maker. He perfected the art of scriptwriting. 'You see, a good film-maker has to have a first-class script in place, since the script is the vehicle through which he makes a statement,' he said in an interview.[21]

The long years as writer also account for Husain's unique voice. As Nasreen Munni Kabir explained, 'You find that directors who have come from another tradition of expression become more interesting. You take Guru Dutt, he worked with Abrar [Alvi, the film writer], but Guru Dutt had one more trick up his sleeve and that was choreography. So he understood the camera and movement. You take Vishal [Bhardwaj], he has come from music. So when you have someone who comes from another tradition, they are very, very interesting. That's why I thought Nasir sa'ab had an individual voice ... Because as a writer when he was doing all those Filmistan films, you could sense that there is something different going on here.' Husain himself admitted to Nasreen, 'Writing and directing are very closely connected. If someone else writes the story, you will have to make changes to it as the director.'

The ultimate influence on Husain at Filmistan was S. Mukerji's. In an article titled 'What the People Want' (*Filmfare*, 4 August 1967), Husain attempted to answer the question that haunts a majority of film-makers who look at cinema as a commercial medium. Through the piece, Husain explained the challenges of producing a film that appeals to Indians across cultural and geographical boundaries. 'A film appreciated in Maharashtra may not be liked

---

[21]Ambarish Mishra, 'I will always be a romantic at heart', *The Times of India*, 7 May 2000.

in Punjab, Delhi, Uttar Pradesh, Bengal or the southern regions of India. A film-maker has to cater to the tastes of the people in India and, at the same time, to the needs of cinegoers in overseas territories,' Husain commented. At the end of the piece, Husain, by that time already the man behind several hit films, wrote, 'I must admit here that this special art of guessing about the people's entertainment needs, I learned very early in my career. My "guru" Mr. S. Mukerjee [sic] ... taught me not only the art of script-writing, but the ingredients of mass appeal in a movie.'

Such was his commitment to entertain that it often got in the way of Husain's business decisions. Subhash Mukerji narrated an episode in this regard. 'He liked only his kind of films – romantic, musical, comedy – the kind he made, my dad made.' One morning, Husain, who had by this time turned film distributor as well, called up Subhash and asked him to accompany him to the trial screening of Asit Sen's *Safar* (1970). Subhash noted that Husain was bored through the film.

'When the movie finished, I was smiling. "*Kyun hans rahey hain aap?* (Why are you smiling?)," he asked me. He had gone there as a distributor to see whether he could take the film for his distribution firm. I said, "*Main isliye hans raha hoon kyunki aapko yeh picture pasand nahin aayee* (I am smiling because you didn't like this film)."'

Husain's reaction was, '*Kya picture hai, cancer se marr raha hai* (What a depressing film, he is dying of cancer).' Subhash replied, '*Yeh picture mein music achhaa hai. Iss director ka yeh strong point hai. Yeh picture chalegi.* (The film has good music. This kind of story is the director's strength. This film will do well.)[22] You must remember, sir, you have come as a distributor and not as Nasir Husain, the director–producer. I guarantee you that this movie will do well.'

---

[22]Sen had made the tear-jerker *Khamoshi* (1969) earlier.

Husain remained adamant. He told Subhash, *'Nahin, nahin. Kya hai itna kuchh...* (No. What's so special about it?).'

On *Safar's* silver jubilee celebrations, Subhash called up Husain to make his point, which Husain graciously acknowledged. *'Haan, haan dekha maine. Silver jubilee kiya hai* (Yes, I can see. The film is celebrating its silver jubilee).'

A few years later, Husain organized a lavish function to celebrate the golden jubilee success of *Yaadon Ki Baaraat* (1973), to which he invited S. Mukerji as chief guest. With a number of people in attendance, Husain took to the microphone. Pointing to Mukerji, who was seated right beside him, Husain said, *'Aaj jo kuchh bhi main hoon, inhi ki wajah se hoon. Aur yeh aisey-waise guru nahin thay, yeh laat-waat bhi maar dete thay, jhaanpad bhi maar detey thay, but shaayad uss waqt humko uski zaroorat thee* (Whatever I am today, I am because of this man. And he is no ordinary teacher, he may have rebuked me, scolded me, but perhaps I needed it at that time).'

Subhash Mukerji, who was present at this function, said, 'I call it the height of loyalty and gratefulness also. To be able to say that in front of 500 people, in a party, was amazing. My uncle was squirming with embarrassment.'

3

'HE WAS SHAMMI KAPOOR'

'People remember that Salim–Javed brought the Angry Young Man, but not many people are aware that this contemporary, modern, dashing hero was created by Nasir Husain. To begin with, with Dev Anand. Then one step forward, with Shammi Kapoor. And this particular image of Shammi Kapoor was taken away by many people – maybe they enhanced it, exaggerated it, turned it into its own caricature whatever, but these two very strong images were created by one writer–director.'

– Writer–poet–lyricist Javed Akhtar

'Nasir Husain's films come out of a conversation with Western cinema.'

– Kaushik Bhaumik, associate professor, School of Arts and Aesthetics, Jawaharlal Nehru University, New Delhi

With India achieving independence in 1947, the dominant narratives in Hindi cinema in the 1950s changed towards nation building and commenting on the inequities that existed in this new, independent state. The classics of this period – *Awara* (1951), *Do Bigha Zamin* (1953), *Shree 420* (1955), *Pyaasa* (1957) and *Mother India* (1957) – reflected these themes. The four film-makers at the forefront in this era were Raj Kapoor, Bimal Roy, Mehboob Khan and Guru Dutt. Dr Rashmi Doraiswamy, professor at Academy of International Studies, Jamia Millia Islamia, explained the politics of these film-makers. 'Guru Dutt is the critic. He is always critiquing. In Raj Kapoor, it's the rich and the poor, the haves and the have-nots, that's the whole dynamics of his narratives with K.A. Abbas and all. With Bimal Roy, again the rural countryside, the city, the transition, migration. And Mehboob again, the whole panoramic, epic view of rural India.'

'Modernity', too, as seen in Mehboob's *Andaz* (1949),[1] had clearly arrived in Hindi cinema around this time. Several films of the 1950s – *Baazi* (1951), *Awara*, *Taxi Driver* (1954), *Aar Paar* (1954), *Shree 420* (1955), *C.I.D.* (1956) and *Howrah Bridge* (1958) – bring the city into sharp focus predominantly as a way of showcasing this tryst with and issues arising out of modernity. As film scholar M.K. Raghavendra commented, 'After 1947, Nehru's dominating nationalist ambition in turn set out to recreate the city for its own purposes: to make it not only the symbol of a new sovereignty but an effective engine to drive India into the modern world. The city was therefore a persuasive emblem for "Nehruvian modernity".'[2]

It was in this milieu that Husain set out to make his first film, *Tumsa Nahin Dekha*, even as *Paying Guest* was being made. 'After my first few stories had proved successful as films, I began

---

[1] *Andaz*'s modernity is underscored by its characters' Western attire, the men (Dilip Kumar and Raj Kapoor) having travelled overseas and Neena (Nargis) handing over the reins of her father's modern-day business empire to Dilip (Dilip Kumar).

[2] M.K. Raghavendra, 'The 1950s and 1960s', *Seduced by the Familiar: Narration and Meaning in Indian Popular Cinema*, Oxford University Press, 2008, p. 133.

to warm up to the idea that I could be even more successful if I became a director.'[3]

The problem for Husain was that when he was writing *Tumsa Nahin Dekha*, his mentor S. Mukerji was not in the country. 'I wanted to narrate *Tumsa Nahin Dekha*'s story to Mukerji sa'ab but he had fallen sick and gone away to London.' So, on Subodh Mukerji's recommendation, Husain went with his idea of *Tumsa Nahin Dekha* to Tolaram Jalan, 'Mr Moneybags' of Filmistan after Rai Bahadur Chunilal had passed away in the early 1950s. 'I told him, "I want to become a director. I am not interested in only writing" ... Tolaram Jalan asked me to narrate the story to him. "*Haan, humko sunaaiye. Hum faisla karengey. Woh kya faisla karengey* (Yes, tell me the story. I will decide. What will S. Mukerji decide?)." I narrated the entire story to him. He liked it. We started work on the film in Mukerji sa'ab's absence. When Mukerji sa'ab came back, he saw what was happening. I told Mukerji sa'ab, "I don't want to work [as a writer]. I want to direct. If you don't want me, sack me. I will try my luck outside Filmistan." He told me to stay on.' The making of Husain's first film, however, was not as easy as this.

Although Jalan had given his approval, he did not have faith in Husain. He gave Husain a shoestring budget for the film. At times, Jalan would force Husain to shoot on sets when the paint on them hadn't even dried. '*Ek sauteley bachchey ki tarah, jaisey palta hai, uss tarah woh picture bani* (The film was given step-motherly treatment),' Husain recalled, the consternation evident in his voice as he said this.

But if dealing with Jalan's penny-pinching ways was a hard task,

Husain had a bigger headache searching for *Tumsa Nahin Dekha*'s hero. The man originally pencilled in for the hero was Dev Anand. The impish, modern hero seemed a continuation of the Dev Anand characters that the actor had already played in *Munimji* and *Paying Guest*. As former editor of *Filmfare* and *Screen*, Rauf Ahmed, said, 'He [Husain] took it for granted because Dev and he had a good equation.' But Anand turned the role down, because he did not want to act opposite Ameeta. 'Ameeta had done a bit role in *Munimji*. So he was not interested. He was doing very well for himself. He said I can get any heroine I want,' explained Rauf.

Ameeta was an aspiring lead actress, working in Filmistan at this time. She had done a few films, including playing the girl (Bela) opposite Pran in *Munimji*. She had been cast as *Tumsa Nahin Dekha*'s heroine on Jalan's insistence. 'Seth ji [Jalan] wanted me to cast her,' said Husain. 'She used to work in the studio.' With Jalan determined to use the film as a launch pad for Ameeta's career,[4] Husain thought it better to move on after Anand's decision rather than stake his big break as a director.

Husain detailed the frustrating hunt for the film's protagonists before Jalan had insisted on Ameeta's name. 'I went to see many prospective heroes. Many heroines as well. I went to see Kishore Kumar. I went to Ajit. He was a good actor. I went to Madhubala … But nobody gives a newcomer a chance. They said they would think about it but they never got back. With great difficulty, Meena Kumari said, "I can give you a couple of days every month." *Jaise ki prasaad batt raha ho* (Like alms were being distributed).'

---

[4]In Rauf Ahmed's book, *Shammi Kapoor: The Game Changer*, 'The Turning Point', Om Publications, 2016, pp. 72-73, Ameeta explained her inclusion in *Tumsa Nahin Dekha* as Filmistan's decision to cut costs after their previous production *Hum Sab Chor Hain* had gone haywire. 'I was legitimately due for a break as a full-fledged heroine, so they cast me instead of an established heroine.'

By this time, S. Mukerji had returned from abroad. Once again, displaying his knack for spotting talent, Mukerji recommended Raj Kapoor's younger brother, Shamsher Raj Kapoor or Shammi Kapoor, to Husain. Husain was appalled. Shammi had done about nineteen films at this point, most of which had failed to click. Many were films like *Laila Majnu* (1953), *Gul Sanobar* (1953), *Mehbooba* (1954) and *Mirza Sahiban* (1957) – costume dramas, in which Shammi played a leaden male romantic lead.

The problem for Shammi was that the beginning of his career coincided with the era of Raj Kapoor, Dilip Kumar and Dev Anand – the Big Three, who were at the peak of their popularity at that time. Almost every other actor played second fiddle to these three men. Also, because of his pencil moustache and the Kapoor surname, audiences couldn't separate him from Raj Kapoor. It didn't help that the female characters in his films, like Shashikala in *Jeewan Jyoti* (1953), were underscoring the similarity by mouthing dialogues like, '*Aiee kitna badal gaya hai tu. Haaye, ab toh moochhein bhi nikal aayee hain. Oh ho jaise bilkul Raj Kapoor* (How different you look. Oh, you have grown a moustache. Just like Raj Kapoor).' The review for *Rail Ka Dibba* (1953), similarly, noted, 'Shammi Kapoor apes Raj Kapoor.'[5]

Aching over a floundering career, Shammi said as much. 'It hurt a lot because I didn't understand what it meant to ape somebody because I wasn't aping. I came from the same school of acting. We were from the same stage and had done the same roles. But it made me realize that it was going to be tough.'[6] Then there was Shammi's marriage to Geeta Bali, a far bigger star than him, after

---

[5]Deepa Gahlot, 'The Beginning of a Dynasty', *Shammi Kapoor: The Dancing Star – The Legends of Indian Cinema*, Wisdom Tree, 2008, p. 14.

[6]Nasreen Munni Kabir, 'Shammi Kapoor: A Star Like No Other', *Bollywood's Top 20 Superstars of Indian Cinema*, edited by Bhaichand Patel, Viking/Penguin Books India, 2012, p. 142.

a whirlwind romance in 1955. 'When I married the star Geeta Bali, I was in even deeper trouble. Then I was no longer only the son of Prithviraj Kapoor, and brother of Raj Kapoor, but I was also the husband of Geeta Bali. That's three-to-one.'[7]

But Mukerji was convinced. Ironically, the same Mukerji had turned Shammi down after a screen test for *Anarkali*, Husain's first successful film. This time, however, Mukerji had seen Shammi play a roguish character, an adventurous playboy who sweeps the heroine off her feet, in a Prithvi Theatres' play, *Kalakaar*, where he had starred alongside his father Prithviraj Kapoor and Uzra Mumtaz. 'On the basis of that, S. Mukerji was very sure that Shammi would do the role well,' Rauf commented.

What must have also helped convince Mukerji is that in 1956, a year before *Tumsa Nahin Dekha*, Shammi had acted in Filmistan's comic caper *Hum Sab Chor Hain*. The film starred Nalini Jaywant as the central character (and in a double role), but also had Ameeta in it. Shammi plays a wealthy, elite, westernized theatre owner, Mr Nath, whose mannerisms often border on the comic. Although he was still sporting his pencil moustache in the film, his character graph veers from a man falling over himself to satisfy the whims of his star performer Fifi (Ameeta) to someone who later fawns over Bimla (Jaywant) since that's where his business interests lie and also because he has fallen for her by the end of the film. All through, Mr Nath utters the catchphrase '*Balley oh balley*' and speaks with the air of an Englishman that would have surely tickled audiences.

Husain remained sceptical. 'I asked Mukerji sa'ab, "*Kar paayega yeh?* (Will he be able to do it?)" I had no faith in him. As an actor he was okay, but he wasn't popular. But Mukerji sa'ab told me to take him. I told him I might as well take Geeta Bali. She was a big star. Mukerji sa'ab told me, "Whosoever you get between

---

[7]Ibid.

the two, we will take that person.'" On Mukerji's advice, Husain narrated the story to both Geeta and Shammi. On hearing the narration, Geeta told Husain, *'Ismein toh mera role nahin hai. Role inka hai* (I don't have much of a role. He has a good role).' Husain concluded, 'That is how Shammi Kapoor got the role.'

Shammi, who had made up his mind to quit films if *Tumsa Nahin Dekha* didn't work out, changed his look for the film. 'I had nothing to lose. I went all out. Changed my image. Changed my style. Shaved off my moustache. Cut my hair short. Got myself a crew cut. And there grew the "Yahoo" image … I made *Tumsa Nahin Dekha*.'[8]

There is something about the year 1957 – one in which Hindi cinema produced classics that broached a number of critical subjects. Mehboob's *Mother India*, an allegory for India living in its villages, was at the very forefront of such films that released that year. The first of Guru Dutt's three tragedies, *Pyaasa*, which ended with a most scathing question asked of an increasingly materialistic society, *'Yeh duniya agar mil bhi jaaye toh kya hai?'* (What does it matter if one gets this world?), also came that year. B.R. Chopra's *Naya Daur* adopted a more buoyant tone and doffed its hat to the idea of Nehruvian socialism. Then there was V. Shantaram's *Do Aankhen Baarah Haath*, very much an embodiment of his commitment to reformist cinema.

Interspersed between these fine films were some other notable ones, which underscore the significance of 1957 as such an

---

[8]From 'Shammi Kapoor, Always in Time', featured in the series *Movie Mahal*, produced by Hyphen films for Channel 4 TV, UK. Interview by Nasreen Munni Kabir, 1987. (https://www.youtube.com/watch?v=b5h5Fs_sbHw)

important reference point in any study on Hindi cinema. There was the comedy *Dekh Kabira Roya* with an ensemble cast, which highlighted the pitfalls of modern love. *Ab Dilli Dur Nahin*, produced by Raj Kapoor, didn't do well at the box office, but made a larger social comment about the impersonal judicial system through the tale of a young boy determined to save his father from the gallows. *Paying Guest* also released in 1957. Nasreen Munni Kabir summarized the year best: 'What was very good with that year, you see the richness of a film industry when there are all kinds of threads of narrative.'

But 1957 has a much larger significance, going beyond the immediacy of the films. It saw the debuts of three directors, who would come to own and define much of Hindi cinema over the 1960s and 1970s. Hrishikesh Mukherjee, having worked as an editor with Bimal Roy, ushered in a new middle-of-the-road cinema with *Musafir*. Over the next two decades, Mukherjee would perfect his art while making us laugh and cry in equal measure with films like *Anari* (1959), *Satyakam* (1969), *Abhimaan* (1973), *Chupke Chupke* (1975) and *Gol Maal* (1979). In the same year, Vijay Anand, Dev Anand's brother, who first wrote *Taxi Driver*, turned director with the romantic thriller, *Nau Do Gyarah*. Vijay's screenplays, music sensibilities and interesting camera techniques resulted in some of the finest films of the 1960s like *Guide* (1965) and *Jewel Thief* (1967). Nine years from his first directorial venture, Vijay's career would overlap with Husain's, with the two joining hands on another seminal film, *Teesri Manzil* (1966). But for now, right at the end of this *annus mirabilis*, with a December 1957 release, Husain made his own debut with *Tumsa Nahin Dekha*.

Husain's directorial debut, which he also scripted and wrote the story and dialogues for, begins with a wealthy landowner, Sardar Rajpal (B.M. Vyas), who lives in Soona Nagar, Ghatpur, Assam.

Rajpal has a dark past as he tells Meena (Ameeta), a girl he raised after he found her abandoned many years ago. Twenty years ago, when he was known as Gopal, Rajpal had fled Shillong, having murdered a supposed friend, who cheated him of all his wealth while gambling. Rajpal is hesitant to return to Shillong because he fears the law will catch up with him. But Rajpal also pines for his wife Kamla (Anjali Devi) and son Shankar (Shammi Kapoor) whom he had left behind. Raising Meena helped Rajpal cope with his personal loss.

Rajpal puts out two advertisements in the newspapers: one seeking a couple of men to protect his estate from the local chieftain Bhola (Kanu Roy), with whom Rajpal has a long-running feud, and the other giving his whereabouts to his wife but in a way that only she knows who he is and can come and find him. On seeing the advertisements, Kamla asks Shankar to go to Soona Nagar to take up the job that Rajpal has advertised. Kamla does not tell Shankar who Rajpal really is since Shankar hates his father because he had left them to fend for themselves.

Meanwhile, the villain of the piece, Sohan (Pran), also makes his appearance. Sohan is Vishnu's (Raj Mehra) son, the brother of the man Rajpal had murdered. Vishnu, having seen Rajpal's advertisements, realizes who he really is. He gives Sohan the background. Sohan then makes his way to Soona Nagar to present himself as Rajpal's long-lost son so that he can usurp Rajpal's property to avenge his uncle's death. Consequently, both Pran and Shammi Kapoor reach Soona Nagar and present themselves to Rajpal as Shankar. Rajpal hires both men, hoping to learn their real identities. Naturally, Shankar and Meena also get acquainted and romance blossoms between them.

Although *Tumsa Nahin Dekha* begins with a crime, and though Rajpal and Meena are left wondering who the real Shankar is, the film has the effervescence that Husain had displayed with his screenplay and dialogues in *Munimji* and *Paying Guest*. Even the conflict that Rajpal has with Bhola over buying land from the government at throwaway rates, but which Bhola's fiancé, Seema (Sheila Vaz), claims belongs to the local communities no matter what is written on paper, is a red-herring. The film doesn't attempt to make any social statement, a departure from the classics of the time.

Instead, with a well-knit screenplay, and with the thoroughly enjoyable exchanges that take place between Shankar and Meena as they fall in love with each other, *Tumsa Nahin Dekha* is a breezy entertainer. The film has a terrific musical score, with some delightful songs, including the title track, '*Jawaaniya yeh mast mast bin peeye*', '*Chhupnewaale saamne aa*' and '*Sar par topi laal*'.

The 31 January 1958 *Filmfare* review called *Tumsa Nahin Dekha* 'A Highly Entertaining Film'. It said, 'Though this story of love and revenge could have easily become a melodrama, writer–director Nasir Husain has succeeded in maintaining a proper balance between the serious and the comic. The dialogue sparkles with wit, and a fast pace is sustained in the narrative from start to finish. This is creditable, in view of the fact that the picture is Nasir Husain's first independent vehicle as a writer and director.' The audiences too loved the film and it went on to become Shammi Kapoor's maiden hit. But the impact of *Tumsa Nahin Dekha* went beyond the reviews and its reception by the masses.

Hindi films of the late-1940s right up to the mid-1950s had the hero and heroine fall in love almost instantly. There was no elaborate courtship between the film's protagonists. The narratives concentrated on what happened after the film's protagonists fell in love or the obstacles that came in the way of realizing their romance. There were exceptions like *Aan* (1952), *Mr. & Mrs. '55* (1955) and *Chori Chori* (1956), but such films were few and far between.

In Dev Anand's *Ziddi*, for instance, his character and Kamini Kaushal's character are shown to fall in love and talk marriage within the first twenty minutes of the film. In *Awara*, Raj (Raj Kapoor) and Rita (Nargis) fall in love with each other the moment they realize they were childhood friends. Filmistan's *Nagin* was perhaps the most bizarre. Here, two ethnic communities are locked in enmity for several years when the film begins. Against this background, Mala (Vyjayanthimala) and Sanatan (Pradeep Kumar), the respective successors to both clans, make grand declarations of heaping more misery on the other community at the start of the film, but take precisely seven cinematic minutes from their first acquaintance to fall in love.

This instant romance irked Husain. He told Nasreen, 'One thing I did not like about the films in those days was that in all the films there was this usual scene that the hero is sitting and the heroine comes from behind. She then puts her hands on the hero's eyes and asks, "*Bolo main kaun hoon?* (Guess, who?)" I don't remember how many times I had seen this scene. *Bezaar ho gaya thaa main.* (I was completely frustrated.) I wanted to do this in a more modern way.'

He did. For him, the wooing was an important part of his narrative. 'It's the process of falling in love that's more exciting than the romance itself,' he said.[9] He would have the lead pair acquainted early in the film, but with the hero (always) initially irritating the heroine with his demeanour or tricks. The heroine would resist the hero, even loathe him, but only until he rescues her from a tricky situation or has built up empathy in her heart

---

[9]Deepa Gahlot, 'It's the chase that is exciting', *Filmfare*, 1-15 November 1984, p. 75.

through one of his ploys (such as terminal illness) after which she reciprocates his affection.

Although this can be seen in *Munimji* and *Paying Guest*, it is in *Tumsa Nahin Dekha* that the romance between Meena and Shankar played out for a far longer duration. Bear in mind that in *Munimji*, Roopa has fallen for Raj before the halfway mark in the film. Something similar happens in *Paying Guest*, where Shanti and Ramesh sing the wonderful duet '*Chhod do aanchal zamaana kya kahega*' just after the forty-five-minute mark. In both films, the storyline takes a different turn once the romance between the protagonists has been established.

Tumsa Nahin Dekha is different. Here Meena and Shankar come into contact quite early in the film. But it isn't until late in the second half, after Shankar has rescued Meena from being held hostage by Bhola, that Meena has a change of heart. Before that, the two are at loggerheads, beginning from the time that they meet at the station and, by sheer coincidence, share a train journey while making their way to Ghatpur. Their constant bickering, moments of madness and battle of wits, even through a song, '*Aaye hain door se*', make *Tumsa Nahin Dekha* a fun film. Take the exchange the two have immediately at Soona Nagar station, fighting for the only tonga available that can take them to Ghatpur, with a hapless tongawallah caught in the crossfire.

> Meena: *Aye, aye! Yeh taanga mera hai. Tum ismey nahin ja saktey.* (Hey, hey! This is my tonga. You cannot take it.)
>
> Shankar: *Kyun nahin ja sakta? Aapse pehley mera saamaan pahuncha hai.* (Why can't I? My luggage was loaded on it before you reached.)
>
> Meena: *Taangeywaaley, mera saamaan rakho.* (Tongawallah, load up my luggage.)
>
> Shankar: *Taangeywaaley, khabardaar! Agar inn madam ka saamaan*

iss taangey mein rakha toh tumhaari yeh lambi moochhey ukhaad loonga. (Tongawallah, beware! If you place this lady's luggage in the tonga, I will rip your long moustache off.)

Taangeywaala: *Yeh kya kar rahe hain, huzoor? Jhagda aap dono ka hai aur dushmani meri moochhon se?* (What are you doing, sir? Why direct your ire at my moustache when it is the two of you fighting?)

Shankar: *Aisa hi hoga. Military mein reh chuka hoon pyaare, pehla waar moochhon pe karta hoon.* (That's how it is. I have served in the military, my dear, I always attack the moustache first.)

Meena: *Sahaab military ke hajaam thay. Tum iski fikra na karo. Mera saamaan rakho warna tumhaara keema nikaal diya jaayega.* (The gentleman was a barber in the army. Don't you worry about him! Load my luggage or I will make mincemeat of you.)

Shankar: *Ha ha, memsa'ab ki gosht ki dukaan hai…* (Ha, ha, the lady appears to be a butcher…)

[Meena cuts Shankar off by lunging for his throat.]

A similar banter between the hero and the heroine played out pretty much in each Husain film. The nok-jhonk between the protagonists kept the audience riveted. The hero's puckishness matched the heroine's feisty, will-tolerate-no-nonsense attitude and formed the bulk of Husain's narratives. 'Add to that good music, a lot of humour and the audience enjoys it,' Husain said.[10]

The crucial point here is that Husain didn't patent the lengthening of the wooing process. It is his style that was different. Films like *Albela* (1951), *Dholak* (1951) and *Mr. & Mrs. '55* had already started breaking from the mould. However, in these films, the onset of romance happened on a slow boil. It wasn't until much later in the film that the crucial admission of love happened.

---

[10]Ibid.

In Husain's films, the hero almost immediately falls in love with the heroine. The heroine hates the sight of him initially only to have a change of heart midway or closer to the film's climax. 'The "hate" or "pretend hate" is not mutual, as in the other films,' noted Madhulika Liddle.

According to Rauf Ahmed, 'He wanted to make the hero bold and aggressive. The hero would have to really fight for her. He will sing and dance. He will not be ashamed of himself. The earlier concept was that singing and dancing were all for women.' But Rauf also recalled Shammi's complaint with this elongated courtship approach pursued by the hero: 'Shammi Kapoor would say, "Yes, I will have to fight for her, but by the time I win, the villain comes. I don't get any time with her."'

But Husain did give his protagonists a few tender moments together. In *Jab Pyar Kisise Hota Hai*, when Sunder (Dev Anand) and Nisha (Asha Parekh) spend a day out in Neelgaon's idyllic environs, Nisha asks Sunder, '*Kahiye, dekhi hai issey zyaada khoobsurat cheez?* (Tell me, have you seen anything more beautiful?)' Sunder responds in the affirmative. When Nisha says he is lying and asks where he has seen such a place, he responds, turning to Nisha, '*Jab gardann ghumaata hoon, dekh leta hoon* (When I turn my head, I see it).' Husain also used poetry in such moments as seen from his dialogues across films. This ability to build romance with a certain delicate touch is what ultimately helped Husain bounce back at the fag end of his career.

Tumsa Nahin Dekha's biggest impact was the change in Shammi Kapoor's fortunes, which in turn changed the persona of the mainstream Hindi film hero. Shammi, initially, couldn't believe that audiences had accepted the film wholeheartedly. At the premiere held at Bombay's Naaz cinema, Shammi was somewhat confused by the audience's constant hooting and clapping. He feared yet another flop. 'He asked me, "*Nasir, kya hua, log gaaliyaan de rahe hain kya?* (Nasir, what's happening, are people jeering?)" I replied, "*Gaali nahin de rahe hain, magar hall mein commotion hai. Tumhaari taareef kar rahe hain* (They aren't jeering, but there is commotion in the hall. They are complimenting you)."

Filmfare said of Shammi, 'Shammi Kapoor playing a gay, carefree role, discards the Kapoor grand manner and invests his portrayal with his own zestful, reckless attitude to life. His performance is more memorable for the effortless ease with which it is put over. It should prove a turning point in his career and help to put him in the ranks of the top-notchers.'[11] Ironically, the film which Jalan had hoped would give Ameeta's career a fillip, boosted Shammi's instead.

The Hindi film hero before *Tumsa Nahin Dekha* bore the weight of the world on his shoulders. A cursory look at the characters played by the heroes of the post-independence era, particularly the 'Big Three' – Dilip Kumar, Dev Anand and Raj Kapoor – leading up to 1957, tells us that they were weighed down either by nation-building narratives (Dev Anand in *Vidya*, 1948; Dilip Kumar in *Shikast*, 1953, and *Amar*, 1954), or their indigent, sometimes amoral state (Raj Kapoor in *Awara* and *Anari*, 1959; Dev Anand in *Baazi, Taxi Driver, House No. 44*), or suffering experienced in romance (Dilip Kumar in *Devdas*, 1955, and *Madhumati*, 1958; Dev Anand in *Ziddi*), or because of their underdog status (Dev Anand in *C.I.D.*,1956) or as protagonists showcasing the evils of society (Balraj Sahni in *Do Bigha Zamin*; Raj Kapoor in *Shree 420* and *Phir Subah Hogi*, 1958; Guru Dutt in *Pyaasa* and *Kaagaz Ke Phool*, 1959, and Dev Anand in *Milap*, 1955).

'The hero before that was actually a bit defeatist,' summarized

---

[11]*Filmfare*, 31 January 1958.

Rauf. 'He was a very emotional man, the sacrificing type, wanting to give his life up like Dilip Kumar used to do in his movies. His good nature is the essence of his character, the starting point. The heroine fell in love with the nice person.'

Consequently, the hero didn't have time for fun or unbridled mirth. All his energies were directed towards achieving the end that would free him of his burden. If he was a complete cynic, a nihilist, like the poet Vijay in *Pyaasa*, he would leave the world to its ways and go his own path. He would even accept defeat like Shambhu (Balraj Sahni) in *Do Bigha Zamin*. But he couldn't laugh or wasn't allowed the luxury to live life with gay abandon.

But Shankar was different. He is introduced in *Tumsa Nahin Dekha* through the enchanting Mohammed Rafi number, '*Jawaaniya yeh mast mast bin peeye*', which sets up his romantic character from the beginning. In the very next scene, when his uncle asks him whether he has found a job, he isn't too perturbed even when his uncle tries to remind him about his mother's long struggle in providing for him. Instead, he asks his uncle to relax and shows him a wad of notes, which spooks the latter considerably.

> Chacha: *Arrey, yeh kahaan se laaya?* (Where did you get this?)
>
> Shankar: *Chacha, yeh mat poochho kahaan se laaya hoon aur kaisey laaya hoon, lekin kamaayee imaan ki hai, Chacha. Chacha, kabhi race ke maidaan par gaye ho?* (Uncle, don't ask me from where and how I got this, but I earned it honestly. Uncle, have you ever visited a racecourse?)
>
> Chacha: *Nahin baba.* (No, my child.)
>
> Shankar: *Kya ajeeb jagah hai woh bhi. Ek taraf ghodey bhaagtey hain aur doosri taraf gadhey chillaatey hain, 'Come on, come on'* [pulls his uncle by grabbing his shawl while saying this] *aur kabhi kabhi Bhagwaan bhi gadhon ki sunn leta hai, Chacha. Arrey waah re Bhagwaan!* (What a strange place it is. On one side you

have horses racing and on the other, you have donkeys egging them on, 'Come on, come on' and sometimes god listens to the donkeys as well, uncle. Praise the lord!)

The exchange ends here, with Shankar leaving his uncle in splits at his retelling of a day at the races. In Nasir Husain's world, the lack of a regular job[12] or a mother's toils don't hold the hero back; neither does his uncle worry for too long. The hero's Teflon-hide and his penchant for flippancy deflect all problems. In *Paying Guest*, similarly, Ramesh's exertions as an advocate don't get in the way of his romantic escapades. He also has no dilemmas in taking money from Shanti to pay the rent to Babu Digambernath.

The Husain hero could, therefore, go and spend a day at the racecourse, sing songs, romance and remain buoyant. All through he portrayed a delightful impishness, a joie de vivre rarely seen in the Hindi film hero, heightened by his sharp-wittedness and sense of humour. As Husain said, '*Humaarey yahaan chat zubaan, zubaan se khelne waala, aise dialogue hua kartey thay. Har ek baat ka ulta jawaab deta thaa, is tarah ka character* (Quick-witted, sharp-tongued, that's the kind of dialogues I wrote. Being irreverent about everything said to him, that's how the character was).'

It must be mentioned here that this waggish character that Husain portrayed seemed greatly inspired from Shafiq-ur-Rahman, one of Husain's favourite writers. The Pakistani humourist and short-story writer, whose stories were all about college romances and first loves, and were often based in idyllic, hill-station settings, time and again presented a male character who had a bit of the devil in him. He could leave you in splits with his quick-wittedness and his absurdities. Nuzhat confirmed this to me. 'All the pranks in Dad's films that the hero does to impress the

---

[12]We are informed that Shankar is waiting for some war to begin so that he can go back to his old job in the military.

girl, to get out of a problem, is very much P.G. Wodehouse and Shafiq-ur-Rahman.' At the same time, Rahman's romances were tender, never deteriorating into anything crude. Husain's dialogues for building up the romance between his protagonists reflected this tehzeeb in Rahman's writing. Javed Akhtar commented, 'I think Nasir Husain was influenced by Shafiq-ur-Rahman. His humour and romance originate there, not that he has plagiarized anything, but I think this chemistry has come from there.'

There was an even more significant aspect to Husain's male hero. Before *Tumsa Nahin Dekha*, the Hindi film hero seldom danced. How could he, for the weight of the entire world was on his shoulders. On the rare occasion that he did, like Raj Kapoor in '*Mud mud ke na dekh*' or in '*Dil ka haal suney dilwaala*' in *Shree 420*, his actions were characterized by a kind of rhythmic one-two, one-two movement that responded to the beat of the song. For a large part, the actor's movements went into enacting the meanings of the lyrics, much like a mime artist, but mostly with his hands coming into prominence. Dilip Kumar did something similar in '*Udey jab jab zulfein teri*' from *Naya Daur*. Besides making his entry in the song, clapping and hopping on one leg, his movements in the song are largely restricted to him performing with his hands.

Dev Anand was possibly the most limited of the three. Whether in his teasing, romantic songs in *Munimji* and *Paying Guest*, or in his lighter but philosophical songs from his earlier films like '*Mere labon pe dekho aaj bhi taraaney hain*' (*Baazi*), '*Chaahey koi khush ho chaahey gaaliyaan hazaar de*' (*Taxi Driver*) or '*Oonche sur mein gaaye ja*' (*House No. 44*), Anand relied solely on his facial expressions and the inimitable way in which he moved his head to enact most of these songs. As author Jerry Pinto pointed out,

'With Dev Anand what you had was a loose-limbed lope.' Even much later, in the 1960s and '70s, it is difficult to think of a Dev Anand song as a 'dance' number. Moreover, there were hardly any situations where these men were allowed to dance with complete abandon. The few exceptions to this were Raj Kapoor exuding a manic energy in '*Main hoon ek khalaasi*' in *Sargam* where he goes absolutely nuts by the end of the song. He flails his arms and smacks himself repeatedly on the head, with the recklessness of a man who has let go of himself completely. Dilip Kumar, too, in *Naya Daur*, feeding off the energy of the bhangra dancers in the latter half of '*Yeh desh hai veer jawaano ka*', exhibits this kind of uninhibitedness.

But such instances were few and far between. Instead, it is the image of Dilip Kumar confined to his bed, singing '*Seeney mein sulagtey hain armaan*' to Madhubala in *Tarana* (1951) while tucked in a blanket, a bandage on his forehead, that is the archetype for a song sequence involving a hero for most of the 1950s. Inanimate, constrained and brooding. Kaushik Bhaumik, based on these visuals, opined, 'The musical culture of the '50s is very different to the musical culture of the '60s. The '50s is very much within the old, theatrical, operatic tradition of music. Music is static. It's coming from a static source. Someone is standing, singing. It's completely operatic in that sense.'

The final song in *Tumsa Nahin Dekha*, '*Sar par topi laal*', made a dramatic departure. Early in the song, after Shankar has sung his half of the mukhda, '*Gorey gorey gaal, gaal pe uljhey uljhey baal, ho tera kya kehna*', he claps along with the junior male artistes for a few seconds, showing a joviality that matches the beat of the song. But then as the song heads into a climax, Shankar hits another gear. He bursts into a series of onomatopoeic sounds, in tandem with his frenetic movements. He is shown dancing on one leg, going back and forth with the male artistes, matching them step for step all the while. He shouts out '*oh sad ke, oh beliyaa*' and flits across the frame. The sheer abandon that characterizes this forty-second-long frenetic finish, helmed very much by Shammi (Ameeta also does her bit), was missing in the hero of the time.

This was not a one-off. In Husain's very next film, *Dil Deke Dekho* (1959), Shammi dances his way through most of the film. Shammi's entire frame features prominently in the songs '*Megha re bole*', '*Do ekum do*', '*Pyaar ho toh keh do yes*' and '*Yaar chulbula hai*', differentiating him from other mainstream heroes. For these heroes, the camera would generally limit itself to the upper half of their anatomy, mid-shots to close-ups, given their penchant for enacting song sequences with facial expressions. But Shammi, with his feline grace and innate sense of rhythm, was shown in long-shots more regularly through the course of a song. This is not to say that Shammi conformed to any conventional dance forms when he performed in these songs. In fact, he even claimed not knowing how to dance[13] but his energy, verve and rhythm in these sequences (and in later films) were unmatched and very different from the norm.

'*Yaar chulbula hai*', interestingly, is very similar in its placement in the film and picturization to '*Sar par topi laal*'. Both numbers are the last song sequences in their respective films. Both songs signify the coming together of the protagonists, after the extended wooing has played out and all misunderstandings have been cleared. Both songs are shot outdoors, with local male and female artistes shown alongside the hero and the heroine. Both songs have a frenetic finish, where the hero dances unfettered and uninhibited.

---

[13]'I do not know how to dance, but I have given expression to my songs.' *The King of Romance: Shammi Kapoor, Part 3*, https://www.youtube.com/watch?v=PkHvc2vg2i8

It is interesting to trace the genealogy of the Nasir Husain hero. Sanjit Narwekar contended that the first leading man in Indian cinema to have a decidedly comic image was Motilal. Although he was known as the man with the Midas touch, having starred in a rush of hit films for Sagar studios in the 1930s, his roles in comic films like *Do Diwane* aka *Gay Birds* (1936) and *300 Days And After* (1938) gave Motilal the credentials of a comic hero. However, for much of the 1940s, Motilal immersed himself in serious films and it wasn't until R.K. Shorey's *Ek Thee Ladki* (1949) that he made a return to comedy. Then followed *Mr. Sampat* (1952) and *Mastana* (1954), where he played the Chaplinesque-lead. Then there was *Jaagtey Raho* (1956), where he played a comic drunk, singing the beautiful song '*Zindagi khwaab hai*'.

'Motilal's greatest asset as a hero–comedian was that he had a natural air of gaiety, which manifested itself on the screen,' wrote Narwekar. 'The glint in his eye, the raffish looks and the debonair charm combined to make him one of the leading stars of his era … Motilal's was a hard act to follow. For a decade there was none who could step into his shoes … The star who did the trick was Shammi Kapoor.'[14] But with Motilal comedy was only a small part of his legacy. He was chameleon-like, adapting to the demands of his character, which explains him playing even villainous roles in later films like *Anari* (1959) and *Paighaam* (1959).

There is also a temptation to think of the Husain hero as an extension of the personas of the actors Bhagwan and Kishore Kumar. This is incorrect. If one is to go by Bhagwan's *Albela* (1951), the only film of any real prominence for the actor, and the song '*Shola jo bhadke*' that featured him and Geeta Bali, Bhagwan displays the same kind of rhythmic, choreographed movements that Raj Kapoor later exhibits in his two songs from *Shree 420*.

---

[14]Sanjit Narwekar, 'The Hero as Comedian', *Eena Meena Deeka: The Story of Hindi Film Comedy*, Rupa & Co., 2005, p. 186.

It would be a real stretch to term Bhagwan's style as uninhibited in this sequence. As Jerry Pinto pointed out, 'He gets his effects from the incompleteness of his movements, the minimalism of the steps.'

Kishore Kumar was actually uninhibited, much like Shammi Kapoor. Watch him in '*Jaaney bhi de chhod ye bahaana*' (*Baap Re Baap*, 1955), '*Hum thay woh thee*' (*Chalti Ka Naam Gaadi*, 1958) and '*C-A-T cat, cat maaney billi*' (*Dilli Ka Thug*, 1958) and Kishore displays tremendous energy and an innate sense of timing even as he enacts cinematic frenzy. There was a madness about him which came through not just in his singing and comedy, but in his dancing as well.

Both Bhagwan and Kishore, however, were seen as pure comic heroes. Audiences did not receive them in the same way as they did the Big Three. To illustrate, Madhulika Liddle quoted her father, who, as much as he loved *Albela*, once said, 'Who wants to relate to Bhagwan?' Narwekar, correspondingly, wrote of Kishore, 'In fact, quite often, his having to also romance the heroine came in the way of his sense of comedy. In many of his films like *New Delhi* (1956), *Dilli Ka Thug*, *Naughty Boy* (1962) and *Ek Raaz* (1963), one can see his dilemma of being a romantic hero cast in the comic mould. Having begun on the funny note in the initial romantic scenes it becomes quite a volte face to get into the more serious climax.'[15]

But Husain's Shankar, and later, Roop/Raja (Shammi Kapoor) in *Dil Deke Dekho*, makes it a point to showcase his virility when threatened by the enemy. At no point does he shy away from the threat posed by Pran or Siddhu (the villain in *Dil Deke Dekho*), but instead fights them with aplomb. As Madhulika Liddle observed in an email exchange with me, 'Shammi Kapoor personified the "hero" one could aspire to be: handsome, debonair, urbane,

---

[15]Ibid., 'The Reluctant Comedian', p. 76.

witty – yet ultimately not a clown. When push came to shove, his character would always end up doing the noble thing, not resorting to antics for anything that wasn't light-hearted to start off with. He was always the *hero*.'

Most notably, Husain broke new ground with *Dil Deke Dekho* in another way as well. When Neeta's (Asha Parekh) friend calls up the Deonar Club and asks the male voice at the other end, 'Are you the drum player?',[16] the nature of this abrupt question is meant to emphasize its significance. Before *Dil Deke Dekho*, it was rare that the hero would be a musician in a Western band. If he played a musician,[17] the character would be rooted in Indian culture. The heroes played Urdu poets, ghazal singers or musical maestros. *Tansen* (1943), *Baiju Bawra* (1952), *Pyaasa* (1957) and *Phagun* (1958) are examples that come to mind. Moreover, there was a general air of condescension towards such figures since music was not seen as a respectable profession. In the 1960 film, *Manzil*, Dev Anand's character, a music composer educated in music in the West, sets out for Bombay from Shimla after he bears the brunt of a series of snide remarks from his father (K.N. Singh) and father-in-law (Manmohan Krishna) such as '*Sangeet se pet toh nahin bharta*' (Music won't give you bread and butter) and '*Gaaney-bajaaney waalon ko toh aaj kal koi ladki bhi nahin deta*' (Nobody wants to let their daughters marry a musician).

---

[16]In fact, before Neeta's friend actually makes the phone call, Shammi's character is referred to as the drum player on five instances, underscoring the novel nature of his profession.

[17]The musician figure in *Dil Deke Dekho* is not to be confused with the protagonists of films like *Albela* (1951) and *Aasha* (1957). In the latter films, the main characters sing and dance because they are employed in the theatre as 'actors' and not as 'musicians'.

In contrast to these films, *Dil Deke Dekho* was a novel enterprise in the commercial mainstream. Here, the hero is a modern, Western-style drummer in a club, at home with rock-'n'-roll, pop and jazz sequences, something of an anathema in the Indian cinema of the era, given its discomfort with 'modernity'. By presenting Shammi Kapoor in this role (and later in *Teesri Manzil*, 1966), Husain pushed the envelope and broke stereotypes. If later films like *China Town* (1962), *Kismet* (1968), *Karz* (1980), *Disco Dancer* (1982) and as recently as Imtiaz Ali's *Rockstar* (2011), use Western-style musician figures at the crux of their plots, credit is owed to Husain for pioneering such characterizations.

The success of both *Tumsa Nahin Dekha* and *Dil Deke Dekho* spurred Shammi on his path to stardom. These films gave him an image distinct from the Dev Anand–Dilip Kumar–Raj Kapoor troika. Mouthing catchphrases like 'yahoo' (first used in *Tumsa Nahin Dekha*) and 'tally-ho' (first used in *Dil Deke Dekho*), here was a distinct Western, modern hero, who didn't carry the burden of the world, who romanced his love interest with flair, who didn't seem to mind using the odd shortcut to get ahead, who danced and shimmied across the screen with abandon, but who ultimately righted all wrongs that had been done to him, with his masculinity coming to the fore. He was quickly dubbed the 'rebel star' and a 'dancing hero' – terms credited to L.P. Rao, then editor of *Filmfare*.

'Most importantly, he exuded an unabashed and irresistible sexuality that was far from the heroes of the time, who projected romanticism but rarely sexuality,' wrote Nasreen. 'With his dreamy eyes, soft voice, charming dialogue delivery and arresting personality, Shammi Kapoor radiated the raw appeal of an Elvis Presley, especially evident when performing songs.'[18]

---

[18]Nasreen Munni Kabir, 'Shammi Kapoor: A Star Like No Other', in *Bollywood's Top 20 Superstars of Indian Cinema*, edited by Bhaichand Patel, Viking/Penguin Books India, 2012, p. 143.

This similarity to Elvis was most apparent in the song '*Kaun yeh aaya mehfil mein*' in *Dil Deke Dekho*, inspired by the Paul Anka classic '*Diana*'. Here, Shammi – wearing a white-patterned jacket knotted at the waist, over a black-coloured turtleneck and black trousers, his hair brushed – sings, dances and serenades Neeta (Parekh) at the Royal Hotel where he has taken up the job of a bandmaster.

Husain admitted to Nasreen that he watched many of the Presley movies and loved Presley's character. 'I loved his dancing style. I loved his dialogue-delivery … His rhythm was a different kind of rhythm, the way he moved his legs.' He told Nasreen that he had a discussion with Shammi and told him that '*Iska andaaz hi alag hai* (He has an altogether different style)'. Husain claimed that he did not ask Shammi to imitate Presley, 'but I told him to look at his movements, to look at his style'. When Nasreen asked him if he thought that Presley, a very American hero, would actually appeal to the Indian audience, Husain's reply was prescient. 'He was an American, but as an Indian, if I liked the way he moved, others would like it, too.'

They did. By the end of the 1950s, a new movie-going audience was taking shape, one that didn't want to be reminded of the experiences of the past. 'The 1950s were too tense. The nation has just come into being and there is this whole ideological kind of thing,' explained Kaushik Bhaumik. M.K. Raghavendra said something similar in an email interview to me while explaining Shammi's appeal: 'Shammi Kapoor's free-spiritedness, I would argue, could only come out of a free nation and not out of a British colony. This has less to do with his appealing to a younger generation than with addressing a younger generation growing up in freedom.' Both statements tied in with Jerry Pinto's comment, who noted in his book *Helen: The Life and Times of an H-Bomb*, 'Any cinema to be successful, must give the nation in which it is born what the nation needs.'[19]

Bhaumik juxtaposed Husain's first few films, with their emphasis on youth, in a larger context, against the Hollywood experience. 'By the time we come to the '60s a new kind of Hollywood cinema is coming about, with youthful characters. Elvis Presley is acting in his films [Presley made his acting debut with *Love Me Tender* in 1956]. There are interesting kinds of experimentation done by the auteurs of Hollywood; film-makers like Delmer Daves, a master western film-maker, shifted ground and made a certain kind of youth-oriented films in the 1960s. So I'm sure these guys are watching these films and adapting them to the Indian context. So at no point does he [Husain] do the Shammi Kapoor films outside the history of respectable global cinema.' When I told Bhaumik of Husain's admission of being in awe of Presley, he remarked, 'Of course. This is precisely what I am saying, the best of popular Indian cinema has always come out of a dialogue with Hollywood genre cinema.'

Husain himself admitted to being conscious of targeting the youth in his films. 'In all my films, I kept note of who watches films nowadays. It's the youth that watches films. Elderly people might watch it once, but will not go for a film again. So when I made films in those days, I paid attention to the youth and to the masses, who were the main consumers of films. I never ignored them. I kept in mind what they liked and what they didn't like. Like songs, I always put special emphasis on them.'

At the same time, Husain stayed clear of being preachy. When Nasreen asked him if he had any idea of how much he changed the image of youth in Hindi cinema, he said he had never thought about it. 'I thought my job was to entertain. Nothing more. I can't change the youth. I can't change their opinion. I can't change

---

[19]Jerry Pinto, 'The Woman Who Could Not Care', *Helen: The Life and Times of an H-Bomb*, Penguin Books India, 2006, p. 45.

anything because people go to the movies to enjoy and not to be a better man. No person goes to the movie house thinking, "Seeing this movie I will be a better man." He goes to enjoy.' On being asked about the impact Shammi Kapoor's character had on the youth of India, Husain responded, 'Yes, there is no doubt that he was liked in the film. His actions were liked. His comedy was liked. It might have reflected somehow on the character of the people. But I never made a film [with this thought] that one will become a better person after seeing this film.'

There is perhaps another more significant reason for the success of the Shammi Kapoor character. There is a deep-rooted connection between the Shammi persona that Husain created and Indian mythology. Lord Krishna, an incarnation of Vishnu, endears himself to Indians for his charm with the gopis of Vrindavan, the melody of his bansuri, his naughty ways as a child, his sharp-wittedness and cleverness. But Lord Krishna is unafraid to bend rules in the name of dharma. He could ultimately rely on his own strength to slay the biggest of demons. It is interesting also that in Hindu mythology, Rama, who is seen as 'Maryada Purshottam' (the Perfect Man), predates Krishna as an earlier avatar of Vishnu. Rama is burdened by duties towards his father, his brothers and ultimately even towards his subjects. It is hard to find moments of sustained joy in his life. This ties in with the genealogy of mainstream heroes of Hindi cinema post-1947, where Dilip Kumar, Dev Anand and Raj Kapoor were weighed down and largely (even in their darker roles) veered to the ideal (by the climax they definitely did). Shammi, who followed the trio, was closer to the Krishna figure.

It is no coincidence, therefore, that in a film like Shakti Samanta's *China Town*, one of the characters played by Shammi (the film has Shammi in a double role) is a hotel singer, Shekhar, who is in love with Rita (Shakila). Rita's father (S.N. Banerjee) doesn't approve of Shekhar's profession. When Shekhar, in the guise of a sadhu, tells Rita's father that his daughter is very lucky for she will marry a very good-looking man and someone who loves music, her father is a little stunned. He asks, '*Sangeet premi?* (Music lover?)' To this, Shekhar replies, '*Sangeet koi buri cheez nahin hai, bachcha. Gau-on ke charhaiyaa, raas rachaiyaa, Sree Krishna kanhaiyaa thay bansuri bajaiyaa* (Music isn't a bad thing, my child. The cowherd, the amorous lover, Shri Krishna played the flute).'

Even the *Dil Deke Dekho* song, '*Megha re bole*', seems to corroborate this theory. Here, Shammi as Raja serenades the women of the countryside in order to show off his singing qualities to Neeta (Parekh). He says, '*Mere gaaney par sunder naariyaan daudi chali aati hain* (Beautiful women come running when they hear me sing).' Although he is a drummer performing in clubs and hotels, Raja's idioms and expressions in the song are distinctively folk and veer towards chaste Hindi. But of course the women respond to him. They are dancing by his side all through the song sequence even as it shifts into the more Western-style '*Bade hain dil ke kaaley*'. This blending of cultures was an essential part of Husain's cinema, and as Bhaumik commented on Raja's reaching out to the women, 'This is the Krishna figure – this is part of what I call the leela model of the Indian hero.'

There is no doubt about Shammi's contribution to the success of Husain's first two films. The audience responded to his image makeover, his physicality, his roguish appeal and his dancing. But cinema is a collaborative exercise, with great films often coming out of a meeting of minds. Had it not been for Husain's screenplay, the charm of the extended wooing process, the banter between the hero and the heroine, the music and the innovatively shot song sequences, things may have come apart for both men.

Both men recognized this. In *Shammi Kapoor: The Dancing Hero*, authored by journalist, critic and writer Deepa Gahlot, Husain acknowledged Shammi's qualities. 'While working with him, I felt he was an all-rounder – he could do comedy, he could play emotions, he could be physical and tremendously musical. It is very rare to find all these talents in one person … I can't say that the dance movements he became famous for were my idea. Of course, I used to make suggestions but the dance movements were entirely his. It was entirely his creation.'[20] Shammi returned the compliment, saying, '*Tumsa Nahin Dekha* was my first big hit. Nasir helped me create my style. The hands-out, flamboyant, westernised Shammi Kapoor was created by him.'[21] In lighter moments, Husain would remind Shammi of his role in shaping the latter's destiny, 'Papaji [Prithviraj Kapoor] just gave birth to you; I am your real god – who has made you.'[22]

But there was more to it. Both men had an innate love for music, with Shammi being classically trained. Shammi listened to a lot of Hindustani classical music, Western classical music and jazz. There is also an episode where he talked about the actress Nargis buying him a gramophone that he wanted. Likewise, Nuzhat, Husain's daughter, told me about Husain yearning for a gramophone during his days in Bhopal. 'He used to stand outside people's windows because when the gramophone first

---

[20]Deepa Gahlot, 'The Turning Point', *Shammi Kapoor: The Dancing Hero – The Legends of Indian Cinema*, Wisdom Tree, 2008, pp. 40-41.

[21]Harneet Singh, 'Shammi Kapoor, India's Elvis, dies', *The Indian Express*, 15 August 2011. (http://archive.indianexpress.com/news/shammi-kapoor-india-s-elvis-dies/832069/)

[22]Deepa Gahlot, 'The Turning Point', *Shammi Kapoor: The Dancing Hero – The Legends of Indian Cinema*, Wisdom Tree, 2008, p. 41.

came to Bhopal, two or three households in Bhopal had it. It was an amazing thing. They used to stand outside and listen to Begum Akhtar.'

Nuzhat also recollected the not-so-noble pursuits of both men. 'My dad was this small-town guy. His "badness" and partying and all that was very small,' she told me in a lighter vein. 'Shammi was the guy who introduced him to the big time, like going out and partying and drinking and having a blast. I mean, Shammi Kapoor was the all-time party animal. So, they were like a couple of bad boys around town. Dad would tell Geeta Bali, "*Isine toh mujhe sharaab peena sikhaaya* (He is the one who taught me to drink)."' Laughing all through this recollection of the relationship, she added, 'So he started drinking at the age of thirty-two, I always remember this, after Shammi Kapoor came into his life.'

So, was Husain living his life vicariously through the Shammi Kapoor character? Not just through his childhood, but in his adult life as well, Husain seemed to be some kind of bon vivant, who had a sense of humour and a jovial personality. As film-maker–producer Aditya Chopra told Nasreen in the context of Mansoor Khan's *Qayamat Se Qayamat Tak* (1988), Sooraj Barjatya's *Maine Pyar Kiya* (1989) and his own film *Dilwale Dulhania Le Jayenge* (1995), 'The three Khans became our muses at an age when we were representing ourselves on the screen. I am quite sure Raj is me, Prem is Sooraj and Aamir's character, who is called Raj in Mansoor's film, is a version of Mansoor.'[23]

When I met Aditya Chopra at his sprawling YRF office for this book, he explained, 'I think what happens with directors is that they live their fantasies through their movies. For passionate film-makers, their heroes embody their aspirations, their way of romancing, their way of dealing with conflict. Especially in the

---

[23] *Aditya Chopra Relives Dilwale Dulhania Le Jayenge: As Told to Nasreen Munni Kabir*, Yash Raj Films Pvt Ltd, 2014, p. 117.

case of writer–film-makers, definitely a very strong part of them does come in [into their cinema]. A body of work can signify a slight commonality, which you can then articulate, you know, this was Nasir sa'ab here.'

Mansoor Khan, Nasir Husain's son and the man who directed some of Hindi cinema's most popular films at the turn of the 1990s, *Qayamat Se Qayamat Tak* and *Jo Jeeta Wohi Sikandar* (1992), concurred. After directing his last film, *Josh* (2000), Mansoor relocated to Coonoor, Tamil Nadu, where he started a twenty-two-acre, family-run organic cheese-making farm.

About his father's cinema, Mansoor said, 'He had tremendous flair, which came out in his heroes. In his initial films, for that particular flamboyant hero, Shammi uncle was the ideal. My dad, if you met him in his younger years, was very flamboyant himself. He was outgoing, an extrovert. That character was the character he himself was and he loved that. And so he needed a hero who could play that. Later, he found that in Rishi Kapoor.'

Nuzhat agreed. 'He was Shammi Kapoor in many ways.'

4

PHIR WOHI STORY LAYA HOON: DECODING THE NASIR HUSAIN FORMULA

'*Aap dekhiye na, unki sabhi kahaaniyaan lost-and-found hain. Tumsa Nahin Dekha se dekho … Yeh unki craftsmanship hai. Wohi cheez aapko de rahe hain, aap phir enjoy kar rahe ho. Phir de rahe hain, phir enjoy kar rahe ho. Jaisey tune mein saat sargam hotey hain: sa, re, ga … usi pe tune banti hai na. Aap humour kahaan se laaogey? Situation change ho jaati hai. Banda change ho jaata hai. Wohi humour phir kaam kar jaata hai* (See, all his films were lost-and-found. *Tumsa Nahin Dekha* onwards … It was his skill that though he was giving them the same thing, they were enjoying it. He presented the same thing again, they still enjoyed it. A music scale has seven notes: do, re, mi … a melody is created from the same seven notes. Where will you get the humour from? Situations change. Actors change. But the same humour can still be used.) What he liked, he did it and did it with conviction. Basically, *aapka conviction hona chaahiye.* (Basically, you must have conviction.) There is nothing stronger than your conviction.'

– Actor Jeetendra

'The "formula" is integral to Hindi films. What exactly it is no one can really tell you, but everyone knows its essential elements.

70

A bit of this – emotion, humour, action, melodrama – and a bit
of that – songs, fights, dances, foreign locations – all sprinkled
in judicious quantities throughout the film. But even if it sounds
simple, it is not a template as dull and lazy film-makers often
think. It requires intelligence to make the perfect formula film
which gives the viewer the all-important feeling of "paisa vasool"
or money's worth.'
                          – Author and journalist Sidharth Bhatia[1]

Before *Tumsa Nahin Dekha*'s release, Husain had asked people
within Filmistan what they thought of the film. The responses
varied. The editor D.N. Pai told him, '*Chhey haftey toh zaroor
chalegi* (It will definitely run for six weeks).' There were others
like Tolaram Jalan, who were a lot more dismissive. '*Waahiyaat
hai, log chappaley maarengey* (It's a horrible film. People will boo
it).' Husain had consequently tempered his expectations from the
film. 'I was surprised. I did not expect it would run. *Maine socha
thaa 8-10 hafte chalegi, toh baahar kaheen toh naukri mil jaayegi.*
(I had thought that if the film runs for 8-10 weeks, I may be able
to get a job outside.) But it celebrated jubilees at so many theatres
in Bombay and Delhi.'

Following *Tumsa Nahin Dekha*'s overwhelming success, Husain
had a fallout with Jalan. Husain even told Jalan, '*Mere bagair
Filmistan nahin chal sakti* (Filmistan won't function without
me).' This angered Jalan, who promptly fired Husain, an episode
Husain believed Jalan later regretted because Husain still had
a few years left on his contract. At the time that Husain left
Filmistan, Shashadhar Mukerji too parted ways with the studio
and formed his own independent production house, Filmalaya, in

[1]Sidharth Bhatia, 'Spicing it up: The Masala Film', *Amar Akbar Anthony:
Masala, Madness and Manmohan Desai*, HarperCollins *Publishers* India,
2013, p. 65.

1958. Filmalaya became a launching pad for several new artistes. Mukerji's son, Joy Mukerji, debuted with *Love in Simla* (1960).

Meanwhile, keen to keep the winning combination going between Mukerji, Husain and himself, Shammi Kapoor suggested that they collaborate on another film. This turned out to be Filmalaya's first film, *Dil Deke Dekho* (1959). In contrast to the exhausting search for *Tumsa Nahin Dekha*'s hero, the problem with *Dil Deke Dekho* was finding its heroine.

I met Asha Parekh along with Nuzhat at her Juhu residence, which was in the midst of some serious renovation. Despite the inconvenience, Parekh played the perfect host, serving us freshly made steamed idlis and some other delectable savouries. In the midst of all this, she also told us how she landed *Dil Deke Dekho*, her first role as a mainstream heroine.

Parekh had already done a few roles as a child artiste, starring in Bimal Roy's *Baap Beti* (1954) and Vijay Bhatt's *Shri Chaitanya Mahaprabhu* (1954). Vijay Bhatt also cast her as his lead heroine for *Goonj Uthi Shehnai* (1959), but sacked Parekh within two days of the film's shooting. 'He said I was not star material. I was thrown out. That's luck,' said Parekh, laughing wryly. Ironically, Parekh's role in *Goonj Uthi Shehnai* went to Ameeta, who faded away shortly afterwards.

Shammi was very keen on Nutan, but Mukerji and Husain felt that *Dil Deke Dekho* required a young, flamboyant, feisty girl. Nutan was also about to get married. Shammi then suggested Waheeda Rehman, but she was busy with *Kaagaz Ke Phool* (also released in 1959).

By this time, the film-maker Nandlal Jashwantlal, who had directed *Anarkali* (1953), had screen-tested Asha Parekh. Husain had seen this screen-test. He was keen on taking her. She had also been asked to hone her acting skills at Filmalaya's acting school, but the idea didn't go down too well with her. 'I felt acting *seekhna kya hota hai* (How can you learn how to act). It's inborn, you know.' Parekh never showed up at Filmalaya.

The other favourite to land the leading role for *Dil Deke Dekho* was Sadhana. She had been going to Filmalaya's acting school. Keen to get cracking on Filmalaya's first film, Mukerji asked that Sadhana be cast in *Dil Deke Dekho*. But Husain had chanced upon Asha Parekh somewhere while on a car drive with the comic actor Rajendra Nath. Husain took the opportunity to convince Parekh to come for the screen-test. 'That's when I went back to Filmalaya studio,' Parekh said.

With Parekh returning, it was decided that both actresses would get screen-tested alongside Shammi. Sadhana would stand in with Shammi for one shot and then Parekh would do the same. Meanwhile, R.K. Nayyar, the director of *Love in Simla*, approached Husain to excuse Sadhana from *Dil Deke Dekho* so that the schedule of his film didn't get affected. This is how the legend of Sadhana's sty was born. The actress didn't turn up on the day of the screen-test, owing to a sty in her eye. As Javed Akhtar noted, 'In English they say, "The sky is the limit." Here it became the sty is the limit.'[2] And Parekh came to be cast in Filmalaya's first production and Husain's second directorial venture (which he also wrote). She would go on to work in every Husain film right up to *Caravan* (1971), with *Manzil Manzil* (1984) being her last film with Husain.

---

[2]Zee Classic's *Classic Legends: Season II*, featuring Nasir Husain.

With *Dil Deke Dekho*, Husain entered a formulaic space which borrowed several strands from *Tumsa Nahin Dekha*. Where the hero was separated from but ultimately reunited with his father in *Tumsa Nahin Dekha*, in *Dil Deke Dekho* it's the mother. Husain would use this basic blueprint, flipping a trope here, inverting a theme there, to produce his next few films, which included *Jab Pyar Kisise Hota Hai* (1961) and *Phir Wohi Dil Laya Hoon* (1963). Even *Pyar Ka Mausam* (1969) was a rehash of these four films.

Although each of these films was a bigger hit than the other, they firmly slotted Husain as a formula film-maker. 'In fact Shammi uncle told me once,' said Mansoor, '"You know, Mansoor, I want to tell you something about your father. He came to Bombay with one file under his arm. He had one script in that file and he consistently used that one script again and again."' The actor Rishi Kapoor, with whom Husain worked in later years, and whom I met in his office at R.K. Studios in September 2014, also remembered Husain saying something similar to him, 'He used to tell me, "*Main Lucknow se bas utni hi kahaaniyaan laaya thaa, usko tod mod ke, ghooma phira ke wohi banaatey rehta hoon* (I had brought only this one story with me from Lucknow, which I rehash, update and remake)."'

The broad outline of Husain's formula films involved some kind of a crime to begin with. The crime led to a parting of the main characters – generally father from son, but could also be mother from son as in *Dil Deke Dekho*. The estranged figure would then play a guardian figure to a girl-child, who would either be abandoned as in *Tumsa Nahin Dekha*, but would mostly be a deceased friend's daughter. The hero would romance this girl, who has been brought up by his estranged father (mother in the case of *Dil Deke Dekho*). As part of the wooing process, which formed the main body of the film, the hero would often assume a disguise or impersonate someone. But in some films like *Caravan* and *Zamaane Ko Dikhana Hai* (1981), the heroine conceals her identity from the hero for purposes other than romance. The villain would attempt to usurp the wealth of the hero's estranged parental figure by claiming to be the long-lost son. This would create some tension between the hero and the parental figure, but the hero would ultimately prevail over the villain and the family members are reunited in the end.

Within this broad framework, Husain used interesting twists in storyline. For instance, in *Jab Pyar Kisise Hota Hai*, there is no lost-and-found element. Instead, Nisha (Parekh) and Sunder (Dev Anand) are promised in marriage to each other as children by their parents, but after Nisha's mother's death, Nisha's father (Mubarak) reneges. Sunder's agenda then is to woo Nisha despite her father's misgivings.

This theme of the children being promised in marriage was essentially a continuation of what had already been seen in passing in *Munimji* (1955), where Captain Suresh tells Ramlal that if he has a daughter he would like her to marry Ramlal's son. Husain then repackaged this element in not just *Jab Pyar Kisise Hota Hai*, but also in *Pyar Ka Mausam* (although here the heroine Seema is betrothed to the character Jhatpat Singh), *Hum Kisise Kum Naheen* and *Manzil Manzil* as well.

There were other variations to the blueprint. In *Phir Wohi Dil Laya Hoon*, Mohan (Joy Mukerji) knows that Colonel Mahendranath (Wasti) is his father and deliberately confronts his estranged father at every opportunity. In *Caravan*, there is no element of lost-and-found, but a girl on the run from the villain, who is looking to usurp all her wealth by having her killed. In *Pyar Ka Mausam*, Sunder (Shashi Kapoor) has been separated from both his parents as a child. Here, it is his grandfather, Sardar Ranjit Kumar (Wasti), who assumes that he is out to marry

Seema (Parekh) only for her wealth. In *Yaadon Ki Baaraat*, there are three long-lost brothers who must be reunited at the climax of the film.

'Yeh poochh kya nahin hai Ooty mein? Khoobsurat pahaadiyaan, rangeen waadiyaan aur meri jaan-e-tamanna oo-oo-oo-oo...'[3]

One of the immediate things that jumps out from Husain's body of work is the near absence of the city in his films. This didn't mean that Husain based his films in villages or showcased rural life as shown in films like *Do Bigha Zamin* or *Mother India*. He opted for hill stations. This distinguished him from his peers like Shakti Samanta, Raj Khosla and Vijay Anand, who made some of their most successful films with a city at the centre of their storyline. Samanta's first few successful films, *Howrah Bridge* (1958) and *China Town* were about the underbelly of Calcutta. Raj Khosla's *C.I.D.* was based in Bombay while *Kala Pani* (1958) was set in Hyderabad. Vijay Anand based *Taxi Driver* (1954, directed by Chetan Anand) and *Kala Bazar* (1960) in Bombay, but turned to Delhi for the delightful *Tere Ghar Ke Samne* (1963). Husain, though, largely eschewed the city.

In *Tumsa Nahin Dekha*, the film's setting is largely Soona Nagar, Ghatpur. In *Dil Deke Dekho*, much of the action unfolds between Nainital and Ranikhet. In *Jab Pyar Kisise Hota Hai*, it is Darjeeling and Neelgaon, while in *Phir Wohi Dil Laya Hoon*, it is Kashmir. *Teesri Manzil* takes us to Dehradun and Mussoorie, while in *Pyar Ka Mausam*, although Sunder (Shashi Kapoor) is adopted by a family in Bangalore, much of the film takes place in Ooty and somewhere near Nandipur gaon. Similarly, we hear of Mahabaleshwar, Nainital, Darjeeling and Shimla in *Yaadon*

---

[3]'Ask, what isn't there in Ooty? Beautiful mountains, colourful valleys and my beloved...' – Sunder (Shashi Kapoor) to Hamid mian (Ram Avtar) in *Pyar Ka Mausam*.

Ki Baaraat, Hum Kisise Kum Naheen, Zamaane Ko Dikhana Hai and *Manzil Manzil.*

Although other directors also moved outdoors at the same time, Husain was one of the key directors who fashioned Hindi cinema's foray into the hills, which became a staple of films right through the 1960s. Yet again, it was that year, 1957, which saw the first signs of this, with *Tumsa Nahin Dekha, Nau Do Gyarah, Do Aankhen Baarah Haath* and *Naya Daur* seeing extended portions showcasing the countryside.[4] Film-makers took to colour to showcase Kashmir, Shimla, Tokyo and Paris in their films. Husain was at the forefront of engineering this move to the outdoors even before the coming of colour.

This didn't mean that Husain stayed entirely away from the city. In *Caravan*, even though much of the film plays out in the open landscape, the protagonists pass through Bombay and Bangalore. *Yaadon Ki Baaraat* is almost entirely Bombay based, with the exception of the Sunita (Zeenat Aman)–Vijay (Vijay Arora) romantic track playing out in Mahabaleshwar before they too come to Bombay. *Hum Kisise Kum Naheen* and *Zamaane Ko Dikhana Hai* have the hero's family operating out of Delhi. We also hear of the thakurs in *Qayamat Se Qayamat Tak* relocating to Delhi after all that has happened in Dhanakpur gaon.

Wherever the city comes into Husain's narrative, there is very little evidence of it. In *Yaadon Ki Baaraat*, although there are references to the city, it isn't until much later in the film that Mumbai's LIC building is shown as visual confirmation of the city. The same is the case with films like *Pyar Ka Mausam, Caravan, Hum Kisise Kum Naheen* or *Zamaane Ko Dikhana Hai*, which have little or no visual confirmation of the protagonists being placed in Bangalore or Bombay or Delhi other than them saying

---

[4]Earlier films like *Andaz* (1949) and *Do Bigha Zamin* (1953) also show the countryside but these were exceptions.

so themselves. Even in *Qayamat Se Qayamat Tak*, there aren't any glimpses of Delhi city.

Phir Wohi Dil Laya Hoon provides some visual confirmation of Delhi when Mona (Asha Parekh) gives Mohan (Joy Mukerji) a tour of the city. But even there, Delhi's Qutub Minar and Red Fort are shown precisely as the sightseeing exercise that they are meant to be for Mohan. Beyond that there are no other markers for Delhi. Only a later film like *Zabardast* (1985) would have visuals of Bombay's Bandstand area and specific references to 'Juhu hotel' and '19th Road Khar'.

When I asked Mansoor why Husain's narratives were usually placed outside the city, he couldn't offer a satisfactory explanation, but gave a very practical reason for the absence of Delhi in *Qayamat Se Qayamat Tak*, saying, 'We never shot it in Delhi.' While this is as good an answer as any, its significance lies in the fact that there was very little reason for Husain to showcase the city. For the most part, the canvas of a Husain film, other than in its song sequences and its climax, restricted itself to indoor spaces: clubs, hotels, coffee shops and homes. This also explains why we don't have evidence of the hill station that the narratives are said to be taking place in. For example, in a film like *Teesri Manzil*, there is no visual confirmation of Dehradun or Mussoorie. Unlike in *Love in Simla*, where Shimla is foregrounded in at least a couple of sequences. Similarly, Asha Parekh told me that the area around Mumbai's Aarey milk colony and the Tulsi Lake stood in for the Darjeeling countryside for a lot of *Jab Pyar Kisise Hota Hai*'s outdoor shooting. *Zamaane Ko Dikhana Hai*, likewise, was shot in the Nilgiris between Coonoor and Ooty and passed off as Darjeeling. *Phir Wohi Dil Laya Hoon* is possibly an exception in that extended portions of it were actually shot in Kashmir.

Perhaps this is why Bombay is mentioned and shown to some extent in *Yaadon Ki Baaraat* and in *Zabardast* because both

Shankar (Dharmendra) and Sunder (Sunny Deol) are part of the city's underbelly in these films. It would have been difficult for Husain to not deal with Bombay city in some way here.

But there were other reasons why Husain situated his films away from the city. Since the time the city came to be foregrounded in the films of the 1950s, it was seen as a place of vice and immorality. Raj Kapoor's *Shree 420* is the perfect example of this where the outsider Raj (Raj Kapoor) pawns his honesty after coming to Bombay. He is on morally slippery ground in the company of Bombay's wealthy elite, who are out to dupe the poor of whatever little they have.

Husain possibly shared this dim view of the city. He saw it as a hostile place, where it wasn't possible to experience love and happiness. In *Tumsa Nahin Dekha*'s opening scene, for instance, when Sardar Rajpal (B.M. Vyas) hears of Meena (Ameeta) wanting to go to the city, he gets anxious. When Meena presses him to explain his anxiety, asking, '*Kya hai shehar mein?* (What is there in the city?)', Sardar Rajpal replies, '*Lootere. Haan! Bhole-bhaaley insaano ki khushi lootney waaley. Jahaan tu ja rahi hai usi shehar mein meri khushi looti gayee.* (Dacoits. Yes! They who rob innocent people of their happiness. The very city that you are going to robbed me of all my joys.)' Sardar Rajpal then goes on to give Meena his backstory.

Husain's most intimate depiction of a city in any of his films comes in *Baharon Ke Sapne* (1967), a film unlike any other Husain film. Needless to say, it is not a happy place that we encounter as Ram (Rajesh Khanna) decides to head to Bombay to look for a job. In that four-minute sequence depicting Ram going from place to place, we see the Gateway of India, Eros cinema, Haji Ali, the LIC Building, as also some crowded Bombay streets. Not surprisingly, it is the rather sombre song '*Zamaane ne maare jawaan kaise kaise*', which translates to 'How many youth has this world claimed', that plays out in this sequence. Ram's appearance turns from clean-shaven to bearded by the end of the song, clearly underscoring the city as a daunting place even for educated individuals looking for a job.

Javed Akhtar offered another stimulating explanation for Husain staying away from the city. 'The city is real. So he would make his own world where he was the God, the commander and the king. He would make his own culture of "kunwar sa'abs" and "thakur sa'abs". It was for him to decide how life was running there and what the norms of that society were. But if he were to have shot the film in Bombay or Delhi, he would have been bound by the city's existing culture and norms. So he decided to be the God of his own environment in the film.'

A world of thakurs, zamindars, estate managers and 'Bambai ke Seth Devidayal'

Akhtar's observation is partially correct because in some of Husain's films, the estranged male parental figure (or the heroine's father) is some kind of a wealthy landlord based in the countryside or in a hill station. This is certainly the case with Sardar Rajpal, who has acquired land after coming to Soona Nagar. Sardar Roop Singh (Mubarak) in *Jab Pyar Kisise Hota Hai* is also a first-generation wealthy landowner. *Pyar Ka Mausam*'s Sardar Ranjit Kumar, too, is an affluent landlord, but he is part of the feudal tradition since he has inherited this wealth from his father.

The parental figures in *Dil Deke Dekho* and in *Phir Wohi Dil Laya Hoon* aren't necessarily zamindars or thakurs. Jamuna Devi (Sulochana Latkar, *Dil Deke Dekho*) operates out of Ranikhet as the owner of Royal Hotel, while Mahendranath (Wasti, *Phir Wohi Dil Laya Hoon*), even though he has ostensibly served in the army, appears to be some kind of a 'khaandaani rayees' living in Delhi. The common thread running through these characters is that they constitute the upper-class elite, who live in these countryside/hill station settings or visit them for vacation and recreational purposes as in *Phir Wohi Dil Laya Hoon.*

Although on his father's side Husain hailed from a family of zamindars in Shahabad, they weren't the kind of Anglophone, upper-class elite that come through in his films. Both Nuzhat and Mansoor guessed that it was only with his coming to Bombay that he became more aware of the urban elite. The kind of cigar-smoking, tweed coat-wearing figures that featured in his films were possibly inspired from his impressions of these people. Nuzhat, however, added that Husain's Bhopal upbringing possibly made him aware of the Bhopal royal family, their lifestyle, the estate managers they had.

In September 2004, Dr Rashmi Doraiswamy presented a remarkable paper titled '"These Days" of Our Modernity: The Cinema of Nasir Husain' at the Film and Television Institute of India (FTII) in Pune. Much of Doraiswamy's thoughts on Husain's films as outlined in this paper (and speaking to her) helped me contextualize many dominant tropes and motifs in Husain's cinema. Writing on the subject of the hill station setting in Husain's cinema, Doraiswamy explained the historical significance of these locations.

The British had created nearly eighty hill stations in India by the nineteenth century and these were being used as summer capitals from the mid-nineteenth century onwards. For instance, Shimla became the summer capital of the subcontinent, and district and provincial administrations moved to Ooty, Mahabaleshwar, Poona, Darjeeling and Nainital during the hot summer months. 'Life in the hill stations helped relive the social experiences of upper middle classes back in England,' wrote Doraiswamy in her paper. 'The range of social activities offered in these stations included fetes, amateur theatre, picnics, balls, hunting and sports.

Elite schools were built here. Hill stations as health and holiday resorts offered ample opportunities for young people to meet, court and marry.'[5]

By the 1880s, Indians had started buying properties in the hill stations and many Indians extended their philanthropic activities to these summer getaways, building hospitals, dharamshalas and sanatoriums, Doraiswamy tells us. Correspondingly, in two of Husain's films, Asha Parekh dances for charitable efforts in these locales. In *Jab Pyar Kisise Hota Hai*, the song *'Nazar mere dil ke paar huyee'* is presented by 'Miss Nisha & Party: In Aid of Bengal Relief Fund' in Darjeeling. In *Pyar Ka Mausam*, the song *'Aap se miliye, pyaar thaa inko'* is advertised as 'In Aid of Crippled Children, National College Society Presents Miss Seema and The Ballet Troupe' and takes place in Ooty.

The Indianization of the hill stations started much before independence, with clubs and hotels, which lent these places their distinctive air, changing their attitudes to Indians. Newer and older hotels opened their doors to Indians. Doraiswamy wrote, 'Husain's characters are the natural heirs to the Indians who entered the hallowed portals of British high culture. It is not just his young protagonists, who freely participate in the spaces of hotel and club, but also the older generation, the fathers and aunts, who are at home in these spaces. He is one director who manages to establish, in film after film, the hill station as a specific metropolitan entity. While other directors used the hills for their natural, visual beauty (as Shakti Samanta did, for instance, in *Kashmir Ki Kali*, 1964), Nasir Husain used the hills ideologically, creating a space of real and imagined metropolitan culture. The city and the hill station/s are names whose signifieds [*sic*] are

---

[5]Dr Rashmi Doraiswamy, '"These Days" of Our Modernity: The Cinema of Nasir Husain', Film and Television Institute of India, Pune, 4 September 2004, p. 4.

"metropolis". There is very little attempt at realistically establishing the one or the other. Both are imaginary constructs based on real histories, serving narrative functions.'[6]

The hill station as a shared space between the remnants of the British raj and the Indian elite also explains the presence of Anglo-looking characters in *Munimji*, in song sequences like '*Jawaaniya yeh mast mast bin peeye*' and '*Aaye hain door se*' in *Tumsa Nahin Dekha* and in the two songs from *Teesri Manzil*, '*O haseena zulfon waali*' and '*Tumne mujhe dekha*'.[7] Asha Parekh's dance face-off against the Western-styled Miss Pony at the Darjeeling Club in *Jab Pyar Kisise Hota Hai* and the blonde-haired Miss Loveleena at the Rainbow Club in *Pyar Ka Mausam* can also be rationalized through these settings.

Locating his characters in the landowning, feudal class made another trope plausible. Here, the father of a boy could promise his son in marriage to a friend, the father of a girl. This, as has already been noted, was the case in several Husain films. Much of Hindi cinema from the 1960s also followed this theme, with the villain being a family relative, whom the heroine is being coerced into marrying.

Caravan onwards, Husain subtly changed tracks. He no longer concerned himself with the wealthy, landowning class in hill stations but with a new industrial class that saw the hero's or heroine's father as a businessman. 'Bambai ke Seth Devidayal' or Sunita's (Zeenat Aman) father (Murad) in *Yaadon Ki Baaraat* and both Kaajal's (Kaajal Kiran) father Kishori Lal (Kamal Kapoor) and Rajesh's (Rishi Kapoor) father (Murad again) in *Hum Kisise Kum Naheen* are examples of this.

---

[6]Ibid., p. 6.

[7]Even though Husain didn't direct this film, the fact that he situated his story in Mussoorie makes it a natural place for such people to visit.

The common link with this entire elite class was that whether they were landlords or businessmen, they needed estate managers or managers. That's where the hero estranged from this parental figure or the villain impersonating the hero came into play as seen in the characters and plotlines of *Tumsa Nahin Dekha* and *Hum Kisise Kum Naheen.*

'Bhagwan Das crorepati ke bete ko kaun nahin jaanta huzoor?'[8]

The use of disguise and impersonation was one of Husain's signature tropes and he used it for different purposes. In *Paying Guest*, Ramesh comes along as the elderly Wajahat Mirza to meet the precondition set by Babu Digambernath that he will only rent out his accommodation to an elderly gentleman. It is through the guise of the Mirza that Dev Anand is able to soften Shanti's heart for Ramesh. In *Jab Pyar Kisise Hota Hai*, Sunder impersonates Popat Lal to get closer to Nisha but Rajendra Nath's character also impersonates Popat Lal so that he can make a quick buck off Sardar Roop Singh. In *Caravan*, Sunita assumes the guise of Soni, a village belle, so that she can fit in with the travelling gypsies, while in *Zamaane Ko Dikhana Hai*, Kanchan gives herself a makeover as Bahadur Singh, so that she can give Ravi (Rishi Kapoor) the slip. Husain used the trope for comedy, deceit, to conceal true identity and to escape the villain's clutches.

Husain's villains, too, made use of the trope to further their agendas. In *Tumsa Nahin Dekha*, *Dil Deke Dekho*, *Phir Wohi Dil Laya Hoon*, *Pyar Ka Mausam* and *Manzil Manzil*, we see the villain trying to pass himself off as the hero so that he can appropriate the hero's wealth and property. In *Zamaane Ko Dikhana Hai* and *Manzil Manzil*, both Shekhar (Kader Khan) and Professor Das

---

[8]'Who doesn't know the millionaire Bhagwan Das's son, sir?' – A steward addressing Anil (Shammi Kapoor) in *Teesri Manzil*.

(Prem Chopra) wear disguises. They appear to be men one can trust before we get to know their backstories.

In fact, *Hum Kisise Kum Naheen* is fascinating precisely because in one segment of the film, three of the protagonists have assumed alternate identities at the same time. Sanjay (Tariq) has taken on the identity of Manjeet so that he can get closer to Kaajal (Kaajal Kiran). Rajesh presents himself as Manjeet to Kaajal since he and Saudagar Singh (Amjad Khan) have forged a plan to settle scores with Kaajal's father. But the elderly, bespectacled, frail and white-haired Saudagar Singh himself is not who he is claiming to be but a dangerous, wanted felon.

The use of disguise is an old dramatic device across cultures. Indian mythological epics are full of instances where gods, demons, sages and apsaras have taken on different forms to further all kinds of purposes. Hindi cinema, consequently, made sufficient use of disguise and impersonation, even before Husain came into the picture. Kaushik Bhaumik remarked on Husain's use of the trope, 'It allows you to circulate in spaces which you couldn't have if you had maintained that identity. To become incognito allows you to become uninscribed of attributed social meanings, which then unmoors you from the societal circle.'

At the same time, according to Jerry Pinto, 'At some level, all of us use the two spaces of adolescence and young adulthood as laboratories of the self. When you leave school and go to college, you can shrug off the familiarities of old friends and neighbourhoods, and put on a new self. This is what Nasir Husain's heroes were always doing: trying out other selves to be more appealing, sexually and socially. And just as the hero is always about to be revealed in his true colours by some misstep, so also one walks the tightrope of a pretended other self.'

'Maayoos hokar mar jaana chaahta thaa toh bhagwaan ne tujhe bhej diya. Tu bhi beaasra thee aur mera bhi koi nahin'[9]

In almost all Husain films, the hero and the heroine have only one parent or parent figure. This is not to be understood as Shankar in *Tumsa Nahin Dekha* being raised only by his mother (because the film is a lost-and-found story, the father cannot be present in Shankar's life from the beginning). Instead, it needs to be seen from the view that Meena (Ameeta), who has been abandoned as a child, is raised by Sardar Rajpal and has no mother figure.

Similarly, in *Dil Deke Dekho*, Neeta only has her father Jagat Narayan (Raj Mehra). Besides Jamuna Devi referring to her mother as a foreigner there is no other mention of Neeta's mother in the film. In *Jab Pyar Kisise Hota Hai*, while Sardar Roop Singh has his sister watch over Nisha, only Sunder's mother is shown in the film. There is no reference to Sunder's father. The same theme plays out in film after film, be it *Teesri Manzil, Caravan, Hum Kisise Kum Naheen* or *Zamaane Ko Dikhana Hai*. Even Vijay (Vijay Arora) in *Yaadon Ki Baaraat* is raised by a solitary father figure, while his youngest brother Monto/Ratan (Tariq) has his nanny, Rosie ma, raise him as a single parent.

The one parent to one male or female protagonist trope is one of the most distinctive and unique themes in Husain's cinema. Again, this is not to say that Husain alone was doing this. A lot of the films right through the 1960s, like *Hum Dono* (1961), *Junglee* or *Aadmi Aur Insaan*, have only one parental figure for the hero or the heroine. But for Husain to have used this theme consistently for nearly three decades in his cinema is fascinating.

Javed Akhtar explained this. 'It becomes unnecessary to have

---

[9]'Having lost all hope, I wanted to kill myself, but then I found you by God's grace. You were an orphan and I too had no family.' – Sardar Rajpal (B.M. Vyas) to Meena (Ameeta) in *Tumsa Nahin Dekha*.

two parents. One parent serves the purpose. That is why there was only one parent. An authoritarian father was required for the heroine; a concerned, compassionate mother was required for the hero – that's enough.' Mansoor echoed the same thought. 'It complicates things. It wasn't really needed. It was purely efficiency. *Kaun waste karey time? Ek aur character ke dialogues aayengey beech mein.* (Why waste time? Another character's dialogues will get in the way.) Writers prefer not to add unnecessary characters.'

'Secretary, kal subah hum Sunita memsa'ab ke saath ghoomney-phirney jaayengey'[10]

In many of Husain's films, the hero and heroine set out on a journey, initially brought together by that wonderful element in Hindi cinema called 'kismet', but then continuing of their own volition or motives. The journey wasn't always a single continuous bit of travel from place A to place B, but often involved the protagonists going to several destinations, at times back and forth, with breaks in between. This often made the journey look more like an adventure trip, but there were instances where the journey was something as short-lived as a day out in the countryside. Correspondingly, in narrative terms, the journey could take up anything between a big chunk of a film or simply a ten-to-fifteen-minute sequence. This was the time during which the hero and heroine sized up each other, indulged in a battle of wits, but mostly fell in love with each other.

In *Tumsa Nahin Dekha*, we get the first glimpse of this trope when Shankar and Meena coincidentally meet at the railway station en route to Ghatpur. They then share a rather acrimonious train journey, trading insults all the way till they reach Soona Nagar

---

[10]'Secretary, tomorrow morning I will head out with Miss Sunita for the day' – Kunwar Vijay Kumar (Vijay Arora) in *Yaadon Ki Baaraat*.

station. Next, they stop over at the colonel's (S.L. Puri) house for the night due to inclement weather before Meena heads out the next day for her home. *Dil Deke Dekho* onwards, however, it is clear that the end of journey will result in love. In this film, Neeta already knows Raja before they set out from Nainital for Ranikhet. By the end of the car ride, much of which has been spent with Raja showing Kailash-babu (Rajendra Nath) up, Neeta is no longer openly hostile to Raja. Similarly, in *Jab Pyar Kisise Hota Hai*, Monto and Nisha spend some time driving around in the Darjeeling countryside and then partake in a train journey from Darjeeling to Neelgaon after which Nisha is seen to be enjoying Monto's company.

Phir Wohi Dil Laya Hoon has the journey play out for the major part of the storyline. Here, Mohan and Mona first go on a sightseeing tour of Delhi and then to Agra where Difu (Rajendra Nath) has supposedly been taken to be treated at the mental hospital. They return to Delhi only to head out for Kashmir. On reaching Kashmir, they also make a day trip to Baramulla, where Mohan sings '*Banda parvar*'. Through all these trips, Mohan has deceived, befriended, irked, romanced and, ultimately, wooed Mona successfully. Something similar happens in *Teesri Manzil* and *Caravan*, with both films dedicating the bulk of their narratives to the shared travels of their protagonists. In contrast to *Phir Wohi Dil Laya Hoon*'s adventures are the shorter, picnic-like drives taken into the countryside by Vijay and Sunita in *Yaadon Ki Baaraat* and Sanjay and Kaajal in *Hum Kisise Kum Naheen*, at the end of which both sets of protagonists are shown to have grown close to each other.

The films that followed, too, had this subplot, with the protagonists of *Zamaane Ko Dikhana Hai*, *Manzil Manzil* and *Zabardast* all going from one place to another, with romance blossoming along the way. In *Qayamat Se Qayamat Tak*, Husain provides a refreshing twist when he makes Raj (Aamir Khan) and Rashmi (Juhi Chawla) undertake the journey to Sitanagar on foot after both have individually lost their way. In the process, the two meet, spend the night in the jungle and indulge in casual banter (mostly with Rashmi speaking), which allows for some of the best moments in this delicate love story to play out.

'Iss baar youth festival mein Kashmir aayee huyee har party ko humaarey saamne haar maan-nee padegi'[11]

Bhaumik sees the connection between the various themes playing out in a Husain film pointing at one essential fact. 'The logic is that of youth. That is what is driving his narrative. In the sense that the young have to run away somewhere in order to celebrate their love. And he also has this sense of nature being connected to romance. It is in this space, places like Darjeeling, that romance blossoms, which is true of a lot of Bengali films in the 1950s, for example, the Uttam–Suchitra films. It may come back to the city but the romance has to happen in bucolic, paradisiacal, nature settings. And it is a trope which is there in Hollywood cinema as well. From the beginning, nature is where romance is most wonderful to think about and feel, the songs take on a certain meaning, there is a freedom of bodily movement, which is very important. There's also the logic of holidays. In the holidays, young people meet. It's part of the generation's thought process about romance that since we belong to traditional families, there will be no possibility of romance in the city because families know everybody else. And so, if you are young and in love, you have to move outside of the city to the countryside and nature.'

Bhaumik's analysis tied in with Husain's own admission of

---

[11]'This time, every team that participates at the Kashmir youth festival will have to accept defeat in front of us' – Mona's (Parekh) friend (Tabassum) in *Phir Wohi Dil Laya Hoon*.

making his films keeping the youth in mind. In several of his films, the 'youthfulness' of the protagonists is emphasized. That is why in *Phir Wohi Dil Laya Hoon*, Mona and her friends head to Kashmir for the 'youth festival'. In *Teesri Manzil*, Sunita relies on her college girls' hockey team to teach Rocky a lesson. It is the youth that will form a 'Rock-'n'-Roll' Club in *Dil Deke Dekho*, swing to 'Prince Monto and The Avengers' in *Yaadon Ki Baaraat* and participate in beauty contests (Kaajal in *Hum Kisise Kum Naheen*). Consequently, when Raj of *Qayamat Se Qayamat Tak* says at his graduating class's farewell, '*Humaarey liye college ka yeh aakhri din hai* (Today is our last day at college)', we know we are firmly in Nasir Husain world – a world of dreamy-eyed youth, bursting with hope, love and an air of cherubic optimism. Aditya Chopra endorsed this sentiment prevalent in the Husain universe. 'One thing that spoke to me very strongly in his films was they were just so young. I used to find it so fascinating that he was just such a young mind. There was a sense of adventure. I remember always feeling happy. His films always gave me a sense of happiness.'

This buoyancy is essentially articulated by the Husain hero. As stated earlier, be it in *Paying Guest* or in *Tumsa Nahin Dekha*, the Husain hero isn't held back by his circumstances. Separated or estranged from his parent, he doesn't wallow in misery. It is the hero indulging in masquerades, disguise and impersonations while wooing the heroine that gives the audience much of their laughs in a Husain film.

And one of the defining traits of youth in a Husain film is never to let circumstances dictate their approach to life. In *Dil Deke Dekho*, Raja is determined to earn money by all means possible to provide for the treatment of his father's blindness. That is why he turns to playing some kind of agony uncle figure in the guise of the delightful quack, Professor Samri. Raja doesn't let his father's health bog him down, like the Shashi Kapoor character in *Waqt* (1965), who makes us acutely aware of his mother's ailing situation and indigent circumstances all through. In *Jab Pyar Kisise Hota Hai*, Sunder uses the news of having found a job to cheer his mother up after Sardar Roop Singh reneges on his promise. *Phir Wohi Dil Laya Hoon's* Mohan, too, gives us a similar moment when after singing '*Laakhon hai nigaah mein*', the hero hands over his first salary, a princely sum of rupees three hundred, to his mother, saying she no longer needs to work. He then goes on to pat his biceps and broadens his chest, signifying that he, who is now at the peak of his youth, shall provide for her and together they will live happily.

These same cheerful traits are seen in *Teesri Manzil's* Rocky, *Caravan's* Mohan, *Yaadon Ki Baaraat's* Vijay and Ratan, and *Hum Kisise Kum Naheen's* Rajesh and Sanjay. Whether he is suspected of being responsible for someone's death or is having to provide for the family or is separated from siblings, or faced with promises being broken and family fortunes being lost, the Husain hero remains ebullient all through. Trading in quips, romancing with a certain panache, indulging in all kinds of trickery and fun became the Husain hero trademark.

Add to this his ability to dance and sing his way past all his problems, all of which became the archetype not just for the 1960s hero, epitomized most by Shammi Kapoor, but for the modern Indian hero, too. Think of so many of the heroes of the 1990s, leading into the early twenty-first century and these are all successors to Husain's male protagonist. In writer–film-maker Zoya Akhtar's directorial debut, *Luck By Chance* (2009), when the teacher at the acting institute (Saurabh Shukla) says, '*Hindi filmon ka hero na sirf acting karta hai, balki gaaney gaata hai, dance karta hai, comedy karta hai, action karta hai* (Not only does the hero in Hindi cinema act, he also sings, dances, does comedy and action as well),' he could be enunciating the DNA of the Husain hero.

Anuradha Warrier, who runs the popular blog 'Conversations Over Chai',[12] told me in an email conversation that the larger takeaway from this frothy element that defined Husain's cinema was his 'celebration of self'. Anuradha posited that by the time Husain debuted, the Partition was long past and nation-building and Independence Day speeches were mere rhetoric. 'The disillusionment with Independence and what was promised had yet to solidify into youthful angst,' wrote Anuradha. 'This was the magic in-between period, where, for once, there was hope ... His heroes appealed to a youth who wanted, even needed, optimistic, aspirational stories. They wanted music, they wanted romance, they wanted colour, the promise that a Nasir Husain hero held out. They didn't want their lives to be lived in stark black and white. They were middle class, they were educated, they wanted to hear that they could also get a job, get a girl, have the romance of their lives, live a life filled with music. They demanded it. They didn't want major conflict; they didn't mind the tiny hurdles that faced the Nasir Husain hero, for they knew things would be all right in the end. That was their idea, their dream, their hope of reality. He was worried not about the nation but about his job. So were they. Their hero was worried about winning the girl of his dreams. He made it possible for them to dream about winning their own beloveds. And if he could achieve all this, hey, so could they! Nasir Husain sold dreams. He traded magic. He offered hope. And audiences lapped it up. The time was just right for celebrating an individual, his journey towards finding his own self. In many ways, they were fluffier versions of the coming-of-age stories that are the modern thème du jour.'

Husain's cinema bucked the dominant discourse of the era

---

[12]http://anuradhawarrier.blogspot.in/

he started out in and set forth its own discourse. Not for him moral platitudes and lofty sermons. If laughter and mirth are the best medicines to treat the ill, Husain's brand of frothy, light-hearted cinema worked like an elixir. As Raghavendra observed, 'The popular film-maker is important because he is much more a national film-maker, because he understands the pulse of the public. The public is speaking through him in many ways. He actually articulates the aspirations, concerns and attitudes of the public. Whereas the artistic film-maker has got a finger only on his own artistic sensibilities. He is not connected to the public.'

'Achha toh maine repeat kiya'[13]

Ultimately, a lot of Husain's cinema was about repetition. The common view was that Husain was only about '*Phir Wohi Story Laya Hoon*'. But a closer look at his films also reveals that Husain even repeated scenes, dialogues and the way characters dressed in several of his films.

Take the '*badmaash, gundaa, lafangaa*' dialogue from *Paying Guest*. The same is repeated in *Tumsa Nahin Dekha* with a slight twist. When Meena discovers that it is Shankar in her compartment on the train instead of her friend, she says, '*Badmaash, gundey, lafangey*' to which Shankar's response is, '*Ji unn sabko doosrey dabbey mein sawaar karaaya hai. Yeh toh khaaksaar hai, artist, lover of beauty* (All of them are travelling in another compartment. I am a nobody, an artist, a lover of beauty).' Similarly, the '*Surat toh buri nahin*' exchange leading to '*Shehnai bajaaney waaley chhutti pe gaye hain*' between Chanchal and Ramesh from *Paying Guest* is repeated verbatim between Mona's friend (Tabassum) and Mohan in *Phir Wohi Dil Laya Hoon*. Elsewhere, Husain played around with the line '*Nafrat mohabbat ki pehli seedi hai*' in several films

---

[13]'Ok, so I repeat.' Colonel Mahendranath (Wasti) in *Phir Wohi Dil Laya Hoon*.

from *Munimji* to *Paying Guest* to *Tumsa Nahin Dekha* to *Teesri Manzil* to *Yaadon Ki Baaraat*.

He would lift entire scenes, too. Take, for instance, the car crash in *Teesri Manzil*, when Rocky's car brakes fail as he makes his way to nab the killers who are plotting his death. The entire crash from the point the car falls off the cliff was copied frame by frame and fitted into *Caravan* to depict Sunita's car accident.

From plotlines to scenes to dialogues, right down to his heroes' wardrobe and having the same character names, Husain repeated it all. Look at Joy Mukerji with his red sweater in *Phir Wohi Dil Laya Hoon* for '*Laakhon hai nigaah mein*'. Shashi Kapoor and Vijay Arora have the same colour sweater slung across their shoulders in *Pyar Ka Mausam* and *Yaadon Ki Baaraat* respectively. Sunita, Sunder, Mohan and Monto play in a loop as character names. His heroes invariably get hurt on the head, but wear their bandaged pates and head (pun intended) bravely into the climax across films – Shankar in *Tumsa Nahin Dekha*, Mohan in *Phir Wohi Dil Laya Hoon* and Sanjay in *Hum Kisise Kum Naheen*.

Akhtar explained Husain's inclination to repeat. 'For Nasir Husain, the story was like a peg on which he could mount his beautiful romantic scenes, funny comic scenes, beautiful songs, dances and other enjoyable moments. He just needed a story to support these elements. For him the story itself wasn't as important as the moments in the film. He had the story so that the moments – light-hearted, engaging, interesting, romantic as they were – could fit in.'

At times, Husain tweaked similar moments just that wee bit to lull the audiences into thinking that they were watching something new. For instance, in *Phir Wohi Dil Laya Hoon*, when Difu (Rajendra Nath) sits down to eat with Mona and her friends in the countryside, it is Mohan who is pinching Difu's food from behind the haystack. This same situation plays out in *Caravan*, too, but with Sunita stealing Mohan's food from under the lorry.

But Husain, very importantly, also tweaked his presentation of the same moment to reflect the changing times. That is why Mohan and Sunder from *Phir Wohi Dil Laya Hoon* and *Pyar Ka Mausam*, respectively, are shown transitioning from the acoustic guitar to the electric guitar with Monto (*Yaadon Ki Baaraat*), Sanjay (*Hum Kisise Kum Naheen*) and ultimately Raj in *Qayamat Se Qayamat Tak*. Husain definitely acknowledged the coming (and passing) of Jimi Hendrix and the Woodstock years to make this change. 'Why am I successful? Because though my themes are basically the same, I modify them with the current trends and attitudes of the young. I believe in moving with the times,' said Husain.[14]

This is perhaps also why we hear of the city more frequently in Husain's films beginning with *Caravan*, because the city makes its return to Hindi cinema in a big way in the films of the 1970s. This updating of traditions, moving with the times, played an important part in keeping Husain relevant across decades.

Repeating themes or following a successful formula was not Husain's unique preserve. Film-makers before and after him followed set patterns once they chanced upon something that clicked with audiences. Shakti Samanta, Husain's peer all through, used the lost-and-found trope quite often in his successful films of the 1960s. Manmohan Desai made a career of peddling the same themes. His *Naseeb* (1981) is nothing but *Amar Akbar Anthony* (1977) redux. In his book on the latter film, Sidharth Bhatia listed the 'Manmohan Desai clichés' such as they came to be known – the lost-and-found trope, the fondness for miracles with mothers, Amitabh Bachchan doing a drunken scene and the

---

[14]Resham Shaam, 'Little Big Man', *Super*, May 1978.

use of animals galore.[15]

Raghavendra explained this fondness for repetition in our cinema. 'In Indian cinema, what will happen is not in doubt but how it will happen is what leaves one curious. Like in classical music, when someone sings a raga, one knows the raga but what one savours is how it will be actually elaborated upon. A major film-maker always has signature devices but how that signature will work out each time becomes important. This happens even when – like Hitchcock – the director is working with suspense and surprise. I used this notion in the title of my first book *Seduced by the Familiar*.'

Bhaumik has no problems with the repetitive nature of Husain's films. 'People making the same film again and again is not necessarily a bad thing. So [Alfred] Hitchcock remakes *The 39 Steps* [1935] as *North by Northwest* [1959]. Hitchcock's preoccupations are the same. But between *The 39 Steps* and *North by Northwest*, he [Hitchcock] has evolved … You watch *The 39 Steps* and *North by Northwest* and get pleasures out of both precisely because genre-theorists have argued that genre is so much about repetition as well as difference. Good genre film-makers know that I am going to tell the same story again and again like John Ford making the westerns. Same story. Spectators are clever enough to understand what is going on, why the same story is being remade and they can see where the differences are.'

Bhaumik also rationalized the repetition element by highlighting how Husain used scale to make the same thing look different. 'Husain is like [Martin] Scorsese who made his gangster films at various scales. I make the comparison from the very particular logic of how master film-makers sometimes play with

---

[15]Sidharth Bhatia, 'The Last Word in Entertainment', *Amar Akbar Anthony: Masala, Madness and Manmohan Desai*, HarperCollins *Publishers* India, 2013, p. 131.

scale. He goes into spectacle in *Hum Kisise Kum Naheen* and he does it at a scale at which no one else could. And he handles the scale extremely well. *Hum Kisise Kum Naheen* really cannibalizes material from *Yaadon Ki Baaraat*, but the scale has expanded.'

To understand Bhaumik's remarks, look at the climactic fight sequence of both films. In *Yaadon Ki Baaraat*, Shankar knocks over Shaakaal's henchmen by taking over the wheel of the van in which he and Sunita have come to the deserted airstrip. Shankar drives the vehicle in reverse, in circles, to knock the men off. The same thing is repeated in *Hum Kisise Kum Naheen*, but on a grander spectacle. Here, Rajesh operates out of a helicopter (instead of a van) and uses the rectangular iron frame that he has tied to the chopper to maim Saudagar Singh's men. The villains can only exhort their men in English ('Come on, Martin, come on. Ranjit, do something,' says Shaakaal. Saudagar Singh says, 'Don't run, damn you! Hold it! Hold it!'), but to little effect.

Husain himself never bothered about the criticism that came his way for rehashing his storylines and plot elements. The success of each film spurred him on to greater peaks and that is all that mattered to him. 'Of course you can repeat the same thing. It depends on the audience and for how long you can bluff them. If you can do it all the time, it's fine.'[16]

Akhtar narrated an episode in this regard. The story goes that once at a party at Husain's house, the actor Randhir Kapoor (he played a small cameo in *Zamaane Ko Dikhana Hai*) jocularly asked Husain, 'Nasir sa'ab, you make such successful films, but all your stories are the same. Why don't you change your storyline?'

Husain responded, 'Tell me something, how many times have you visited my house?'

'Several times,' replied Randhir.

---

[16]Deepa Gahlot, 'It's the chase that is exciting', *Filmfare*, 1-15 November 1984, p. 75.

'And each time you come, you tell me, "Nasir sa'ab, you must serve us that same delectable biryani from last time." Why do you always ask for the same biryani and not something new?'

'I love the biryani.'

'That's precisely the point. People like my stories, so why should I give them something else?' said Husain.[17]

---

[17]Zee Classic's *Classic Legends: Season II*, featuring Nasir Husain.

Nasir Husain's career as writer–director–producer in Hindi cinema was spread over five decades. *Courtesy: NH Films/Nuzhat Khan*

'Husain had an individual voice,' said Nasreen Munni Kabir. 'He was not copying anyone.' *Courtesy: NH Films/Nuzhat Khan*

Anarkali (1953), the first film for which Husain got independent credit for story.
Courtesy: Sumant Batra

Song booklet, *Dil Deke Dekho* (1959). The posters for his early films emphasized the musical nature of his cinema. *Courtesy: Sumant Batra*

Song booklet cover, *Baharon Ke Sapne* (1967). With this film, Husain broke the mould of his formula films. *Courtesy: NH Films/Nuzhat Khan*

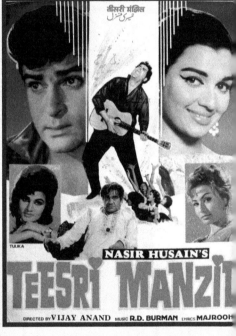

Poster, *Teesri Manzil* (1966). The lead pairing of Shammi Kapoor and Asha Parekh in the film itself is a distinct Husain influence. Vijay Anand had not worked with either actor before. *Courtesy: Sumant Batra*

Poster, *Hum Kisise Kum Naheen* (1977). Husain delivered three hits in the 1970s, but without Amitabh Bachchan, the reigning star of that era. *Courtesy: NH Films/ Nuzhat Khan*

The good times with Shammi Kapoor. Also seen in the picture are Rajendra Nath and Tahir Husain. *Courtesy: Rauf Ahmed*

From L to R: All Husain's heroes – from Dev Anand to Joy Mukerji to Shammi Kapoor. *Courtesy: NH Films/Nuzhat Khan*

The good old days: Husain is seated third from right with Vijay Anand, Shakti Samanta and Anand Bakshi to his right. On Husain's left are Majrooh Sultanpuri and Madan Puri. S.D. Burman is standing in the centre, while son R.D. Burman is on the extreme right next to Mrs Nasir Husain (in black). *Courtesy: Ashim Samanta*

From L to R: S. Mukerji, O.P. Nayyar and Husain. Husain acknowledged Mukerji's influence by referring to him as his 'guru'. *Courtesy: NH Films/ Nuzhat Khan*

With Dev Anand: Husain gave Anand a modern, urbane makeover in films like *Munimji* (1955) and *Paying Guest* (1957). *Courtesy: NH Films/ Nuzhat Khan*

The *Jab Pyar Kisise Hota Hai* (1961) team. Extreme left: Yash Johar, Raj Mehra (third from left), Dev Anand (centre), Nasir Husain (third from right) and Pran (extreme right). *Courtesy: NH Films/Nuzhat Khan*

The bon vivant, musical
hero was a constant trope of
a Nasir Husain film.

Above: Joy Mukerji in
Phir Wohi Dil Laya Hoon
(1963);

Right: Shashi Kapoor in
Pyar Ka Mausam (1969).

*Courtesy: NH Films/Nuzhat
Khan*

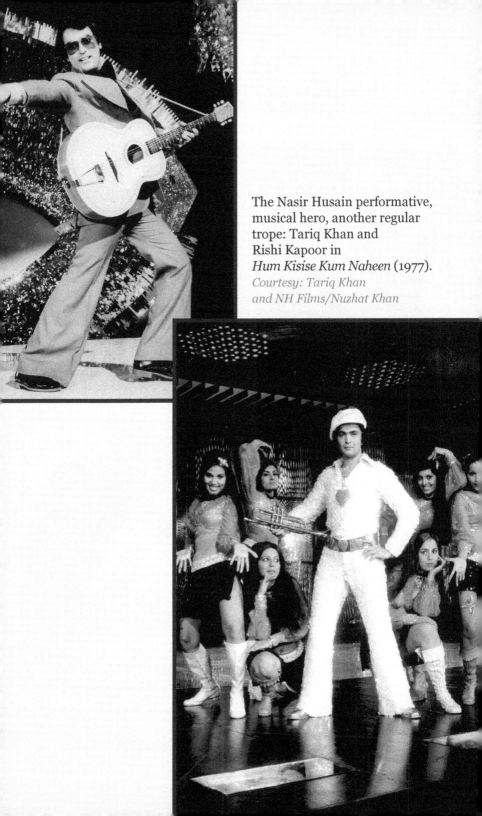

The Nasir Husain performative, musical hero, another regular trope: Tariq Khan and Rishi Kapoor in *Hum Kisise Kum Naheen* (1977).
Courtesy: Tariq Khan and NH Films/Nuzhat Khan

The *Dil Deke Dekho* (1959) team with Sulochana Latkar, Nasir Husain, Tahir Husain, Asha Parekh and S. Mukerji (standing behind Parekh in white). Sadhana, a Filmalaya discovery, is also seen in the picture. *Courtesy: NH Films/ Nuzhat Khan*

With Mrs Indira Gandhi. Asha Parekh is to Husain's left and wife Ayesha Khan is on the extreme right. *Courtesy: NH Films/Nuzhat Khan*

5

SAR PAR TOPI LAAL, GIRLS ON TREES AND COLOUR IN THE COUNTRYSIDE

'Bhai iskey baarey mein toh O.P. Nayyar kaha kartey thay ki, "Main jab dhunein banaata hoon toh logon ko meri dhunein bahut haseen aur rangeen nazar aati hain lekin usmein asli kamaal hai Nasir Husain ka jo picturization itni khoobsoorti ke saath kartey hain, ki woh gaana aur zyaada colourful lagta hai."' (O.P. Nayyar used to say that, 'When I compose my songs, people consider them very beautiful and vibrant, but the real magic in them is woven by Nasir Husain, who picturizes them so well that the song looks even more colourful.')

— Actor and television personality Tabassum

During Husain's days at Filmistan, S. Mukerji soon realized that the young writer also had a wonderful ear for music. He entrusted him with the additional responsibility of vetting tunes composed by music directors working on films being made at Filmistan. 'You decide whether the music is good or not,' Mukerji is supposed to have told Husain.

At that time, S.D. Burman was doing a number of films for Filmistan. Mukerji sent Husain to listen to Burman's tunes. Burman senior knew that Husain had been sent to him on the 'boss's' instructions. Perhaps with the intention of softening up

Husain, Burman insisted that Husain first partake of the food that had been sent from his house for lunch. Husain was only delighted to tuck in the fine Bengali cuisine that had come from Burman's home. Burman then opened another tiffin box and asked Husain to also help himself to some wonderful rasgullas that had come all the way from Calcutta. Husain, once again, happily took up his host's offer.

Only after this sumptuous spread did Burman play Husain a few of the tunes. But Husain didn't like what he heard. He didn't know how to say this to Burman, who was much senior to him. He remained quiet for some time. Burman insisted that he speak up and not be afraid. Husain hesitantly told Burman, '*Dada mujhe yeh tunein kuchh theek nahin lagi* (Dada, I didn't like the tunes much).' Burman got angry. He spoke aloud in Bengali, 'What a strange man! He ate my food, the rasgullas that I got and he is now dismissing my tunes.' Narrating this incident on Zee Classic's *Classic Legends*, Javed Akhtar noted, laughing, '*Beharhaal, khair yeh toh ek mazaak ki baat thee* (Anyhow, this was just in jest),' but then stated the seminal truth about Husain, '*lekin yeh haqeeqat hai ki unka selection, music ka, bhi bahut achha thaa* (But this is a fact that he had a terrific sense of music).'

Akhtar's assessment is possibly an understatement. Look at the history of Hindi cinema and it's hard to think of a director whose films consistently had great music over twenty-five years. Barring his last two films as director, Husain gave hit soundtrack after hit soundtrack from *Tumsa Nahin Dekha to Zamaane Ko Dikhana Hai*. The only other film-maker with a comparable record would be Raj Kapoor. Film-makers like Shakti Samanta, Raj Khosla or Yash Chopra, perhaps more prolific than Husain, generally had good music in their films, but also had films which were complete duds musically. In contrast, Husain had popular or good to great songs even in the least of his commercial successes, *Baharon Ke*

Sapne and *Pyar Ka Mausam*, songs which continue to resonate with listeners in the new millennium.

Music was the most important element of Husain's 'formula'. As Sidharth Bhatia remarked of Husain's films succeeding despite retelling the same story, 'My only theory is the songs. Every film of his. He was a master at this.' Husain admitted to the emphasis he placed on music. 'I give a lot of importance to music in all my films. I have an ear for it. In fact, even when I was working with S. Mukherjee [sic], he used to ask me to help him select S.D. Burman's tunes. And S.D. would use me to recommend certain tunes to S. Mukherjee. My judgment rarely failed.'[1]

Notwithstanding his ear for music, however, Husain's song sequences, just like his films, follow a pattern. Not only do they emerge at certain similar moments across films, but their themes and, in some cases, the picturization are also a redux of what Husain had already done previously. This shouldn't surprise us since if Husain's story was the same, the song situations would also, logically, not be too dissimilar.

'Bachna ae haseeno, lo main aa gaya'

The first song of a Nasir Husain film generally introduces the hero or establishes his musical credentials. In *Tumsa Nahin Dekha*, we see Shankar (Shammi Kapoor) for the first time with the camera teasing us as it focuses on his feet. It then cuts for a couple of shots to the girls picnicking in the garden, cuts back to Shankar and makes its way up from his feet, past his waist before it moves close up and shows us a debonair Shankar. It is only then, with the camera emphasizing Shankar's good looks from such close quarters, that he starts singing, '*Jawaaniya yeh mast mast bin peeye*'.

The same sequence is virtually repeated in *Phir Wohi Dil Laya Hoon* (although this is the second song in the film). Here, Mohan

---

[1]Resham Shaam, 'Little Big Man', *Super*, May 1978.

(Joy Mukerji) is introduced with the camera first focusing on his feet, then moving to a long shot of the women in the garden, before cutting back to Mohan, who turns to the camera at that exact instant and starts singing, '*Laakhon hai nigaah mein*'. Similarly, the first time we see Raj (Aamir Khan) in *Qayamat Se Qayamat Tak*, he too is with guitar in hand as he gets ready to sing '*Papa kehtey hain*' at his college farewell.

In films like *Dil Deke Dekho*, *Teesri Manzil* and *Hum Kisise Kum Naheen*, the songs – the title track of *Dil Deke Dekho*, '*O haseena zulfon waali*' (*Teesri Manzil*) and '*Bachna ae haseeno*' (*Hum Kisise Kum Naheen*) – tell us that the hero is a musician. In such films, the hero can sing and dance at any point since the 'musical' aspect of his character has been established. In *Yaadon Ki Baaraat*, the youngest brother's role as a musician is integral to the narrative as he renders the title track, which will ultimately help reunite the brothers at the climax. Mansoor put down his father's fascination for the musician character to the simple fact that, 'Well, my dad was extremely fond of music.'

The common thread that runs through all these songs is that they emphasize the importance of love and romance, and position the hero as the central peg of Husain's films. Whether it is '*Jawaaniya yeh mast mast bin peeye*' or '*Laakhon hai nigaah mein*', it is the hero who sets out to find the woman of his dreams amidst so many beautiful, young women. By the time we get to '*Bachna ae haseeno*', the hero's tone is a little more aggressive, narcissistic perhaps, but the emphasis is still on 'husn', 'aashiq' as in the earlier songs, which were about 'sanam', 'haseen', 'shama', 'parvana' and 'dil'. Even '*Papa kehtey hain*', which begins with someone becoming an 'engineer' and someone doing well in 'business' in the future, ultimately talks about the hero looking for his ladylove amongst a bevy of beauties in the antara '*Mera toh sapna, hai ek chehra*' and making a name in this '*dil ki duniya*'.

'*Ladies and gentlemen, naach-gaaney ke iss muqaabley mein...*'[2] Husain's song situations invariably have his hero and heroine responding to an informal challenge related to music and poetry or participating in a formal musical competition as a prelude to wooing.

His first film, *Tumsa Nahin Dekha*, has an episode where Shankar disguises himself as a poet, Virumal Aryapremi Lahorewaale, and accepts Meena's invitation to a '*muqaabla – bol ke badley bol*'. The song '*Aaye hain door se, milne huzoor se*' follows, where the two engage in a battle of poetic wits. Raza Mir, author of *The Taste of Words: An Introduction to Urdu Poetry*,[3] and a self-confessed fan of Husain's cinema, told me that such exchanges were in the tradition of 'bait-baazi', which is repartee in Urdu poetry. 'It is a very famous and traditional form of flirting and romance,' Mir said. 'Bait-baazi is like antaakshari. In the formalized bait-baazi, people use the last letter to create the sher, but in the more informal ones, it's more like you recite a sher, and then someone responds with another, a repartee of sorts.'

As already mentioned, in *Dil Deke Dekho*, Raja charms the women in the countryside with '*Megha re bole*' in order to prove to Neeta how good a singer he is. A similar situation takes place in *Pyar Ka Mausam*, but here Sunil (in the guise of Pyarelal) challenges Seema to win over the women and establish who is the better singer. They engage in light-hearted banter:

Sunil: *Kyun, kaun hai yeh? Lata Mangeshkar hain?* (Why, who is she? Is she Lata Mangeshkar?)

Seema: *Aap bhi Mohammed Rafi nahin hai.* (You too are no Mohammed Rafi.)

---

[2]A line during the 'All India Pop Competition' in *Hum Kisise Kum Naheen*.
[3]Penguin Books India, 2014.

After which comes the wonderful duet '*Ni Sultana re, pyaar ka mausam aaya*', with Sunil winning the bet by bribing the women with some cash.

When the hero himself is not singing or indulging in poetry, he works the heroine into envy over some dancing beauty performing in a club. The heroine and this dancer will then compete so that the heroine can establish both her superiority and the hero's poor judgement. *Jab Pyar Kisise Hota Hai*'s '*Tum jaise bigde babu*', taking place at the Darjeeling Club, and *Pyar Ka Mausam*'s '*Aap chaahein mujhko*' at the Rainbow Club fall in this category of songs.

These are instances of an informal face-off, but *Phir Wohi Dil Laya Hoon* and *Hum Kisise Kum Naheen* have formal competitions to rationalize the song sequences. In *Phir Wohi Dil Laya Hoon*, Mona and Kamini Devi compete to the classical-based song '*Dekho bijli dole bin baadal ke*'. Asha Parekh told me that the prelude to the song is the 'Lakshmi taal'[4] and was composed by the film's choreographer Gopi Krishna. More interestingly, the actor Tabassum, who is seen singing the song with two other girls, has a very young Saroj Khan (the choreographer) seated to her left. In *Hum Kisise Kum Naheen*, Rajesh (in the guise of Manjeet) and Sanjay participate in the wonderful medley, one of the iconic song sequences in Hindi cinema, which is part of the 'All India Pop Competition' taking place at the Nainital Club.

'Ajeeb khushk insaan hain aap bhi. Gaana mat gaao, mohabbat ki baatein na karo. Aakhir yeh raasta katega kaisey?'[5]

In Husain's cinematic world, no journey undertaken by the hero and the heroine is complete without a song. This was a

[4]Refers to the fifty-second-long instrumental prelude to the song.

[5]'You are a most boring person. Don't sing, don't indulge in any kind of romantic conversation. How will the journey pass?' Shankar (Shammi Kapoor) in *Tumsa Nahin Dekha*, which leads to the film's title track.

continuation of a certain Hindi film tradition, where protagonists sang while on the move, predominantly while making their way from the village to the city. Any number of Hindi film songs like '*Mausam beeta jaaye*' (*Do Bigha Zamin*) and '*Mera joota hai Japani*' (*Shree 420*) validate this. The starting point for this theme (as with several other Husain tropes such as disguise, a modern flamboyant hero) in Husain's films is perhaps *Munimji* where Raj bursts into '*Jeevan ke safar mein raahi*' while driving Roopa home after she has arrived from abroad. After much haggling with Roopa, who at first stops him from singing and then from driving fast, Raj tells her, '*Kuchh na karoonga, toh yeh raasta kaise katega* (If I don't do anything, how will I endure the journey),' which explains all such sequences in a Husain film. There can be no journey without music.

Subsequently, almost every Husain film has a song on the move. *Paying Guest* has Ramesh teasing Shanti with the enchanting '*Maana janaab ne pukaara nahin*' as they make their way from Shanti's college to her home in Lucknow's Aminabad neighbourhood. The *Munimji* moment is repeated almost identically in *Tumsa Nahin Dekha*, when Shankar and Meena finally decide to use the same tonga after reaching Soona Nagar station. Meena warns the tongawallah and Shankar that she will not tolerate any singing, but this doesn't stop Shankar from going ahead and rendering the title track of the film. In *Jab Pyar Kisise Hota Hai*, Monto sings the film's title track from atop a jeep while he and Nisha are travelling to Neelgaon from Darjeeling. Mohan renders '*Banda parvar, thaam lo jigar*' in *Phir Wohi Dil Laya Hoon*, when Mona and her friends decide to head to Baramulla for the day. The banjaras led by Mohan in *Caravan* sing '*Arrey ho, goriya kahaan tera des re*' while making their way to Pune where a theatre owner has promised them good money to put up a big show. Raj and Rashmi sing '*Gazab ka hai din*' in *Qayamat Se Qayamat Tak* when they are trying to find their way to Sitanagar.

If the journey in a Husain film provides the backdrop for romance between the hero and the heroine to blossom, it is the song that generally facilitates the process. It is in this sequence that we see the hero flirting with the heroine while she fumes, or winning her over by the end. As an example, look at '*Hoga tumse pyaara kaun*' from *Zamaane Ko Dikhana Hai*. Before the song, Kanchan (Padmini Kolhapure) rants and rages at Ravi (Rishi Kapoor) for coming into her life. Even though she says her final goodbye to him ('Bye, you rich, filthy lover boy'), Ravi has her in his arms by the end of the song.

Nasreen Munni Kabir explained the significance of the journey in these songs. 'I think the train or any other means of transport is a way of showing movement – that the characters are going places. Like, say, the famous scenes with the scooter in *Roman Holiday* [1953]. It is the little space you get, away from reality. Where do people tell each other everything? They can to total strangers on a journey, because you have not arrived and this could well be a passing acquaintance. In that space you don't have the heaviness of the Indian tradition, the Indian family. Questions like "is she going to be the right wife for me" do not matter.'

The song on the move is usually preceded by a sequence where the car, in which the protagonists are travelling, breaks down. The genesis of this, too, goes back to *Munimji* where Roopa is forced to ride with Raj after her car meets with an accident. In *Dil Deke Dekho*, Raja sings '*Raahi mil gaye raahon mein*' to Neeta as they make their way to Ranikhet after the car that she and Kailash (Rajendra Nath) are driving in meets with an accident. *Jab Pyar Kisise Hota Hai* has a near identical episode where the protagonists sing '*Yeh aankhein, uff yumma*' after their truck is involved in a crash.

In *Teesri Manzil*, the car doesn't actually break down but serves as a convenient excuse for the protagonists to break into a song. Twice. While going to Madanpur, Sunita (Parekh) hears her friend signalling to her frantically from the boot. She asks Anil (Shammi) to stop the car, on the pretext that the vehicle's engine needs water because it heats up far too quickly. As Anil sets out to look for water, Sunita lures him far away from the car, leading to Anil singing the beautiful ballad, '*Deewaana mujhsa nahin*'. Then on their way back to Mussoorie, Sunita asks Anil to help her with the car, which she can't get to start. She then pretends to sob and begs Anil to forgive her – Anil had rescued her from bandits the previous night and she is feeling well-disposed towards him – which he eventually does. This gives Sunita enough reason to sing '*O mere sona re, sona re*'.

Yaadon Ki Baaraat follows a slightly different path. Here, the car which Vijay (Vijay Arora) and Sunita (Zeenat Aman) are using for their day out in the countryside has genuinely broken down. Vijay uses this to his advantage and gets Sunita to stay the night with him at a garage after faking a sudden bout of unconsciousness. The next morning, Sunita even goes to a nearby temple to pray for his recovery. Seeing her genuine love for him, Vijay admits that his whole cancer ruse[6] was a charade. Sunita gets upset with Vijay for lying to her, but her anger is only momentary for Vijay eventually charms her with the magical '*O meri soni, meri tamanna*'.

These songs once again highlight Husain's ability to repackage and rehash the same situation with a fresh approach. If the song played out in a tonga the first time, it shifted to a car the second time and a train next. At times, it was a car breaking down that led to a song sequence, while at other times, the protagonists had to lose their way for the song to happen. Sometimes the boy sang to the girl, with the pair of them on bicycles in monochrome settings, while in other instances, the protagonists just expressed their joy

---

[6]Vijay lies to Sunita earlier in the film that he is dying of cancer to win her affection. She thinks his falling unconscious is linked to his terminal illness.

in the beauty of the countryside in the company of feisty, spirited banjaras while riding colourful bullock carts. What was '*O mere sona*' in one film became '*O meri soni*' in another.

Film songs for long have been looked at and critiqued within the rather narrow view of how the triumvirate of composer–playback singer–lyricist combine to produce a song. But the manner in which a melody is composed, embellished with lyrics and then sung is only one part of a song's role in Hindi cinema. The visual aspect of the song – the set design, the choreography, the manner in which it is performed and its picturization – has hardly been written about. This is indeed a tragedy since the song sequence is the one site that has exemplified originality and artistic collaboration in a Hindi film.

Further, if we consider cinema as a primarily visual medium, it is song sequences that steer it to cinema's original objective. Is it even possible to think of *Mughal-E-Azam*'s '*Jab pyaar kiya toh darna kya?*' without the imposing grandeur of K. Asif's Sheesh Mahal accompanying it? Entire careers have been made of song and dance, with no less than a name like Helen shining across four decades in Hindi cinema on the strength of how wonderfully she sashayed, shimmied and swayed across the camera. It is not possible to think of the 'Bollywood experience' without song sequences, and film-makers like Guru Dutt, Raj Kapoor, Vijay Anand and Shakti Samanta really did some pioneering work in this area, often elevating it to high art. So did Husain.

I met actor–producer Aamir Khan on more than one occasion to discuss Husain's cinema. Aamir is Nasir Husain's nephew. Aamir's father, Tahir Husain, is Nasir Husain's youngest sibling. One of the first things that Aamir confirmed to me were Husain's budgetary constraints in shooting *Tumsa Nahin Dekha*. And so when I asked him about the title track's picturization, Aamir pointed out to the use of back projection by Husain to overcome that limitation. Back projection by itself was quite a common phenomenon in the industry by that time. But Aamir explained how Husain used back projection innovatively to give the viewer an outdoor feel to the song. One would actually have to view the song to fully appreciate Husain's craft in the song.

'They didn't have a budget for outdoor,' Aamir said. 'So he innovated and tried to do the best with the resources that he had. And it's very difficult to convey that these people were actually travelling in the tonga. So they were restricted to shooting just the actors, with the background moving. That's why a lot of it is in close-ups.'

But Husain's creative genius comes to the fore in the few seconds before the second antara of the song, '*Tum bhi haseen, rut bhi haseen*', begins. It is just after the women in the countryside are shown and the camera cuts to the wheel of the tonga.

Aamir described the moment. 'There is one very clever shot. It starts with the wheel moving and then it tilts up to them so it gives you the illusion of the tonga moving. So *yeh do, teen shot, baahar ke passing shots le liye hain – yeh move ho raha hai, toh lagta hai ki woh log road pe jaa rahey hain* (So they have taken a few passing outdoor shots and since the wheel is moving, it gives the impression that they are travelling on the actual road).'

Then, just as the second antara draws to a close with the words '*peeye bina, aaj humey chadha hai nasha*', we see Shankar turn upside down, with his head now a few inches above the moving ground. This was yet another trick conjured by Husain to give the impression of an outdoor shoot. Aamir explained, 'Now this is a very difficult shot. He is hanging from the tonga. So underneath him has to be the road, but back projection is not shot downwards.

You can't project on the floor. You have to project on the screen. So Shammi uncle had to pretend that he was leaning backwards and hanging, but actually he was not. Because the screen is at the back. So the shot will come at the back only, but he [Husain] created an illusion that he [Shammi] is dangling below. We get the feeling because even the air is blown into his hair to give that impression.'

The extent of Husain's innovations with 'Tumsa nahin dekha's picturization needs to be seen against other popular songs of that time, which used back projection. Munimji's 'Jeevan ke safar mein raahi', Paying Guest's 'Maana janaab ne pukaara nahin' and Naya Daur's 'Maang ke saath tumhaara' – all three songs have their protagonists singing with back projection. But the camera in all three songs largely operates in clichéd ways. In the Paying Guest song, it actually does nothing except for pulling out from a medium shot of Dev Anand to get both Nutan and Dev Anand in the same frame. In the Naya Daur song, the camera cuts to long shots of the tonga going by in the countryside since they are in the actual outdoors. There are close-ups of Dilip Kumar and Vyjayanthimala as well, but little else that excites the eye or stimulates the imagination.

In contrast, Husain cut frequently and presented different camera angles to suggest a lot of action in his song. There is a frontal view of Ameeta and Shammi with the tongawallah's back to the viewer, side-on views of both Ameeta and Shammi, several close-ups of both and ultimately even a frontal view of the tongawallah when Shammi comes in front. There is the added joy of watching Ameeta knock Shammi Kapoor on the head in perfect timing to the 'ting' sound that punctuates the song. Madhulika Liddle gushed over the song's picturization in contrast to the Naya Daur song. 'Nasir Husain's song picturizations are never boring. The people involved do interesting things other than merely lip-synching to the song. There's action. Even within the very confined space in which the song plays out, there's so much going on.'

It is easy to attribute the action in the song purely to Shammi Kapoor's physicality. Jumping around the tonga, turning upside down and going in front to sit beside the tongawallah may well have been integral to his screen image in later years, but while shooting for this film, Shammi only had a number of flops behind him. Husain would have had to green-light his mannerisms while thinking of how to bring it all together. Also, if one is to look at '*Piya piya piya*' from *Baap Re Baap* (1955), the song's picturization is insipid despite the presence of Kishore Kumar, whose physicality and theatrics were at par if not more than Shammi's. The *Tumsa Nahin Dekha* song is proof, therefore, that cinema is definitely a collaborative exercise where it took two to 'tonga'.

Tumsa Nahin Dekha's title track is the only song in the film that was written by the noted poet–lyricist Sahir Ludhianvi. Actually, Husain had sought Sahir to write all the songs for his debut film. But Sahir clashed with Husain and quit the film. 'In those days, Guru Dutt's *Pyaasa* was being made. We were making *Tumsa Nahin Dekha*. Sahir would tell me, "Look at *Pyaasa*. What songs." I would tell him our song situations and he would talk about *Pyaasa*. I told him, "*Woh apne type ki picture bana rahe hain, main apne type ki picture bana raha hoon* (He is making the film he wants to make and I am making the film I want to make)." Because of that we had a falling out.' The episode was more proof of Sahir's egotistical behaviour. Sahir often spoke his mind, but at times he overstepped the norms of propriety and displayed hubris. Just after *Pyaasa*'s release, he clashed with S.D. Burman over the success of the film's songs, which led to Burman refusing to work with him again. His break-up with composer Jaidev, with whom he collaborated on two memorable soundtracks, *Hum Dono* (1961) and *Mujhe Jeene Do* (1963), is similarly well known.

But Husain remained an ardent admirer of Sahir's poetry. In *Dil Deke Dekho*, Kailash (Rajendra Nath) attempts to charm the person he thinks is Neeta (but is actually Neeta's father, his face hidden from Kailash), while reciting lines ('*Tum aa rahi ho zamaane ki aankh se bach kar...*') from Sahir's famous anti-war poem, 'Parchhaiyaan' (Shadows). 'Sahir Ludhianvi was a great poet, but in those days he would only talk about *Pyaasa, Pyaasa, Pyaasa*. Everywhere he went, he only spoke about *Pyaasa*. If we hadn't fought, he would have been writing the songs. That is why I got Majrooh [Sultanpuri] sa'ab. I hit it off instantly with Majrooh sa'ab. He wrote a lot of songs for me.'

Before we get to Husain's relationship with Majrooh, another inspired song sequence from Husain's first four directorial films needs to be discussed: the title track of *Jab Pyar Kisise Hota Hai* – '*Jiya ho, jiya o jiya kuchh bol do*'. The song, one of the many outstanding Shankar–Jaikishan compositions for the film, was written by Hasrat Jaipuri. Here, too, Husain made a concerted effort to give the feeling of movement rather than just relying on Dev Anand bobbing his head and lip-synching his way through the song, most of which involved back projection.

Husain shot some portion of the song on location in Darjeeling, which is established in the long shots of the train and the car moving parallel to each other. Separate shots – of the railway tracks, the wheels of the train, Popat Lal (Rajendra Nath) and his secretary (Aamir Khan's father, Tahir Husain) leaning out of the window to see a pair of donkeys in the countryside, the camera moving up the car to where Dev Anand is seated and then moving from the back of the car to the right and from the front of the car to the left – all give the impression of actual movement.

Sadanand Warrier, Anuradha's husband and Hindi film music buff, gave an even more detailed explanation of how Husain best picturized Shankar–Jaikishan's score to heighten the train's 'in motion' effect. 'Notice how the music starts when Dev jumps off the train seemingly to his death and Asha Parekh finds that he is on top of the car. Prior to this scene in the dialogue, Dev Anand is speaking in very theatrical tones and the only sound you hear is the agitated chuff-chuff of the engine. It grows louder as he jumps. After the jump, he's on top of the car and there is a rush of strings followed by the accordion, and the music slows imperceptibly before picking up with a combination of accordion and guitar playing the melody and then the bongos come in. From this point onwards, the rhythm reflects the train's chuffing. The music drives the scene forward, and if you pay attention to the bongos and maracas, they are actually simulating and accentuating the steam engine's wheezy rhythm.'

Sadanand observed something else that accentuates the feeling of movement. 'When Mohammed Rafi sings "*Jiya ho, jiya o jiya kuchh bol do*", there is a very high-pitched flute (piccolo, penny-whistle? I think there are two of them because it has a double-reed effect) which plays a very noticeable part. It's like a birdcall, you can't miss it as it is repeated at the same time always in the mukhda. This is the sound you hear when a bird goes trilling past your window. The sound doesn't have a location. You get the same effect when you are in a train and a stationary or flying bird utters the same sort of cry. It adds to the feeling of motion ... The song ends with the bongos still driving the tune along, the music continuing to play the refrain, long shots of the train still moving, all these giving an impression of being in motion.'

Doraiswamy saw another brush with modernity in this song. 'It is Nasir Husain's desire to touch up the modern with a little "more modern" that also explains the song sequence "*Jiya ho, jiya*

o jiya kuchh bol do" shot on a car and train running parallel to
each other. Horses running along trains are a common enough
motif in action films that thrive on the thrill in the different kinds
of speed of animal and machine. Here, however, we have a car
and train go along together harmoniously ... He [Husain] revels,
almost in a child-like manner, in the technical devices that allow
the "this modern" (the car) and the "this modern" (the train)
to run alongside each other: the back projection, the cut that
covers up the improbable jump from the train compartment on
to the roof of a car and back again. This sequence is literally and
metaphorically a romance with modernity. Not just on the part of
the characters in the film and the director, but also of the music
director who translates the beat and rhythm of the wheels of the
train and the sonority of its whistle into the music.'[7]

More significantly, prior to this, Hindi film songs that featured
the train either had the character singing from within the train
– like in '*Aao bachchon tumhe dikhaayein*' from *Jagriti* (1954) or
'*Apni toh har aah ek toofan hai*' from *Kala Bazar* (1960) or '*Dil
thaam chaley hum aaj kidhar*' from *Love in Simla* (1960) – or
had the song as a voiceover – like in '*Dekh tere sansaar ki haalat*'
from *Nastik* (1954) or '*Main hoon Jhum Jhum Jhum Jhumroo*'
from *Jhumroo* (1961). The *Jab Pyar Kisise Hota Hai* title track,
in contrast, is one of the earliest instances[8] where one character

---

[7]Dr Rashmi Doraiswamy, '"These Days" of Our Modernity: The
Cinema of Nasir Husain', Film and Television Institute of India, Pune,
4 September 2004, p. 13.

[8]An earlier song that attempted a feeling of thrill and spectacle was
'*Chal meri gadiye tu chhuk chhuk chhuk*' from *Ek Do Teen* (1953). But
in that song, the picturization involves mostly wide shots of the moving
train and mid-shots of the characters. Also, all three characters are very
much part of the moving train. They don't sing to each other from any
vehicle moving parallel to the train.

is singing from outside the train to another character seated inside and the train is very much part of the sequence. The novel picturization imparted a definite thrill, a feeling of adventure and spectacle to the song.

Stylistically, '*Jiya ho*' pre-empted another great 'train–car' song sequence from Hindi cinema – '*Mere sapnon ki rani kab aayegi tu*' from *Aradhana* (1969). In this song, Rajesh Khanna sings the song from within a jeep driven by Sujit Kumar to Sharmila Tagore, who is seated inside the train. The picturization is clearly in '*Jiya ho*' territory. When I met Ashim Samanta, son of *Aradhana*'s director Shakti Samanta, and asked him if his father, who knew Husain well and was friendly with him, had possibly been inspired by Husain's picturization for his song, Ashim replied, 'My father never discussed it, but I am sure all of them were influenced by each other's style.'

Returning to *Tumsa Nahin Dekha*, the last song in the film, '*Sar par topi laal*', also needs to be closely examined. As the song heads to a frenetic finish, Husain captured and heightened the change in tone through some interesting camera techniques, shot-taking and editing.

Beginning from the moment where Shankar finishes singing '*Gorey, gorey gaal, gaal pe uljhey, uljhey baal, ho tera kya kehna*' for the last time, and where Meena and her co-dancers are shown clapping in the next frame, Husain resorted to a Dutch angle (the camera is at an angle) to capture the moment. As the pace picks up, Husain cut frantically to match the beat of the song. He used the Dutch angle once again to show Shankar going back and forth with his male co-artistes. He then presented a series of quick cuts to show the junior artistes clapping their hands, dancing on one foot, shaking their hips, with close-ups of Shammi, Ameeta and some of the junior artistes each time the playback singers exercise their vocal chords. The series of cuts, barely lasting a few seconds in each shot, enliven the sequence and perfectly articulate O.P. Nayyar's frenetic finish to the song.

This frenzied closure to a song is a recurring motif in Nayyar's music. Just around the time *Tumsa Nahin Dekha* released, Nayyar did something similar in '*Yeh desh hai veer jawaano ka*' (*Naya Daur*) and '*Mera naam Chin-Chin-Choo*' (*Howrah Bridge*, 1958). But in both these films, the camera stays at a fair distance from the artistes. The cuts are not as quick, with the directors of both films (B.R. Chopra for *Naya Daur* and Shakti Samanta for *Howrah Bridge*) content to allow the bhangra dancers and Helen alone to provide the spectacle in these sequences.

By no means does this suggest that Husain patented the Dutch angle. Dutch tilts were used in Hindi cinema from much before. Dutch tilts are generally used to create a sense of 'off-balance', to portray a moment of tumult either in the character's mind or a catastrophic moment, but it was not unusual for directors to use them in songs as well (as an example, '*Suno gajar kya gaaye*' in *Baazi* uses a Dutch tilt momentarily towards the end of the song). Filmistan, certainly the place where Husain would have learnt it, flogged the technique to death, using it in several films in succession: in *Sargam* (1950), after the ship capsizes at the end; *Anarkali* (in war sequences); *Munimji* (in the song '*Zindagi hai zinda*'); and *Paying Guest* (at the climax in the courtroom when Shubha Khote's character is confronted by the return of Yakub's character, who she thought was dead).

The *Sargam* song, '*Main hoon ek khalaasi*', which has the rare instance of Raj Kapoor dancing unfettered, comes close to Husain's style as it resorts to a Dutch tilt at the precise moment the pace picks up at the end. But the cuts here are nowhere near as quick as Husain's cutting and the shots of the artistes are generally mid-range rather than extreme close-up. Interestingly, the otherwise sombre *Do Aankhen Baarah Haath*, from the same year as Husain's film, has the song '*Taka taka dhoom dhoom*' end with a series of quick cuts, but here it is only the character's heads or their full frame that come into focus to portray their abandon. There are no Dutch angles in this song, and neither do the characters' arms or legs specifically come into focus.

Husain was different in that he used a combination of Dutch angles, extreme quick cuts and close-ups of the artistes, their hands, their feet or any other part of their body that moved, to not only convey a wholesome feeling of ecstasy, abandon and hysteria, but also to amplify the composition's feverish climax. It gives the feeling that the composition, which is actually pre-recorded, is possibly emanating from the actions of the artistes, as part of the mise-en-scène.

The way the song was picturized invited Tolaram Jalan's wrath. 'The producer came and said, "What have you done? Are you mad? People will get chakkar (dizzy)." *Woh time pe itna fast cutting hota hi nahin thaa.* (There wasn't a lot of fast cutting in those days.) Almost like flash cuts,' Aamir told me.

Husain went on to make this one of his signature song picturization styles. In most of his films, there is at least one song which builds up towards a frenetic finish. And in his three films following *Tumsa Nahin Dekha*, Husain replicated the '*Sar par topi laal*' experience at the end of each of these songs. In '*Yaar chulbula hai*', '*Do ekum do*' (both songs from *Dil Deke Dekho*), '*Tum jaise bigde babu*' (*Jab Pyar Kisise Hota Hai*) and '*Dekho bijli dole bin baadal ke*' (*Phir Wohi Dil Laya Hoon*), we see a series of flash cuts, quick panning of the camera, the artistes approaching the camera, and close-ups of the artistes, their hands and feet, all of this to accentuate the experience of the frenzied climax.

Intriguingly, Husain used the Dutch angle in a variety of ways, but mostly in song sequences. In another fine song from *Tumsa Nahin Dekha*, '*Chhupnewaale saamne aa*', he made use of Dutch angles between the mukhda and both the antaras of what is essentially a soft romantic song. Of particular delight is the interlude between the mukhda and the first antara, when Seema (Sheila Vaz) is shown dancing around Shankar. The exact instant where she completes her circular routine around Shankar, the camera pans to the left (in a single shot) but tilts ever so gently as well, to show the other artistes in the sequence. Here the Dutch tilt is in sync with the lightness of the moment, the overall mood of the song. Anuradha Warrier admired the entire treatment of the song. 'The softness of the song itself, the pretend romance with the village girl, *manaofying* the "hidden" heroine – just the whole vibe of the scene. It never fails to make me smile. You know the girl is going to give in, you are, in fact, waiting for her to give in, willing her to give in. How can she resist?'

Husain did the same in '*Sar par topi laal*', giving a few Dutch angles early in the song after the mukhda has been sung. The primary role of the technique, though, in this song and in '*Do ekum do*' and '*Tum jaise bigde babu*', is as a marker (as it was in *Sargam*), to indicate the precise moment from where the song shifts gears. In '*Dekho bijli dole bin baadal ke*', however, he used the angle to portray the feeling of dizziness that Mona's opponent experiences as she fails to keep up with Mona, signalling the moment of Mona's victory. Similarly, in *Yaadon Ki Baaraat*, Husain used the Dutch angle right at the beginning of the scene when Monto (Tariq Khan) is shown for the first time, cavorting around the stage with his electric guitar, to bring out his rock-'n'-roll-style character.

Speaking on the history of the musical genre in American cinema, eminent film-maker Martin Scorsese paid homage to the great Hollywood director–choreographer, Busby Berkeley. It was with Berkeley that the musical came into its own in the late 1920s and 1930s. Referencing one of Berkeley's milestone films, *Gold Diggers of 1935*, which had more than one song sequence (refer '*Lullaby of Broadway*') that used Dutch tilts extensively and had several interesting close-ups of the tap-dancing artistes' feet, Scorsese said, 'A former dance instructor, Berkeley was the first to realize that a movie musical was totally different from a staged musical. On film everything was seen through one eye, the camera. In designing his production numbers, he would, therefore, rely on unusual camera movements and angles. The camera itself would partake in the choreography. Berkley's ballets could not have existed outside the movies. They were pure cinematic creations.'[9]

Looking at Husain's camera techniques and angles in these songs, it is almost as if Scorsese spoke for him, too.

The tight budget for *Tumsa Nahin Dekha* may have constrained Husain from venturing into an actual hill-station location for the film. But in *Dil Deke Dekho* and his own home productions, starting with *Jab Pyar Kisise Hota Hai*, he showcased the outdoors in all their splendour. The beauty of '*Pyaar ki kasam hai*' (*Dil Deke Dekho*) and '*Yeh aankhein, uff yumma*' (*Jab Pyar Kisise Hota Hai*) lies not just in the mellifluousness of both compositions, the way they are sung and in their lyrics, but in Husain's picturization as well. He placed his protagonists in fields blooming with daisies, made them serenade each other in the mist, in sylvan settings, and took wide shots of the valleys – all to synchronize the ethereal, romantic flavour of the songs with nature's exquisiteness.

---

[9]Martin Scorsese, The Musical – A Personal Journey Through American Movies (1995) –https://www.youtube.com/watch?v=N028ZvX8bdM

In a sense, Husain was prescient. If *Junglee* (1961) popularized the outdoors, having been shot in 'Eastman Color', Husain's first three directorial ventures celebrated the outdoors, particularly, in song sequences, despite being shot in monochrome. He had already made himself familiar with the contours, the dynamics and the coordinates of the open landscape in his initial films. But Husain was also anticipating the use of colour. We know that because of *'Sar par topi "laal"'*. And so by the time he actually worked with colour in *Phir Wohi Dil Laya Hoon*, we see a master at work in this space. For his songs in *Phir Wohi Dil Laya Hoon*, not only did he showcase the beauty of Kashmir, with its colourful shikaras, houseboats, the beautiful valleys and gardens, but he brought in scale and spectacle as well.

As an example, look at *'Laakhon hai nigaah mein'*. It is actually the same song as *'Jawaaniya yeh mast mast bin peeye'* from *Tumsa Nahin Dekha*. Both songs introduce the hero, are about him looking for that one singular beauty from amongst so many and are shot outdoors. Both songs were composed by the same person (O.P. Nayyar), sung by Rafi and written by Majrooh Sultanpuri. Even in terms of their picturization, of how the songs begin and end, they are similar. But in the *Tumsa Nahin Dekha* song, Shammi Kapoor doesn't go beyond the garden setting. The song begins with him entering the garden and ends with him exiting it, waving goodbye to the many young people, mainly women, in it. The song is symptomatic of Husain's scale in the film. It is small, with Husain having to make do within a narrow canvas.

'Laakhon hai nigaah mein', in contrast, begins with Joy Mukerji singing in a garden (possibly Srinagar's iconic Shalimar Bagh), then has him shift to a shikara, admiring the many beauties in the Dal Lake who are swimming and surfing, only for him to sing the last antara in a big field (part of the erstwhile Oberoi Hotel in

Srinagar) against the backdrop of several balloons going up in the air. Husain expands his protagonist's world (from garden to lake to field) and brings in spectacle through several elements (colour, scale, beautiful shikaras and balloons). The last shot of the song – a single, wide shot – has Mohan running down a hillock just as several balloons are released in the sky. The moment he makes his way down the short incline, Mohan turns to wave his arms (just as Shankar does at the end of '*Jawaaniya yeh mast mast*'), but the impression created is that he is saying goodbye not just to the people releasing the balloons, but to the entire spectacle around him. Only after doing this does he exit the frame to bring an end to the song. 'Same introduction, same style, but it works both times. Both songs were super hits,' concluded Javed Akhtar.[10]

Similarly, in '*Humdum mere khel na jaano*', Husain placed Joy Mukerji, Asha Parekh and the other accompanying artistes in snow-covered terrain. He made the women prance with balloons in their hands and then had them release them. He finally shifted to the top of a houseboat, with all his protagonists, to give the entire sequence a sense of vibrancy, dynamism and colour. For '*Banda parvar*', he had a number of women run in an open field against the backdrop of snow-capped peaks. He made them stand against trees, even placed them on the trees and finally lined them up on either side of the road (in three separate shots) to wave at the passing tongas, with scarves in hand. 'His [Husain's] wife and I went to colleges [in Kashmir] to ask for girls to be sent for "*Laakhon hai nigaah mein*",' Asha Parekh told me about the hunt for the extra artistes in these songs. The emphasis in both songs is clearly on spectacle, to delight the audience with the array of colours and scenery on display.

---

[10]Zee Classic's *Classic Legends: Season II*, featuring Nasir Husain.

Neelam Mukerji added perceptively that while there was a lot of colour in these sequences, the reason Husain had the girls running around was because, 'He built the hero up. There are no males there. It's just the women. They are props to build the hero's romantic image. He was such a clever director … It was a subtle indication of sex and the male gaze.' She further elaborated that Husain's use of colour, with the scenic locations et al, was a continuation of the S. Mukerji school of film-making. 'Baba [S. Mukerji] used to say, when there is a romantic story, handsome man, beautiful girl, you must have good music, the rest of your props must be colourful. The public enjoys that. It's good to their eyes … The films will survive on the good looks of the lead pair, the beauty and the melody of the songs, the ambience and the scenery which go with it.'

An essential distinction must be made between Husain and Shakti Samanta here. Samanta's *Kashmir Ki Kali* (1964) released only a year after *Phir Wohi Dil Laya Hoon*. In one of the most memorable song sequences from that film, Samanta had Shammi Kapoor deliver a zest-filled performance in '*Yeh chaand sa roshan chehra*'. The song focuses on the local women of the Kashmiri countryside to bring out its colour and beauty. This is understandable since Sharmila Tagore's character in Samanta's film belongs to this demographic. But despite the songs in *Phir Wohi Dil Laya Hoon* also being situated in the Kashmiri countryside for a large part, Husain totally avoided referencing the local women. It can be argued that this is because Parekh's character is that of an urban girl. Her friends have to be of a similar background. But to not have a single shot of native women, while they are waving out to Mohan in '*Banda parvar*' or among the many beauties on view in the garden or in the lake in '*Laakhon hai nigaah mein*', clearly underscores Husain's affinity towards modernity instead of the traditional. This is not to say that

Husain avoided such representation completely. We see it in his songs like the *Tumsa Nahin Dekha* title song or '*Megha re bole*' or in a later song like '*Hoga tumse pyaara kaun*' when Ravi (Rishi Kapoor) waves out from the top of the train in *Zamaane Ko Dikhana Hai.*

Rashmi Doraiswamy observed, 'Look at *Kashmir Ki Kali.* It has the element of the local colour. Nasir Husain doesn't give a damn. He just doesn't care ... When people go into locations, they tend to use folksy music, but that's not the case with him, except in "*Megha re bole*" where you have these tribal girls dancing. This is unique because this is something that everybody uses, especially when you go into the hills. But he does not go into all that, which is very good in a way because it also shows that he is not into a particular kind of exotica, in a sense of showing the local people ... And that's what makes him so different.'

To this extent, Samanta and Husain were different. For most of the 1960s, Samanta's films foregrounded a certain 'exotica'. Be it *Howrah Bridge, Singapore* (1960), *China Town, Kashmir Ki Kali* or *An Evening in Paris*, the film names themselves gave a hint of Samanta's ambitions. Husain's cinema didn't tread such places. Even while in the countryside, hill-station setting, his characters represented the Anglophone Indian elite. None of his protagonists were ever truly native. Compared to Samanta's films, Husain's were also, as Sidharth Bhatia observed, 'breezier in terms of storytelling'.

Bhaumik sees Husain's foray into the Kashmiri countryside not just as part of a larger trend, but also something that allowed for a certain kind of song picturization. 'In the '60s, outdoor shooting becomes so important, principally because of colour, music becomes very dynamic. It allows for this thought that music can float around in space ... In the sense that valleys allow for resonance and echoes. There is celebration of lovers serenading each other across hilltops.'

To illustrate Bhaumik's observation, look at how Husain picturized the beginning of '*Humdum mere khel na jaano*'. When Mohan starts singing the prelude to the song with, '*Door bahut mat jaaiye, leke qaraar humaara…*', the camera zooms out (at the very moment the words '*Door bahut mat jaaiye*' finish – in perfect sync) to give away his position on a snow-capped hill. The camera cuts to Mona, who is implied to be at a fair distance down below. Mona responds, '*Paas raho ya door tum, tum ho saath humaarey…*' (Whether near or far away, you are by my side). The moment she utters the word 'door', the camera zooms out to give a wide view of '*yeh khaamosh nazaarey*' (these silent, stunning environs), which is the last line of the prelude. In both cases, there is hardly any accompanying instrumentation to go with the voices of Rafi and Asha Bhonsle. Yet, the words sung by Mohan and Mona appear to have traversed the entire distance between the two. It is only then that the camera cuts to a close-up of Mohan and he starts singing '*Naazneen, bada rangeen hai waada tera…*', which then leads into '*Humdum mere khel na jaano*'.

Such song sequences, however, have invited the ire of critics and a certain condescending attitude towards Hindi cinema. Their disparaging comments stem from the view that the moments in these songs or the sudden episodic appearance of the song itself out of nowhere is 'unreal' and 'escapist'. After all, where do we find girls perched on trees or men and women singing out to each other, with several artistes accompanying them in their song and dance routine?

This is a facetious argument. The objective of a film isn't to reflect reality. The idea is to create a world which is consistent in its narrative, its character portrayals and its overall look and feel. For instance, look at Wes Anderson's fine 2014 film, *The Grand Budapest Hotel*, which is a homage to a certain hotel culture that existed in a time long gone. It would take a brave man to say that the look and feel of Anderson's film mirrors 'reality', but within the world that Anderson creates, there is a remarkable evenness through all the elements that make the film.

Husain, too, created (for the most part) a world of his own. In such youth-oriented, romantic narratives, it was absolutely 'logical' for his characters to burst out into song and dance and climb trees. His films were, after all, about the thrill of young love. It was the celebration of that love that allowed Husain to let his characters run around in the countryside, wave their scarves and sing songs to each other out in the open. The vibrant spectacle in *Phir Wohi Dil Laya Hoon*, exemplified by balloons of all colours taking off in the background all too frequently, is a manifestation of the same. If anything, the moments in which Husain stepped out of 'this buoyant world' and ventured into 'another space' – like the attempted historic but artificial set where Mohan sings the otherwise minimalistic composition, '*Aanchal mein saja lena kaliyaan*', or when Mona sings the rather morose '*Meri berukhi tumne dekhi hai lekin*' at the climax – jar vis-à-vis the overall presentation of *Phir Wohi Dil Laya Hoon*.

In doing so, Husain (or for that matter several Hindi film-makers before and after) again echoed what Scorsese said of film-maker Vincente Minnelli's milestone film *Meet Me In St. Louis* (1944), which despite being a musical, made a clean break from the Broadway settings of musicals in previous years. The protagonists in the film are members of a middle-class household. 'They did not need to be professional performers,' said Scorsese. 'Anyone could sing and dance. They felt like it. Singing and dancing became as natural as breathing or talking. Also, the tunes were designed to further the plot and reveal the characters. They expressed the ebb and flow of personal emotions.'[11]

Likewise, Husain proved to be a master in using songs to advance his narratives. He said so himself. 'For me songs were a part of the story. It wasn't *ki aap gaaney ko nikaaltey hain, toh story ko farak nahin padega. Aisey gaaney nahin hotey thay.* (That if you eliminate the songs, it won't affect the story. These weren't that kind of songs.) They moved the story forward.'

While the advertisements for his initial four films clearly emphasized the musical nature of his cinema, with musical notations jumping out of the ads, Husain rationalized the presence of the songs in the narrative all through. The competition songs (or the informal face-off ones) invariably had a build-up to them. The songs in the countryside were based on the logic of celebrating love. The songs on the move were very much within the Indian cinematic tradition of singing while setting out on a journey. Other numbers like '*Chhupnewaale saamne aa*' or '*Dekho kasam se*' from *Tumsa Nahin Dekha* or '*Hum aur tum aur yeh samaa*' from *Dil Deke Dekho* were crucial to the process of courtship and the '*roothna-manaana*' routine that was part of the same. Nasreen acknowledged Husain's skill in integrating songs. 'I would say that most film-makers cannot do without the song. But some people do it better ... Nasir sa'ab had it from day one. He knew the rules of Hindi cinema very well. His songs were absolutely integrated because they tell you something. Like "*Chhupnewaale*" tells you a lot about this [Shammi Kapoor] character.'

The other clever thing that Husain did very well, which

---

[11]Martin Scorsese, The Musical: A Personal Journey Through American Movies (1995), https://www.youtube.com/watch?v=N028ZvX8bdM

explained the many songs in his films, was making use of the 'performance within a performance' ruse. This is when the protagonist is expected to sing (and/or dance) on stage or in a club or hotel or even at an informal gathering such as a party within the narrative of the film. The key element here is that there is a two-tier audience in such sequences – the audience within the film in front of whom the character is performing and the audience outside the film itself. The 'performance within a performance' theme has been a part of Hindi cinema all through with songs in clubs, hotels, at parties, poetry competitions, weddings, on anniversary and birthday celebrations, etc., serving up a whole bunch of reasons for the film's protagonists to put on a show.

Having musician figures as protagonists provided them the logic/rationale to break into music any time. But the use of the 'performance within a performance' motif allowed Husain to create occasions such as '*Yaum-e-Azaadi*' ('*Tumne mujhe dekha*' in *Teesri Manzil* or '*Hai agar dushmann, dushmann*' in *Hum Kisise Kum Naheen*) or the charity event shows or the formalized competition songs, which further sanctioned musical forays by his protagonists. Similarly, '*Teri zulfon se judaayee toh nahin maangi thee*' in *Jab Pyar Kisise Hota Hai* arises out of the need for Sunder (Dev Anand), attending a party at his employer's house, to sing and provide a rejoinder to Nisha's scathing, poetic jibes. Most of *Caravan*'s songs are performed for an audience. '*Papa kehtey hain*' in *QSQT* is part of the college's farewell celebrations.

One of the best examples of Husain's skill at moving the narrative forward came courtesy a 'performance within a performance' song in *Dil Deke Dekho*. In a late moment in the film, Raja is once again reminded by Jamuna Devi not to address Neeta by her name for she is soon going to be his employer, the owner of Royal Hotel. In a couple of scenes before this, Jamuna Devi also asks Neeta to accompany her to Royal Hotel for a programme taking place there that evening. When Neeta arrives at the hotel later that evening, Raja sings '*Dilruba meri Neeta*' in full view of Jamuna Devi and Neeta's father, as an open admission of his love for Neeta and in absolute defiance of Jamuna Devi's diktats.

Dil Deke Dekho's music best exemplified Husain's music sensibilities and presentation skills from amongst his early films. Just as an example, consider the song, '*Do ekum do*', whose significance, in the context of Husain's legacy, extends on several fronts. What is discussed here is just one aspect that emerges from this very important song, which also, coincidentally, doubled up as a 'performance within a performance' song.

The song begins as some kind of informal challenge between Mirza Changezi (Raja in disguise) and Neeta's friends. Changezi is supposedly a famous qawwal and shaayar from Delhi and Neeta wants him to recite his poetry. But Neeta's friends, part of her 'Rock-'n'-Roll' Club, want the elderly Changezi to rest and leave the singing and dancing to them. Changezi is affronted and quotes a few lines, suggesting that he is still young at heart ('*Maashooq kahen aap humaarey hain buzurg, naacheez ko yeh din na dikhaana yaa rab*'). To this riposte, the girls dare Changezi to compose a song to their words, which are '*Do ekum do, do dooni chaar, rock, rock, rock!*'. Changezi agrees to the 'muqaabla'.

Neeta's friends dance in the interludes and begin each of the antaras ('*Do teeya chhey, do chaukey aath*' and '*Do sattey chaudaah, do atthey solaah*'), with Changezi finishing them off. But as the song heads into its frenetic climax (the Dutch angle signals its onset), after Neeta and Changezi sing the mukhda one last time, it's Neeta's friends – part opponents but also audience – who

SAR PAR TOPI LAAL, GIRLS ON TREES...   129

become integral to the crazy, heady climax. This is different from '*Sar par topi laal*' or '*Yaar chulbula hai*' where the extras are restricted to dancing alongside the hero and heroine and have no role in the narrative. '*Do ekum do*' arises out of a challenge between Neeta's friends and Changezi. Their proactive participation at the culmination makes the madness palpable.

'*Do ekum do*'s climax laid the blueprint for the finish in a lot of Husain songs such as '*Daiyya yeh main kahaan aa phansi*', the *Yaadon Ki Baaraat* sequence ending with '*Dum maro dum*', '*Bachna ae haseeno*', '*Dil lena khel hai dildaar ka*' (*Zamaane Ko Dikhana Hai*) and '*Papa kehtey hain*'. In each of these songs, the audience becomes a participant either by cheering or singing along or just dancing with the protagonists. At times, it is the hero who asks the audience to join in – like Rajesh in '*Bachna ae haseeno*', who asks his audience 'Will you all join me?' before breaking into his mad, mad '*chhuk-chhuk-chhi-chha-chhi-chhuk-chhuk*' routine. At other times, the spectators just feed off the protagonist's frenzy and end up lighting sparklers and chanting '*Yaar ka, yaar ka*' like in '*Dil lena khel hai dildaar ka*'.

The madness or frenzy at the end of these 'performance within a performance' songs which infected the audience within the film, was, one suspects, Husain's attempt at passing on the same vibe to the larger audience watching the film.[12] Mansoor corroborated this. 'He liked this whole thing of "crowd participation". I

---

[12]Again, this is not to suggest that Husain patented this participation by the audience at the end of songs. Just as an example, Raj Kapoor's '*Mud mud ke na dekh*' from *Shree 420* also had the onlookers joining in at the end of this club song. Also, a number of Shammi Kapoor songs such as '*Suku suku*' (*Junglee*), '*Meri jaan balle balle*' (*Kashmir Ki Kali*) and '*Dekho ab toh*' (*Janwar*, 1965) followed this blueprint of a lively energetic finish, but it is mostly in Husain's sequences that the climax is further heightened by quick cuts and close-ups.

learned this word from him. And crowd participation implies not just the crowd singing along, but also an exchange. There is an interaction. It feels like a real scene. And then he pulls up the girl and Zeenat Aman comes up on stage and then Vijay Arora comes up [in the song "*Aap ke kamrey*" leading to the "*Dum maro dum*" sequence in *Yaadon Ki Baaraat*]. A give and take leading to the medley dance competition in *Hum Kisise Kum Naheen*.' Nuzhat further substantiated Husain's predilection for getting the audience involved. 'He did have this need to create a situation where everybody gets involved so that you as the cinema-going audience also almost got the feeling that you are part of it and you are dancing with the protagonist on-screen.'

It goes without saying that Husain's first four films had quality music. In his National Award-winning book, *Bollywood Melodies: A History of the Hindi Film Song*, Ganesh Anantharaman termed the compositions of *Tumsa Nahin Dekha*, 'the most youthful score of the decade [1950s]'.[13] Subhash Mukerji narrated the following anecdote to explain just how popular Husain's music was in its time and vis-à-vis the competition: 'For *Junglee's* outdoor shooting, they would sing *Jab Pyar Kisise Hota Hai* songs – Shammi Kapoor, my dad – everyone used to sing "*Sau saal pehley mujhe tumse pyaar thaa*", "*Jab pyaar kisise hota hai*". In fact, *Jab Pyar Kisise Hota Hai's* music, according to me, was better than *Junglee's*. Nasir sa'ab's music was always fantastic.' What higher accolade for Husain's music sense can there be than from someone whose father made *Junglee*, a spectacular success in its time. *Junglee's* soundtrack, too, has its own place in the annals of Hindi cinema.

---

[13]Ganesh Anantharaman, 'The Melody Makers', *Bollywood Melodies: A History of the Hindi Film Song*, Penguin Books India, 2008, p. 52.

Most of the songs from these films continue to remain popular. They have stood the test of time. Not only was the score essential to each of the film's success, but it was, as many people reiterated, the defining ingredient of Husain's magical formula. Working with O.P. Nayyar (*Tumsa Nahin Dekha* and *Phir Wohi Dil Laya Hoon*), debutant Usha Khanna (*Dil Deke Dekho*) and Shankar–Jaikishan (*Jab Pyar Kisise Hota Hai*), Husain was able to extract the very best from his composers. From the mellifluous '*Pyaar ki kasam hai*' to the impishness of '*Aaye hain door se*' to the zest of '*Banda parvar*', Husain got the perfect song for each occasion from his composers.

As good as the music is in these initial films, it is difficult, however, to see the Nasir Husain stamp on them. If anything, it is O.P. Nayyar's distinctive rhythms that shine through in Husain's early films. Even Usha Khanna admitted in an interview that with *Dil Deke Dekho*'s score, 'O.P. Nayyar himself was surprised to hear the remarkable similarity to his own music.'[14] Nayyar's characteristic 'tonga' beats also come through clearly in *Tumsa Nahin Dekha*'s title track and '*Banda parvar*', among other songs. And if as Ganesh Anantharaman noted of the composer's style, 'O.P. Nayyar's music epitomized the brighter side of life, the possibility of joy amidst life's vicissitudes,'[15] Nayyar perfectly articulated the essence of Husain's films except that it didn't allow Husain the opportunity to leave his own mark on the music of these films.

Aditya Chopra explained the possible dynamics at play between Husain and Nayyar. 'O.P. Nayyar's music always had one theka. He had a slightly Punjabi style of music. So there was always a very strong Punjabiyat. But in the works of O.P. Nayyar with

---

[14]Dr Mandar, 'Meeting Usha Khanna', http://www.cinemasangeet.com/ hindi-film-music/interviews/meeting-usha-khanna.html

[15]Ganesh Anantharaman, 'The Melody Makers', *Bollywood Melodies: A History of the Hindi Film Song*, Penguin Books India, 2008, p. 50.

Nasir Husain, the Punjabiyat was slightly diminished. In the Nasir Husain work of O.P. Nayyar it seemed that, he [Nayyar] was, very strangely, more modern. It seemed that there was a younger mind at play with O.P. Nayyar, but the younger mind was still under Nayyar. I don't think he [Nasir Husain] could have been assertive enough. Obviously O.P. Nayyar was the more senior, the bigger man. So he was still leading and Nasir sa'ab was just making sure that the joy factor in the music came through.'

If anything, it is *Dil Deke Dekho* whose music most exemplifies Husain's sensibilities. This is not just because of the distinct Western influences – three of the songs in the film are straightforward imitations of Western numbers (the title song is based on the McGuire Sisters' *'Sugar in the morning'*; *'Dilruba meri Neeta'* is a copy of Paul Anka's *'Diana'* and *'Pyaar ki kasam hai'* is taken from Ivory Joe Hunter's *'Since I met you baby'*) – but perhaps because the music didn't conform nearly as much to the music of Husain's other three films. With their pop, rock-'n'-roll and jazz-style tunes, *Dil Deke Dekho*'s music is an early indicator of the Western influences and music sensibilities that informed his later films.

Sadanand noted, 'The point I suppose could be that the two movies with O.P. [Nayyar] and the one with S–J [Shankar–Jaikishan] did not stand out differently as a "new Nasir Husain-influenced" music. You could recognize the style of both OP and S–J. There were no Nasir Husain inputs as such. With poor Usha Khanna almost all the songs in *Dil Deke Dekho* are copies of some Western pop song or a traditional Western melody. I think she was too young and so while she had talent, she may not have had the clout to resist her arrangers, Nasir Husain, etc.'

Instead, the more definitive association that Husain forged on the music front in these initial films was with Majrooh Sultanpuri, who was the lyricist in three of Husain's first four films. Majrooh had come to the industry in the late 1940s and had shot to fame in his debut film itself, *Shahjehan* (1946), with the K.L. Saigal song, '*Jab dil hi toot gaya toh*'. Since then, he had found much success, having written a number of frothy songs for films like *Aar Paar, Mr. & Mrs. '55, C.I.D.* and *Paying Guest*. Perhaps, the fun quotient in Majrooh's song-writing appealed to Husain's film-making sensibility and that is why the two struck a fine collaboration.

But Majrooh also had a strong poetic lineage. Early in his life, he had been groomed by the eminent Urdu poet, Jigar Moradabadi. He was also a member of the Progressive Writers' Movement. As a Progressive poet, he spoke out against the evils plaguing society, but as film songwriter, he wrote comfortably about husn, mohabbat and ishq. Consequently, he often drew a lot of flak for his film work from the Progressive community. Nonetheless, his standing as a poet must have endeared him to Husain, who was a keen lover of Urdu poetry himself.

'Dad read a lot of poetry,' said Nuzhat. In film after film, Husain reflected this romance with Urdu verse. We already know that Husain had quoted Faiz Ahmad Faiz (in *Munimji*) and Sahir (in *Dil Deke Dekho*). He also quoted poets Amir Minai ('*Unko aata hai pyaar pe gussa, humey gussey pe pyaar aata hai*' in *Paying Guest*) and Faiyyaz Hashmi ('*Tasveer teri dil mera behla na sakegi*'[16] – this line is used in both *Dil Deke Dekho* and *Phir Wohi Dil Laya Hoon*). The Mirza Changezi character in *Dil Deke Dekho* is more proof of Husain's familiarity with the stalwarts of Urdu poetry, since Mirza Wajid Husain Changezi, who died in 1956, was among the

---

[16]This non-film song written by Hashmi was sung by Talat Mehmood in 1944, which made the singer an overnight sensation.

leading poets of the early twentieth century, who lived for most of his life in Lucknow.

However, Husain used shers (couplets) towards other ends such as comedy too. In *Pyar Ka Mausam*, Rajendra Nath's character (as the fake Jhatpat Singh) quotes none other than the pre-eminent Mirza Asadullah Khan 'Ghalib' when he is asked to introduce himself:

> *Poochhtey hain woh ke Ghalib kaun hai?*
> *Koi batlaao ki hum batlaayain kya*
>
> (They ask: who is Ghalib?
> Someone tell them for how do I introduce myself)

In an altogether different take, Raj Mehra's character is seen nailing Sohan (Pran) for the murder of Nisha's friend in *Jab Pyar Kisise Hota Hai*, with the following couplet by Amir Minai:

> *Jo chup rahegi zubaan-e-khanjar*
> *Lahu pukaarega aasteen ka*
>
> (However much the murderer tries to conceal his crime
> The blood on his sleeve will give him away)

The recent film *Rockstar* (2011) had the lyricist Irshad Kamil earn plaudits for his reference to twelfth-century Sufi poet, Baba Farid's lines, '*Kaga sab tann khaiyyo, mera chun chun khaiyyo maas, do naina mat khaiyyo, mohey piya milan ki aas*' (Oh raven, feast on my body, savour every piece of my flesh, leave but my eyes alone, I yearn to behold my beloved) in the song, '*Oh naadaan parindey*'. But Husain had referenced these two lines way back in *Paying Guest*, when he had Shanti (Nutan) use them against Chanchal (Shubha Khote) in their debate on marriage for love or for materialistic comforts. The debate itself concluded with a fine back and forth between Shanti and Chanchal, with the two making their arguments through Urdu couplets and dohey.

Ramesh, who is watching the entire proceedings from the comfort of a tree, appreciates the exchange saying, '*Subhaan Allah*', which almost appears as if Husain was lauding himself on his choice of poetry as dialogue in the sequence.

The ultimate proof of Majrooh and Husain sharing the same wavelength when it came to poetry lies in the couplet uttered by the booming voice each time the 'NH Films' banner comes on screen at the beginning of every film produced by Husain (beginning with *Phir Wohi Dil Laya Hoon*). The couplet goes:

Kya husn ne samjha hai, kya ishq[17] ne jaana hai?
Hum khaaq-nasheenon ki thokar mein zamaana hai

(What has beauty understood and what secrets has love unravelled?
The world is at the mercy of us dust-dwellers alone)

The couplet is from Jigar Moradabadi's, Majrooh's ustad, famous ghazal, '*Ek lafz-e-mohabbat*'. The essence of the ghazal, best highlighted by this sher, perfectly articulates the spirit of a Nasir Husain film, with its emphasis on love and romance. It is entirely possible that Majrooh recommended this couplet to Husain when he was looking for an appropriate voiceover to feature along with the 'NH Films' banner. Equally, Husain could have already been familiar with the ghazal in its entirety because of its popularity. In *Dil Deke Dekho*, Husain used another charming sher from the same ghazal when Neeta has to win Raja over:

Hum ishq ke maaron ka itna hi fasaana hai,
Rone ko nahin koi, hasney ko zamaana hai

(Here then, the tale of the lovelorn
None to cry over our passing and the world to laugh at us)

---

[17]Interestingly, the voiceover introducing the NH banner interchanges the words husn and ishq and recites the couplet as shown at the beginning of this book. This could have only happened unwittingly but Husain stuck with this same incorrect recitation of the sher through each of his films.

Javed Akhtar explained the meeting of minds between Husain and Majrooh. 'He had great respect for Majrooh sa'ab. These people had respect for words. The problem nowadays is that most people don't know language, how can they respect words? They don't know the nuances. And he [Husain] was totally confident of and dependent on Majrooh sa'ab for obvious reasons. Majrooh sa'ab's sensibilities matched Nasir Husain's. He understood what Nasir Husain wanted.'

Aamir concurred with Akhtar's assessment of the two men sharing a similar wavelength. 'The one advantage that Majrooh sa'ab and Nasir sa'ab had as a team was that Nasir sa'ab himself was very good at Urdu. For example, when Majrooh sa'ab worked on *Qayamat Se Qayamat Tak* and *Jo Jeeta Wohi Sikandar*, he had a lot of disdain for Mansoor and me. He was like "*Tum logon ko kya pata? Tum logon ko zubaan ke baarey mein kya knowledge hai?* (What do you people know? What do you know about language?)" He would throw that at Mansoor and me. Of course, our Urdu was not as good as Nasir sa'ab's. So we would keep quiet,' Aamir told me, laughing, before adding, 'But he [Majrooh] never felt that with Nasir sa'ab because Nasir sa'ab had a fine understanding of language.'

It was this rapport between the two that resulted in many beautiful songs. Majrooh didn't just pen words that summarized the essence of Husain's characters, his films, but also introduced humour that was so integral to Husain's films. Take, for instance, the lyrics of one of the stanzas of '*Chhupnewaale saamne aa*':

Door khadi hairaan hai kya,
Daant mein yun ungli na daba

(Why are you standing far away, surprised?
Don't bite your finger thus)

Elsewhere, in '*Do ekum do*', when Neeta's friends invite Mirza Changezi's riposte to '*Do nam atthaarah, do daham bees*', he wrote, '*Ho gaya gaana ab lao meri fees*' (The song is over, now pay me my fees). Equally, in these light-hearted, up-tempo songs, Majrooh's poetic lineage is discernible. For '*Sar par topi laal*', one of the antaras has this interesting exchange between Shankar and Meena. Shankar sings:

> *Mera dil oh jaaney jaan,*
> *Chura ke chali kahaan,*
> *Nashey mein bhari bhari*
>
> (My heart, oh beloved,
> Where do you steal and go,
> Leaving me in a trance)

To which Meena responds,

> *Churaaoon main dil tera,*
> *Jigar bhi nahin mera,*
> *Umar bhi nahin meri*
>
> (To steal your heart,
> Neither do I have the guts,
> Nor am I old enough)

In *Dil Deke Dekho*, where Majrooh had to work on tunes borrowed from the West, his lyrics gave the songs a makeover. It is indeed a tragedy that in Hindi cinema when a tune is copied, the song is dismissed by critics in its entirety. Lost in the criticism are the lyrics, written entirely in the context of the film, and which sometimes stand out on their own,[18] like Majrooh's words in the first antara of the title track:

---

[18]Or consider Majrooh's lyrics for '*Ae dil hai mushkil*', which gave this track from *C.I.D.* an entirely different identity from the original song, '*Oh my darling, Clementine!*' from which the tune was lifted. The *C.I.D.* song has gone on to become an anthem of sorts for the city of Bombay.

Poochho, poochho, poochho parwaane se zara,
Dheere, dheere jalney mein kaisa hai mazaa?

(Ask the moth if you so care
How it delights in perishing ever so slowly in the flame)

Javed Akhtar, though, is most complimentary about Majrooh's
'Aankhon se jo utri hai dil mein' in *Phir Wohi Dil Laya Hoon*. The
song is picturized on Mona (Parekh) when she is gushing over
Mohan's good looks in a photograph. 'Most Urdu poetry is from
the male point of view,' said Akhtar. 'It is the male gaze, and you
talk of the beautiful damsel and so on. But a girl remembering
a young man and fantasizing [about] him and describing him is
very, very difficult because poetry doesn't have that tradition. It's
a very well-written song.' Majrooh's versatility while retaining an
overall poetic sensibility is what must have earned him Husain's
confidence.

Together, the music, the lyrics and the picturization of the
songs completed the Nasir Husain film experience. Along with
the general breezy nature of his films, the song sequences were
essential to the 'entertainment' aspect. Perhaps, this was another
reason why Husain paid so much attention to the music and their
picturization, because the tunes and the way they were presented
needed to transcend the geographical and cultural barriers that
are omnipresent in a country like India.

Just as Husain was being inspired from Western tunes, the
Tamil film *Ethirigal Jakirrathai* (1967) included the song *'Aahaa
aahaa indru then nilavu'*, which was a rehashed version of *'Aaja
aaja main hoon pyaar tera'* from Husain's *Teesri Manzil*.

On to *Teesri Manzil* then.

6

COSMOPOLITANISM, CLUBS AND R.D. BURMAN – MÉLANGE MAGNIFIQUE

'His films were all about celebration. And his villain was never really much of a threat. And the culmination of it was not the problem. It was the holiday romance. Everyone took off. It was always fun and games. It would be one scenic locale, and there were these great songs, picnics and there were these clubs, and the Anglo-Indian culture ... the atmosphere created was so chic.'

– Film-maker and producer Karan Johar

According to M.K. Raghavendra, 'I don't think there has ever been noir in Hindi cinema. One of the things about noir is that it has to be very pessimistic in some way. There has to be moral decline on the part of the hero.' Going by this strict, classical view of American noir, it would be difficult to slot more than a handful of Hindi films as noir. However, if as Raghavendra further explained that instead of the noir element in the narrative, we consider Hindi films that make use of noir imagery – 'In their imagery, they have something which is taken from American noir – shot in black-and-white, cigarette smoke, chiaroscuro lighting, starkly lit, dark interiors' – there are a larger number of Hindi films that can be branded as noir.

Madhulika Liddle also added the all-important prefix 'Bollywood' to define the noir genre in Hindi cinema. 'Bollywood is emotion and escapism and all that erases – even if only for three hours – the dull reality of life. So noir, Bollywood style, has the shadowy photography and some of the sleaze, but it's easier to relate to for an audience that likes its singing and dancing around the trees, its pretty ladies and its happy endings.'[1] This view that blends noir imagery with the musical Hindi film, gives Indian noir a distinct identity of its own. It includes a number of films like *Mahal* (1949), *Baazi* (1951), *C.I.D.*, *Howrah Bridge* (1958) and *Bees Saal Baad* (1962). *Teesri Manzil*, which released exactly a decade after *C.I.D*, perhaps best epitomizes the genre.

Teesri Manzil, which incorporated elements from Alfred Hitchcock's *Strangers on a Train* (1951) and *To Catch a Thief* (1955), is a 'whodunit' drama about a young girl Sunita (Parekh), who sets out from Delhi for Mussoorie to find a drummer named Rocky (Shammi Kapoor), whom she holds responsible for the death of her sister, Roopa. The general belief is that Roopa committed suicide a year ago, having jumped from Park Hotel's 'teesri manzil' (the third storey) where Rocky worked. Rocky, who gets acquainted with Sunita while on a train journey (recalling *Tumsa Nahin Dekha*) to Dehradun, gets to know of Sunita's agenda fairly early. He conceals his identity and presents himself as Anil Kumar 'Sona', a crorepati's son, to Sunita with the ambition of winning her affection. He even reveals his entire story and his version of events to Sunita after the two get romantically involved, but Sunita is heartbroken and distraught at his confession. It is only when CID Inspector Das (Iftekhar) reveals to Rocky that Roopa did not commit suicide but was murdered that an uncanny

---

[1]Madhulika Liddle, 'Villains and Vamps and All Things Camp', *The Popcorn Essayists: What Movies Do To Writers*, Edited by Jai Arjun Singh, Tranquebar, 2011, p. 151.

set of events unfold, leading Rocky to Roopa's real killer. With some fine performances from the leads, the supporting cast, which included Helen, Prem Chopra, Prem Nath, Rashid Khan and even K.N. Singh (in a blink-and-miss appearance) and a soundtrack that has been hailed a turning point in Hindi cinema, *Teesri Manzil* is an absolute humdinger of an entertainer.

Directed by Vijay Anand, the film marked the first instance of Husain handing over the directorial reins to someone else in a Nasir Husain production. For Vijay Anand, too, it was the first time he happened to direct a film which was being produced by and starred someone other than his elder sibling, Dev Anand.

Following *Dil Deke Dekho*, which was a Filmalaya production, Husain was keen on launching his own production house. As Rauf Ahmed told me, Husain had a script ready and was introduced to composers Shankar–Jaikishan by Shammi Kapoor. The composers were at the peak of their success then. Their hectic schedule prevented them from committing to Husain immediately. However, a few days later, Husain called up Shammi to tell him that he had roped in Shankar–Jaikishan to do the music for the film. Asha Parekh, too, was on board. Husain wanted to know whether Shammi would like to join the team. Shammi felt slighted that Husain had to even ask him. After all, he had introduced S–J to Husain. Affronted, Shammi walked out of Husain's film. 'Shammi said, "It was a very idiotic thing I did but I got very upset because we were very close … He should have taken it for granted that I am with him because we were together in two other projects,"' Rauf recalled Shammi Kapoor telling him.[2]

Aamir gave me another version based on what Husain himself had told him. According to Aamir, when Husain approached

---

[2]The same episode is also detailed in Deepa Gahlot, 'The Rebel Arrives', *Shammi Kapoor: The Dancing Hero – The Legends of Indian Cinema*, Wisdom Tree, 2008, pp. 50, 52.

Shammi for dates for *Jab Pyar Kisise Hota Hai*, the actor was a little high-handed and remained noncommittal. 'Chachajaan was a little hurt that Shammi uncle was not giving him the due that their relationship really deserved. So Chachajaan backed off and said, "*Chalo theek hai* (It doesn't matter), no problem," and signed Dev sa'ab.' Aamir added that while he didn't really know the exact details, he felt that Shammi must have been upset that Husain didn't wait for him. '"*Main free nahin thaa toh Nasir ruk jaata. Usney Dev ke saath film kyun bana di? Ab main bhi kaam nahin karoonga.* (Nasir should have waited if I wasn't free. Why did he have to make a film with Dev? Now I won't work with him)." And Nasir sa'ab was like, "*Tumhaarey paas mere liye time nahin hai? Mere liye time nahin hai? Toh phir main jaata hun baahar* (You don't have time for me? Fine, I will look elsewhere)."'

Where human egos are involved, such things happen. After all, wasn't the S.D. Burman–Sahir Ludhianvi break-up post *Pyaasa* nothing but a clash between two heavyweight, artistic personalities? Mansoor lent credence to this view when he said, 'My dad, like any person, had a sticky ego himself. He must have felt jilted even if Shammi uncle might have said let me hear the script. He would have then said, "I'll do it on my own steam. I don't need you." He must have felt that, "I am the maker. I made you."'

Thus, Shammi Kapoor and Husain parted ways after *Dil Deke Dekho*. Around the same time, in a separate turn of fate, and which yet again highlights the curious workings of the Bombay film industry, Dev Anand bowed out of a film initially titled *Mr. Hitler*, being directed by Subodh Mukerji. Husain then offered *Jab Pyar Kisise Hota Hai* to Dev Anand and the star agreed to do the film since he was keen on working with Husain again. Meanwhile, Subodh Mukerji signed up Shammi Kapoor, with *Mr. Hitler* becoming the 1961 blockbuster, *Junglee*.

Which brings us back to *Teesri Manzil*. Indeed, the more

popular version is that Husain had offered the film to Dev Anand. This is borne out by the fact that there are stills available of Dev Anand sitting before a drum set for *Teesri Manzil*. Vijay Anand, who was an established director by then, was brought on board to direct his brother. But some time into the shooting, Dev Anand and Husain had a showdown and Husain ousted Dev Anand from the film. Vijay Anand, who had no problem with Husain, continued in his role and directed the film.

But Rauf Ahmed has another version of how Vijay Anand came on board to direct the film, one that was corroborated by all members of the Husain family. According to this other sequence of events,[3] Husain, who had struck up a friendship with Vijay Anand, had picked him initially to direct *Baharon Ke Sapne*, the film that followed *Teesri Manzil* a year later. Meanwhile, Husain was to direct Dev Anand in *Teesri Manzil* himself.

Dev Anand, though, wasn't very happy with Husain's decision to give his brother a black-and-white, 'arty' film to direct, starring a newcomer,[4] while Husain himself was directing the bigger, more commercial *Teesri Manzil*. Dev Anand's comments didn't go down well with Husain and the two had a rather public confrontation at a party, supposedly hosted by R.K. Nayyar and Sadhana. The next day, Husain decided to replace Dev Anand. And to make an even bigger point to Dev Anand, he handed over the reins of *Teesri Manzil* to Vijay Anand and decided to direct the smaller

---

[3]On 15 August 2011, in a *Hindustan Times* article titled 'To Shammi uncle, with Love', Nasir Husain's grandson, the actor Imran Khan, reiterated this version as part of his homage to Shammi Kapoor, who had died the previous day. The article can be seen at http://www.hindustantimes.com/news-feed/entertainment/to-shammi-uncle-with-love-imran-khan/article1-733386.aspx

[4]That newcomer in *Baharon Ke Sapne* was Rajesh Khanna, who would become Hindi cinema's first superstar by the turn of the 1970s.

Baharon Ke Sapne himself. Enough time had also passed to heal whatever acrimony existed between Husain and Shammi Kapoor post *Dil Deke Dekho*. Consequently, Husain didn't lose much time and approached Shammi for *Teesri Manzil*, who readily agreed to do the film. But were Dev Anand and Shammi Kapoor really interchangeable?

Dev Anand once admitted to Rauf Ahmed in an interview, 'I created my biggest rival. With every film I let go, he [Shammi Kapoor] shot to fame.' While this may be true, considering that Husain's *Tumsa Nahin Dekha* was written keeping Anand in mind and that both *Junglee* and *Teesri Manzil* turned out to be spectacular hits in Shammi's career, the two actors were quite unlike.

In most of Dev Anand's films, particularly the ones he is most remembered for, Dev Anand's profession is always foregrounded, giving his characters a semblance of seriousness. In films like *C.I.D.*, *Paying Guest*, *Solva Saal* (1958), *Hum Dono*, *Tere Ghar Ke Samne*, *Jewel Thief* (1967), *Johny Mera Naam* (1970) and even *Hare Rama Hare Krishna*, his profession – ranging from lawyer to journalist to army officer to CID inspector to architect to gemologist to pilot – is integral to his character and, in most cases, essential to the climax of these films. Even in his 'amoral' roles – *Baazi*, *Jaal*, *Taxi Driver*, *House No. 44*, *Kala Bazar* and *Guide* (of course, this film is an adaptation of R.K. Narayan's book) – what Dev Anand's character does for a living is in sharp focus and that helps to bring out the upheaval or makeover his character faces by the end of the film. In *Taxi Driver*, he brings his occupation to the audience's attention in the most direct way possible when he says, '*Main sharaabi hoon, goonda hoon, mawaali hoon, taxi driver hoon, taxi driver* (I am a drunkard, a goon, a scoundrel, a taxi driver, a taxi driver).'

Contrastingly, the occupational pursuits of the characters played by Shammi Kapoor in *Tumsa Nahin Dekha, Dil Deke Dekho, China Town, Professor, Bluff Master* (1963), *Budtameez* (1966), *An Evening in Paris* (1967), *Brahmachari* (1968) and *Tumse Achha Kaun Hai* (1969) were all frivolous and on the margins of society. His lack of a serious profession (and a musician certainly didn't count as one in the India of the 1950s and 1960s) made him a bit of an outsider, an *aberrante* compared to the heroes before him. This allowed Shammi to be a bit of an insouciant before things turned serious at the climax. Even his characters in *Junglee* and *Kashmir Ki Kali* are red herrings. In the former, he breaks out of his serious, industrialist avatar to turn into a wild, spirited young man, while in the latter, he realizes halfway through that he is not the heir apparent to a wealthy mill owner's fortune.

This distinction is important in the context of Husain's cinema. Husain's heroes (except *Baharon Ke Sapne*) remained bon vivants – be it as musicians, tour guides, estate managers, lorry owners-cum-nautanki artistes or just frothy romantics – all through (up to *Hum Kisise Kum Naheen*), which made Shammi much more of a natural fit in Husain's films than Dev Anand. Interestingly, the one time Husain's hero had some kind of a serious profession was in *Jab Pyar Kisise Hota Hai*, where Sunder (Dev Anand) is an engineer.

Then there was Shammi Kapoor's physicality, his verve, his energy and his dancing style that is so important to *Teesri Manzil*. In one of my conversations with Mansoor, he said that it is 'very unusual' that Shammi Kapoor is a drummer in *Teesri Manzil* since, 'the guitar is more tempting because it's a very portable instrument. You can dance with it. With drums, you can't do that.' It is important to remember, though, that Rocky substitutes his friend (the writer Salim Khan) in his place before '*O haseena zulfon waali*' begins,[5] so as to shimmy and 'shake it like Shammi' in the song. But what is remarkable is that in a few scenes before the song, when Rocky is shown playing the drums with Ruby (Helen) dancing before him, Shammi puts on a virtuoso drum performance without sitting down. Even the restrictions placed on him as a drummer cannot confine his physicality. Perhaps, it was because he grasped Shammi's physicality that Husain handed the guitar and not the drums to his other heroes like Joy Mukerji or Shashi Kapoor thereafter.

Nasreen noted, 'I don't remember people quoting Shammi Kapoor's dialogues at all … But the physicality compensated for the fact that you didn't pay that much attention to dialogue.' This physicality, too, is vital to Husain's films as it signified, what Kaushik Bhaumik termed, 'a certain *élan vital*'[6] that was there in abundance in his cinema – in the demeanour of his heroes,[7] the music and even in his sense of comedy. On the other hand, try and imagine Dev Anand in '*O haseena zulfon waali*' and '*Aaja aaja main hoon pyaar tera*', with him bobbing his head from side to side. Even in the lesser-known *Manzil* (1960), a rare instance

---

[5]Actually, Salim Khan is shown as Rocky only when the curtains are drawn open. Before that, the man playing the drums behind the closed curtains is Leslie Godinho, one of the most well-known jazz drummers and percussionists in the industry at that time. Godinho also played in many jazz bands and introduced the triple congas in the film industry.

[6]Élan vital is a term coined by French philosopher Henri Bergson to explain the vital force or impulse of life. Bhaumik used the term to describe the manic energy of *Teesri Manzil* as an example of the overall physicality in Husain's cinema.

[7]It is this physicality that is on view when Mohan (Joy Mukerji) shows off his biceps to his mother while making the 'ho ho ho – ha ha ha ha' sounds to announce his landing a job in *Phir Wohi Dil Laya Hoon*.

where Anand played a musician figure,[8] his role is restricted to that of a music composer instead of the kind essayed by Shammi either in *Dil Deke Dekho* or *Teesri Manzil*.

Husain also preferred Shammi to Dev Anand. He said so in as many words to Nasreen. When Nasreen asked him in what way, he replied, 'Comedy. I have done it with Dev Anand also in *Jab Pyar Kisise Hota Hai* but Shammi has acted well. It is a question of understanding. Shammi would hear the full story, read the scene before coming to the sets and he would ask me, "*Tum kis tarah karogey?* (How would you do it?)" I would tell him my style.'

The emphasis on Shammi and Husain's use of Shammi do not in any way discount Vijay Anand's influence on *Teesri Manzil*. It is his visual sensibility that gives *Teesri Manzil* the edge that makes it such a fine suspense film. As Doraiswamy observed, 'Vijay Anand uses circularity in sets and camera movements throughout the film to emphasize the peephole/pupil-of-the-eye effect, for every character in the film is watching and spying on the other.'[9]

The opening scene of the film establishes Vijay Anand's shot-taking sensibility as distinct and far more evolved than Husain's. After Sunita's father (Raj Mehra) is shown speaking in the initial frame, the camera cuts to Ramesh (Prem Chopra). For the next eighty-five seconds, the camera, through a series of dolly track movements, while moving away from and towards the many

---

[8]In this film, too, the focus is very much on Dev Anand's profession, detailing Dev Anand's quest for acceptance by his father for his decision to choose a career in music.

[9]Dr Rashmi Doraiswamy, '"These Days" of Our Modernity: The Cinema of Nasir Husain', Film and Television Institute of India, Pune, 4 September 2004, p. 13.

characters, going from the drawing room in Sunita's house to inside her bedroom, shows us the entire gamut of people being spoken to and about (even a picture of Sunita's dead sister makes its way into the frames) in one single, long take. The shot ends only after Sunita is spooked by Ramesh's presence (after he greets her with the words, 'Hello Sunita') in her bedroom, thus coming a full circle, since the shot begins with Ramesh and ends with the camera cutting to him.

Such lengthy, uninterrupted shot-taking was not unusual for Vijay Anand. As Jai Arjun Singh observed on his blog, 'Jabberwock', a song like '*Tere mere sapne*' (*Guide*) that lasts more than four minutes, 'is made up of only three shots, which increase progressively in length – in other words, there are only two cuts in the whole scene.'[10]

Husain's cinema didn't go anywhere near this level of sophisticated cinematography. Barring his song sequences, where his desire to create spectacle and a certain dynamism came to the fore, his cinematography was fairly basic, focusing purely on his characters as they spoke. He generally didn't make any statements (except in *Yaadon Ki Baaraat*, where he does so with a grand cinematic shot) in these moments either with complex dolly track movements or long takes, which could have, perhaps, stemmed from a desire to remain invisible, at times a conscious call made by film-makers. Mansoor explained this lucidly when he told me that Husain's cinematography was, 'very practical. It wasn't so much about the cinematography or the cinematic look. Okay, he may take one or two grand shots once in a while, but his emphasis was not so much on that. Even the kind of cinematographers that he worked with were people who were more practical … My dad's perspective maybe was not so much "visual cinema". Even I don't

---

[10]Jai Arjun Singh, '"Tere Mere Sapne", a visual treat', 18 March 2014, http://jaiarjun.blogspot.in/2014/03/tere-mere-sapne-visual-treat.html.

have that. I'm just trying to get the moment out. And so when he had someone like Jal Mistry [the cinematographer for *Baharon Ke Sapne*], his influence would have been very strong in shaping the visuals that way.'

Asha Parekh further elaborated on the different styles of both directors. Speaking on Husain, she said, 'The greatest thing about him was that he did his homework. That saved a lot of time while he was shooting. He would do his shot divisions at home. He had his idea of what the set was because he knew where he was shooting. What he would do is take shots of one side, *jo aaney waaley hain* (which would feature), and then he would turn the camera and go to the other side because he had his homework done.' In contrast, 'If Vijay Anand was shooting, he would not think like a producer. He would shoot one side, then he would come to this side, then again he would go back. So the time consumed was more because the lighting had to be shifted whereas Nasir sa'ab was a producer–director. He [Husain] would think of everything. That's why I said, he was the only director who used to come with his homework done among all the directors that I have worked with. He had everything written down in his book to the last detail. One would know how many shots he was taking.'

Husain's writing, too, contributed to the suspense and the many fine moments of romance and humour in *Teesri Manzil*. For instance, consider the scene which has Sunita, Rocky and the actor Ram Avtar, referred to as 'motey' (fatso), travelling by train to Dehradun early in the film. The comedy in this scene arises not only from Rocky's exchange with Sunita and Ram Avtar's rotundness, but also from the manner in which Rocky has Sunita believe that she has killed Ram Avtar so that he can milk the situation to his advantage.

This at some level is a microscopic view of *Teesri Manzil's* storyline where one person is suspected of being responsible for another person's death and there are characters around (like Ruby) to use this to their advantage. Through a comic situation involving a person who has been allegedly murdered, viewers are primed into what happens at the climax. '*Khoon ka muqadamma hai aur adaalat hai jahaan ke mujhe bayaan dena hai, ki khoon kisne kiya* (It is a murder case and there will be a court of law where I will be called upon to testify as to who committed the murder),' Rocky tells Sunita in this scene. But this remark could have easily been made by Ruby (Helen) to Rocky in one of the many scenes in the film where she insinuates that his 'raaz' (secret) is safe with her provided he does her bidding. This is an exemplary specimen of screenplay writing, where the gist of the film is articulated in one sequence, ironically a comic one.

Similarly, Husain even updated his philosophy on romance to heighten the *Teesri Manzil* premise when he had Anil Kumar Sona tell Sunita, '*Mere dadaji marhoom kaha kartey thay, beta milaap ki teen manzilein hoti hain – Pehli manzil, nafrat aur ladaayee, doosri manzil – dosti aur safaayee. Teesri manzil, pyaar aur sagaai* (My late paternal grandfather used to say that there are three stages in a relationship – first of hatred and argument, second – friendship and honesty. The third, love and marriage).'

Elsewhere, the dialogues build up the romance between the protagonists ever so beautifully, in quintessential Husain style. Take the exchange between Anil and Sunita on 'Crane Hill' when Sunita is expecting Rocky (whom Anil has presented as his friend), but has to deal with Anil who has turned up in Rocky's place:

> Sunita: *Dekhiye Mr Anil, na mujhe aapki daulat se koi waasta hai, na aapke chacha ke bangley se. Mujhe sirf itna bata dijiye, Rocky ne kya kehelwaaya hai?* (Look, Mr Anil, neither am I interested in your wealth, nor in your uncle's bungalow. I just want you to tell me, what did Rocky say?)

Anil: *Oh I see. Yaani ke Rocky ka message. Ji haan, of course. Rocky ne kehelwaaya hai ke … kya jaadubhari aankhein hain aapki!* (I see. You mean Rocky's message. Yes, of course. Rocky has said … what enchanting eyes you have!)

Sunita: *Yeh Rocky ne kehelwaaya hai?* (Is this what Rocky said?)

Anil: *Ji nahin, yeh toh main keh raha hoon.* (No, that's what I'm saying.)

Sunita: *Toh Rocky ne kya kehelwaaya hai?* (Then what has Rocky said?)

Anil: *Oh Rocky ne? Khoob yaad dilaaya. Rocky ne kehelwaaya hai ke, ke … Kya pyaari surat hai aap ki!* (Oh Rocky? Glad you reminded me. Rocky has said … what a beautiful face you have!)

Sunita: *Yeh Rocky ne kehelwaaya hai?* (Is this what Rocky said?)

Anil: *Ji nahin yeh bhi main keh raha hoon.* (No, that's me again.)

Sunita: *Toh Rocky ne…* (Then what has Rocky…) [Gets completely agitated and walks off]

'It's a lovely, romantic scene with humour in it as well,' said Aamir, who counts this as one of his favourite scenes and as an example of Husain's terrific writing.

Teesri Manzil also brought the jungle into sharp focus in a Husain film. As part of the film's storyline, Anil and Sunita travel to Madanpur, but lose their way during the journey. They have to spend the night in the jungle, which is where Sunita has a change of heart about Anil after he saves her from some dacoits.

The jungle first appears in *Munimji*, with Raj (Dev Anand) frequenting that space. Most of his dalliances with Roopa (Nalini Jaywant) are in the jungle itself. In *Tumsa Nahin Dekha*, Sardar Rajpal has relocated to the jungles of Assam. In *Caravan*, Soni

(Parekh) flees from Rajan's (Krishen Mehta) henchmen midway through the film and escapes into the jungle. The jungle features at the climax of *Pyar Ka Mausam* and *Hum Kisise Kum Naheen* as well. In *Manzil Manzil*, Sonu (Sunny Deol) is a forest officer and so the climax may logically play out in the forest.

One aspect of the jungle's continued presence in Husain's films is that it reinforced the hero's masculinity. In most of the aforementioned films, the heroine needs to be rescued by the hero when in the jungle. Whether Raj saves Roopa from the tiger in *Munimji* or Sunita is saved by Anil or Raj defends Rashmi from the gang of four unruly boys (led by the character played by Makarand Deshpande) while on their way out from the jungle in *Qayamat Se Qayamat Tak*, each of these instances underscore the heroine's dependence on the hero. As Jerry Pinto observed, 'I suspect it had to do with a return to the primeval where the male–female equation is reinscribed in its traditional pattern and the woman gets to realize she is dependent on the man.'

But the move into the jungle is also consistent with the overall mobility quotient of Husain's cinema. We have already seen how Husain's protagonists fall in love over a journey in the course of his film, but this, too, is part of a larger, continuous movement between places in narrative terms in his films. *Teesri Manzil* begins in Delhi, moves to Dehradun and then to Mussoorie. There is the trip to Madanpur and back after which the climax of the film is resolved in Mussoorie. *Pyar Ka Mausam* begins in Ooty (where Sardar Ranjit Kumar is introduced), then shifts to Nandipur (Bharat Bhushan's and Nirupa Roy's characters are established), then to Bangalore (where Shashi Kapoor is introduced), then back to Ooty (where Sunil remembers meeting Seema from a year ago) and then shuffles between Ooty and Bangalore before the climax is finally played out in Ooty.

Hum Kisise Kum Naheen begins in Delhi. Beirut airport, where the all-important diamonds are handed over by Rajesh's father to Kaajal's father, makes an appearance (even if superficially so). The story then shifts to Nainital after which Rajesh takes us to London to give us the backstory of his relationship with Sunita (Zeenat Aman), before returning to Nainital from where it shifts to a place three hundred miles on the other side of the Indian border where the climax take place.

All of Husain's films, be it *Dil Deke Dekho, Phir Wohi Dil Laya Hoon, Caravan* or *Qayamat Se Qayamat Tak,* have this element of travel as part of the unfolding screenplay. This in itself gives the films a sense of dynamism and prevents the plotline from stagnating in any one place. 'You are right. That getting on the move brings in a lot of excitement,' Mansoor said. Aamir commented, 'That's what I mean when I say that his films have a holiday feel to it. That's why his stories were travelling to those places. But I don't know why they were built into his scripts. It wasn't like they were going there just for a song. The story travelled there.'

One of the more nuanced explanations for this theme in Husain's cinema came from Kaushik Bhaumik. 'It's about celebrating modernity, mobility. That's why I say he is a progressive film-maker. It's a thrill, it's adventure. It allows you to posit a certain logic about how India has changed and what is happening and trying to talk about that class in his early films, which is defined by mobility – motorcars, holidays, that kind of stuff. It also celebrates feminine mobility, modernity, modernization of all kinds of things. It allows you to then talk about a number of things. It's a purely cinematic thing as well. The thrill of movement, it allows for a certain kind of story to be told, a certain kind of complexity. Also, the audience loves the fact that *mujhe kitna kuchh dikh raha hai* (I am getting to see so much). That's why I say cinema is a contract where the film-maker promises that you will be taken into some kind of magical world. It is fulfilling that contract as well. Through a number of registers – commercial, ideological, just cinematic – all kinds of things are being fulfilled. And that's precisely the thing about his progressiveness – in accepting change, modernity, and seeing them positively. That things will change because people are getting more confident in moving around. It's also showing that people are now confident of being on their own, the young travelling on their own. So it's celebrating the new youth.'

This movement from hill stations to the jungle to the city (even if only fleetingly) in Husain's films marks not only a seamless transitioning between topography and terrain, but between cultures as well. Be it *Teesri Manzil*'s Rocky or *Munimji*'s Raj or *Dil Deke Dekho*'s Raja, they are as much at ease as in the Indian countryside as they are in clubs and hotels, one of the most conspicuous spaces of Western modernity. It is this that allows the thakurs of Dhanakpur gaon in *Qayamat Se Qayamat Tak* to migrate to Delhi without any hassle or emotional attachment.

Rashmi Doraiswamy wrote in this context, 'The narrative movement in Nasir Husain's films thus does not encapsulate binary oppositions of city / village, high / low city or rich / poor city, but leads to higher versions of the same: urban metropolis to metropolis in the hills. What this shift offers in narrative terms is scenic location without a compromise on modernity. Nasir Husain is in a hurry to get his protagonists to the hills so that their romance can unfold in sylvan surroundings with the modern social spaces and milieu that only hill stations can offer. The curving hill roads, the picturesque beauty of the mountains, the open spaces were as important to him as the clubs, bungalows and hotels that the hill stations provided … The people native to these parts appear in the song sequences, involved in their agricultural or other activities, in a ready camaraderie with the protagonists.'[11]

This easy cosmopolitanism is also evident in Husain's competition songs. In *Dil Deke Dekho*, we have already seen how Raja charms the native women in his Krishna avatar when he sings '*Megha re bole*'. But this composition, which Sadanand Warrier called a 'mish mash of folk styles', effortlessly switches to '*Bade hain dil ke kaaley*', which has a 'typical European folk lilt in the beginning, a 2/4 rhythm, followed by a sort of slight jazz influence'. Even the interludes in the song 'are very Western', remarked Sadanand. It is worth mentioning that while the entire sequence begins with Raja wanting to establish his singing credentials by wooing the local women, there is an easy comfort between these women and Neeta's own skirt-and-pant-wearing friends that is established by the end of the sequence. The locals have integrated themselves into this segment and are shown dancing in the Western interludes with complete ease alongside Neeta's friends.

Doraiswamy observed in the context of this song, 'The prologue sums up the entire song-situation with its binary oppositions: single boy and group of girls in a playful mood, tribal women and urban girls, traditional and modern lyrics and music … This is one of the most benign juxtapositions of two modes of being and two modes of music. It is also symptomatic of Nasir Husain's vision of modernity that the man playfully sings the "traditional" song "*Megha re bole*" and the woman a more westernised "*Meri jaan wah, wah, wah*". While the second song is saturated with a sense of playfulness, the other song is imbued with an exquisite

---

[11]Dr Rashmi Doraiswamy, '"These Days" of Our Modernity: The Cinema of Nasir Husain', Film and Television Institute of India, Pune, 4 September 2004, p. 6.

and subtle sense of irony, evident to the tribals as well, brought about by the "modern" Shammi Kapoor, with his distinctive body-language, singing a song about nature.'[12] For this reason, Doraiswamy contributed this song to the anthology *Defining Moments in Movies*, writing, 'This multiple song sequence signals the future style of an important Hindi film director.'[13]

Something similar happens in *Jab Pyar Kisise Hota Hai*'s '*Tum jaise bigde babu*' and *Pyar Ka Mausam*'s '*Aap chaahein mujhko*'. At one level, it is possible to read these songs as Asha Parekh's 'Indian-ness' helping her show the other lady up (Miss Pony in the former song and Miss Loveleena in the latter). But the more significant thing is that it is the urban Indian elite that is seen consuming and enjoying both kinds of performances. In *Jab Pyar Kisise Hota Hai*, Miss Pony is shown dancing to, as Sadanand explained, 'a Boogie-woogie, rock-and-roll rhythm, heavily influenced by the swing jazz bands. It is more Boogie-woogie than straight jazz, a mixture though,' before Neeta breaks into '*Tum jaise bigde babu*'. In *Pyar Ka Mausam*, Miss Loveleena is dancing to a 'Latin-influenced number. Sort of the salsa-influenced stuff that was in vogue in the Western pop and jazz scene then,' observed Sadanand. It is from here that Seema takes over to perform '*Aap chaahein mujhko*'. That these Indian, regular Hindi film song sequences can follow Western musical rhythms and styles and that, too, in a club-like space[14] is indicative of Husain's idea of cosmopolitanism.

---

[12]Ibid. p. 12.

[13]*Defining Moments in Movies: The Greatest Films, Stars, Scenes and Events That Made Movie Magic*, edited by Chris Fujiwara, Cassell Illustrated, 2007, p. 296.

[14]Interestingly, in *JPKHH*, when Monto (Dev Anand) tells Nisha (Asha Parekh) that he is going to the Darjeeling Club to watch Miss Pony, he says that there is a 'jam session' taking place over there. This, too, is a Western cultural influence but is consumed by an Indian audience.

Teesri Manzil also showcases Husain's cultural egalitarianism in another way. In the film, although Rocky is a Western-style musician, performing in clubs and hotels, a la *Dil Deke Dekho*, he passes himself off as Anil Kumar 'Sona' to escape Sunita's wrath. Anil tells Sunita and her friend that 'Sona' is his takhallus (pen name), which establishes him as an Urdu poet. In this guise, Anil claims to have written a song, which is to be performed by Rocky. But the drummer can't sing since he is unwell and has sought Anil to perform the song, which then leads to '*O haseena zulfon waali*'.

Rocky passing himself off as an Urdu poet not only brings to the fore Husain's love for poetry, but is also another example of the cosmopolitan element in Husain's cinema. It has already been established that Husain often had his characters quote famous Urdu poets for various purposes. At the same time, Husain's protagonists are also found switching to the English language all too frequently in the course of a film. Phrases like, 'Stay there, you blooming rascal', 'Good Lord!', 'Don't talk rubbish', 'I am sorry, I thought you were my fat mother', 'You go to hell!' or the use of English by the villains in *Yaadon Ki Baaraat* and *Hum Kisise Kum Naheen*, or Shammi Kapoor (in *Dil Deke Dekho*) and Rishi Kapoor (*Hum Kisise Kum Naheen*) constantly using English is a motif across many Husain films.

Two scenes underscore this motif most. In *Tumsa Nahin Dekha*, Ameeta's character momentarily steps out of the train, which is going to Soona Nagar, to buy magazines. She speaks to the newspaper–magazine vendor, saying, 'I'll take this, this and this. How much?' which the vendor understands clearly and replies to. The other scene is from *Yaadon Ki Baaraat* where Sunita, praying for Vijay's well-being, puts forth her prayers to Lord Krishna in a temple in a mishmash of Hindi and English, using words like 'life', 'system', 'fault', 'daddy' and full sentences such as 'I know it is a bad practice', 'But please forgive me. Please!' and 'because

I love him. I really, really love him'. These moments indicate the cosmopolitan nature of India, where an educated girl will converse with a newspaper vendor in English and another Western-attired girl will visit a temple – a space Hindi cinema normally reserves for Hindi-speaking, traditionally dressed, sari-clad women – and also make her supplications in English.

Doraiswamy commented, 'The languages used in Nasir Husain's films testify to the social milieu of the metropolitan culture his narratives are set in. His characters speak in excellent Hindi, Urdu and English. Linguistic code-switching is part of the essential make-up of his protagonists. He is a director who uses English phrases that belong to the register of a younger generation. He does not consider it necessary to translate them into Hindi immediately.'[15]

Bhaumik said this is why he likes Husain's films. 'There is a denial of modernity and a denial of cosmopolitanism in the literary space. For example, in Hindi literature, in a serious Hindi novel, you won't find this kind of stuff. This is recording something which has not been recorded elsewhere. There is so much guilt about cosmopolitanism because the nationalists and the intellectuals still think that this is a poor country. Therefore, we must not at all have anything to do with our own cosmopolitanism being expressed in any public sphere. As compared to that, at least there is an acknowledgement in Hindi cinema of what is happening in society. And one enjoys Nasir Husain's films precisely because of that – that there is a very easygoing understanding and there's no tradition–modernity divide in that sense … And the reason why Hindi cinema succeeded so well while India was modernizing is precisely because it could show both ends of things. And the films

[15]Dr Rashmi Doraiswamy, '"These Days" of Our Modernity: The Cinema of Nasir Husain', Film and Television Institute of India, Pune, 4 September 2004, p. 11.

talked about such characters. Hindi cinema actually shows up a truth in terms of language identities, which is far more precious than what high-brow literature was doing for India at that point in time. That's why Nasir Husain is fascinating. Nasir Husain and Mansoor Khan, the Husain family – they are wonderfully at home in all kinds of cultures and all kinds of idioms.'[16]

But to return to *Teesri Manzil*, the idea that a Western-style, rock-'n'-roll musician can actually double up as a poet, with a takhallus, re-emphasizes this blurring of lines between tradition and modernity. The idea itself is a redux of a smaller moment in *Dil Deke Dekho* where Mirza Changezi has to improvise his poetry to match up to the 'rock-'n'-roll' generation of Neeta's friends in '*Do ekum do*'. And Changezi does so with great success, with Neeta's friends applauding his ingenuity during the song. In one smooth sequence, Husain merges the world of an Urdu shaayar with that of the rock-'n'-roll generation.

Bhaumik gave a wonderfully detailed insight into the larger statement Husain made through a sequence like this. 'Comedy is always about the absurd. That's what I like about these films or the films of the '50s and '60s – they are very canny – generically. You can say, I can do this because this is a comic sequence and nobody is going to ask any questions about it and people will believe whatever I do because it has to be zany and it has to be nonsensical and it has to be fun. But while doing that, they are actually making quite significant socio-cultural commentary on what India has become, what are the kinds of worlds that are

---

[16]In light of Bhaumik's remarks here, just think of how well Mansoor Khan brought out the different worlds of the boys from Rajput College and Model College in *Jo Jeeta Wohi Sikandar*.

blending in real life. There are two ways of reading it and both readings are happening at the same time – on one hand, you are saying India *mein yeh hota hai* (this happens in India), this meeting of cultures – so it's a meta commentary – so Urdu poets are writing the rock-'n'-roll songs. All the great rock-'n'-roll songs [in Hindi cinema] are written by the Urdu poets – so that is one way of looking at it.

'At the other end it is saying, the young are talented enough that they are picking up Urdu poetry. It's also talking about the youth culture, which is smart enough to speak Urdu or Hindi or Hindustani at home and speak in English outside and is also able to do shaayari while being equally comfortable with rock-'n'-roll. This also shows a new generation, which is not making this distinction, which is comfortable living in multiple worlds. There is a commentary about the outside, about India as a whole – so there are three levels of commentary actually. There is India, then there is a commentary about the film industry itself where cultures are blending – how the Hindustani, Urdu writers are writing the rock-'n'-roll songs. And then there is a comment about the young and how they are smart and how they are happy to inhabit these different worlds and are not necessarily finding any contradiction within that, which probably is true because if we think about ourselves, we actually have been like that. We have listened to all kinds of music and we have not made that distinction.'

Teesri Manzil's 'O haseena zulfon waali' is similar to the '*Do ekum do*' episode. Here, Anil Kumar Sona, who is actually the musician Rocky but is pretending to be a poet, responds to Sunita's jibes of having to listen to '*kisi besurey bongey ka gaana*' (a man who sounds like a tin drum). The result is a knockout number where terrific lyrics merge with a novel musical arrangement, the kind of which hadn't been experienced since the advent of the Hindi film song in 1931. To put it succinctly, the words of a poet from the world of high Urdu literature, Majrooh Sultanpuri, weave themselves into a song composed by a musical maestro from a much younger generation, R.D. Burman.

In *Dil Deke Dekho*, we also see Raja responding to an advertisement given out by Royal Hotel (the business owned by Jamuna Devi), which seeks out a bandmaster, '*jo Hindustani aur vilaayati music jaanta ho*' (who knows Hindustani and Western music). Even Neeta is said to be the daughter of Seth Jagat Narayan, but who married a 'vilaayati' (foreigner) lady. Both incidents are a vindication of Husain's approach to the East/West debate, which didn't find the need to segregate between Hindustani and Western musicians or bear any suspicion towards a man who has married someone from the West, at times a matter of concern in Hindi cinema.

In Guru Dutt's *Mr. & Mrs. 55*, for instance, Lalita Pawar's character is lampooned because she takes up the cause of feminism, which, we are told in the film, she imbibed from European and American women. Likewise, actor–film-maker Manoj Kumar's *Purab Aur Pachhim* (1970) shows the West as the source of all things evil. Even Sooraj Barjatya's *Maine Pyar Kiya* (1989) has Prem (Salman Khan) fall for the more traditional (therefore good) Suman (Bhagyashree) compared to the more modern (hence evil) Seema (Pervin Dastur). But in Husain's world, two disparate cultures and traditions could not only coexist or merge into one, there was also no need to view modernity or Western influences pejoratively.

Husain showcased this comfort with modernity in another way as well. *Teesri Manzil's* setting is predominantly Park Hotel, Mussoorie. It is from this place that Roopa has allegedly jumped and committed suicide. It is here that Rocky performs. Roopa's death, and the subsequent suggestion of murder, reinforces Hindi cinema's stereotyping of hotels and clubs as places from where vice, evil and sleaze emanate. As Jerry Pinto noted, 'Almost everyone in the hotel business, according to Hindi cinema, is a murderer or a smuggler at worst; an obsequious and smarmy hanger-on at best ... Villains own hotels as a cover for their activities. Lesser fry check into hotel rooms with their suitcases full of gold, diamonds, drugs or cash. The comedians arrive disguised as room service and the maids are thieves or fair game.'[17] A number of Hindi films like *Baazi, Footpath, Taxi Driver, Shree 420, Howrah Bridge, China Town, Phool Aur Patthar* (1966), *An Evening in Paris* and *The Train* (1970) show the hotel or the club as a place from where the villain operates, or as a space that belongs to the vamp, or as a place where the morality of simple Indian folk will be compromised. Directors like Shakti Samanta and N.A. Ansari exploited this notion to the hilt. Even a Manmohan Desai film like *Naseeb* (1981) shows the hotel to be owned by the villains, which is why it has to burn down, a bit like Ravana's Lanka, before righteous men can take it over.

On the contrary, Husain celebrated the club/hotel as a place of fun and music, where audiences – be it the youth or the elite – were entertained. Whether it is *Jab Pyar Kisise Hota Hai*'s 'Darjeeling Club' or *Pyar Ka Mausam*'s 'Rainbow Club' or *Hum Kisise Kum Naheen*'s 'Nainital Club', these were places of mirth and music for Husain. Even when Regent Club '*ki mash-hoor cabaret dancer*', Monica, performs the lively '*Piya tu*' in *Caravan*, the audience in attendance is sophisticated. It is not a place of scandal and crime.

Yaadon Ki Baaraat is the clincher in this argument. In this film, 'Park Hotel' is a front for Shaakaal's illicit activities, but that is

---

[17]Jerry Pinto, 'The Woman Who Could Not Care', *Helen: The Life and Times of an H-Bomb*, Penguin Books India, 2006, p. 54.

more a Salim–Javed influence. In a number of Salim–Javed films, most prominent amongst which are *Deewaar* (1975), *Don* (1978) and *Shakti* (1982), the hotel is a world inhabited by the likes of 'Daawar', 'Saamant', 'JK' and 'Don' himself. But even in *Yaadon Ki Baaraat*, Husain established the hotel as a place for the youth to come and enjoy and swing and groove to the longish song sequence beginning with '*Aap ke kamrey mein koi*'. This sequence takes place in Hotel Blue Heaven where Monto (Tariq Khan) is introduced. This is separate from Shaakaal's world, which is Park Hotel. In Hotel Blue Heaven, Monto, the musician figure, so central to Husain's narratives, is the ringmaster in that it is he who directs proceedings. Music is at the centre of this universe. In '*Lekar hum deewaana dil*', which takes place at Park Hotel, Shaakaal's intermittent appearances in the song clearly establish this space as distinct from Hotel Blue Heaven.

Teesri Manzil too builds up Park Hotel as a place of intrigue, with people constantly spying on each other. This is nothing but a decoy because the actual villain in the piece, Kunwar Mahinder Singh (Prem Nath), isn't running some kind of crime syndicate from the hotel. He kills Roopa because she has discovered that he killed his own wife. In the process of eliminating Roopa, Kunwar sa'ab chases her down to Park Hotel, where he throws her off from the hotel's teesri manzil. Besides this, there is nothing else to suggest that Park Hotel is a world inhabited by the morally corrupt. Before this, two of the film's best songs, '*O haseena zulfon waali*' and '*Tumne mujhe dekha*', have been performed in this very place, the latter on the occasion of 'Yaum-e-Azaadi'. Husain also (by writing it into the script) has Anil and Sunita dance the hysterical '*Aaja aaja*' at the Rock-'n'-Roll Club, a space mentioned in the film purely for this song sequence. In fact, the biggest testimony to Husain's unabashed love for the club/hotel space is *Dil Deke Dekho*, where the film's narrative shuttles between Deonar Club and Everest Club and Radio Club, with Royal Hotel in Ranikhet also shown as a place which doesn't offer anything other than song and dance.

This celebration of the club culture, a distinct legacy of the British, and the hotel space, a modern Western phenomenon (as opposed to the serai/musaafirkhaana[18] experience) along with Husain's comfort with showcasing different languages, their idioms ('*Zameen jumbad, aasmaan jumbad, na jumbad Gul Mohammed*'[19] – the earth and the sky may shift, but Gul Mohammed will remain stubborn) and the mobility quotient in his films, established Husain as a champion of modernity.

The presence of clubs and hotels in Husain's films is significant in another crucial way. While decoding Husain's formula, it has been mentioned that Husain had an inclination to show only one parental figure for both the hero and the heroine. But as Doraiswamy commented in her paper, 'Nasir Husain consistently debunked the spatial/ideological notion of home vis-à-vis the hero as well as the heroine in his films ... The hill station milieu was important to him precisely because in it the hotel was not posited as a space against the home and community. If most Hindi films of the time posited the hotel as a "profane" space, the natural habitat of the villain and the vamp, Nasir Husain, drawing on the hill station milieu, gave us hotels free of all negative valency. Raj Kapoor's *Shree 420* is a typical example of this binary positing of space, where the home of the traditional community, even if it is the street, is opposed to the space of the hotel, the hub of Western values and by implication of a corrupted modernity.

---

[18]A serai/musaafirkhaana is a place where travellers can stay for the night. In the 1957 film *Aasha*, this dichotomy between the hotel as a separate space from the serai is re-emphasized when the hotel manager asks a female guest to leave the hotel because she isn't able to settle the bill. '*Yeh hotel hai, serai nahin* (This is a hotel and not a serai),' he says.

[19]Rocky says this to Sunita in *Teesri Manzil*.

'Nasir Husain set his films in the hill station precisely because those values of a "westernized" modernity that he wished to represent within the space of the hotel or club, could be done here without creating an equal and opposite space of "tradition" or home. The band, the drummer, the music, the body language and verbal language of young people enveloped in the modernity of the rock-'n'-roll generation, could only be adequately represented in the hill station. This liberation from home also accounts for Husain's fascination for scenes in the train as in *Jab Pyar...* and *Teesri Manzil*.'[20] Husain's use of the hotel as a non-domestic space further allowed him to present the hero as a musician figure who could give free rein to his West-inspired tunes and dances. 'Two birds with one stone,' Doraiswamy concluded.

It was this move away from the 'home' that made Husain do away with the need for both parental figures. Doraiswamy explained this to me in detail during our meeting in Delhi. 'He was not really involved in the problematics of home. He was not bothered with that. Creating the space of the home, with all its coordinates, he never did that. Home means a family. Home means father, mother, brother, sister. Home means values – he was not interested in that. The modernity he was envisaging is not the modernity that fits in easily with the other versions of modernity.' Doraiswamy even took off in Hindi to express her frustration with the one-dimensional understanding of Husain's cinema in this context. '*Yeh jo log kehtey hain ki yeh baar baar ek hi story sunaata hai, unko samajh hi nahin aayee hai baat.* (These people who say that he told the same story again and again, they haven't understood him at all.) He was the only man who left the home [behind in his cinema]. He didn't give a damn about it. There

---

[20]Dr Rashmi Doraiswamy, '"These Days" of Our Modernity: The Cinema of Nasir Husain', Film and Television Institute of India, Pune, 4 September 2004, p. 8.

will be a father, there will be all kinds of things happening – "My sister is dead, I am going to look for my sister [*Teesri Manzil*]" – whatever, there will be some ruse, but you move away from the home. That is why, for me, he is so unique ... he is the one person who said to hell with the home. None of the others could do that.'

Equally, *Teesri Manzil* is a terrific meeting of minds between Vijay Anand and Nasir Husain. Both men had very modern sensibilities when it came to film-making and placed a special emphasis on music. Like Husain, some of Vijay Anand's best films (*Tere Ghar Ke Samne, Jewel Thief*) dealt with the urban elite. Madhulika Liddle summed this up best. 'I think *Teesri Manzil* is an excellent example of the blending of two genres, the frothy romantic drama with a crime angle (which Nasir Husain was the master of) and the predominantly suspense film (which Vijay Anand was very good at: I'm thinking specifically here of *Nau Do Gyarah* and *Jewel Thief*). Both men were brilliant at creating gripping, extremely entertaining cinema – and that is what *Teesri Manzil* is. They bring their own individual skills together here – Nasir Husain's love for the prolonged courting, the outdoors, the comic relief, the impersonation, the prettiness and Vijay Anand's excellence at building up suspense.'

This meeting of minds is better understood by how Vijay Anand shaped Husain's idea for *Teesri Manzil*, fine-tuning it against his own sensibilities. Narwekar told me that the basic premise for *Teesri Manzil* came from a scene that Husain had in his head, which he wanted to flesh out into a story. The scene was, 'There is this girl at a petrol pump. She is filling petrol and she is telling her saheli (girlfriend) that my sister was murdered last year and I'm searching for the man who killed her. And that man is at the petrol pump overhearing this. [Though] that scene did not make it into the film eventually, the story of *Teesri Manzil* originated from this.'[21] Narwekar, who is also a big fan of Vijay Anand's work, and who spent a lot of time with him while the director was alive, said that Vijay Anand looked at Husain's idea of film-making as a set of building blocks. 'He [Vijay Anand] said that, "I realized that he [Nasir Husain] had certain stock characters – the dancer, the sidekick, the secretary. I identified with a lot of things but I liked a screenplay which was well integrated and not having all this side-humour."'

Perhaps, this explains why *Teesri Manzil* didn't have a comic sidekick like the characters played by Rajendra Nath in most of Husain's films and why *Teesri Manzil* also makes a departure from Husain's favourite lost-and-found trope. Even in terms of song picturization – '*O mere sona re*' from the film seems to have shaped Husain's own picturization of '*O meri soni*' in *Yaadon Ki Baaraat*. In *Teesri Manzil*, when Sunita begins singing the first antara – '*O meri baahon…*', the shot has her moving parallel to Anil, with the camera dolly tracking this movement. Husain repeated this same shot in *Yaadon Ki Baaraat* when Vijay sings the mukhda for the second time at the beginning of '*O meri soni*'. Given how similar the first few words of the two songs are and how alike they are in terms of their situation and placement in the film, Husain could have also done this deliberately. One protagonist is trying to win the other over in both songs, which are also rendered in the countryside after a car has broken down.

But the reverse is also possibly true – that Husain influenced Vijay Anand in some way. For instance, look at '*Aaja aaja*' from *Teesri Manzil*. The song stems from Husain's '*Do ekum do*'

---

[21]Vijay Anand even admitted to this being the genesis of *Teesri Manzil*'s storyline in an interview to the journalist Roshmila Bhattacharya for her article in *Screen*, 'Murder and Melody', 12 April 2002.

episode in *Dil Deke Dekho* where Neeta's friends are part of the 'Rock-'n'-Roll' Club. In *Teesri Manzil*, '*Aaja aaja*' is performed at the Rock-'n'-Roll Club. The picturization all through is vintage Vijay Anand as the director 'pushes his fondness for frames within frames witnessed earlier in the "*O haseena zulfon waali*" song to the limit by giving an improbable, impossible "point of view" shot from within the guitar...'[22] This happens at the end of the song, when the pace picks up and the onlookers at the Rock-'n'-Roll Club join in to become part of this wild, wild crescendo.

In two earlier films directed by Vijay Anand – *Nau Do Gyarah* and *Tere Ghar Ke Samne* (1963) – the director had song sequences filmed in the club space: '*Kya ho phir jo din rangeela ho*' in the former and '*Dil ki manzil*' in the latter. In both songs, the tempo picks up at the end, particularly in '*Dil ki manzil*'. But Vijay Anand doesn't indulge in rapid cuts of the Husain kind to match this enhanced tempo. In contrast, and very much in keeping with Husain's picturization of such moments (as seen in '*Sar par topi laal*' or '*Yaar chulbula hai*' or '*Do ekum do*'), Vijay Anand resorts to extremely fast cutting, giving us close-up shots of the artistes, their hands and legs, the guitars, before Sunita's friend falls to the ground, exhausted, signalling an end to the manic '*Aaja aaja*'. The audience joining in at the end is in itself a repetition of '*Do ekum do*'. Vijay Anand had never done anything like this before. It was the ultimate hat-tip Vijay Anand, a man far more accomplished at shot-taking and picturization, could have paid Husain.[23] A year

---

[22]Dr Rashmi Doraiswamy, '"These Days" of Our Modernity: The Cinema of Nasir Husain', Film and Television Institute of India, Pune, 4 September 2004, p. 13.

[23]Vijay Anand also admitted to not being a very big advocate of frequent cuts during a song. In an interview to Nasreen Munni Kabir, which was reproduced in *The Indian Quarterly*, 'The Goldie Standard',

(Contd...)

later, Vijay Anand would repeat this while giving a montage of close-ups at the feverish finish of *Jewel Thief*'s '*Hothon pe aisi baat*'.

Teesri Manzil's greatest significance in Husain's career was that it marked the beginning of his collaboration with Rahul Dev Burman. RD was the only child born to music composer S.D. Burman and Meera Dhar Gupta, a classically trained singer and also prolific lyricist who wrote a number of SD's Bengali songs. RD, who had assisted his father from very early in his life, made his film debut with *Chhote Nawaab* (1961). He then gave the music for a few other films, *Bhoot Bangla* (1965), *Teesra Kaun* (1965) and *Pati Patni* (1966). Although the odd song from these films like '*Matwali aankhon waale*' (*Chhote Nawaab*), '*Aao twist karein*' (*Bhoot Bangla*) and '*Pyar ka fasaana*' (*Teesra Kaun*) became popular, it's difficult to believe that RD's career was poised for far bigger things based on his music for these films. What was not in doubt, though, was his talent.

Pancham's fifth film turned out to be *Teesri Manzil*. Both Husain and Vijay Anand were keen on collaborating with the youngster. However, as Anirudha Bhattacharjee and Balaji Vittal detail in their National award-winning book, *R.D. Burman: The Man, The Music*, with Shammi Kapoor's entry into *Teesri Manzil*, the actor was keen on having either O.P. Nayyar or Shankar—

(...contd.)
Volume 4, Issue 1, October–December 2015, p. 80, Vijay said, 'Some choreographers have a limited understanding of editing. They want too many cuts and do not allow the shot to be held long enough ... Nowadays, film editors are in love with the rhythm. They don't allow you to see the faces of the heroine or hero.' And Husain, as we know, was cutting only to match the beat of these songs as they went into their frenzied climax.

Jaikishan as composer because their music had been an integral part of Shammi's successful films. Aamir also said, 'I remember Nasir sa'ab telling me that when Shammi uncle came on to the film, he was very particular about who was doing the music. I think he [Shammi] was keen on Shankar–Jaikishan. Pancham uncle was fairly new at that time. So Nasir sa'ab told Shammi, "Trust me. This guy is damn good. And just to satisfy you, I'm going to call him and you hear all the songs."' The crucial thing to note over here is that *Teesri Manzil*'s songs had already been composed by RD and recorded for the film. So when RD sang the songs from the film for Shammi Kapoor at Husain's house, 'Shammi uncle got so excited on hearing the songs that he got up and started dancing,' said Aamir. That's how RD became a part of *Teesri Manzil*.

Husain's role, therefore, in getting Shammi to listen to RD and the subsequent success of the film's music mean that he deserved as much credit as anyone else. Aamir agreed. 'I would say that the music of *Teesri Manzil* is of course created by Pancham uncle. Goldie uncle being the director would have interacted very strongly with Pancham uncle. But in this case the producer was as strong musically and the three of them would have worked together. I cannot imagine Nasir Husain being disconnected from the music of *Teesri Manzil*.' Mansoor said something similar. 'My dad was involved. I don't know who had the upper hand but I'm pretty sure that my dad was involved to a great degree.' Asha Parekh articulated it perfectly when she said, 'I would give the credit to all three. Goldie also had a great sense of music. So it was Shammi Kapoor, Goldie and Nasir sa'ab – the three together. That is why the music is outstanding in that film.'

Teesri Manzil should hence be viewed as a fine coming together of not just Vijay Anand's and Nasir Husain's sensibilities, but a film that drew on the talents of Shammi Kapoor, R.D. Burman,

Majrooh Sultanpuri and N.V. Srinivas (the film's cinematographer) as well. It is cinema at its collaborative best. As Bhattacharjee and Balaji wrote of RD's music, 'So even as Vijay Anand was conjuring up the thrills, Pancham was designing his personal blend of rock, jazz, Latino and twist to create a sound, the likes of which was unheard of in the then thirty-five-year history of Hindi films.'[24] Majrooh responded to the suspense-oriented premise of the film and Sunita's quest for vengeance with lyrics like '*Woh anjaana dhoondhti hoon, woh deewaana dhoondhti hoon, jala kar jo chhup gaya hai, woh parwaana dhoondhti hoon*' (I look for that stranger, I search for that crazed soul, who remains hidden having caused grief, I search for that lover) for '*O haseena zulfon waali*'.[25] At the same time, Shammi Kapoor, who lost his wife, Geeta Bali, just when '*Tumne mujhe dekha*' was being filmed, recovered well enough to imbue the song with just the right emotion that makes it such a fine sequence to watch even today.

In a sense, *Teesri Manzil* was a film where a kind of 'passing-

---

[24]Anirudha Bhattacharjee and Balaji Vittal, 'The Pancham Manzil', *R.D. Burman: The Man, The Music*, HarperCollins *Publishers* India, 2011, p. 50.

[25]Also, consider Majrooh's lyrics for '*Dekhiye sahibo*', possibly, the least of *Teesri Manzil's* fine songs if one were to go by popular opinion. But look at what Majrooh writes in the last stanza for both Sunita's and Anil's characters: Sunita sings '*Haaye haaye dekho toh isko, boley hi ja raha hai, Uljhi baaton mein zaalim, sabko uljhaa raha hai*' (Look, look at him, he just keeps talking, The brute is confounding matters by talking non-stop). Anil responds to this with '*Sach bann gaya agar uljhan, phir kahiye janaab-e-mann, meri kya khataa? Mujh par yakeen ab kam sahi, Main saada-dil mujrim sahi...*' (If the truth has become complicated, tell me, respected onlookers, how am I to blame? You may not trust me entirely, I am innocent, but guilty in your eyes...) This exchange is another subtle reflection of *Teesri Manzil's* storyline where Anil is determined to prove to Sunita that he did not murder her sister.

of-the-baton' happened in Husain's film-making. It marked the
last time the film-maker worked with Shammi Kapoor, largely,
because of the actor's dramatic decline (owing to his wife's death)
by the end of the 1960s. Shammi's over-the-top persona, so crucial
to the spirit of Husain's films, needed to be replaced by someone
with an equal manic energy in his work. That person turned out
to be R.D. Burman, who, beginning with *Teesri Manzil*, forged a
formidable collaboration with Husain right up to the turn of the
1980s. Together, the film-maker–composer duo worked on nine
films right up to 1985, which defined the very best of Hindi film
music for at least the next fifteen years.

Bhaumik attributed this collaboration with RD to Husain's
prescience. 'His understanding that RD was going to do something
different precedes the film itself. He knows that this guy is going
to do something interesting. I mean in 1966, RD is still very
young and learning. He's still four–five years away from his real
glory days from '71 onwards. But Nasir Husain realizes that RD's
score for *Teesri Manzil* is a transition. There's a realization that this
is all leading up to something other than Shankar–Jaikishan. It's
leading up to some other kind of mood, energy and percussion
and syncopation and bodily movement, a certain kind of youthful
élan vital, particularly in the duet dance numbers ['*O haseena*'
and '*Aaja aaja*']. There is a very canny understanding of that …
He must have been watching RD, listening to his music, and he
must have picked up something interesting there that this guy is
going to be the future at the level of youth culture, which is what
defines RD in the years to follow … It's all about youth, it's not
about westernization.'

Just as an example, listen to the drumming in the opening
few seconds of *Dil Deke Dekho*'s title track and '*O haseena zulfon
waali*'. While the drumming establishes a link between the two
films, and is also another clear signifier of Husain's influence on

Teesri Manzil's music score, the drumming in the *Teesri Manzil* song is twice the length of '*Dil deke dekho's* drum rolls and clearly much more manic. This signified a transition from the world of Husain's earlier composers to R.D. Burman. As good as the music is in Husain's first four films, there is something distinctive about the music in his films with RD. To term that distinctiveness simply 'Western' is flippant since film composers right from the late 1940s were using Western-style tunes and musical arrangements in their films. Husain's meeting of minds with RD happened not just at the level of the song, but in the way that it was picturized and at the level of the narrative as well, where music got more closely integrated into the film's screenplay.

Before discussing the Husain–RD association further, it is important to talk about another film that Husain released shortly after *Teesri Manzil*. With this film, Husain broke the mould of his formula films in no uncertain terms.

7

BREAKING THE MOULD,
THE GANDHIAN WAY

'When the public comes to see a Manmohan Desai film, they expect full entertainment. They want to see the same things over and over again. They want to see lost-and-found. They want to see a good song. They want to see well-picturized songs. They want to see action. They want to see some new item in the film. What they've seen before, they must see it again. That's definite. Like there's a brand. When you go to see a [Alfred] Hitchcock film, you go with a definite mind that you are seeing a murder mystery. You are not going to see a romantic Alfred Hitchcock film. When you go to see a Cecil B. DeMille film, you go with the expectation that you are going to see big grandeur. They cannot deceive the audience. You cannot play the fool with them. Like Billy Wilder has said in his book. Never cheat an audience. Don't try to change the image of the actor too much. They come fully prepared that they have come to see a film with this thing in mind. If it's a Hitchcock film, it's a murder mystery. Give it to them.'

– Film-maker Manmohan Desai[1]

'I think a film-maker who becomes a brand promises certain things to his audience tacitly. This automatically implies the

---

[1]Documentary on Manmohan Desai's films on Doordarshan: https://www.youtube.com/watch?v=AspspTDxJOw

segment of the public he caters to. This means that he can neither reach below nor above himself if his films are to be accepted. [Alfred] Hitchcock's *Under Capricorn* (1949, a historical drama) was a flop. If Chetan Bhagat tries to write philosophy, he will obviously destroy his own career.'

— Author and film scholar M.K. Raghavendra

Going back to Husain's college days, an Urdu magazine, *Aaj Kal*, published a short story written by Husain. The story went on to win the first prize in a competition featuring students from Lucknow, Allahabad and Aligarh universities. 'I adapted that story into my film *Baharon Ke Sapne*,' Husain said. With this film, whose shooting commenced only a few months into *Teesri Manzil's* production, Husain consciously broke away from his usual cinema, which the critics often described as candy-floss, one that didn't attempt to propagate any social or political ideology.

Asha Parekh continued as heroine in this offbeat Husain film. But Parekh, who was doing her fifth successive film with Husain, told me that Husain had initially offered her role to Nanda. This may have been because Parekh was starring in Husain's other production, *Teesri Manzil*, which was still a work-in-progress. Parekh was also very much at the peak of her professional career by this time. Besides her success in Husain's films, she had also starred in hits such as *Ziddi* (1964) and *Mere Sanam* (1965). Parekh was very much in demand and working with top-notch directors like Pramod Chakravorty (*Love in Tokyo*, 1966), Raj Khosla (*Do Badan*, 1966) and J. Om Prakash (who produced *Aaye Din Bahar Ke*, 1966).

'Actually, I didn't have dates to give him,' Parekh said. 'He went to Nanda and narrated the subject. She wanted to do glamorous roles. So she was not very keen on *Baharon Ke Sapne*. She somehow made an excuse. And I got a firing from Nasir sa'ab for sending him to Nanda. He came back and said, "Why the hell can't you do it?" I said, "I can't do it because I don't have dates." So he said, "If I adjust the dates with you?" Then my mother said if you adjust the dates, we can do it. That's how I was brought into the film.'

The bigger casting story, as with most Husain films, concerned the film's hero. The male protagonist was a relative newcomer, but his meteoric rise a few years after *Baharon Ke Sapne* would give Hindi cinema its first true superstar. That newcomer was Rajesh Khanna, winner of the Filmfare–United Producers Combine contest. The United Producers were a group of twelve eminent film personalities, featuring the likes of B.R. Chopra, Shakti Samanta, Bimal Roy and Husain. The idea behind the contest was to promote new talent, with the winner getting the opportunity to act in a film produced by each member of the United Producers Combine. Having witnessed Khanna's acting abilities in the talent contest and since the actor had little baggage in terms of an on-screen persona, Husain must have found Khanna ideal to play the lead in his film, a strong socio-political drama. *Baharon Ke Sapne*, consequently, turned out to be Khanna's third release following *Aakhri Khat* (1966) and *Raaz* (1967).

The contemplative tone of *Baharon Ke Sapne* is set by the tribute at the start of the film, which reads, 'This film is dedicated to the sacred memory of one of the greatest sons of India, MAHATMA GANDHI, the apostle of PEACE & NON-VIOLENCE.'[2] Shot

---

[2]Interestingly, the usual 'NH Films' banner, which is shown after the initial dedication to Gandhi also has a relatively more sombre voiceover for '*Kya ishq ne samjha hai*'. There is no drum roll accompanying the recitation of the couplet. But the couplet ends with the same emphatic drumbeat as in other Husain films.

in monochrome, the film is about 'A small industrial town near Bombay', where Bhola Nath (Nana Palsikar) lives with his wife (Sulochana Latkar) and four children, including Champa and Ram (Rajesh Khanna). Bhola Nath has been a poor millworker at the local mill (National Mills Ltd) for the last thirty years. His only hope and source of pride is Ram,[3] who has completed his BA. Bhola Nath is certain that Ram will land a big job soon because he is a graduate.

This doesn't happen. Stung by failure and his inability to find a job, Ram finds solace in the company of Geeta (Asha Parekh), his childhood sweetheart. Bhola Nath, meanwhile, tries to secure a job for Ram at the mill by having a word with the manager (Prem Nath). But the manager insults him and warns him about being slack on the job. Successive setbacks and the pain of his father's tribulations (Bhola Nath loses his job) lead Ram to Bombay in search for a job, but he returns disappointed. Unknown to his family members, Ram takes up a job at the mill as a daily wage-earner, but spends most of his money and time drinking at an illicit liquor den after working hours.

Soon, Ram is introduced to Das Kaka (P. Jairaj), a trade-union leader, who is inspiring the workers at the mill to fight for their rights. Motivated by Das Kaka, Ram soon becomes the leader of the disgruntled workers and takes on the establishment. But Das Kaka seeks militant trade unionism. He is determined to burn down the mill to teach its greedy owners a lesson. Ram doesn't share this view and believes that the workers cannot destroy the very means to their livelihood. He believes in the Gandhian principle of non-violence. The climax of the film deals with how

---

[3]Several references to the film, including online and print publications, suggest that Khanna's character was named Ramaiya. But this is incorrect. The DVD version refers to Khanna as Ram all through the film.

Ram stands up to Das Kaka and his men even though he and
Geeta are shot at in the process. While Das eventually dies, Ram's
and Geeta's lives are saved by doctors. The final scene of the film
depicts Ram and Geeta walking together into the sunset, with the
song 'O more sajna', playing in the background.

However, this was not the ending Husain had originally
filmed. The original ending had Ram and Geeta dying of bullet
injuries. This was followed by a scene showing their bodies being
carried away, with the song 'Zamaane ne maare jawaan kaise kaise'
playing in the background. But the initial response to the film
was underwhelming. Filmfare termed the film 'Drab back-street'
in its review, saying, 'Baharon Ke Sapne is a fairy tale narrated in
pseudo-realistic fashion.'[4] Another review was equally trenchant
and described the film as 'Nasir Husain's Fake Workers'. The
reviewer went on to say, 'As a film it is as flippant as any boy-
meets-girl melodrama of the Indian cinema.'[5] Husain attempted
to cover his losses by changing the ending to a happier one within
a week of the film's release. But the damage had already been done.
After five straight successes since Tumsa Nahin Dekha, Husain
was humbled at the box office. The film wasn't a total disaster but
its collections certainly paled in comparison to Husain's earlier
films.

Baharon Ke Sapne's critical and commercial reception is not a
true reflection of the film's quality. With the benefit of hindsight,
the film has several admirable elements, including its overall
theme. The performances by the lead characters are indeed notable.
Nana Palsikar as Bhola Nath is particularly poignant, maintaining
a brave face despite his mounting struggles and shattered dreams.

---

[4]Filmfare, 4 August 1967, p. 41.

[5]This review is dated 6 August 1967 and is sourced from the National
Film Archive of India. The publisher of the review, however, could not
be determined.

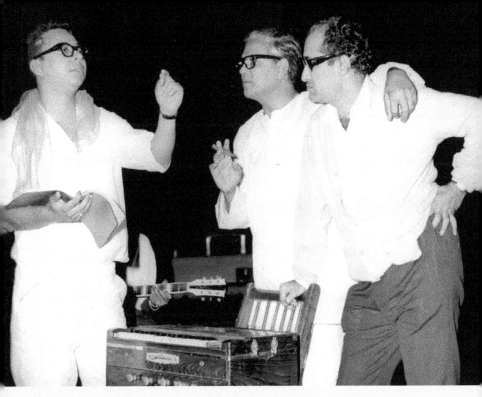

With R.D. Burman and
Majrooh Sultanpuri, the
men who articulated
the leitmotif of Husain's
cinema through their
compositions and lyrics.
Courtesy: NH Films/
Nuzhat Khan

With the cast and crew of *Teesri Manzil* (1966), a film where some of
the finest minds in showbiz came together to create a wonderful noirish
musical drama. *Courtesy: NH Films/Nuzhat Khan*

The song '*Aap se miliye*' from *Pyar Ka Mausam* (1969) showcased a mélange of cultures, signifying the 'vasudhaiva kutumbakam' element in Hindi film songs. *Courtesy: NH Films/Nuzhat Khan*

With *Tumsa Nahin Dekha* (1957), Husain provided Shammi Kapoor's career the impetus it needed after multiple flops. He perhaps best understood Shammi Kapoor's physicality, which couldn't be constrained even as the drummer figure in *Teesri Manzil. Courtesy: NH Films/Nuzhat Khan*

While Dharmendra's track in *Yaadon Ki Baaraat* (1973) reflected the Salim–Javed influence, the Zeenat Aman–Vijay Arora track was vintage Nasir Husain. *Courtesy: NH Films/Nuzhat Khan*

The song *'Lekar hum deewaana dil'* is arguably *Yaadon Ki Baaraat's* pièce de résistance, its lyrics and picturization providing a microcosm of the film's storyline. *Courtesy: NH Films/ Nuzhat Khan*

Nasir Husain with Asha Parekh and Rajesh Khanna on the sets of *Baharon Ke Sapne* (1967). *Courtesy: NH Films/Nuzhat Khan*

With cinematographer Munir Khan (wearing hat) on the sets of *Hum Kisise Kum Naheen*. *Courtesy: Shamir Khan*

In keeping with his penchant for the spectacular in his songs, Husain put Kaajal Kiran on a crane in *'Yeh ladka, haaye Allah' (Hum Kisise Kum Naheen)*, thereby creating the illusion that she was actually up in the sky with the hot-air balloons. *Courtesy: NH Films/Nuzhat Khan*

Husain with Rishi Kapoor and Kaajal Kiran during the shooting of the song *'Humko toh yaara teri yaari' (Hum Kisise Kum Naheen)*. *Courtesy: NH Films/Nuzhat Khan*

With son Mansoor Khan. Mansoor assisted Husain on *Zamaane Ko Dikhana Hai* (1981) but claimed to be bumming around on the sets of *Manzil Manzil* (1984) and *Zabardast* (1985). *Courtesy: NH Films/Nuzhat Khan*

A young Aamir Khan, who assisted Husain on *Manzil Manzil* and *Zabardast*. *Courtesy: NH Films/Nuzhat Khan*

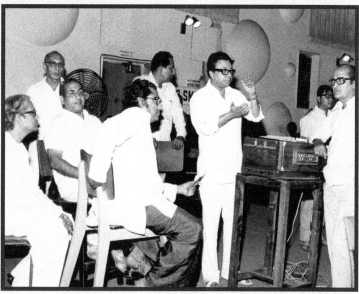

From L to R: Majrooh Sultanpuri, Mohammed Rafi, Kishore Kumar, R.D. Burman and Nasir Husain – the many geniuses behind *Hum Kisise Kum Naheen*'s fine soundtrack.
Courtesy: NH Films/Nuzhat Khan

Scriptwriters Salim–Javed with Husain. As Javed Akhtar said, 'Yaadon Ki Baaraat is a Nasir Husain hyphen Salim–Javed film.' *Courtesy: NH Films/Nuzhat Khan*

Husain was a master at writing dialogues. The exchanges between Raj and Rashmi in *Qayamat Se Qayamat Tak* (1988) brought out the overall tehzeeb and nazaaqat of the film. *Courtesy: NH Films/Nuzhat Khan*

Top: According to Jerry Pinto,
'Nasir Husain was only focused
on the song, the romance
and the heroine ... the biggest
memory today we have of
Zeenat Aman is ...
"*Chura liya hai*" ... dressed in
Western clothes ... strumming
a guitar ... in the middle of
a party.' *Courtesy: NH Films/
Nuzhat Khan*

Right: Nasir Husain songs were
a spectacle:
'*Hoga tumse pyaara kaun*'
took the Hindi film hero to
serenade his heroine on top of
a train long before
'*Chhaiyyan chhaiyyan*'.
Courtesy: NH Films/Nuzhat Khan

In one heart-wrenching scene, he is lying in bed, having lost his job, uttering the following prayer, '*Tu hi hai bhagwaan sabke purdeh dhakne waala. Jab daant na thay, tab doodh diye hu. Jab daant diye, kya anna na dego?*' (You are the Almighty, who provides succour to everyone. When we didn't have teeth, you gave us milk. Now when we have teeth, will you not provide us food?).

In contrast to *Teesri Manzil* and her other roles in Husain's films, which had her play feisty, well-heeled characters, Parekh comes up with a remarkably understated performance as a small-town girl, who is also the breadwinner in her family. There are shades of her *Do Badan* performance in this film, with Parekh walking the tightrope between conveying emotion and not going over-the-top.

The real star is, undoubtedly, Khanna. In playing Ram, who experiences rejection and failure for the most part, but then finds new meaning to his life as the leader of the millworkers' struggles, Khanna delivers a sensitive, nuanced performance. What perhaps worked for Khanna is that he was still at the beginning of his career and a long way off from getting stuck in the one-dimensional manner of emoting that makes him a mimic's delight for his 'Pushpa, I hate tears'[6] style of dialogue delivery. Most importantly, as Ashim Samanta confirmed, it was Khanna's performance in *Baharon Ke Sapne* that convinced Shakti Samanta to cast him in *Aradhana* (1969), the role that made Khanna a superstar. 'As a United producer, [Shakti Samanta] had selected him [Khanna], but to doubly confirm, to reassure himself, he went and saw some portion of the rushes. He was very impressed and signed him.'

The soundtrack yet again established Husain as a connoisseur in selecting the right tunes for his films. From the lilting '*Aaja piya tohe pyaar doon*' to the delightfully naughty '*Chunari sambhaal gori*' to the simple but hummable '*O more sajna*' to the inherently

---

[6]Khanna's character's signature dialogue from *Amar Prem* (1972).

delicate '*Kya jaanu sajan hoti hai kya gham ki shaam*' to the abject
strains of '*Zamaane ne maare jawaan kaise kaise*', Husain got the
right song for every moment. The one song that does jar with
the overall theme is the rather rambunctious '*Do pal jo teri*', but
Husain may have deliberately played this up as a way of portraying
the gaudy, materialistic side of the wealthy elite against whom
Ram lashes out after the song.

The picturization matches the mood of each song. While
'*Zamaane ne maare jawaan kaise kaise*' plays out even as Ram
looks in vain for a job in Bombay, '*O more sajna*' is shot against
the backdrop of salt beds somewhere in the interiors of
Maharashtra. As eighty-five-year-old Sulochana Latkar, who
played the role of Ram's mother in the film and Jamuna Devi in
Dil Deke Dekho, noted, when I met her in her Prabhadevi home,
'There has never been such a song in Hindi cinema. That setting
itself was unique. And it was a love song. People normally shoot
such songs in gardens.' The innovative setting led Anirudha
Bhattacharjee and Balaji Vittal to term it 'a piece of Dresden art'.[7]
Aamir explained Husain's thinking behind the song. 'I would
imagine because the setting of the film has a lot to do with labour.
He would have probably wanted it to be in the environment that
they are living in, the characters coming from that basti, from a
poor background, a lot of them are unemployed, or at least he
[Ram] is unemployed. It would hardly be possible for them to
go out into the mountains. He would want to keep the setting of
the song within the same class that they belong to and yet make
it outdoors.'

'*Chunari sambhaal gori*' is classic Husain territory. The song has
a long prelude and finishes with the characteristic flourish seen

[7]Anirudha Bhattacharjee and Balaji Vittal, 'The Pancham Manzil',
R.D. Burman: The Man, The Music, HarperCollins *Publishers* India,
2011, p. 59.

in several of Husain's earlier songs. Husain resorts to a series of flash cuts, with the camera constantly shifting between the male and female junior artistes' feet. A swish pan also lends dynamism to the song's climax. By the end of the sequence, the character artistes Anwar Husain, Rajendra Nath and Manorama also join, which again is standard Husain practice of involving the audience within the song at the finale.

The song that brings *Baharon Ke Sapne*'s fine cinematography into focus is '*Aaja piya tohe pyaar doon*'. The lighting for the song (as for most of the film) is unique and unlike any other Husain film. Through the song, Geeta is often framed through a series of circular dolly track shots and for the most part between a pair of trees or vines, which is a most unusual framing style for a character in a song compared to any of Husain's other films ('*Piya tu*' in *Caravan* is perhaps an exception). The song is a declaration of Geeta's unflinching love for Ram. But the picturization shows Geeta attending to household chores. While the words present Geeta as a strong woman, who would provide for Ram, she is also shown to be held back by the duties of the home.

Baharon Ke Sapne was shot by well-known cameraman Jal Mistry, Fali Mistry's younger sibling. Both brothers did some pioneering cinematography since their coming to the film industry in the 1940s. Fali Mistry worked on seminal films like *Babul* (1950), *Nagin* (1954) and *Guide* while Jal Mistry helmed the cinematography for *Barsaat* (1949) and *Uran Khatola* (1955). Faroukh Mistry, Fali Mistry's son and Jal Mistry's nephew, spoke to me over a Skype conversation in March 2015. Faroukh himself is a cinematographer, having graduated from the FTII and the American Film Institute. He has worked in film and television for several years in India and abroad.

Speaking on Jal Mistry's work in '*Aaja piya tohe pyaar doon*', Faroukh told me that it was 'classical Hollywood lighting styles. It's basically very high contrast work. At the same time, it maintains its glamour ... If you look at *Barsaat*, Jal sa'ab's first film, with Raj Kapoor, you will see a similarity in this work and *Barsaat* in terms of lighting. This is his style. He was known for this.'

This high contrast work, which works at several levels in bringing out the conflicting situations Ram finds himself in through the film, won Jal Mistry a Filmfare Best Cinematography Award, making it the first of his four Filmfare Awards in this category. *Filmfare* noted, 'The camera is about the best thing in the film, the lighting just right whether it falls on a room in a slum or dramatically highlights a mob of strikers in the night or spreads a warm white aura across a sand dune.'[8] Aamir said that Jal Mistry's work in *Baharon Ke Sapne* reminded him of the work of ace cinematographer and Dadasaheb Phalke Award winner V.K. Murthy, who worked with Guru Dutt on films such as *Pyaasa* and *Kaagaz Ke Phool* (1959).

As Faroukh explained to me, Murthy worked as an assistant to Fali Mistry and Jal Mistry in his early years in the film industry. 'The same contrast is there in Murthy sa'ab's work. The same extreme contrast – he pushed it even further in *Pyaasa* because of the subject he was dealing with. Especially in all Guru Dutt's films, the contrast is pushed even more. Murthy sa'ab was assisting Fali sa'ab. Jal sa'ab started with Fali sa'ab as well. Jal sa'ab went on to do *Barsaat* and my dad went on to do *Mela* (1948).'

The other song in which Jal Mistry and Husain worked innovatively to bring out the essence of the moment in the film's screenplay is '*Kya jaanu sajan hoti hai kya gham ki shaam*'. The song was shot in colour. It is the only such segment in the film, possibly because it is a dream sequence where Geeta speaks of finding true bliss with Ram. The sequence takes place at a mela, which Geeta and Ram go to. The song begins and ends against

---

[8] *Filmfare*, 4 August 1967, p. 41.

the backdrop of a Ferris wheel, which is part of the mela. But the main body of the song was shot at Filmistan studios.

Asha Parekh explained the different shooting backdrops. 'Actually, when this song was shot, I was working in the day for *Teesri Manzil* and in the night for *Baharon Ke Sapne*. I had just come back from Benares after a dance conference. It was the same set as the "*Dekhiye sahibo*" song in *Teesri Manzil*.[9] So in the night we used to shoot there [for *Baharon Ke Sapne*] and in the morning we were shooting for *Teesri Manzil*. The set was at Chena Creek – it was terrible, it was a lonely place at that time. And I collapsed one day on the sets, the second day of shoot. I was brought back home at two in the night. And after that I could not get up. I had typhoid. So they had to dismantle the set and the rest of the song was shot in Filmistan.'

The manner in which Husain and Jal Mistry underscore the dream sequence effect is important. Right at the beginning of the song, we see Rajesh Khanna dressed in a tux. The camera zooms in on him from high above after which it goes into some kind of multi-prism with the Ferris wheel. The next shot has Khanna turning towards the camera after which there's a pull back from the stars and then there is another zoom into Khanna, which is basically the same shot at the beginning of the song. After a couple of quick shots, we see the camera zoom into the stars at the precise moment that Lata Mangeshkar again starts singing the alaap. These repeated zooms and the use of the multi-prism effect give the song the required dream sequence impact.

As Faroukh Mistry explained, zooms weren't in vogue in Hindi cinema in the mid-1960s. 'Zooms were only used for a certain effect. And this is all to create that dream effect. Therefore you

---

[9]If one looks carefully, one can see the same 'Wills' stall featuring in both songs.

had the multi-prism.[10] And the zoom, even the zoom-out from the stars, it's to create a certain effect within limitation.' It's only in the 1970s that zooms started being used in a big way in Hindi cinema. According to Faroukh, 'In the '70s, when the multi-starrers came in, zoom was a time-saving element because actors would give you two hours. You know you pull back from a close-up, you come to a long shot. From the long shot you come out, you go into a close-up. So we used that element for economics.'

Barring this sequence, *Baharon Ke Sapne* is a black-and-white film. It's interesting to speculate why Husain chose this texture for the film, when he had already forayed into colour with *Phir Wohi Dil Laya Hoon*. Even *Teesri Manzil*, which was being shot almost simultaneously with *Baharon Ke Sapne*, was a colour production. It's not that black-and-white films were not being made in the late 1960s. In fact, Rajesh Khanna's first film, *Aakhri Khat*, was shot in monochrome. As late a film as *Khamoshi* (1969) was made in black-and-white. But most of the big-ticket producers and directors – Navketan, B.R. Films, J. Om Prakash, Shakti Samanta, Ramanand Sagar, Pramod Chakravorty, Raj Khosla and Hrishikesh Mukherjee – had transitioned to colour by the mid-to-late 1960s.

'I think it was purely a budget thing,' Mansoor said. 'He was making a film that did not have the scope to earn a lot. He knew he was making a slightly more serious film, which is not the genre he had explored or he was yet comfortable with. My dad used to be very practical about cost and budgets. He wanted to make it viable. It's not like serious films have not been shot in colour, but I think this was more of a budget thing.'

Aamir gave a different perspective. 'I would imagine that partly

---

[10]Husain himself used the zoom quite sparingly initially, such as to amplify the echo effect in '*Humdum mere khel na jaano*' in *Phir Wohi Dil Laya Hoon*. The multi-prism, according to Faroukh, 'are multiple image filters made out of prisms that would create multiple images'.

it may have been a budget decision, but I don't think that would be the only reason ... I feel that the subject was that kind – at least at that time when the transition was happening from black-and-white to colour – I can see why he chose black-and-white for a film like this because it is more real, more depressing, more stark, and thus suited the subject.'

Baharon Ke Sapne was a film close to Husain's heart. He had, after all, carried the story with him since his college days, a story that won an award too. After the many successful films that he had helmed as director, he felt that he could now risk an atypical subject. Film-maker Karan Johar, whose father, the producer Yash Johar, served as 'chief production secretary' on *Jab Pyar Kisise Hota Hai* and is seen for a passing moment as a hotel receptionist in that film,[11] echoed this. When I met Karan at his Dharma Productions office in early 2015, he remembered Husain telling his father over a meal that, 'his [Husain's] big passion was to make *Baharon Ke Sapne*'. Mansoor added, 'He was doing it with a different intention. He was trying to show that I can also make a thoughtful film.'

Husain affirmed this when he wrote, 'With *Baharon Ke Sapne*, I stand at the crossroads of my career. I have achieved unprecedented box-office success as a maker of escapist entertainment. *Baharon Ke Sapne* is altogether a new experiment for me. Whatever it may or may not be, I assert that it presents life in its barest and cruellest form. Whether it sets a trend for my future films depends on the verdict of the people.'[12]

---

[11] This is the scene when Sunder (Dev Anand) comes to the hotel where Nisha (Asha Parekh) is staying in Darjeeling and presents himself to the receptionist as Popat Lal.

[12] Nasir Husain, 'What the People Want', *Filmfare*, 4 August 1967, p. 33.

To be fair to Husain, the film broached several crucial social concerns. Besides raising the issue of using violence to achieve one's means, it also focused on the stark divide between the 'haves' and the 'have-nots'. The film had elements of Guru Dutt's *Pyaasa* in the subplot of the local prostitute, who is forced into becoming a sex worker due to circumstances. It is also an early precursor to Yash Chopra's *Kaala Patthar* (1979), with Rajesh Khanna donning Amitabh Bachchan's angst-ridden persona when he takes on the management on behalf of the workers.

There is a touch of *Naya Daur*, too, as the National Mills' manager (Prem Nath) makes a brutal case for mechanization and says how being old and weak is a curse in a mill whose machines are operated best by energetic, young hands. Husain's own concerns on employment after his graduation that he articulated to Nasreen Munni Kabir were at the heart of *Baharon Ke Sapne*'s premise. The mill manager extends the same rationale to Bhola Nath when he says, '*BA, BA, BA! Kya samajh rakha hai tumney BA pass ko? Yahaan hazaaron, laakhon BA pass jootiya chatkaatey phirtey hain. Woh zamaana gaya jab BA pass ki koi keemat thee. Aaj woh takey ser bikta hai. Bojha dhota hai sar pe. Rickshaa khenchta hai. Joota polish karta hai.* (BA, BA, BA! What do you think a BA is going to do? There are thousands of BAs doing menial jobs here. That era is gone when a BA had any value. Today it is worthless. They work as coolies. As rickshaw-pullers. They polish people's shoes.)'

The venerable Urdu progressive writer Rajinder Singh Bedi was enlisted to write the dialogues of the film. Bedi worked as writer on several landmark Hindi films (*Madhumati*, 1958, and *Satyakam*,[13] 1969, to name a few) before writing and directing

---

[13]This Hrishikesh Mukherjee film, too, appears to pay tribute to Gandhi, since it begins with a quote from the Mahatma. Interestingly, as author

(Contd...)

the critically acclaimed *Dastak* (1970), which incidentally is a monochrome film. *Baharon Ke Sapne*'s subject appealed to Bedi's progressive lineage. He took it as a compliment when Husain, a successful writer himself, asked Bedi to write the dialogues. Bedi wrote of Husain, 'Discussions followed and I found Nasir's was no mere doctrinaire understanding of the life of the poor and the downtrodden. He felt for the millworker, the petty shopkeeper, even the small town whore, and this lent reality to the life shown in *Baharon Ke Sapne*.'[14]

Bedi was equal to Husain's expectations, using a variety of writing styles ranging from satire (*'Kaisa sona ladka thaa, taaleem ne satyanaash kar diya'* – What a gem of a boy. Education ruined him), to poetic metaphors (*'Lachhu, yeh kaala aasmaan dekhta hai aur iss pe chamaktey huey taarey bhi? Aisa lagta hai ki jaise bhagwaan ne makhmal ka kaala libaas pehan rakha hai. Iss par taaron ke button lagey huey hain'* – Lachhu, can you see the black sky and the stars shining against it? It looks like God has worn a black velvet coat. The stars appear as buttons on the coat), to abject despondency (*'Main laash kaise ho gaya?'* – How did I turn into a living corpse), to articulate the politics of the film.

Joining ranks with Bedi was Majrooh Sultanpuri. *Baharon Ke Sapne* is the only Husain film that gave him the opportunity to showcase his progressive ideology and Majrooh didn't disappoint. His fine lyrics embellished RD's tunes, bringing out the hopelessness of Khanna's ambitions (in *'Zamaane ne maare jawaan kaise kaise'*):

(...contd.)

Jai Arjun Singh noted in his book on Mukherjee's cinema, *The World of Hrishikesh Mukherjee: The Filmmaker Everyone Loves*, the film was, 'not coincidentally I'm sure,' timed to release in Gandhi's birth centenary year, viz., 1969. Interestingly enough, *Satyakam*, arguably among Mukherjee's finest films, failed at the box office.

[14]Rajinder Singh Bedi, 'Nasir Husain and I', *Star & Style*, 1 August 1967.

Paley thay jo kal, rang mein, phool mein
Kahin kho gaye, raah ki dhool mein
Huey dar-ba-dar kaaravaan kaise-kaise

(They who were brought up with such love and care
Lie lost in the dust on the ground
How such caravans have lost their way)

But in keeping with the progressive ideology, Majrooh left Husain's
audience with hope (in '*Chunari sambhaal gori*'):

Pal chhin, piya pal chhin, ankhiyon ka andhera
Raina nahi apni, par apna hoga kal ka savera
Arrey, rain kaun si jo na dhal jaaye re

(Momentary is the darkness caused by blinking, my dear
The night may not be ours, but the dawn tomorrow will be
Which night doesn't come to an end?)

The other defining feature about *Baharon Ke Sapne* is the way
it highlights the secular element in Husain's cinema. Husain
consistently made secular references, either by incorporating some
character from the minority community or using some other
device (such as dialogues, disguise or song-writing) to establish
his egalitarian approach towards different religions.

In *Dil Deke Dekho*, Raja repairs the punctured tyre of Neeta's
car, but only after he has uttered the words, '*Bajrang bali ki jai. Ya
Maula kar madad!*' Sunil's best friend in *Pyar Ka Mausam* is Hamid
mian (Ram Avtar). In *Yaadon Ki Baaraat*, Shankar is inducted into
a life of crime by Usmaan bhai 'Baatliwala' (Ravinder Kapoor)
while Vijay's best friend is Salim (Jalal Agha), whose '*badey saley
bhai*' is 'Dr Munir Khan sa'ab'.

Similarly, Sharif mian (Amjad Khan) alias 'Sharafat Ali
Karamat Ali Salamat Ali Wajahat Ali' befriends Ravi in *Zamaane*

Ko Dikhana Hai. Not surprisingly, Raj and Shyam's (Raj Zutshi) best mates from college in *Qayamat Se Qayamat Tak*, with whom they regularly venture out on their 'shikaar' (hunting) trips, are Shahid and Hamid. Similarly, when Maqsood Ghoda (Aditya Lakhia) and Ghanshu (Deven Bhojani) spot Devika (Pooja Bedi) for the first time in *Jo Jeeta Wohi Sikandar*, their expressions are, '*Ya Allah! Ya Allah!*' and '*Har har Mahadev! Mahadev!*'

In *Caravan*, the song that introduces Mohan (Jeetendra) has a pundit and a maulvi face-off against each other before the last antara, with each one using his own religious incantation to assert himself over the other. But so dogged are they in their agenda that soon enough the pundit starts saying, '*Allah Allah Allah*' and the maulvi, '*Hari Hari Hari*'. This leads Mohan to sing (in the song '*Hum toh hain raahi dil ke*'):

> *Pundit Mullah daantey, par hum sab ka dukh baantey*
> *Saarey hain apney pyaarey, bolo kiska gala kaatey*
> *Ramu ya Ramjani, apni toh sabse yaari, arrey ho suno zara*

> (The pundit or the maulvi sermonize, but we share everyone's grief
> Everyone is dear to us, who do we kill
> Be it Ramu or Ramzani, we are friendly with everyone, hear what we say)

The depiction of characters from the minority community is an old ploy in Hindi cinema to broaden a film's appeal across ethnic and religious lines. As Jerry Pinto noted, 'If political secularism arises out of arithmetic, the secularism of cinema arises out of commerce.'[15] Several film-makers such as Guru Dutt, who cast the comedian Johnny Walker in films like *Mr. & Mrs. 55* and *Pyaasa* in such roles, lived out this axiom. Manmohan Desai went even

---

[15]Jerry Pinto, 'The Woman Who Could Not Care', *Helen: The Life and Times of an H-Bomb*, Penguin Books India, 2006, p. 51.

further as he foregrounded the different religious identities that contribute to the idea of India through his male protagonists, particularly in films like *Amar Akbar Anthony* (1977) and *Naseeb* (1981).

But unlike Desai, Husain's secularism was hardly conspicuous primarily because his secular references, whether in terms of character portrayals or dialogues, were mostly for comic purposes. In these lighter moments, it is easy to lose sight of the larger message that Husain was conveying. But the ease with which Ramesh (Dev Anand) turns into the old Wajahat Mirza and is able to rent Babu Digambernath's accommodation in *Paying Guest* or Raja (Shammi) is able to turn up as Mirza Changezi and is warmly welcomed by Neeta's father[16] into his house in *Dil Deke Dekho*, might offer a clue to the kind of India Nasir Husain dreamed of. The eminent journalist Siddharth Varadarajan even referred to the *Paying Guest* episode, saying, 'Seeing the film 52 [sic, 58] years later, one is struck by how improbable this scenario is in the urban India of today … If *Paying Guest* were remade today, a "Muslim" Dev Anand would have to knock on many, many Hindu doors in a city like Delhi or Mumbai in order to find a room for rent. Along the way, he would be told by prospective landlords that he can't be taken in because he may eat meat.'[17]

Baharon Ke Sapne, however, sees Husain make an emphatic secular declaration. In the film, we are introduced to John, the

---

[16]Neeta even tells her father that Mirza Changezi and his daughter will be staying at their house overnight, to which Jagat Narayan has no problem.

[17]Siddharth Varadarajan, 'Why can't Mr. Zaveri live where he wants?', *The Times of India*, 12 April 2015, http://timesofindia.indiatimes.com/home/sunday-times/all-that-matters/Why-cant-Mr-Zaveri-live-where-he-wants/articleshow/46893676.cms?utm_source=facebook.com&utm_medium=referral&utm_campaign=TOI

man who runs the illicit liquor den, where Ram turns up for his daily fix. The first time that Ram is seen drinking at this place is in the company of Lachhu (Anwar Husain). Right behind Ram's head one can see a crucifix. The significance of the crucifix, 'Father, forgive them for they know not what they do,' is clear. Later, when the police arrest John, Ram empathizes with a disconsolate Mary, John's niece. Ram's and Mary's names are enough of a marker to highlight Husain's agenda, but Husain goes the extra step. We hear Ram ask the girl, 'Mary, *tumhaara kya hoga?* (Mary, what will happen to you?),' to which Mary only points at her rosary. At this moment, church music starts playing in the background. Ram knows that all will be well. He puts his hand on Mary's shoulder, smiles and leaves her with the words, 'Okay Mary, bye!' It is a most tender scene, where the refuge Mary finds in her own faith, while being offered solace by someone from the majority community, emphasizes the secular idea of the Indian state.

'He was entirely secular,' said Nuzhat. 'He used to say, "I have a personal equation with God." He never talked about religion. He was never, "I'm a Muslim and a Muslim should do this." Every morning, he would say his namaaz once. Because he drank. He would say, "Under the influence of alcohol, you can't be saying your prayers. Early in the morning I am clean. At that time I can say my prayers." And he never missed that.' Mansoor agreed. 'He was not rubbing it in your face because his themes were not about that. But he found a certain warmth in showing these relationships which are subtle. He was very cosmopolitan in his views and not preachy. My mother was a Catholic. I have married a Catholic.'

Despite these touches, *Baharon Ke Sapne* performed below expectation. The reasons varied. The film, perhaps, broached one subject too many instead of focusing solely on one core theme. The climax, too, appears a never-ending one. Here, Ram's long, didactic sermonizing, while he is saving the mill from Das Kaka's attempts to burn it down and after he has been shot, goes against the serious, understated tone of the film. 'Mansoor and I always felt that he fluffed it at the end,' said Nuzhat.

Then there is the matter of bringing Geeta and Ram back to life in response to the audience's rejection of the film. Had Husain stuck to the original ending, perhaps, the film would have been viewed far more favourably today. Mansoor explained, 'In the film, Rajesh Khanna and Asha Parekh, their characters, die, which is the tragedy, which is the premise of the film. He should have had a little patience with the film. The right audience would find it eventually. It happens. They may find it ten years later. So many of Mehboob Khan's films or Raj Kapoor's films have found recognition years later. At that time, they would have been counted as failures. He went and shot that happy ending but it made no difference to the fate of the film.' Nuzhat agreed with her brother's assessment. 'We feel really bad that he felt the pressure to change it [the ending]. He lost his nerve.'

The other big factor at work was that Husain represented a certain brand of cinema in the audience's minds. The movie-going janta had come to the theatres, expecting frothy song and dance, experience the hill-station settings, the holiday romance, but *Baharon Ke Sapne* had none of Husain's standard tropes. The hero here didn't indulge in any theatrics while wooing the girl. Instead, he spent most of his time brooding and raging over his fate. In many ways, Ram was the complete antithesis to Husain's flamboyant hero from his earlier films. *Baharon Ke Sapne* was a tragic family drama, the very kind that Husain stayed away from.[18]

---

[18]*Baharon Ke Sapne* is one of the few Husain films which has both sets of parent figures for its protagonists.

Aamir mentioned an interesting episode to highlight the audience's dissonance: 'He used to go to the theatre to watch the audience's reaction. He told me that when he went to see *Baharon Ke Sapne*, he was in the men's room after the movie ended. He overheard one person telling another, "*Film achhee hai lekin Nasir Husain nahin hai ismein.* (The film is good but it lacks Nasir Husain's touch.)" He caught on to that line. He realized that his audience, after his first four films, expected a certain kind of cinema from him. And he didn't want to disappoint his audience. That is why he never attempted that kind of cinema – realistic, issue based – ever again.'

Kaushik Bhaumik elaborated. 'Cinema is like a contract of entering a fantasy world. You buy a ticket, you know that you are entering a space where extraordinary things will happen. The contract is something even Ashish Rajadhyaksha [author, film academician] talks about – that it is an actual contract between the film-maker and the audience, that you can't show me something that breaks the contract. Nasir Husain was connected in the audience's minds to a certain kind of spectacular entertainment, songs and scene-scenery and all that. Nobody would have accepted that kind of shift in registers. It's like Manmohan Desai turning around and doing some serious-realist cinema, which people wouldn't be able to digest.'

The tepid response to *Baharon Ke Sapne* affected Husain. Nuzhat remarked, 'He decided that he never wanted to make that kind of film again because it was not good business. He was very clear. That's the only film where he looked at such sombre topics so openly. He never said that he shouldn't have made the film. He never said he wished he had made it another way. I don't think he regretted the film, but he must have thought about what he had come to Bombay for. He decided that he was not going to express his more serious, political, cultural ideas in this forum.

Not that he didn't have them. In fact, I have a feeling that if it had done well, he might have been encouraged to do more of it.' Sulochana Latkar endorsed Nuzhat's thoughts. 'Had the film done well, he would have made more such films. Later, when people mentioned to him that he had made a beautiful film and why didn't he make more such films, he said that such films didn't do well, so what was the point?'

In the final analysis, *Baharon Ke Sapne* is an important film. The film holds its own for several different reasons discussed in this chapter. It is also a terrific example of the sometimes narrow prism through which film-makers are viewed – that because they represent a certain kind of cinema, they would almost definitely be incapable of representing any other kind of sensibility.

Mansoor has the last word. 'One day, when my mum was no more, Daddy was sitting alone and watching this film. It was on television. I was on my way out and then I started watching. I watched one scene, two scenes and then I got engrossed in it. I sat and watched it till the end. It was so engrossing that I forgot where I had to go. And then when it came to the end, it suddenly fell apart, with this patchy, sort of an apologetic end. I told my dad, "See, Daddy, had it ended the way you had originally written it [with the protagonists dying], what an impact [it would have made]." He agreed with me.'

8

COMEDY, COMPLICATED PLOTS AND SOME NASHA DAULAT KA

'If you don't have humour, you can't be a writer ... the more wicked you are, the better.'

– Film-maker and composer Vishal Bhardwaj[1]

'Nasir Husain brought in an element of playfulness in cinema that infected everything – from the way songs were sung, the kind of music that was there, the general attitude of people, comedians like Rajendra Nath – everybody was half an octave higher in Nasir Husain's movies. That is what makes his movies so delightful and different.'

– Author Raza Mir

Baharon Ke Sapne's disappointing reception possibly forced Husain to return to his usual 'formula' film, which is why he made *Pyar Ka Mausam* immediately afterwards. This was a rehashed version of Husain's initial directorial ventures, particularly *Jab Pyar Kisise Hota Hai*, but with the lost-and-found ingredient tossed in.

---

[1]From Pragya Tiwari's, editor-in-chief at The Big Indian Picture website, interview with Vishal Bhardwaj: (http://thebigindianpicture.com/2014/03/vishal-bhardwaj-tbip-tete-a-tete/)

Going by several accounts, Husain is said to have had quite a sense of humour. His actors and other crew members, invariably, remember him as a man who kept them all in good spirits with his witticism and ready repartee. The actor Jeetendra told me that during the *Caravan* shoot, there was a punctured-tyre scene. Jeetendra took a few seconds longer than usual to enact it. Husain's reaction to this was, 'Eh cut, cut … *Kya Jeetu kya kar raha hai tu? Tyre se poochh raha hai, kyun puncture hua hai?* (What are you doing, Jeetu? Are you asking the tyre why it has got punctured?)' Subhash Mukerji recalled, 'He once came to our house. We had two Spitz. One of them was Pixie. She used to bark a lot. He walked up and Pixie was barking. I said, "Pixie, shut up. Go inside." He looked at me and said, "We know barking dogs don't bite, but does the dog know it?"' Aamir mentioned that when he was younger, all the children from Husain's family and extended family would gather in Husain's bedroom and hang around there till late. While Husain always indulged them, when he finished dinner and wanted to sleep, he would signal for them to leave with his famous snarky words, '*Chaliye, badi khushi huyee aap logon se milkey.* (On your way now, it was a real pleasure meeting all of you.)'

This innate talent for a 'line-a-minute'[2] can be seen in Husain's work all through. His wisecracks could be sophisticated and satirical. Look at the *Teesri Manzil* scene where Sunita (Parekh) visits Park Hotel for the very first time with her friend, Meena. They run into Anil Kumar 'Sona', who starts chatting up both women. Meena warms up to the suave young man, but Sunita warns her not to engage with him:

> Sunita: *Eh Meena, inhe zyaada moonh lagaogi toh sar par chadh kar baith jaayengey.* (Meena, if you encourage him, he will sit on your head.)

---

[2] As Nuzhat described her father's sense of humour.

But Anil doesn't mind the barb. He replies with customary insouciance (and to Meena's delight) that he is not in the habit of sitting on heads and that his chair is perfectly comfortable.

Anil: *Meena ji, aap inki baat ka bilkul yakeen mat kijiye. Main jahaan bhi baitha hoon badey aaraam se baitha hoon. Aur sar par chadhney ki na toh meri aadat hai, na meri practice.*

But Husain could be cheesy and earthy with his humour, too. In an early scene in *Jo Jeeta Wohi Sikandar*, when the absolutely good-for-nothing Sanjay Lal Sharma a.k.a. Sanju (Aamir Khan) confronts his brother Ratan (Mamik) about switching his original mathematics examination answer papers that he had so diligently stolen, he vents at his brother. He tells him now he will be responsible for his misery ('*Ab main fail ho jaaoonga aur iske zimmedaar tum hogey*'). Ratan tries to impart a moral science lesson to his younger sibling but also ribs Sanju by continuously addressing him as 'Munna'. Unwilling to heed his brother's sermons and irked sufficiently by the constant '*Munna*' reference, Sanju finally blows his fuse. He says: '*Aur yeh kya Munna Munna laga rakha hai, Mr Tunna ... Haan, haan, tu toh imaandari ki top hai, Tunna. Mahatma Gandhi hai Tunna. Sarojini Naidu hai Tunna.*' (Why do you keep calling me Munna, Mr Tunna ... Yes, yes, you are the epitome of honesty, Tunna. You're Mahatma Gandhi, Tunna. You're Sarojini Naidu, Tunna.)

Needless to say, the humour does not translate well. What does Tunna mean? Nothing. It exists only because it rhymes with Munna. And because Hindi often uses nonsense rhyming words, this works in a way that you cannot imagine unless you read the words out loud or hear them on screen.

This rhyming wordplay was a distinctive element in Husain's comic arsenal. Although, the dialogues of *Munimji* aren't solely credited to Husain, we see examples of this kind of humour in the film. When Amar (Dev Anand) goes to look for Ratan (Pran), dressed as a hermit while riding an elephant, he is stopped by the police. In what is an early version of rap, Amar's plea to allow him to enter the jungle rests on a series of crisp rhymes:

> *Hajoor, haathi bhookh se **marey** hai*
> *Ghar mein hai thun-thun Gopal, socha jungle mein **charey** hai*
>   *toh **bachey** hain…*
> *Hajoor, jungle mein nahin **gaye** hain, toh haathi **marey** hai*
> *Gareeb ka haathi **marey** hai, toh gareeb kya **karey** hai?*

> (Sir, the elephant is starving.
> There's no food at home. I brought him to the jungle to eat…
> If he doesn't enter the jungle, he will die.
> What can a poor man do without his elephant?)

This is a recurring theme. In *Jab Pyar Kisise Hota Hai*, when Nisha (Parekh) meets the impostor Popat Lal (Dev Anand) for the first time, she is bowled over by his appearance. When Dev's character greets her with a 'Hello', Nisha, dazed by the sight of a man who belies her own expectations of him,[3] just mumbles, '*Mr Po-Po-Popat Lal.*' To this, Sunder responds, '*Iss mein bahut se po nahin, sirf ek po.* (There aren't so many Po's, just one Po in my name.)'

When Sunita in *Teesri Manzil* tells her friend Meena of her plan to get the girls' hockey team from her college to give Rocky a sound thrashing for his role in her sister's death, she enunciates her idea with a distinct lyrical meter:

> '*Rocky aur hockey*
> *Qaafia jama nahin?*'

> (Rocky and hockey,
> Don't they rhyme perfectly?)

---

[3]Nisha tells her friends that a man named Popat Lal would obviously be '*Rang kaala, kad chhota, tond kurtey ke baahar*'. (Dark complexioned, a midget and pot-bellied.)

In *Hum Kisise Kum Naheen*, when Kaajal realizes that Rishi Kapoor and not Tariq Khan is Manjeet, she gets upset. When Rishi Kapoor as Manjeet asks her whether she isn't happy to see him, she lies and says that she has a headache. To give her some relief, Rishi gets her a tablet, which he peddles in a most advertising jingle-like fashion:

'*Lijiye deviji, dard-e-sarr ke liye*
Hong Kong *ke mash-hoor doctor*
King Kong *ki woh goli hai jisey aadmi khaatey hi*
*bilkul **ping pong** bann jaata hai...*'
(Here, my lady, for your headache,
The acclaimed doctor from Hong Kong,
King Kong prescribes this pill, which makes a person
Bounce like a ping pong ball...)

Nuzhat explained that Husain often found great humour in sounds. 'He would do that even in personal life. In fact, he was so politically incorrect [laughs], like if there was a character called Jhunjhunwala in a film, he would say, "*Yeh jhunjhuna bajaata hai kya?*"[4] Mansoor and I used to cringe.' But perhaps more importantly, as Jerry Pinto observed, 'By skilfully inflecting these words, Husain pointed up a certain ridiculousness while the logic was impeccable. And this is how the hero would generally appeal to the world: clothed in humour, but invested with an impervious Edward Lear-like logic.'

It is possibly towards this end that Husain blended his liking for phonetic humour with the use of catchphrases. In *Dil Deke Dekho*, Neeta's father, Jagat Narayan (Raj Mehra), constantly uses 'Jolly good, jolly good' as some kind of a *taqia-kalaam*.[5] Subsequently,

---

[4]This means, 'Does he play the rattle', with Husain using the word 'jhunjhuna' to play on the name Jhunjhunwala.

[5]A catchphrase or an expression which is used very frequently by its speaker.

Mirza Changezi mocks Jagat Narayan for this idiosyncrasy by responding to everything he says with 'Hollywood, Hollywood'. In *Qayamat Se Qayamat Tak*, when Raj (Aamir) and his cousin Shyam (Raj Zutshi) are sent to Dhanakpur to represent their family in the court proceedings against Randhir Singh (Goga Kapoor), their lawyer (Ajit Vachhani) uses 'fataafat' every other word. This is a clever repetition of an earlier episode from *Pyar Ka Mausam*, where Sardar Ranjit Kumar (Wasti) is told of Seema's betrothal to a character named 'Jhatpat' Singh and the subsequent wordplay that happens around the word 'jhatpat'.

'He loved taqia-kalaams,' said Aamir, laughing. 'He was fond of writing these humorous characters. So even if it's a small part like in *Qayamat Se Qayamat Tak*, the lawyer's role is hardly one scene, but he gave him a taqia-kalaam and also made him eat paan. So each time he said "fataafat", he would spray us with the paan spittle. In that short scene, he wanted to make the character quirky. He used to embellish his film with these things.'

Entwined with the catchphrases were Husain's attempts at lampooning English-speaking characters. So the Colonel Sa'ab (S.L. Puri) in *Tumsa Nahin Dekha*, at whose house Shankar and Meena spend the night when their tonga crashes en route to Soona Nagar, is caricatured by his constant use of the phrase 'my foot'. Husain revisited this figure and presented him as Colonel I.M. Tipsee (Om Shivpuri) in *Zamaane Ko Dikhana Hai*, whose pet expression is 'Jolly good, my foot'. While Husain's wordplay on 'I.M. Tipsee' isn't to be missed, such instances may be seen as poking fun at the remnants of the British raj in quintessential '*Angrez chale gaye, inhe chhod gaye*' (the British have gone but have left their offspring behind) style. Hindi cinema often had this caricature-oriented relationship with such emblems of colonial rule. The actor Asrani's cameo in *Sholay* (1975), with his trademark line '*Hum Angrezon ke zamaane ke jailor hain*' (I am a jailor from British times) and the background score (an instrumental rendition of '*For he's a jolly good fellow*') that plays out the first time he is seen in the film, is a perfect example of this. At the same time, Husain also delighted in the trials of the aspirational class, who saw English as a language of social mobility. In *Caravan*, Mohan (Jeetendra) is seen making a fool of himself using words and phrases like 'untoocation' (for education), and '*Shame not coming you me?*' (meaning, aren't you ashamed of yourself?). Mohan's character, possibly, resonated with a section of the English-educated Indian elite, who sniggered at the attempts of the lower middle class to attain class equality merely by learning English.

A concise summary of all this can be seen in one of the scenes towards the end of *Phir Wohi Dil Laya Hoon*. Here, Difu (Rajendra Nath) smokes a pipe and repeatedly responds to Colonel Mahendranath's comments with a rather imperial, 'I see'. Difu then blunders his way through the conversation, pronouncing and spelling words like 'position' as 'p-o-t-o-n', 'repeat' as 'r-e-p-a-tey-e' and 'compliment' as 'c-o-m-p-a-n-tey-e' before finally leaving the colonel in splits with the question, 'Don't you know English?'

Disguise and impersonation was another source of humour in Husain's films. One part of this was situational comedy, a popular trope in Hindi cinema, 'in which a character is suddenly placed in a strange situation, where he is uncomfortable because he is unsure of the "rules of behaviour". The classic scene in Hindi films is that of the mistaken identity.'[6] We see this kind of humour in *Caravan* where Mohan thinks Soni is an ordinary village belle and wishes to

[6]Sanjit Narwekar, 'Prologue', *Eena Meena Deeka: The Story of Hindi Film Comedy*, Rupa & Co., 2005, p. ix.

marry someone more educated than her. It's only later in the film that a longish rant in English by Soni leaves Mohan dumbstruck and shakes him out of his misconceptions. Similarly, in *Qayamat Se Qayamat Tak*, Raj being mistaken for Roop Singh (Rashmi's fiancé-to-be) in Dhanakpur at Rashmi's birthday celebrations is also an example of this situational comedy.

What is significant is that Husain actually invoked a certain Wodehousian world, possibly as homage to one of his favourite writers, through disguise and impersonation. Be it Professor Samri of *Dil Deke Dekho* or Sunder impersonating Popat Lal in *Jab Pyar Kisise Hota Hai*, the shenanigans of these characters delighted the audience. In *Dil Deke Dekho,* when Professor Samri lands up at Nisha's house as Mirza Changezi, what follows is a series of misconceptions, mix-ups and confusions deliberately created to suit the interest of one character, namely Raja (or Samri or Changezi). The entire drama appears scripted from a P.G. Wodehouse novella as Changezi engineers a series of deceptions to upset Jagat Narayan and put down Neeta's prospective suitors (Kailash and Chandra), even as the background score reaffirms this sequence as an absurdly comic one.

Another Wodehousian episode plays out for far longer in *Zamaane Ko Dikhana Hai.* Here, Ravi (Rishi Kapoor) is interested in romancing Kanchan (Padmini Kolhapure). But Kanchan is not keen on their relationship and begins to avoid him. She leads Ravi to believe that she is actually Colonel Tipsee's daughter. Also, to make ends meet, Kanchan disguises herself as a young boy and takes up a job as a Nepali caddy, Bahadur Singh, at the very hotel that Ravi is staying in. The interactions that follow between Ravi and Bahadur Singh are hilarious. Ravi, unaware of who Bahadur Singh actually is, treats him like his man Friday. He calls Bahadur Singh his 'bosom friend' and displays his affection towards him in the most intimate ways, by often kissing and hugging him.

However, Colonel Tipsee's wife, a coquettish woman, is also named Kanchan. She believes herself to be the Kanchan Ravi is looking for. She calls Ravi and plans to meet him on the sly. Ravi gets excited that he will finally meet Kanchan, the girl he thinks to be Kolhapure, after a long time. But Kolhapure as Bahadur Singh takes advantage of the misconception between the two and lands Ravi in hot water with Colonel Tipsee for chasing his wife. The cigar-smoking Colonel Tipsee, who speaks in a distinctly sonorous Anglicized accent while raging at Ravi with his usual 'Jolly good, my foot' rant, invokes a character who could have only been from a Wodehousian universe.

According to Doraiswamy, 'Masquerade, that's an essential part of his stories. That you pretend to be somebody else. You can masquerade because you're a spy, but that would be more of a thriller thing. But if you are just masquerading to fool the person you love, it's more innocent and that is extremely Wodehousian.'

Subodh Mukerji, director of *Munimji* and *Paying Guest*, which Husain wrote, remained a regular figure of humour in these films. This was possibly some kind of inside joke since Husain had used this trope in an earlier film, *Love Marriage* (also directed by Subodh Mukerji), where he was the sole dialogue writer. Here, when Sunil's (Dev Anand) boss enquires about their company's bowling attack for their friendly cricket fixture, a third person replies, '*Spinners mein Shankar hai, Jaikishan hai aur pace bowling mein Nayyar* (The spinners are Shankar, Jaikishan and the pace bowler is Nayyar)', a clear reference to the famed composers Shankar–Jaikishan and O.P. Nayyar.

Husain's caricaturing of Subodh Mukerji, though, was more in the nature of him getting back good-naturedly at the latter for invariably coming up trumps in their tennis matches in real life.

After presenting him as an alibi for Sunder's acquittal in the case of Shanti's (Nisha's friend) murder in *Jab Pyar Kisise Hota Hai*, Husain portrayed Subodh Mukerji as a villainous character in *Phir Wohi Dil Laya Hoon*. He is the doctor who collaborates in the plan to pass Ramesh (Pran) off as Colonel Mahendranath's son, Mohan. In *Pyar Ka Mausam*, too, the character at the Rainbow Club, who first gets Seema drunk and then tries to take advantage of her, is also named Subodh Mukerji.

But from *Caravan* onwards, Subodh Mukerji becomes a tennis racquet-wielding character, who swings the racquet around madly, like a fly swatter. In that film, he is 'Subodh Mukerji *theatrewallah*' for whom Mohan and Soni present '*Daiyya yeh main kahaan aa phansi*'. When Madan Puri's character in the film first refers to him as '*Jhansi ka rehney waala hai*' (He is a native of Jhansi), Husain resorted to his fondness for phonetic humour and lampooned Mukerji, with Mohan quipping, '*Jhaansa dene aaya thaa kya?* (Had he come to swindle[7] us?)' In *Hum Kisise Kum Naheen*, there is Colonel Subodh Mukerji, to whose house Sanjay leads Kaajal's bodyguards and has the colonel believe that they are there to rob his house instead. A Subodh Mukerji character features in *Zamaane Ko Dikhana Hai* and *Manzil Manzil* as well.

'They were buddies. They used to play tennis every single day in the morning at Khar Gymkhana,' Nuzhat said. 'Subodh Mukerji was a [tennis] fanatic. After that [*Love Marriage*], they never collaborated on a film, but they had that connection every single day.' Subhash Mukerji chimed in on Husain's portrayal of his father. 'He [Subodh Mukerji] was lucky for him. And he used to present Baba as complete opposite of what he was in real life.

---

[7]While the word 'jhaansa' translates 'to swindle', Husain was punning on the word Jhansi, the name of the place the Subodh Mukerji character is said to belong to in the film. Subodh Mukerji actually belonged to Jhansi.

He used to make a caricature of what Baba was ... He [Husain] used to wear two knee supports, elbow supports. He would tell Baba, "*Aaj Asha* [Ayesha Khan] *dekh rahi thee jab main yeh pehan raha thaa, apne pair aur haath par sab laga raha thaa. Keh rahi thee iska ek suit banwa lo na. Aasaan rahega.* (Asha was watching me wear all this, on my knees and elbows. She said, why don't you make a suit out of this? It would just be convenient.)" He was not a very good tennis player. He wasn't a sportsman basically.'

The one time that the Mukerjis struck back was in *Abhinetri* (1970). They presented a character in the garb of a tiger, who introduces himself as '*Main Nasir Husain behrupiya hoon*'. (I am Nasir Husain, the impersonator.) 'How could he object, after all that he had done to my dad?' asked Subhash.

Beginning, with *Dil Deke Dekho*, where he starred as Kailash (Harichand's son), Rajendra Nath appeared in every one of the films directed by Nasir Husain right up to *Pyar Ka Mausam* (1969). His last appearance in a Nasir Husain film was in *Zabardast*. Rajendra Nath's presence once again highlighted the feudal nature of the Bombay film industry. He was the actor Prem Nath's brother and since their sister, Krishna, was married to Raj Kapoor, they had very close ties with the Kapoor family as well. Rajendra Nath worked on the stage at Prithvi theatres. Although he had done a few films before, one of his earliest comic roles was in *Hum Sab Chor Hain*, which also featured Shammi Kapoor. 'They were great friends, Shammi and Rajendra Nath. Every Shammi Kapoor film had Rajendra Nath,' commented Rauf Ahmed, which probably explained Rajendra Nath's coming into Husain's *Dil Deke Dekho*.

Although Rajendra Nath does provide a few laughs in *Dil Deke Dekho*, it is as Popat Lal in *Jab Pyar Kisise Hota Hai* that the actor hit the big league. Asha Parekh revealed how Husain hit upon the idea for the character's name. 'Oh my God, that's a very funny story. You see, my jeweller's name was Chimanlal Popat Lal. I must have said it two or three times, "We went to Chimanlal Popat Lal. We went to Chimanlal Popat Lal." That name came from there.'

The first sight of Popat Lal in *Jab Pyar Kisise Hota Hai* has him dressed in a floral nightie and wearing a ladies' hat. Speaking in an exaggerated, 'loud' tone, Popat Lal indulges in all kinds of histrionics, with his burlesque routines. The character was a big hit. Sanjit Narwekar named Popat Lal as one of the '10 mad characters we would like to meet in real life'. He wrote of him, 'A character given to wearing "nighties" and other outlandish costumes, he is obviously modelled on Lou Costello, complete with the pantomime walk and puppet-like gestures. Neither the fans nor the producers allowed Rajendra Nath to get out of his character all through his screen life.'[8]

Narwekar hits the nail on the head. The Popat Lal that we see in *Jab Pyar Kisise Hota Hai* isn't very different from the characters played by Rajendra Nath in *Phir Wohi Dil Laya Hoon* and *Pyar Ka Mausam* (or in other non-Husain films). In *Jab Pyar Kisise Hota Hai*, for instance, he establishes a comic routine which is repeated in *Pyar Ka Mausam*. While in the former, Popat Lal keeps calling out for his 'secretary', in *Pyar Ka Mausam*, there is an inversion of this theme as here it is the secretary, played by R.D. Burman, who responds to everything Jhatpat Singh says with 'very true'. This, according to Narwekar, illustrated a kind of comedy seen in Hindi cinema where 'the concentration has always been on the gag-related comedy in which a kind of visual (and often a verbal ad-libbing) routine is developed between the hero and his comic sidekick (all through the 1950s and 1960s) or two comedians

---

[8]Sanjit Narwekar, 'Appendix 2', *Eena Meena Deeka: The Story of Hindi Film Comedy*, Rupa & Co., 2005, p. 296.

who are woven into the story for comic relief and generally have a separate track unrelated to the main story'.[9]

The characters played by Rajendra Nath in Husain's films, be it Kailash or Popat Lal or Difu, always found themselves at the receiving end of the heroine's ire. She would either openly fire her verbal salvos at him – 'You are a fool' (*Dil Deke Dekho*), 'You clumsy goat' (*Jab Pyar Kisise Hota Hai*) – or push him around quite literally in films like *Jab Pyar Kisise Hota Hai* and *Phir Wohi Dil Laya Hoon*. Dressed in nighties, shorts and vests, the bumbling, animated Rajendra Nath stands out in stark contrast to Husain's self-assured, confident hero. Jerry Pinto summarized these presentations of Rajendra Nath as 'Freudian shorthand for the underdeveloped male' and not very dissimilar from how comedians in this time were made to dress: 'heightened colours, shorts, knickerbockers, all associated with childhood'. Pinto stated that these presentations of Rajendra Nath, like any sidekick's, were meant to 'underscore the hero's masculinity with his own inadequacies'.[10]

The larger point about Rajendra Nath's characterization is that it meshed well with Husain's cinema. The now defunct website 'passionforcinema' noted on Rajendra Nath's passing, 'Probably the first actor in Hindi cinema to bring physical energy into straightforward comedy where the laughter came in from his bending those funny knees a few inches, making tight fists, bending in elbows as if he was gonna [sic] throw in a few wild punches...'[11] This physicality was on view pretty much everywhere in Husain's films.

---

[9]Ibid., 'Prologue', pp. viii-ix.

[10]Jerry Pinto, 'The Comic Comes Courting', *Helen: The Life and Times of an H-Bomb*, Penguin Books India, 2006, pp. 135, 139, 144.

[11]'Farewell Rajendra Nath: Laughter has left the building': (https://archive.is/KeuMK#selection-775.0-775.255)

Be it Shammi Kapoor's or Rishi Kapoor's characterizations; the exchange between Meena and Shankar in *Tumsa Nahin Dekha* when they threaten each other, wooden logs in hand, while dressed in bed linen; the Chaplinesque routines such as when Raja changes the punctured tyre in *Dil Deke Dekho*; Sunder and Nisha laughing hysterically after eating the spiked laddoos in *Jab Pyar Kisise Hota Hai*; the pie fights at the clubs in *Jab Pyar Kisise Hota Hai* and *Pyar Ka Mausam*; the jokes over 'fatness' (often centred around the rotund figure of Ram Avtar such as at the beginning of *Teesri Manzil*); the fuming colonels of *Tumsa Nahin Dekha* and *Zamaane Ko Dikhana Hai*; the automobile-ignition-like-sound made by Mona's friend (Tabassum) all through *Phir Wohi Dil Laya Hoon*; the bald, marching bodyguards and their '*jamaal gota*' episode in *Hum Kisise Kum Naheen*; the Subodh Mukerji character's fly-swatting mannerisms or the use of disguise leading to dramatic change in physical appearance and resulting in exaggerated characterizations such as Wajahat Mirza, Professor Samri, Mirza Changezi or Bahadur Singh – physicality was at the core of Husain's brand of comedy.

Seen against these visuals, Rajendra Nath being kicked by a donkey, sitting on a piece of cake, his bizarre attire, stuffing himself with food and burping, falling over in a pond while in a jeep, fleeing Chaplin-like with his secretary in *Jab Pyar Kisise Hota Hai* and in *Pyar Ka Mausam*, appear entirely consistent with the comic quotient in Husain's film universe. Wondering if Husain had been inspired by the West in this regard, Madhulika Liddle wrote, 'There was the pie-in-your-face sort of slapstick comedy that was fairly popular in Hollywood in the 1940s and 1950s, which I think does find an echo in some of the antics we see in Husain's films.'

A lot of this slapstick humour is regressive and politically incorrect. The jokes about fat people or the racial stereotypes like every other girl in Darjeeling being named 'Kanchan' in *Zamaane Ko Dikhana Hai* do not hold up well. However, he wasn't the only one to do this. Many actors made their careers out of playing fat foolish characters. A fat woman lusting after the hero who would be unavailable to her, a fat man tripping and falling over were par for the course in many films of the 1960s and '70s. The problem is that Husain didn't need to do this. He had other ways to be funny, a rare appreciation of what pure language could do. Here he was stooping to conquer.

Among the more prevalent theories advanced for the popularity of Husain's brand of comedy is that audiences back then weren't nearly as sophisticated as the ones today. At the same time, these people also reflect back at the films and songs of 1950s and 1960s with a certain avuncular fondness. They suggest that the kind of cinema and literary song-writing in that era was precisely because people had a far more evolved sensibility. The inherent contradiction in these views leads to the conclusion that not much has changed between how Hindi cinema was received by audiences 'then' and 'now'. There is a certain delight that audiences have always taken in bodily humour (*Delhi Belly*, 2011; *Piku*, 2015), the faux angrezi-speaking-desi (*Namak Halaal*, 1982; *Bol Bachchan*, 2012) and slapstick (any one of Rohit Shetty's films). The success of television's *Comedy Nights with Kapil* among India's great middle class is proof of all these elements still being celebrated.

The only conclusion one can draw is that Husain had mastered the science of handling these comic overindulgences in his cinema. They did not jar with the overall tonality of his films, which as Raza Mir noted, was 'half an octave' higher all through. Bhaumik aptly remarked, 'What I really like about him is a certain raw energy that he brings into his films ... And the fact that he can balance that excess. He somehow manages to integrate that energy in a very sophisticated urban manner, which is a remarkable feat.'

Moreover, as Jai Arjun Singh observed, humour, be it of any kind, is important. 'We are creatures of many moods, all of us. Some of us don't acknowledge this. Some of us like to think that we are only the sort of people who appreciate sophisticated, subtle humour. There are many people like that. Many critics, many middle-brow people, but to me at least, the human personality is such that, generally speaking, humour is one of the most important things in life. And the human personality is such that you are in a particular mood on one day, you will be in the mood for some really delicate, really sharp, subtle Woody Allen-like humour, which is very sophisticated wordplay. Another day, your synapses might be working in such a way that the only thing that can work for you is David Dhawan humour. And yet another day, you could be in the mood for something completely different. And I really feel that all of these serve their own unique functions.'

Husain, with his wordplay, his general wit, which could be sharp as well as wry, and his Rajendra Nath characterizations served every one of the many human moods.

The Rajendra Nath character in Husain's films, while comic, always had a materialistic agenda. In *Dil Deke Dekho* and *Phir Wohi Dil Laya Hoon*, he is presented as a possible suitor to Parekh's character, but is ultimately bought over after he has been assured of half of Jamuna Devi's property in the former and given a handsome cheque by Colonel Mahendranath in the latter. In *Jab Pyar Kisise Hota Hai* and *Pyar Ka Mausam*, he claims to be Popat Lal and Jhatpat Singh so that he can cheat Sardar Roop Singh and Sardar Ranjit Kumar of some money. But his plans go completely awry as he and his secretary are exposed in both films.

These Popat Lal/Jhatpat Singh impersonations again invoke a

certain Wodehousian feel, where characters present themselves as someone else for all kinds of devilish purposes but not for anything really evil. It also leads one to the broader point that nothing is really straightforward in Husain's films. If mathematics tells us that the shortest distance between two points is a straight line, Husain always took the most circuitous route to bridge the gap between starting point and finish. His plots use several classic elements – crime, separation, suspense, romance, song-and-dance and humour – to get to the resolution.

Look at *Dil Deke Dekho*, for instance. The backstory that unfolds at the beginning is so complicated that it takes at least a few viewings before one can get around the twisted plot. In the opening scene of the film, Harichand (Wasti) has driven down to Nagina's (Indira Billi) house where he tells her that he has hit upon a novel plan to create acrimony between Rana Raghuvir (Surendra) and his wife, Jamuna Devi (Sulochana Latkar). A stranger who had come to visit Harichand for a job the previous night had a heart attack and died. Since this person resembles Harichand in height and build, Harichand plans to pass off this man as himself. After shooting the dead man through his face so that it is completely disfigured, Harichand leaves a letter, addressed to Jamuna Devi, on this dead man's person. The letter suggests that Harichand has committed suicide because he and Jamuna were having an affair. Harichand's letter hits its mark as Rana Raghuvir leaves his wife, convinced that Harichand's son, Kailash, is Jamuna's son from her affair with Harichand.

Harichand explains to Nagina that he has engineered these circumstances to get even with Rana Raghuvir. When Harichand lost his wife, from whom he had his son, Kailash, Jamuna had not yet been married. Harichand had developed a liking for Jamuna and was hoping to marry her. But then Rana entered Jamuna's life. The two fell in love and got married. Then Nagina came into

Harichand's life and just as he was beginning to get over his failed romance with Jamuna, Nagina, too, became besotted by Rana. Unwilling to let Rana Raghuvir steal his lady love a second time round, Harichand stages this diabolic scheme to indict Jamuna and ruin her marriage with Rana. Harichand also has the added incentive that his son Kailash, whom he has asked Jamuna to look after through the suicide note, will inherit all of Jamuna Devi's property once her marriage with Rana Raghuvir breaks up. So convoluted is the plan that when Harichand first reveals it to Nagina, he even warns her, '*Badi gehri chaal hai. Zara gaur se suno*! (It's a very complicated plan. Listen carefully).' Because of Harichand's actions, Rana walks out on Jamuna with his son Roop (whom he later starts addressing as Raja), while Harichand makes his way to Rangoon with Nagina from whom he has another son, Sohan. This sets the stage for *Dil Deke Dekho*'s lost-and-found story.

Consider *Hum Kisise Kum Naheen* as well. Here Saudagar Singh (Amjad Khan) puts on a disguise and convinces Rajesh (Rishi Kapoor) of how Kishori Lal (Kamal Kapoor) has the diamonds that Rajesh's father had hoped to pass on to him. Saudagar Singh also shows Rajesh a letter, which suggests that Saudagar Singh's son is being held captive by Kishori Lal for a ransom of rupees thirty lakhs. Instead of approaching their common enemy directly, Rajesh then comes up with a most complex plan. He tells Saudagar Singh that instead of brazenly kidnapping Kishori Lal's daughter, he will win her over with his charm. Once this happens, they will hold her captive and get what is due to them from Kishori Lal. Why Saudagar Singh, a hardened criminal, does not engage with Kishori Lal directly is a moot point. Entwined within this broad storyline is Sanjay's childhood romance with Kaajal and how their paths eventually converge.

'I think misunderstanding and impersonation are very exciting,' remarked Mansoor on his father's attempts of concocting the dramatic mixture. 'Yes, these things were deliberately interlinked because one plot element by itself is not impactful enough ... You need crime, impersonation, the hero's search for his parents, etc. He wove these things together.' Madhulika added, 'I think Husain's preference for complicated plots was another reflection of his penchant for masala films – a complex plot allowed you to weave in lots of romance, drama, comedy, crime, song-and-dance, etc., in a fairly plausible way.' Aamir endorsed this view, saying, 'I think he believed in putting all these elements in his films. He liked to make his films thick with various themes and various tracks going on.'

The plots of *Dil Deke Dekho* and *Hum Kisise Kum Naheen* bring to the fore one of Husain's pet devices, the letter. In film after film, Husain used the letter for a variety of purposes – to help the villain in his crafty plan of presenting himself as the lost son (*Tumsa Nahin Dekha, Dil Deke Dekho, Pyar Ka Mausam*), to create drama (*Dil Deke Dekho, Teesri Manzil, Hum Kisise Kum Naheen*), for confession (*Teesri Manzil*), as incriminating evidence of a murder (*Jab Pyar Kisise Hota Hai, Caravan*), as proof of resignation (*Dil Deke Dekho*), employment (*Jab Pyar Kisise Hota Hai*), for trickery (*Dil Deke Dekho, Teesri Manzil, Pyar Ka Mausam*), to blackmail (*Yaadon Ki Baaraat*) or simply to communicate (*Pyar Ka Mausam, Yaadon Ki Baaraat, Qayamat Se Qayamat Tak*). While the use of a letter in Hindi cinema isn't a novel phenomenon, the fact that letters changed hands repeatedly all through a Husain film make them a fascinating plot device. And these weren't necessarily letters that made use of the postal service, but '*aisey hi haath se aa jaatey thay* (they would be delivered by hand),' Mansoor chuckled and said. 'Like internal mail.'

While these letters worked towards various ends, perhaps the most important aspect was to make the audience a part of the story even while the story worked itself to the point where the audience waited to see how the contents of the letter would be received. A good example of this is *Teesri Manzil*, where Rocky, in order to reveal everything about himself to Sunita, writes her a letter. The contents of the letter are revealed to the audience even before it reaches Sunita. The gist of it is that on reading the letter, if Sunita turns up for Rocky's performance in the evening, Rocky will think she has forgiven him. If she doesn't turn up, it will be his death. Rocky gives the letter to Datta (Rashid Khan) and asks him not to give it to anyone else but Sunita. Datta, instead, takes the letter to Ruby (Helen) and reads it out to her. On Ruby's instructions, Datta delivers the letter to Sunita, but only after she has come for the 'Yaum-e-Azaadi' celebrations, just as Rocky's performance is about to begin. While Sunita is devastated at Rocky's revelations, Rocky thinks that she has forgiven him. The next five minutes then hinge on how Sunita will react once Rocky has finished singing '*Tumne mujhe dekha*' and the two come face-to-face.

Mansoor offered a brief explanation on Husain's use of the letter. 'It's more dramatic than a scene because it breaks the moment. It creates a little bit of a rift in time between when she knows what has happened and he is still singing the song … When you write in films, you are trying to make your plot work. You use whatever devices you can. This was a very convenient device, maybe it fit very well into the genre that my dad was exploring and he used it to its fullest.'

M.K. Raghavendra volunteered a similar opinion. 'This is a device not specifically from Indian cinema. The advantage of using a letter or a messenger as a way of communication is that it allows for miscommunication in a way that an actual physical confrontation would not. Another way is to use an object, which is given a wrong significance by someone. The miscommunication is a way of creating problems/complications required for the plot to be finally resolved and such complications are crucial to melodramas. If I'm not mistaken, Shakespeare often used the letter or the messenger to create misunderstandings between characters in his plots. A letter arrives at the wrong moment or a messenger arrives too late. In *Othello*, a handkerchief causes a misunderstanding. In *Sangam* [1964], Sunder [Raj Kapoor] misunderstands a letter written by Gopal [Rajendra Kumar] to Radha [Vyjayanthimala] when Sunder was presumed killed in war. It is obvious that directors rely on favourite devices in their films – as Hitchcock used the "MacGuffin". A newspaper announcement could serve another purpose, which is due to its impersonality. Two people far apart would receive the same communication and simultaneously plan courses of action, which come into conflict later.'

The last part of Raghavendra's comments are corroborated in films like *Tumsa Nahin Dekha*, *Phir Wohi Dil Laya Hoon* and *Zabardast*, where Husain used newspaper advertisements to disseminate information and build up drama. In *Manzil Manzil*, Malhotra (Kulbhushan Kharbanda) hands over his cigarette case, inscribed with the words, 'I owe you ten lacs. Malhotra,' to his friend Gautam (Danny Denzongpa). It is this cigarette case which is used by the villain later in the film, to present an impostor to Malhotra.

One final, near omnipresent element in Husain's cinema is class conflict. (His entire repertoire of English-language jokes can be read in this way as a marker between the haves and the have-nots.) Generally, whenever the hero disguises himself, it is for the purpose of advancing his social status. It is for this reason that Sunder in *Jab Pyar Kisise Hota Hai* becomes Popat Lal. He claims to have returned from England and presents himself as Seth Mafatlal's son to Nisha. Mohan (Joy Mukerji) does something similar when he presents himself as Difu's London-returned friend in *Phir Wohi Dil Laya Hoon*. Rocky in *Teesri Manzil* becomes Anil Kumar Sona, '*Bhagwan Das crorepati ka beta*' (Bhagwan Das crorepati's son) and Vijay turns into Kunwar Vijay Kumar in *Yaadon Ki Baaraat*.

Once the hero's disguise is blown, he no longer belongs to the same elite, privileged class as the heroine but still remains educated and middle class. Javed Akhtar opined, 'But class conflict was also backlit. It was not real because the hero, who was supposed to be poorer than the heroine's father, was also an extremely well-dressed person. It is not that he was living in a slum.' Additionally, with the happy ending in Husain's films, the hero ends up rich when recognized as heir to the estranged parent figure's fortune. Consequently, the romance that plays out in Husain's films isn't of the 'man-on-the-street-meets-the-Duchess-of-Kent' kind or between the local village rustic who charms the Anglophone, patrician girl from the city a la *Jab Jab Phool Khile* (1965).

Madhulika observed, 'I actually prefer this style over the "diametrically opposite" hero–heroine of films like *Nadiya Ke Paar* [1948], *Geet* [1970], *Kanyadaan* [1968], *Himalaya Ki God Mein* [1965], *Madhumati* [1958], etc. – mainly because I find it hard to believe that two people of such widely differing upbringings, beliefs, etc., could find enough common ground to fall so wildly in love. Always a little hard to swallow for me. This is why I find it easier to accept Husain's less stark contrasts. I believe they're more realistic; the fact that a Shammi Kapoor of *Tumsa Nahin Dekha* or *Dil Deke Dekho*, or a Joy Mukerji of *Phir Wohi Dil Laaya Hoon*, while not very wealthy, is educated, urban and urbane, puts him on a much more equal footing with a sophisticated Ameeta or Asha Parekh, respectively. It becomes easier to understand why this woman would fall for a man who isn't as wealthy as her, but would appeal to the values/style/upbringing she's familiar with.'

However, before the hero's true antecedents are established, his lower social status invariably riles up the heroine's guardian figure. This elder person takes it upon himself/herself to remind the hero of his place on the social ladder. Consequently, Raja in *Dil Deke Dekho* is warned by Jamuna Devi about his dalliance with 'Miss' Neeta. '*Woh is hotel ki maalik hain,*' she says. '*Aur tum uskey mulaazim. Woh tumhaarey barabari ki nahin.* (She is the owner of this hotel and you her employee. You are not her equal.)' Colonel Mahendranath, similarly, in *Phir Wohi Dil Laya Hoon* isn't surprised by Mohan's temerity when he tries to buy him off. He blames it on Mohan's DNA ('*tumhaara kasoor nahin, tumhaarey khoon ka hai*'). S.K. Nanda (Shriram Lagoo) in *Zamaane Ko Dikhana Hai*, likewise, is unhappy with his son Ramesh's (Randhir Kapoor) marriage to a girl from a lower social background because, embittered by his father's experience, he believes all such women to be gold-diggers. In *Jab Pyar Kisise Hota Hai*, Sunder implores Sardar Roop Singh to allow Nisha to marry him because Roop Singh was also once poor.

Often, the hero or his father are disgraced for such temerity. In *Pyar Ka Mausam*, Sardar Ranjit Kumar humiliates Sunil for entertaining the idea of romancing Seema. He dismisses him from the job, but only after Sunil has entertained Sardar sa'ab's guests with a song at the engagement celebrations of Seema and the impostor Sunder. Things get a little more confrontational in *Hum Kisise Kum Naheen*. Here, the now wealthy industrialist Kishori Lal brazenly reneges on his promise to Ram Kumar (Om Shivpuri) of Kaajal marrying Sanjay since circumstances have changed. '*Lekin woh waqt aur thaa, yeh aur hai* (That was then, this is now),' he tells Ram Kumar. There is also a suggestion that Rajesh's romance with Sunita doesn't meet with her father's approval because Rajesh's family has fallen on hard times. A rare exception is *Yaadon Ki Baaraat* where Sunita's father tells her that he may be wealthy, '*magar woh baap nahin jo apni aulaad ke sukh aur chain ka sauda soney chaandi ki taraazu se karta ho* (but I am not a father who mortgages his daughter's peace and happiness for gold and silver)'. But by the time Sunita's father's says this, Vijay has made his exit, believing himself to be unequal to Sunita's elite status.

In *Hum Kisise Kum Naheen*, Sanjay, who presents himself as Manjeet to Kaajal initially, taunts her later for rejecting his affections because of his lower social status. This comes to the fore in at least two of the songs sung by Sanjay in the film. The first is in the medley sequence where Sanjay responds to Manjeet's '*Aa dil kya mehfil hai tere*' with '*Tum kya jaano*'. As part of this musical composition, Sanjay makes his case to Kaajal:

Suno kehna humaara
Ameeri hai sitaara
Garibi ek aansu
Yeh aansu hai mohabbat
Mohabbat zindagi hai
Bas itna jaan le tu

(Listen to what I say
Wealth is a star
Poverty, a tear
That tear stands for love
Know this:
Love stands for life)

But when she refuses to hear him out, Sanjay launches his most savage attack on Kaajal in the second verse of '*Kya hua tera waada*':

Oh kehney waaley mujhko farebi
Kaun farebi hai yeh bata
Woh jisney gham liya pyaar ki khaatir
Ya jisney pyaar ko bech diya
Nasha daulat ka aisa bhi kya
Ki tujhe kuchh bhi yaad nahin

(You who call me a cheat
Do you not see who the cheat is?
He who suffers for love?
Or she who peddles her love?
What this fascination for wealth
That you remember nothing)

Tariq Khan, Husain's nephew, speculated that Husain's liking for the class-conflict theme may have owed to his formative years. Tariq, who made his acting debut in Husain's *Yaadon Ki Baaraat* (1973) as the youngest brother Monto/Ratan, retired as an executive from a courier company in early 2014. Dressed in a kurta pyjama when he met me, Tariq appeared a distant memory of the young man whose popularity had surged rocket-like following *Yaadon Ki Baaraat* and *Hum Kisise Kum Naheen*.

'Everybody wanted to portray himself as a rich man to win the affection of the girl and to find acceptance in society,' said Tariq. 'If you go back to his school–college background, to present yourself to a nawaab–begum, you had to be somebody for the nawaab to meet you. Commoners couldn't interact so freely with the maharajas in those days. That's the basic reason … The hero had to change his identity to be presentable to society. To be seated among the gentry. He just can't be a commoner. *Entry hi nahin milegi. Wahaan se watchman bhaga dega aapko. Toh woh bhes badal ke aaney ka, ki hum bhi koi nawaab hain, kunwar hain.* (You won't be allowed to enter. The watchman would shoo you away. So you had to change your guise, and present yourself as a nawaab or a prince.) He may have been thrown out somewhere in Bhopal. *Ho sakta hai* (It's possible).'

Mansoor agreed with his cousin's hypothesis. 'Yes, he identified with the hero there. He became successful later, but when he came to Bombay he came from rags to riches. Well not really rags but he definitely was the underdog in his sentiment.' Aamir offered a more philosophical line of thought. 'This class conflict comes from the same space of him and his background and his sher that comes before every film of his, "*Hum khaaq-nasheenon ki thokar mein zamaana hai*". He saw himself as a khaaq-nasheen. We are nobody but *zamaana humaari thokar mein hai*. He had that arrogance … It was not a negative arrogance. It was not a bad arrogance. Nasir sa'ab was not like that but there was a lot of self-pride in his abilities, his self-worth. I think that amount of arrogance is needed for good creative work.'

On the whole, Husain rarely let the film's storyline veer out of control. This was true of most of his directorial ventures right up to *Hum Kisise Kum Naheen*. He combined all his staple elements to produce wholesome, commercial, musical entertainers. 'We could call him "sofa-cum-bed", which means he was a writer–director,' said Zafar Sultan, who worked as an independent editor on Husain's films, beginning with *Zamaane Ko Dikhana Hai*. 'If by chance he found that something was missing somewhere, he would change it immediately.' Mansoor echoed this thought. 'His editing would be in his screenplay itself. That's the point of a screenplay. That if you already understand editing, you have to incorporate that thought in your screenwriting.'

Madhulika wrote that even if the plots were very convoluted, 'You realize that just about everything – every fact shared, every letter written, is there for a purpose: it is referenced somewhere later in the film, or affects what happens somewhere later in the film.' A good illustration of this is in *Caravan* where Nisha (Aruna Irani) is indulging in target practice when one of the knives that she hurls lands in Subodh Mukerji theatrewallah's racquet. Nisha's actions appear inane since they serve more as an introduction to the Subodh Mukerji comic character. However, when Mohan has been left to hang on a tree by Rajan at the climax, it's Nisha's knife-throwing skills that save him from near death.

'One of the things I was really bad at was a compactness of a scene and making sure that the audience understands what you are talking about,' Mansoor said on what he learned from his father in terms of screenplay writing. 'You think that you have communicated something, and so you can have a rambling scene of four minutes, but you haven't really. Being a screenplay writer he would constantly make me aware *ki ismein toh yeh baat samajh mein hi nahin aati hai* (that this doesn't explain anything). This was my learning curve in *Qayamat Se Qayamat Tak* and in *Jo Jeeta* also.'

Nuzhat revealed Husain's thought process more clearly. 'Everything had to be justified. If we can't explain it, we don't do it. You could call it backstory if you want, but everything had to have enough of a justification for it to belong where it was. We used to argue for hours. "Why is she saying that at this point? Because she thinks this…" You can't be just writing anything in a scene. The other thing we took from there is that each character cannot be cardboard. Each character has to have depth. It has to be a full person.'

The cardinal rule, Nuzhat said, that Husain maintained was, 'If it's not written, it can't be on screen.'

9

CARAVAN, THE WOMAN AND WHAT-A-CABARET

'The girls were always very modern. They were never the *abla naari* type, which was the norm in the days he was making movies. The women were all go-getters, of course they were still only falling in love and singing songs, but they weren't the weepy types. They were on equal terms with the guys.'

— Film-maker and choreographer Farah Khan

The years between the mid-1960s right up to 1973 witnessed great churning and experimentation in Hindi cinema. Not enough has been written about this, but the death of three eminent film-makers – Mehboob Khan in May 1964, Guru Dutt in October 1964 and Bimal Roy in January 1966 – within a span of two years, certainly contributed to this. Not very much later, K. Asif, the man behind *Mughal-E-Azam*, passed away in 1971. Madhubala's illness and death in 1969, as also Meena Kumari's demise in early 1972 added to the turmoil. Simultaneously, the dominant trio of the 1950s – Raj Kapoor, Dilip Kumar and Dev Anand – stepped into the autumn of their careers as mainstream heroes by the late 1960s. The failure of films like *Dil Diya Dard Liya* (1966), *Mera Naam Joker* (1970) and *Prem Pujari* (1970) signalled a paradigm shift in audience tastes. Shammi Kapoor,

222

too, had faded by the early 1970s. The lyricist Shailendra's death in late 1966 also shocked the industry, as did Jaikishan's in 1971, which brought an end to the Shankar–Jaikishan collaboration, arguably the most successful of all composers in the 1950s and 1960s. Yash Chopra's split from his brother B.R. Chopra's banner, B.R. Films, in the early 1970s, made headlines as well.

It's difficult to assess the direct impact of these developments on Hindi cinema, but what is interesting is that newer forces came to the fore just as the old withered away. The first graduates from FTII, which was established in 1960, started making their way into the film industry around this time. The birth of 'art house cinema' or the parallel cinema movement can be traced back directly to 1969 as Mrinal Sen's *Bhuvan Shome* and Mani Kaul's *Uski Roti* released in the same year. Making his acting debut in that very same year was a lanky, young newcomer named Amitabh Bachchan, who starred in K.A. Abbas's *Saat Hindustani*, but who would catapult into stardom only some years later with Prakash Mehra's *Zanjeer* (1973). Mehra's film itself was written by a pair of young writers, who were looking to get a foothold in the industry at that time. *Zanjeer*'s success following *Haathi Mere Saathi* (1971) and *Seeta Aur Geeta* (1972) established Salim–Javed as the flavour of the season in no uncertain terms. But the biggest phenomenon of that period was Rajesh Khanna, whose ascent into 'never-seen-before' stardom with *Aradhana* in 1969 and dramatic descent just as quickly best highlighted the tumult in Hindi cinema in this period.

Contributing to this very interesting phase in Hindi cinema was Husain. Following the limited success of *Pyar Ka Mausam*, Husain made *Caravan*, a film which celebrated the 'road' and was replete with itinerant gypsies and music. *Caravan* is the rare instance of a 'road film', a genre not much in vogue in Hindi cinema. The last successful 'road' film had released way back in *Chori Chori* (1956), starring Raj Kapoor and Nargis. For this reason alone, *Caravan* is an important milestone in Hindi cinema. But the film also gives us the opportunity to look at the woman in Husain's cinema since this was the first Husain film where the female character, played by Asha Parekh, took centre stage for much of the film.

Caravan begins with a girl named Sunita (Parekh) talking about events in her recent past that have led her to run away from her husband Rajan (Krishen Mehta). Rajan was working as a manager for Sunita's father, but when Sunita's father, Mohandas (Murad), learns that Rajan has siphoned off some money, he issues an ultimatum to Rajan to return the money by the next day. Rajan, instead, murders Mohandas by throwing him off a balcony a la *Teesri Manzil*. Sunita is greatly disturbed by her father's death and in this state of mind, she writes over her entire property to Rajan should she die. But Rajan, portraying himself to be a sympathetic figure to Sunita in this hour of crisis, tells her that more than the property, he is interested in keeping her father's last wish, which is that Sunita marry him.

Consequently, Rajan and Sunita get married and drive to Khandala to spend their wedding night. But when they reach their cottage in Khandala, Sunita meets Monica (Helen), a cabaret artiste, who tells Sunita all about Rajan's Machiavellian ways and how he is responsible for her father's death. Sunita takes off in Rajan's car but realizes only later that Rajan has sabotaged the vehicle's brakes. Fortunately, she jumps out of the car before it crashes into a ravine. The rest of the film deals with how Sunita, who disguises herself as a village belle called Soni, meets Mohan (Jeetendra) and some feisty, jovial banjaras, and how their lives get entwined before Mohan helps set Sunita free from Rajan's evil clutches.

With *Caravan*, Husain made a break from the world of the aristocratic elite and instead placed his story amidst these banjaras, whose earthy lifestyle (even if superficially depicted) is at complete odds with the world inhabited by the characters of Husain's previous films. It is the one Husain film (barring *Baharon Ke Sapne*) where the hero, even while retaining his buoyant demeanour, suggests that he is struggling to make ends meet. The fact that *Caravan* is also a road film all through, with its storyline moving from Bombay to Khandala to Bombay to Pune to Bangalore and back to Bombay before finishing somewhere in the countryside, makes it very different from Husain's earlier films.

Asha Parekh offered some very interesting insights into the genesis of the film. 'There was a book called *Paprika* based on which Guru Dutt-ji wanted to make a movie with me. It was lying with me [but then] Guru Dutt-ji decided not to make the film. So I gave this book to Nasir sa'ab. He read it. Actually, Aruna Irani's was to be the heroine's role. I was supposed to be playing Aruna Irani's role as Paprika in Guru Dutt-ji's film. So he [Nasir Husain] got a little bit of the idea from *Paprika* and he made *Caravan*.' Parekh claimed that Guru Dutt gave her the book during the making of *Bharosa* (1963), which starred Guru Dutt and Parekh. Nuzhat told me, 'Dad used to speak about that book all the time. That was a huge source of inspiration for him.'

Paprika is the story of a girl born in the chilli fields who turns violent every full-moon night. 'It was a beautiful story, which Guru Dutt-ji wanted to make, but I was not very keen on it because the heroine is shown as a vamp. Every time she got into that full-moon thing, she would get the hero beaten up. I don't remember the exact story, but he was inspired by it,' Parekh recalled. Simultaneously, Parekh claimed that Husain was inspired by the premise of the film *Girl on the Run* (1953), directed by Arthur Beckhard and Joseph Lee. 'He had seen this film, and that's where my track, which had me running from these people, came from … he incorporated these two [the book and the film's title] and made *Caravan*. The *Paprika* role was given to Aruna Irani. And I became the "girl on the run".'

While Parekh's remarks help in understanding Husain's immediate reference for *Caravan*, Kaushik Bhaumik made a keen observation about the kind of films Rajesh Khanna was doing at the time, which may have subconsciously also spurred Husain into doing a film like *Caravan*. 'Rajesh Khanna is such a misunderstood star. He is squarely remembered for his Shakti Samanta films and then a few films which have great songs. People forget there is a lot of violence in Khanna's films. There is a huge amount of mobility across the nation in his films. He is always peripatetic. Rajesh Khanna is the road movie star at that point of time. He is doing the maximum number of roles as truck driver and this and that. ... I think *Caravan* is very much a response to Rajesh Khanna's peripatetic kind of films: *The Train* [1970], *Dushman* [1971] and *Roti* [1974]. *Caravan* is a response to that zeitgeist of some churning, like *Mera Gaon Mera Desh* [1971], there is a certain movement of the hero from the city to the village and that kind of thing. There is some kind of fantasy happening about this movement into the countryside with the banjaras, looking at the countryside in a certain way.'

Even Khanna's earliest hit songs like '*Mere sapnon ki rani*' (*Aradhana*, 1969) and '*Zindagi ek safar hai suhaana*' (*Andaz*, 1971), which were integral to establishing his iconic romantic persona, show him to be very much on the move. Similarly, in Shakti Samanta's 1970 film, *Kati Patang*, while the major portion of the film plays out in Nainital, Khanna runs into the character played by Asha Parekh for the very first time while he is in his jeep, on the way to Almora in the capacity of a forest officer. Bhaumik also pointed to *Uski Roti*, where a truck driver is among the key characters in the film's narrative. 'So popular cinema is beginning to respond to certain demands within Indian society for a new kind of cinema which starts to look at the reality of India, even if superficially,' said Bhaumik. A few other films around this time that had the 'road' element in it were the Jeetendra–Sharmila Tagore starrer, *Mere Humsafar* (1970) and *Bombay to Goa* (1972). Neither film, though, matched *Caravan*'s box-office reception.

Rashmi Doraiswamy found consistency in Husain moving away from the hotel–club space and basing *Caravan* on the road through the itinerant banjaras. 'The road, like the train, the hotel, the club, is a secular and carnivalesque space where all kinds of people, who would not run into one another in regimented everyday life, meet, mingle and interact.'[1] When I met Doraiswamy, she explained, 'Because the road is another way of moving away from the home. Basically, you don't want the home. This is my central argument about Nasir Husain. For me it's not such a break that he is looking at the road and not at the hotel because the road is also away from home.'

Looking at the woman figure in Husain's cinema, it's safe to conclude that his heroines always played second fiddle to his heroes. While the men mostly changed their guise in the pursuit of love, the heroine did it because she felt threatened and wanted to keep her identity under wraps. She, like Soni in *Caravan* and Kanchan (Padmini Kolhapure) in *Zamaane Ko Dikhana Hai*, did it from a position of weakness. The romancing itself was the prerogative of the hero. It is he who made the first move and initiated the entire process of wooing. The heroine would

---

[1]Dr Rashmi Doraiswamy, '"These Days" of Our Modernity: The Cinema of Nasir Husain', Film and Television Institute of India, Pune, 4 September 2004, p. 9.

invariably be at the receiving end of his pranks, his tomfoolery, before she came around to acknowledging the hero's love. As Nuzhat remarked, 'There is always a taming of the shrew element in it.' In this regard, Husain's cinema lived up to what Jerry Pinto wrote: 'The hero in mainstream cinema is the pivot on whom the plot turns. He is the one who does and to whom is done. And the heroine is usually only his love interest.'[2]

Even in *Caravan*, while Sunita garners maximum screen time, she needs Mohan by the end of the film to save her from Rajan. Further, when Mohan resigns himself to a life without Soni after Rajan has been dealt with, it is Parekh who returns as Soni, indicating her willingness to forego a life of material wealth, embodying the *sachcha sukh* concept that Hindi cinema repeatedly evangelized in these years. Anuradha Warrier opined, 'Jeetendra is shown to be "noble" because he has resigned himself to a life without Asha. What is so noble about going away from the woman you love because she is wealthy? If the positions were reversed, wouldn't they have had him benevolently "accept" her? Would Nasir Husain have shown Jeetendra sacrificing his wealth in order to share Parekh's poverty? But it is okay for a woman to *thokkar maaro* her riches to marry the man; but the man, playing King Cophetua, will only "raise" her to his level, not "stoop" to hers!'

Anuradha compared Husain's heroines to how they were presented by other film-makers. 'Raj Kapoor's heroines were much more fiercely independent – the women in *Aag* [1948], Nargis in *Awara* and *Shree 420*; so were V. Shantaram's – look at Shanta Apte in *Duniya Na Mane* [1937]. Watch Bimal Roy's heroines – traditional, often rural, yet with a strong vein of self-respect, and very, very independent within the constraints of the society they live in. Not Nasir Husain ... The heroine's only job is to be

[2]Jerry Pinto, 'The Making of an H-Bomb-I', *Helen: The Life and Times of an H Bomb*, Penguin Books India, 2006, p. 30.

tamed by the hero, fall in love with him, and then dance to his wishes.' Nasreen Munni Kabir agreed with this sentiment. 'All I know is, you don't think of Nasir sa'ab's heroines. There's a reason why. They have not made a deep impression. He didn't create an immortal heroine.'

Much of these perspectives on Husain's heroines are correct. His female protagonists are hardly remembered. They aren't like Radha in *Mother India* or Rosie from *Guide*, who defied all kinds of odds or the prevalent societal norms and are looked upon as some kind of iconic female representations in Hindi cinema. But whether these characters were necessarily progressive is another matter.

Radha in *Mother India* has to go through a trial by fire to be seen as a woman of substance. The corollary to this is: would she have been a lesser woman if she hadn't made it past all her odds? In many Raj Kapoor films, including *Awara*, violence towards the woman is propagated as a convenient way of making her fall in love with the hero. As stated earlier, Guru Dutt's *Mr. & Mrs. '55* glamorized the idea of the 'Indian' woman finding happiness only within the institution of marriage. B.R. Chopra, the man behind the fairly progressive *Sadhana* (1958), also made *Gumrah* (1963), which put the entire onus of preserving the sacred institution of marriage on the woman. The point, therefore, is whether such representations are truly progressive.

But Husain's portrayal of women wasn't necessarily stereotypical, nor did he reduce them to curios. In his own discreet way, he freed the heroine from many of the taboos of Hindi cinema. In most Husain films, the heroine is an educated, modern-day woman, who dresses in a manner and has a lifestyle that is distinctly westernized. She drives cars (*Dil Deke Dekho, Phir Wohi Dil Laya Hoon, Teesri Manzil, Yaadon Ki Baaraat, Manzil Manzil*), goes out picnicking with her friends (*Dil Deke Dekho,*

Pyar Ka Mausam, Yaadon Ki Baaraat) and travels freely (*Jab Pyar Kisise Hota Hai, Phir Wohi Dil Laya Hoon*). The club–hotel space that Hindi cinema had designated as full of vice, is available to Husain's heroines without any fear, be it in *Dil Deke Dekho* or *Teesri Manzil*.

In fact, *Teesri Manzil's* 'Aaja aaja' that takes place at the Rock-'n'-Roll Club, and has Sunita wearing a sleeveless, fuchsia pink shimmery blouse and black leggings, is one of those rare portrayals in Hindi cinema before the 1970s where an A-list heroine, dressed in Western attire, could sing and dance in a club space uninhibitedly without inviting trouble or being judged on her character.[3] A year before *Teesri Manzil*, Asha Parekh's character in Amar Kumar's *Mere Sanam* (1965) is seen dancing with another man in a club to make Biswajeet's character envious. However, no sooner does Parekh start dancing with this stranger than he has his hands all over her. Biswajeet has to intervene to save her from the clutches of this man in this supposedly decadent space. *Teesri Manzil's* Rock-'n'-Roll Club, on the other hand, is a space where Sunita can dance with complete abandon.

Even before this, in the *Dil Deke Dekho* song '*Do ekum do*', the fact that Neeta and her friends could be part of a song with a distinct Western element was atypical for the time. All through the 1950s, there are very few instances of the heroines dancing within their homes in the presence of their parents. A film like

---

[3]One of the few examples before '*Aaja aaja*' is Rajshree dancing with Shammi Kapoor in '*Dekho ab toh*' in *Janwar*. But while the *Janwar* song, an imitation of the Beatles' '*I wanna hold your hand*', is a mutual declaration of love, '*Aaja aaja*'s' lyrics are far bolder. '*Palkon mein aao chhupa loon, naazuk tann hai tumhaara* (Come let me behold you, your body is too delicate),' sings Anil to Sunita. The picturization, too, establishes a sizzling sexual tension between Sunita and Anil. Also, Rajshree didn't enjoy the same stature as Parekh at the box office.

Namoona (1949) even has the father figure express his unhappiness when his daughter takes to song and dance. There followed a reconciliation with Indian-style classical dances or folk dance routines, while Western dancing became the new anathema for the Hindi film heroine. As late a film as Mehboob Khan's *Son of India* (1962) has the heroine's father rebuke her strongly on seeing her do a 'tap dance' routine. He even vents his disgust at a couple doing the tango in a club a few scenes later. He argues that this is not part of Indian culture.

There was some kind of a double standard at work here. While the mainstream rarely allowed the 'good woman' to be employed in theatre or be professionally involved with song and dance, the comic films, whose narratives were far removed from tropes of nation-building, allowed their heroines to operate in such spaces. Therefore, actors like Geeta Bali, Shyama and Vyjayanthimala could be part of some terrific song sequences in '*Shola jo bhadke*' (*Albela*, 1951), '*Aashiqon ko ishq ne ulat pulat kar diya*' (*Shrimati Ji*, 1952) and '*Eena meena deeka*' (*Aasha*, 1957). But never at home.

Moreover, Maya (Nadira) in *Shree 420* or Edna (Madhubala) in *Howrah Bridge* can participate in the club songs only because the former is the vamp while the latter, even though she is the good girl, isn't from the mainstream community. Similarly, Leena (Geeta Bali), Star Club's famed dancer, has to die towards the end of *Baazi*. The crux of Jerry Pinto's book on Helen's emergence is that she represented the very opposite of all that the Hindi film heroine could do and the places she could inhabit. Contrary to this dominant stereotype, Husain presented Neeta, wearing a checked blouse and pants in '*Do ekum do*' and had her dance in the presence of her father, at home, without any hullabaloo.

But dancing alone cannot justify Husain's progressive depiction of his women characters. We also have to consider that Husain allowed them to step out of their homes confidently, whether it was to avenge a sibling's death in *Teesri Manzil* or negotiate a land deal in *Jab Pyar Kisise Hota Hai* or venture out alone to the city on some work (as Meena does for Sardar Rajpal in *Tumsa Nahin Dekha*). Doraiswamy remarked, 'The heroine leaving the house for whatever reason – to meet Mr. Popatlal to finalise an old land deal (*Jab Pyar...*), or to find the drummer in "Park Hotel, Mussoorie" (*Teesri Manzil*) are important chronotopic moments of narrative. The girls on an excursion are into the holiday spirit and freely frequent clubs and hotels. This liberation from the constraining space of the home is what makes the heroine and her friends seem to be on a perpetual picnic in Husain's films. To him goes the credit of creating a special type of the "outdoors" girl, having fun holidaying with friends, headstrong and mistress of her actions. (Heroines like Nargis in Mehboob's *Andaz* [1949] loved the outdoors, but had to return "home" after horse-riding and partying.)'[4]

For another seminal moment in Husain's cinema, we have to look at the Sunita character in *Yaadon Ki Baaraat*. This is when she is reproaching Vijay's father (Shivraj) about his lackadaisical preparations in hosting her friends. This in itself is something of a red flag, since the heroine in Hindi cinema could hardly have the temerity of telling someone older and far more timid than her, '*Manager sa'ab, aap badey dheeley dhaaley aadmi hain* (You are fairly inefficient, Mr Manager).' While Vijay's father tries to put up a stoic defence, saying that he has made arrangements for food '*aur cold drinks ka bhi* (and soft drinks as well)', Sunita delivers the punchline, '*Oh my God, main hot drinks ki baat kar rahi hoon. Mere kuchh dost whiskey aur beer bhi peetey hain* (I am talking about liquor. A few of my friends drink whiskey and beer,

---

[4]Dr Rashmi Doraiswamy, '"These Days" of Our Modernity: The Cinema of Nasir Husain', Film and Television Institute of India, Pune, 4 September 2004, p. 9.

too.)' The manager is caught out by Sunita's frankness. He has no option but to hurriedly cater to these new orders.

In *Hare Rama Hare Krishna* (1971), which came a couple of years before *Yaadon Ki Baaraat*, Zeenat Aman had played Janice, a liquor-drinking, drug-consuming hippie. Even though her heart was in the right place, she had to die by the end of the film, because Hindi film morality didn't allow such women to live. Their redemption lay in their death. In *Yaadon Ki Baaraat*, Husain handled Sunita asking for liquor to be arranged for her friends without depicting her as some kind of depraved woman. Later, when Vijay and Sunita have their day out, the two are casually implied to have had a swim together, probably a first for Hindi cinema. When Vijay photographs Sunita at the precise moment that she bends to dry herself with a towel, while in a one-piece swimsuit, Sunita is absolutely comfortable with her sexuality. She acknowledges Vijay's actions laughingly, without any embarrassment, saying, 'You naughty. *Maaroongi* (I'll beat you)!'

Bhaumik commented, 'It is a coming-to-terms with the fact that the girl and the boy are now equal, that the parents have at some point in time decided to give the daughter all the freedom that they would give a son. That's why these films are in a sense progressive. They are all putting forward women who are modern, contemporary and also acknowledging the fact that if you educate your girls, they are going to be urbane, they are going to be mobile, they are going to be free in all categories of life not just romance but everything else.'

Bhaumik also explained the feisty courtship that played out in Husain's films because of this modern, mobile woman. 'There is an acknowledgment that if you have given her freedom, she will be pampered, she will be wayward and then the hero comes and tames her. That follows the older mode of the Howard Hawks's films, the screwball comedy kind of thing. It's kind of adapting screwball comedy to the Indian form of courtship. There is an erotic frisson there because the girl is not submissive. The very fact of mobility is shorthand for sexual maturity as well. It's about balancing these things in a certain way. And one would have to go back to the screwball tradition to understand this trope of the active, modern girl and how do you then reconfigure coupledom because she is not willing to settle down into coupledom just like that. She has a mind of her own and then how does the boy get her to focus on him.'

An offshoot of this is the idea that Husain's heroes somewhere indulged in stalking. After all, when the hero himself utters the words, '*Nafrat mohabbat ki pehli seedi hai*' (Hatred is the first step in love), it is an admission of this kind. Madhulika Liddle noted, 'Seriously, if I were in the place of any of those women, I'd never have fallen for a man who constantly followed me about, forced me to ride with him.'

But this is only partially true. While Hindi cinema has always popularized the notion that a woman's refusal to play along is only temporary and that she will eventually fall in line, 'stalking' certainly wasn't on Husain's agenda. In Husain's films, the hero almost always withdrew from the heroine after a point, sometimes leaving behind a letter explaining his actions. Further, for every such male protagonist, who could be accused of harassing the heroine into submission, there must also be an acknowledgment of the femme fatale who actually indulged in 'stalking' in Husain's films.

Sunita's sister in *Teesri Manzil* tries to seduce Rocky to the point that when she actually reaches out to him, he ignores her cries for help. Similarly, Ruby (Helen) in *Teesri Manzil*, Chanchal (Shubha Khote) in *Paying Guest* and Nisha (Aruna Irani) in *Caravan* are far more diabolical in their pursuit than any of Husain's heroes. Jerry Pinto succinctly commented, 'There is charm. The men try to be charming, sometimes in disgusting ways like in *Hum Kisise Kum Naheen* where he opens that girl's [blouse] – I remember thinking even then that this is not terribly funny, but overall the men were not stalkers. They were not obsessive lovers. They were just lovers. They were respectful. It was a nicer, kinder, gentler romance. And sometimes I miss it a great deal.' Anuradha Warrier endorsed this view. 'In my opinion, there was a basic decency about that stalking. One knew that it was playful, never disrespectful.'

Another important aspect to Husain's heroine was her open defiance in choosing the man she loves. Consider *Qayamat Se Qayamat Tak*. For much of the film, Rashmi is afraid of doing anything against her father's wishes. But when it comes to choosing between Raj (Aamir Khan) and the man she is engaged to, Rashmi makes a clean break from her family and heads out with Raj. Her father's violent temperament, *khaandaan ki izzat*, et al, cannot hold her back. Something similar happens in *Jab Pyar Kisise Hota Hai* where Nisha decides to marry Sunder despite her father's emotional threats of killing himself if she marries anyone other than Sohan (Pran). On the day of her wedding to Sohan, Nisha openly, in full view of the many attending guests, walks out on her father to show her love for Sunder.

And this independence isn't limited to the new, younger generation in Husain's films. In *Pyar Ka Mausam*, Jamuna (Nirupa Roy) goes against her father's wishes to marry Gopal (Bharat Bhushan). Likewise, in *Jab Pyar Kisise Hota Hai*, Sunder's mother reminds Sardar Roop Singh of the time when his wife went against her father's wishes to marry him.

These aren't the *Dilwale Dulhania Le Jayenge* Simran kind of women, whose fate is determined by the father's actions. As Aamir said, 'The decisions of her life, right or wrong, are being taken by her. And all his heroines have been modern right from his first film. Even if you look at their costumes. His heroines have never been conservative. They visit clubs, they visit pubs, they dance, they drink, they do what they want to do.'

Even more significantly, in a Husain film, the woman separating from her husband doesn't lead to a life of misery. Both Shankar's mother in *Tumsa Nahin Dekha* and Mohan's mother in *Phir Wohi Dil Laya Hoon* have raised their sons into fine men. They aren't victims. On the contrary, a woman like Jamuna Devi (Sulochana Latkar) is in firm control of her business empire in *Dil Deke Dekho*. She even rebukes her manager and Kailash (Rajendra Nath) for misappropriating funds. She cannot be duped. Likewise, in *Baharon Ke Sapne*, Geeta is the breadwinner in her family but also stands her ground against her stepmother's tyrannical behaviour. She is the one who often shows Ram the right path (the significance of her name is reinforced here) in his moments of weakness.

Phir Wohi Dil Laya Hoon probably best exemplifies this strong woman not hitherto seen in Hindi cinema. It begins with Mohan's father, Colonel Mahendranath, being strongly advised by his doctor friend (Mona's father) to bring back Mohan's mother, Jamuna, since his suspicions (these aren't explained) about her have been proved to be false. But instead of allowing her husband the opportunity to ask for forgiveness, Mohan's mother orchestrates her own son's abduction from the colonel's house. Mohan's mother is shown to be the master of her own fate. She is not pining for her husband's change of heart. Neither is she reduced to an overbearing, cruel mother figure, but is shown to be doting over her son for much of the film.[5]

Doraiswamy wrote, 'Nasir Husain also dispensed with the

---

[5]Since Jamuna repeatedly rebuffs Mahendranath's apologies in the film, could it be that she parts with her mangalsutra, the ultimate emblem of all *pativrata naris* in Hindi cinema, without any *rona dhona*, instead of a mere gold chain as fees to Mohan's abductor at the station?

traditional role of the mother, with all the emotional, ideological and melodramatic baggage she usually carried in Hindi cinema. In most of his films the mother is literally absent, with an aunt or ayah doing the role of chaperone. In other films (*Tumsa Nahin Dekha, Dil Deke Dekho, Phir Wohi Dil Laya Hoon*), the wife is separated or estranged from the husband. This contributed in no small measure to the "dehousing" of his protagonists.'[6]

This didn't mean that Husain was championing women's lib or that he gave his women equal or more agency than his leading men. In *Caravan* itself, we have Meetha Lal Tota (Madan Puri), the leader of the banjaras, beating his wife for serving him burnt food. In this film, and also in *Hum Kisise Kum Naheen*, the heroine, based on some bizarre idea of romance, is made to consume liquor in order to prove her love for the hero. But neither did Husain take an entirely dim view of his female characters, where the men determined the norms of maryada for them. On the contrary, Mohan's attempt at forcing a relationship between Bhola (Anwar Ali) and Nisha (Aruna Irani), leads to Nisha rejecting Bhola in no uncertain terms. Going back to *Paying Guest*, when the chips are down for Shanti's family, she works in a theatre company and Ramesh cleans the dishes. There is an easy understanding between the two that these are their roles if the home is to be run. Even when Chanchal asks Ramesh about this, he is candid with her about doing the dishes. As Nuzhat told me, 'Well, he didn't want to marry a regular, stay-at-home Bhopali girl. He married a very independent kind of person. She was not educated, but she was in every sense a modern, forward-looking woman. He didn't have these things about religion, caste or that women cannot do this. I never heard him being dogmatic about power structures in that

[6]Dr Rashmi Doraiswamy, '"These Days" of Our Modernity: The Cinema of Nasir Husain', Film and Television Institute of India, Pune, 4 September 2004, p. 9.

way. Of course, he was a very manly man in many ways. There was
no question that my father was the man [of the house] and my
mother was the woman type of thing. In our lives, for instance,
he allowed us to do what we wanted. In our extended family, our
home was the haven of liberal values, ideas, thinking. Discussion
was possible. Argument was possible.'

Among the many wonderful things about *Caravan* was that it
brought the banjaras back into focus in mainstream Hindi cinema.
Although present in many B- and C-grade films of the 1960s,
Phagun (1958), which had Madhubala playing the banjaran
character Banani, was the last successful Hindi film to present
the banjara community. Husain, too, had depicted the gypsy
community briefly in *Pyar Ka Mausam*, in the song, '*Che khush
nazaare*', referring to them as 'khaanaabadosh', a synonym for
banjaras. But following *Caravan*'s success, the gypsy community
started featuring prominently through important characters and
sequences in Hindi cinema all through the 1970s and 1980s. Films
like *Dharmatma* (1975), *Mehbooba* (1976), *Dharam Veer* (1977),
Ek Chadar Maili Si (1986) or the '*Mehbooba*' song in *Sholay* (1975)
vindicate this. Husain himself made use of the banjaras again in
Manzil Manzil in the song, '*Yeh naina yaad hai piya*'. As Bhaumik
remarked, 'That is Nasir Husain's absolutely original intervention
in *Caravan*, this banjara kind of figure.'

With *Caravan*, Husain may have also been acknowledging
director Bibhuti Mitra's influence on his own craft. Having
worked for Mitra as a writer during his Filmistan days on films
like *Shabnam*, *Shabistan* and *Shart*, Husain certainly seemed to
have incorporated some of Mitra's narrative elements for *Phagun*
into *Caravan*. *Phagun* had composer O.P. Nayyar coming up with
another polished effort with the film's score. Most of the songs

were integrated seamlessly as Banani is presented as the girl on whose singing and dancing skills rest her qabila's fortunes. In one moment in the film, Banani's father pleads with her to put up her best performance at the mela so that the banjaras may earn their meal, which then leads to the wonderful '*Ek pardesi mera dil le gaya*'.

This scene plays out in *Caravan*, too, but in a slightly different manner. Mohan and Nisha come together to perform '*Chadhti jawaani meri chaal mastaani*' on the request of the leader of the banjaras for a gathering of people. *Phagun*'s male protagonist, Bijan (Bharat Bhushan), is shown with a flute from the very beginning and that gives him the licence to break into music. In *Caravan*, Mohan is a part of the banjaras' nautanki troupe, which legitimizes his foray into song and dance.

But these similarities apart, *Phagun* and *Caravan* are very different films. While the former is more comic and deals with caste issues, doomed love and rebirth, *Caravan* keeps the viewer glued to his seat with Sunita, disguised as Soni, evading Rajan and his men even as the film moves from one terrific song to another. Speaking of *Caravan*, Javed Akhtar said, 'From whatever little that I know about screenplay writing, I would say, *Caravan* is a remarkable screenplay ... It is entirely to the screenplay's credit, how Nasir Husain as a writer managed to keep the story interesting right to the end.'[7]

Caravan is vintage Husain. While the overall premise of the film involves Sunita running away from Rajan, there are several other subplots that add to the narrative: Mohan falling in love with Soni even as she struggles with the idea of being married to Rajan; Nisha who loves Mohan and is willing to go to any length to have him. Calling *Caravan* 'a landmark film' because of its complexity, Bhaumik said, 'Narratively, it's the most complex film

---

[7]Zee Classic's *Classic Legends: Season II*, featuring Nasir Husain.

he ever made. The form is really so open-ended, so experimental. To reconcile the open landscape with melodrama of that kind is a technical feat. It's not easy to do. The reason melodramas always happen in closed rooms is because it is convenient, technically. It's like a theatrical space. To reconcile something that happens in closed theatrical spaces as genre convention with openness of landscapes, is fascinating. It's his most ambitious film precisely because of this tension between melodrama and landscape.'

Caravan's biggest ace is undoubtedly its music. R.D. Burman and Husain took another giant step as an iconic composer–filmmaker pairing with the film's score. Husain had been advised to replace RD following the lukewarm response to *Baharon Ke Sapne* and *Pyar Ka Mausam*, but fortunately Husain didn't give in. *Caravan*'s reception at the box office ensured there was no turning back on the collaboration between the two men. As Balaji and Bhattacharjee wrote, 'Between "*Daiyya yeh main kahaan aa phansi*", which straddles a few scales, the honky-tonk Kishore solo "*Hum toh hain raahi dil ke*", the festive and folksy "*Goriya kahaan tera des re*", the joie de vivre of "*Chadhti jawaani*", the frothy "*Ab jo mile hain*", the nights-of-nomads "*Dilbar dil se pyaare*", and the conventional 1960s-style "*Kitna pyaara waada*",[8] the sheer variety on offer in the film's soundtrack is exceptional. While some of these songs are discussed later, the one song that needs to be detailed right away is the Helen number, '*Piya tu*'.

To rewind a little, Husain's and Helen's destinies had been entwined twenty years before *Caravan*'s release. By most accounts,

---

[8]Anirudha Bhattacharjee and Balaji Vittal, 'The Last Word in Cabaret', *Gaata Rahe Mera Dil: 50 Classic Hindi Film Songs*, HarperCollins *Publishers* India, 2015, p. 197–98.

Helen's first film where she featured as a junior artiste is said to be Bibhuti Mitra's *Shabistan*, for which Husain was credited as a dialogue writer along with Qamar Jalalabadi. Then as Husain hit the big league with *Tumsa Nahin Dekha*, Helen shot into fame shortly afterwards with '*Mera naam Chin-Chin-Choo*' in *Howrah Bridge* (1958). She also had a fairly meaty role in *Teesri Manzil*. It is her delicious opening line as the credits roll, 'Rocky, *tumhey wahaan nahin jaana chaahiye* (Rocky, you shouldn't go there)' that sets the stage for a most intriguing film. With '*Piya tu*', Husain got his first opportunity to direct Helen in a song sequence. The result is a sizzling, hot number.

The song happens once Soni reaches Bombay with Mohan's help. She changes back into Sunita's attire and then goes to what is ostensibly Regent Club, the place where Monica works. All through, she is full of anxiety, perhaps for fear of being spotted by Rajan and his men. The patrons here, both men and women, are all fashionably dressed, with the attending stewards also looking immaculate in their white bandhgalas and black trousers. Helen is introduced to these patrons as '*Hindustan ki mash-hoor cabaret dancer* (India's famous cabaret dancer), *one and the only one, Monica*'.

'*Piya tu*' is a typical Nasir Husain song, made up of two distinct parts. The first is a longish prelude before the actual song begins. A few couples are dancing in what is deemed to be some kind of European public square before the camera cuts to Helen. In quintessential Nasir Husain style, we aren't shown Helen's face right away. Instead, the camera languidly works its way up her feet, past her fishnet stockings and her fiery-red flamenco outfit and only then reveals Monica. This, very much like the introduction of Husain's heroes in *Tumsa Nahin Dekha*, *Phir Wohi Dil Laya Hoon* and *Teesri Manzil*, establishes Helen (even though we have seen her earlier in the film) as the *chef protagoniste* in this sequence.

Everyone else is secondary to her from hereon. Then as the clock strikes twelve, and the couples leave, 'middle-class Cinderellas all',[9] Monica downs the half-filled glass of liquor in front of her and collapses on the bar. It is here that the prelude ends and only then does the main part of '*Piya tu*' begin, with a series of high-pitched, almost off-key synthesizer notes.

Over the next five-odd minutes, Monica shimmies, pants, thrashes, gyrates, thrusts, twirls and writhes about in this space, indicating longing, desire and sexual ecstasy all in the name of dousing her '*tann ki jwaala*'. At one point, when her flamenco outfit gets stuck at the bar, she rips it off to reveal a gold halter blouse and half skirt, scandalous outré for the gentry in attendance, but not out of place for Monica, a woman freed of all inhibition. Manil Suri, author and professor of mathematics at the University of Maryland Baltimore County, and who once performed '*Piya tu*' himself in costume,[10] wrote of Helen's performance, 'Over the years, Helen's dance from *Caravan* has perhaps become her most iconic … All that comes through is Helen having a ball, in all her campy glory, magically imbuing even the racier bits with vivacity rather than crudeness.'[11]

[9]Jerry Pinto, 'A Book on Helen, the Dancer?', *Helen: The Life and Times of an H Bomb*, Penguin Books India, 2006, p. 2.

[10]Manil did the performance as part of a reading at the Brooklyn Book Festival in New York in September 2008 where after the reading each invited writer had to 'take a risk' – perform something on the public stage that they'd never done before. 'I'd always wanted to dance like Helen, do a homage to her. What better excuse would I ever get?' wrote Manil. His performance was captured and can be viewed with a simple YouTube search, 'Manil Suri Bollywood dance'.

[11]Manil Suri, 'My Life as a Cabaret Dancer', *The Popcorn Essayists: What Movies Do to Writers*, Edited by Jai Arjun Singh, Tranquebar, 2011, p. 32-34.

Jerry Pinto began his National Award-winning book on Helen with a description of '*Piya tu*'. When I met Jerry in June 2015, he told me that he started his book with this song because, 'For me, one of the most exciting things about this song is its creation of a modern world. In the time that we are talking about in *Caravan*, we all needed introductions to modernity. Now how do you imagine the West? You imagine the West as this pastiche of things. There is a square. There is a clock tower. There are flamingos standing in one corner [*laughs*]. There is this rather surly bartender and there is this woman, Monica. For me, Nasir Husain, at that point, was actively generating a way of looking at the West and looking at modernity.'

In this context, it is interesting to look at the song '*Aap se miliye*' in *Pyar Ka Mausam*. The song is a mélange of cultures as it invokes some kind of high Lucknawi nawaab ethnicity in the first antara. It then forays into Arabian Nights territory in the second verse, but with Egyptian sphinxes and pyramids as part of the set design. In the third antara, Asha Parekh, on whom the song is shot, is a Spanish senorita with a toreador. When the mukhda is sung right at the end, the song moves into the Spaghetti Western space, with Parekh now dressed as a cowboy with guns in her hands.

This easy cosmopolitanism is on view in '*Piya tu*' as well. While Husain probably referenced Monica and the toreador (the character singing '*Monica, oh my darling*') from the *Pyar Ka Mausam* song, the clock tower is possibly an allusion to London's Big Ben, but against Bombay city's skyline with its accompanying signage. The bartender, too, looks like a remnant of the British raj. Jerry observed, 'What's underlying that is the belief that *vasudhaiva kutumbakam* – the world is my oyster. The world is my family. I can borrow from it liberally and freely and bring it all into this one song … Every single thing is fascinating to me. Why is he dressed like a toreador? Is this supposed to be Spain? What is this night culture that is being evoked here? It's a fascinating song because you cannot tell. This is what I call classic Bollywood, high camp Bollywood where nothing is denied to the creative impulse on the basis of some foolish notion of logic. You don't worry about logic, you worry about impact.'

In terms of narrative, 'Piya tu' works at two levels. One is the story that Monica is enacting, which is about reunion with her lover. Jerry commented, 'Hidden in this is also a moral tale because what is happening here is lust. It is very clear. It starts with birha – he is not coming, he is not coming, but as soon as he arrives, she rips her clothes off with her teeth, when she can't get them off. She is willing to confront her need. So you feel that naming her is significant. She is not just a dancer. She has a name, Monica. When he comes over the horizon, he calls her name, "*Monica, oh my darling*". She does not call his name. So for the first time in a patriarchal cinema, her identity is more important than his. He is not named. She is named. Even in "*Mera naam Chin-Chin-Choo*" [*Howrah Bridge*], she announces herself.'

At the other end, as Husain interspersed Monica's performance with shots of Sunita, it is a reminder of the danger that Sunita is in. And therein lies a contradiction. 'So the gypsies should be amoral and sensual and the settled people ought to be a little more civilized. But it's actually the reverse. The caravan is full of people who are trying to help Asha Parekh, not comfort her so much, but protecting her in their own way. And this is the area of danger. For society, it was exactly the opposite. The gypsy, the banjara is dangerous and the person who is settled is supposed to be safe,' said Jerry.

Technically, too, 'Piya tu' offers an interesting critique of Husain's song picturization. Unlike *Teesri Manzil*'s 'O haseena zulfon waali' where Vijay Anand, instead of intermittently cutting to the audience within the song, integrated some of them (Sunita and her friend) within the performance itself, Husain generally cut to show his audience in separate shots. This is the technique he followed in songs like '*Dekho bijli dole bin baadal ke*' or '*Aap se miliye*' and '*Piya tu*' where performer and the audience are shown in separate shots. This is in line with Asha Parekh's assessment of Husain: 'What he used to do is take shots of one side and then he would turn the camera and go to the other side.' Mansoor felt that showing the audience separately in '*Piya tu*' was 'quite unnatural'. In '*O haseena*', on the other hand, since the audience is shown within the same frame as the performance, Mansoor remarked that 'It made it [the sequence] more real so you don't feel like it's [the audience] always a cut away.'

Vijay Anand acknowledged this. In an interview to Nasreen Munni Kabir in 2001, Vijay Anand told her that in cinema, 'It is the camera that is the audience and the camera angles must change in every shot. So you cannot have a strict division between performance and audience. Unlike a stage dance, the film director has to divide the dance into shots. If you compose for the stage, you are also confined to a small space. The dance movements are restricted ... usually within 20x20 feet. And cinema does not want to confine itself to space. It can go anywhere.'[12] Consequently, in '*O haseena zulfon waali*', Vijay Anand cleverly shot Shammi Kapoor and Helen from several directions. The pair aren't performing to the audience within the song, but for the camera.

While Husain has distinct shots of the audience in '*Piya tu*', he does take into account the camera. Considering that the café space is directly in front of the Regent Club audience, when Monica utters '*Piya tu ab toh aa ja*' slowly for the first time, she is facing the camera, but her back is to the audience. Similarly, two minutes into the song, when RD sings out '*Monica, oh my*

---

[12]Nasreen Munni Kabir, 'The Goldie Standard', *Indian Quarterly*, Volume 4, Issue 1, October–December 2015, pp. 79-80.

darling' a couple of times at full throttle, Monica is picturized in
full view from the side opposite the wall painted with flamingos,
with a parallel dolly tracking shot. But for the audience, she is
only moving away from them in a series of side-on movements.
Then as she contorts her body backwards under the slide, it is yet
again solely for the benefit of the camera, for the audience can
hardly see her behind the slide. Taking off from Vijay Anand's
comments, such picturizations possibly imbued the sequence
with greater dynamism than what simply framing the performer
solely from the point of view of the audience would have done.

Jerry concluded, 'Here you see an auteur at work. His camera
is never invasive. It's at a sedate distance from Helen, but it's a
narrative camera. It's not an invasive male gaze. It's not getting
on her dress, buttocks, etc. It's staying at the distance of telling
a story. It's quite a performance actually even from the point of
view of technique because she must have actually rehearsed for
this song. Normally it was eight hours for a song. A whole Helen
song would be done in an eight-hour shift. This could not have
been done in eight hours.' In her interview to Nasreen Munni
Kabir for the weekly *Movie Mahal* series, Helen admitted, 'It took
us about ten to twelve days to shoot that dance.'[13]

Ultimately, everything – from Helen to RD's score to art
director Shanti Das's set design to Munir Khan's cinematography
– worked in near-perfect tandem to give Hindi cinema one of
its finest song sequences ever. Considering what Jerry suggests
in his book – 'The arrival of R.D. Burman's music and Asha
Bhonsle's voice also gave Helen's career as a vamp [in the 1970s]
a new dimension. The fusion R.D. infused into Hindi film music
demanded a new vocabulary of movement. Who else could

---

[13]*Movie Mahal* aired on England's Channel 4 from 1987 until 1989.
'Movie Mahal 38: Helen Part 1', the thirty-eighth in the series, first aired
on 7 May 1989 (https://www.youtube.com/watch?v=OZfFYS3Uq5c).

dance to Pancham's irresistible beats?'[14] – Husain was perhaps being perceptive as he gave Helen a near blank canvas to do her thing against the backdrop of RD's score. The song itself is a rare occurrence among Husain's many song sequences since it doesn't feature either the film's hero or the heroine. From Helen's point of view as well, she seldom got such an uncluttered space, free of junior artistes around whom she would often enough have to foolishly cavort, and where she didn't have to work her seductive charms on the film's hero. No wonder then that Balaji and Bhattacharjee rightly termed '*Piya tu*' 'The Last Word in Cabaret' while including it in their book, *Gaata Rahe Mera Dil: 50 Classic Hindi Film Songs*.[15]

Caravan proved to be Husain's last film with Asha Parekh in a lead role. While he had planned another film with her after *Hum Kisise Kum Naheen*, he had to eventually abandon that project. Parekh then played the role of the hero's mother in *Manzil Manzil*. The two shared a tremendous working rapport and Husain deserves much credit for catapulting Parekh into stardom with *Dil Deke Dekho*. While Parekh enjoyed success in films working with film-makers such as Raj Khosla, Pramod Chakravorty, J. Om Prakash and Shakti Samanta, it is her work in Husain's films that forms the main part of her oeuvre. Sidharth Bhatia told me that it was Husain who shaped Parekh's 'tomboy image'. Jerry contended that it was Parekh 'who prepared the way for Zeenat Aman and

---

[14]Jerry Pinto, 'Main Gud ki Dali', *Helen: The Life and Times of an H Bomb*, Penguin Books India, 2006, p. 83.

[15]Anirudha Bhattacharjee and Balaji Vittal, 'The Last Word in Cabaret', *Gaata Rahe Mera Dil: 50 Classic Hindi Film Songs*, HarperCollins *Publishers* India, 2015, p. 193.

Parveen Babi' owing to the 'rock-'n'-roll' image that she got in Husain's films. Together, Husain and Parekh also formed a film distribution company, called Movie Gems, beginning with *Baharon Ke Sapne*. In all, they distributed twenty-one films under Movie Gems, including *Saraswatichandra* (1968), *Caravan*, *Raampur Ka Lakshman* (1972), *Hum Kisise Kum Naheen*, *Abdullah* (1980) and *Zamaane Ko Dikhana Hai*.

Complimenting Parekh in a *Filmfare* article, Husain said, 'Asha is one of the most disciplined of actresses. She's punctual, very cooperative ... With Asha by your side, you feel you are working with a close friend rather than a top star. She shares your smiles and tears, your difficulties and trials. And she's an asset to a producer because she takes on herself all responsibility for her costumes, jewellery, hair-do and so on ... Asha's charm, according to some, lies in two features – her innocent face, and her infectious laughter. In fact, Asha's laughter like Dev Anand's smile has an indefinable magnetism. When Asha laughs, you just can't help joining.'[16]

Aamir put the working relationship between film-maker and actor in proper perspective. 'Certainly, just by the fact that they have done so many films together, it tells us that they did have some sort of special relationship, one would understand that. That way, Nasir sa'ab also had a special relationship with Pancham uncle and with Majrooh sa'ab. He worked consistently with them over many, many films.'

---

[16]Nasir Husain, 'Thanking My Stars', *Filmfare*, 25 November 1966, p. 29.

10

OF BICHHDEY HUEY BHAI AND MUSICAL SCREENPLAYS

'Nasir sa'ab didn't seem preoccupied by any kind of ideology. So what was his forte? To me, it was his understanding of music. He knew that music was the main entertainer. I would say, his cinema was in the real tradition of the Hollywood musical.'

– Author and documentary film-maker
Nasreen Munni Kabir

'The bonding of the three brothers is critical to the film [*Yaadon Ki Baaraat*] and that's been expressed very well in the film, in that moment when Tariq bhai says I am going to sing the song, which I always sing, once again. Until now no one has ever joined me and Vijay Arora gets up ... *raungtey khadey ho jaatey hain* (it gives you gooseflesh).'

– Actor–producer Aamir Khan

For *Caravan*, Husain collaborated with film writer Sachin Bhowmick on the film's screenplay. Bhowmick was among the eminent screenplay–story writers of the 1960s, having scripted several successful films like *Ziddi* (1964), *Aayee Milan Ki Bela* (1964), *An Evening in Paris* (1967) and *Aradhana* (1969). Husain also worked with Bhowmick on his later films right up to

249

Zabardast. 'Sachin-da was a storehouse of plot points,' Mansoor said. 'But even then, my dad would do the fundamental writing. The fitting and the structure was what my dad was doing. Sachin-da was complementary. A lot of screenplays of a particular kind require a teamwork of three or four people.' Nuzhat elaborated, 'Earlier on because Dad was working on his own and he needed someone to talk to, Dad himself used to say, "I need a sounding board." Sachin Bhowmick's strength was that he had probably read every book in the world and seen every film in the world. His library had all the best-sellers, all the novels and love stories. His mind was like an encyclopaedia. Whatever Dad said would spark off something in him. And he would say, "You know I read a book once…," some situation and then somehow, something would be taken from that. This is how Sachin Bhowmick was very helpful. Dad would take him and they would go and sit in Lonavala, Panchgani – one week, two weeks and every morning after breakfast, they would sit outside and Dad would keep talking and then Dad would do the actual writing.'

Another pair of writers, who appeared at the end of the 1960s, were Salim–Javed. Although the duo would come to own the 1970s, Salim–Javed had a difficult time establishing themselves. Gautam Chintamani noted in his best-selling book on Rajesh Khanna that the pair's 'screen credit in the early days was often devoured by a title card that read "Sippy Films Story Department".'[1] It is only after the success of *Haathi Mere Saathi* and *Seeta Aur Geeta* that the duo emerged from the shadows as a formidable writer duo. It was to this pair that Husain turned for scripting *Yaadon Ki Baaraat,* a blockbuster commercial success.

Yaadon Ki Baaraat is essentially a revenge drama. The film begins with a couple celebrating their anniversary. To mark the

[1]Gautam Chintamani, 'That God Feeling', *Dark Star: The Loneliness of Being Rajesh Khanna*, HarperCollins *Publishers* India, 2014, p. 55.

occasion, the mother sings the film's title track, '*Yaadon ki baaraat*', the same song that she sings every year on this day, with her husband, an artist, Gulzar (Nasir Khan), strumming the guitar and her three sons singing along with her.[2] One night, Gulzar stumbles upon Shaakaal (Ajit) and his henchmen committing a murder. Afraid that Gulzar has seen him, Shaakaal reaches Gulzar's house and kills him and his wife. Shaakaal also wishes to eliminate Gulzar's three sons so that there is no trace of his crime, but the children escape and are separated from each other.

The eldest son grows up to be Shankar (Dharmendra), a professional thief. Vijay (Vijay Arora), the middle sibling, who is found lying unconscious by the railway tracks while running away from Shaakaal, is raised by Mr Verma (Shivraj). Vijay grows up to romance Sunita (Zeenat Aman). Ratan (Tariq Khan), the youngest brother, who is saved by the children's governess, grows up to be a musician. Ratan performs under the name Monto and regularly sings the song '*Yaadon ki baaraat*' at his various performances as a way of finding his brothers. Shankar, who is scarred most by the memory of his parents' murder and separation from his siblings, makes it his life's mission to avenge their death by finding the elusive Shaakaal. Ultimately, the brothers are reunited through the song.

Before delving into the many fine aspects of *Yaadon Ki Baaraat*, it is important to trace the genealogy of the lost-and-found theme, a very popular motif in Hindi cinema. Indian mythology

---

[2]According to film journalist Rajiv Vijayakar, this '*Yaadon ki baaraat*' track is sung by Padmini Kolhapure and sister Shivangi besides Lata Mangeshkar. Music directors Jatin–Lalit, too, sang in the chorus. Rajiv Vijayakar, 'Adieu Nasir Husain', *Screen*, 22 March 2002, p. 16.

is rich with tales of separation such as Dushyant–Shakuntala and Karna and Kunti. Gyan Mukherjee's *Kismet* (1943) is amongst the earliest known Hindi films that made use of this device. *Awara* (1951), likewise, is another reworking of the lost-and-found Ramayana story but where, 'this pregnant Sita who is thrown out by her husband due to suspected loss of honour, lands up not in the lap of nature, but in the slums of the big city of Bombay'.[3]

Several directors such as Shakti Samanta, Husain and Manmohan Desai used the theme quite frequently in their films. Ashim Samanta mentioned that the influence of Gyan Mukherjee, with whom his father had worked as an assistant, probably explains the use of the trope in films like *China Town*, *Kashmir Ki Kali* and *An Evening in Paris*. Husain could have absorbed the idea from S. Mukerji, who was with Bombay Talkies when *Kismet* was made. For instance, *Hum Sab Chor Hain* (1956), which was produced by Filmistan and had Nalini Jaywant in a double role, is the story of twin sisters separated in their childhood reuniting at the end of the film.

Rashmi Doraiswamy justified the fascination for the motif in her paper on Husain. 'The lost-and-found theme has a range of associations with myths as well as resonances of contemporary social and political upheavals that cause families to be split. It functions often as a trope of the unnameable or the repressed, of the trauma of the Partition of the Indian subcontinent, of displacement, uprootment and the losing of one's kith and kin in the mayhem. While the theme is prevalent in Hindi cinema even before Independence/Partition, its enduring appeal in Hindi cinema is probably explained by the cluster of associations of

---

[3]Dr Rashmi Doraiswamy, '"These Days" of Our Modernity: The Cinema of Nasir Husain', Film and Television Institute of India, Pune, 4 September 2004, p. 10.

traumatic loss and separation – conscious and unconscious – that it evokes.'[4]

The interesting thing is that while Indian mythology hardly has any tales of sibling lost-and-found, Hindi cinema is replete with such tales. Initially, though, the films were only about two siblings being separated. Yash Chopra's *Waqt* (1965) was the first film to show three brothers being reunited along with their parents at the film's climax. M.K. Raghavendra explained the popularity of the sibling lost-and-found plot in Hindi cinema. 'One purpose in having siblings thrown apart by circumstances is to suggest two different social trajectories taken by two people who were once in the same social situation. The trajectories correspond to different social experiences, and the difference signifies a divided society. But if you look at most of the Indian films you mentioned, you will also find that one brother is in conflict with the law. This is also true in *Kismet* in which he [Ashok Kumar] is a thief. The "division" may then be understood as being between state authority (i.e., the law) and the citizen who is drawn into conflict with it.'

In most lost-and-found films, the reunion happens through an ornament, either a locket or a taveez or some kind of shared memory. This too is a continuation of mythological tradition, for example, in the case of Dushyant–Shakuntala, where a ring reunites the couple. There are scant instances of music being used towards this end in mythology. A rare exception is the Buddhist legend of Emperor Ashoka reuniting with his blind son Kanishka, a musician, when the former hears the latter sing in the streets of Patna.[5]

Correspondingly, the use of music to bring about reunion in Hindi cinema is also sporadic but present nonetheless. In

---

[4]Ibid.

[5]Michael Wood, 'The Power of Ideas', *The Story of India*, RHUK, 2008, pp. 110-111.

Albela (1951), Bhagwan's character finds his family members when he hears the song, '*Dheere se aa ja ri ankhiyan mein*', the song his sister used to sing to him. In the lesser known *Beti Bete* (1964), while the youngest brother is reunited with his eldest sister by means of a locket, the middle sibling identifies his sister when he hears her sing, '*Aaj kal mein dhal gaya*', a song brother and sister had sung in childhood. In *Hare Rama Hare Krishna* (1971), while Prashant (Dev Anand) is aware of his sister Janice's (Zeenat Aman) identity, he sings '*Phoolon ka taaron ka*' right at the end of the film to make her aware that he is her brother.

Husain, too, used music to connect Sunder and his parents in *Pyar Ka Mausam*. Sunder's father Gopal sings '*Tum bin jaaoon kahaan*' regularly to Jamuna since before their marriage. After they are separated, Sunder hears Gopal singing this song on the streets in Ooty and learns it from him. When Sunder sings this song at Sardar Ranjit Kumar's house, Jamuna, recognizing the song, speaks for the first time after twenty long years. On their part, Salim–Javed had used the lost-and-found trope in *Seeta Aur Geeta* where the sisters (played by Hema Malini in a double role) are separated at birth.[6] The woman who has raised Geeta as her own child reveals her identity to Raka (Dharmendra).

Salim Khan, one half of the famed writing pair, and who acted in Husain's *Teesri Manzil* as Rocky's friend, talked about their collaboration with Husain. 'Yes, he approached us. Naturally, knowing his style, we told him a story that would suit him,'

---

[6]Salim–Javed had taken the theme from *Ram Aur Shyam* (1967), while cleverly changing the hero's double role to the heroine. They also used the lost-and-found theme in their later films: *Haath Ki Safai* (1974) and *Chacha Bhatija* (1977).

said Salim. 'We gave him the basic idea that the brothers find each other with a song. We knew we couldn't make *Deewaar*, *Sholay* or *Shakti* with Nasir Husain. We knew we had to blend it with music. As professional writers, we had to know what each person wanted. We catered to different directors. If we were writing for K. Asif, we would have written a film suiting his style. Song sequences were his [Husain's] forte. His story moved with the song.' The film's title once again showed Husain's fondness for poetry as it was borrowed from the famed poet Josh Malihabadi's autobiography by the same name. 'Most of the titles for our films were ours – like *Seeta Aur Geeta*, *Haathi Mere Saathi*, *Zanjeer* and *Sholay*. But for this film Nasir sa'ab gave the title,' Salim told me.

'It was a Nasir Husain hyphen Salim–Javed film,' Javed Akhtar added. 'Generally, we used to work on our own and hand over the complete screenplay to the director, but *Yaadon Ki Baaraat* was made along with him. All three of us sat together and developed the screenplay. As a matter of fact, Nasir sa'ab's name could also come in the screenplay. Dialogues were entirely his.'

Akhtar's admission is concrete proof of Husain's signature touch to the film. While Shankar's obsession with avenging his parents is necessarily a Salim–Javed plotline, and a near replica of their storyline for *Zanjeer*, Vijay's romantic pursuit of Sunita and the musician figure of Monto are vintage Husain. Mansoor remarked, 'Yes, that is a fact. I know that the premise of the film, and the main story of Shaakaal and Shankar, he got from them. That is the body of the film. Dharmendra's character is very dry and intentionally so. Where would the entertainment come from? That's the difference between *Zanjeer* and *Yaadon Ki Baaraat*. *Yaadon Ki Baaraat* is broader in its sweep of entertainment, both through Vijay Arora and his romantic antics and Tariq bhai and his musical performances. I can understand that he liked Salim–

Javed's plot. But he had to shape it with his forte. He wouldn't have been able to render it purely as a single thread, vendetta film and throw in some songs for Dharmendra. To keep the integrity, the sombreness of that character [Shankar's], while retaining the entertainment quotient, you needed these other characters.' Akhtar agreed with this assessment. 'If you look at the script, it is indeed a great mix of Nasir Husain's films and Salim–Javed's films.'[7]

Among the more definitive Salim–Javed influences on *Yaadon Ki Baaraat* is the presence of the train and its symbolism in the film. The film begins with a shot of (and sound made by) a slow-moving train, before the camera zooms out and moves right to show the courtyard in which the family members have gathered to celebrate. Then, when the young Shankar and Vijay escape from Shaakaal, Shankar gets on board a moving train while Vijay is left behind. Throughout the film, Shankar is haunted by the memory of his brother hopelessly running after the train, screaming '*bhaiyya, bhaiyya*'. Later in the film, Jack (Satyen Kappu), one of Shaakaal's accomplices on the night Gulzar and his wife are killed, is murdered by the railway tracks by Shaakaal. At the climax, although Shankar is involved in a prolonged fight sequence with Shaakaal at a deserted airstrip, he chases Shaakaal to the nearby railway tracks. Shaakaal's foot gets stuck in the railway tracks and he is run over by a speeding train. The final scene of the film shows Shankar reunited with his brothers on the very railway tracks that have represented trauma and misery for him all these years.

Right through the 1950s and 1960s, the train and its associated emblems (the railway tracks, the noise made by it, the platform) served as a place of romance in Hindi cinema and had a jolly, romantic vibe to them. The many wonderful songs from this

---

[7]Zee Classic's *Classic Legends: Season II*, featuring Nasir Husain.

period like '*Hai apna dil toh awaara*' from (*Solva Saal*, 1958), '*Main chali main chali*' (*Professor*, 1962) and '*Mere sapnon ki rani*' (*Aradhana*) establish this. Husain also was at the vanguard of showing the train as a place where strangers meet (*Tumsa Nahin Dekha, Teesri Manzil*) and love blossoms ('*Jiya ho*', *Jab Pyar Kisise Hota Hai*). The train gives these song sequences a certain sense of dynamism and vitality and provides a showcase for Hindi cinema's tryst with the countryside with the advent of the '60s. The train was also a symbol of national unity. M.K. Raghavendra noted, 'The imagery of passing railway stations' in films like *Devdas* (1955) and *Jailor* (1958) gave it this identity.[8] *Aashirwad's* (1968) remarkable '*Rail gaadi, rail gaadi*' accentuates this as it mentions the various places that the Indian rail network traversed. It is this symbolism that allowed the wonderful song from *Jagriti* (1954), '*Aao bachchon tumhe dikhaayein*', a salutation to the idea of India, to take place from within the train. On the odd occasion, the train turned into a place where a strong philosophical or social comment was made – as seen in '*Dekh tere sansar ki haalat*' (*Nastik*, 1954) – precisely because, ideologically, it hadn't come to represent vice or evil in the mainstream yet. Films like *Shart* or *Aar Paar*, both from 1954, or Pramod Chakravorty's *Passport* (1961), all of which depicted the train for various sinister motives were, however, the exceptions.

With the coming of the '70s, however, the train acquired a much more diabolical presence. In a sense, this was a return of a certain tradition that had previously shown Fearless Nadia (Mary Evans) fighting off goons on the top of a train (*Miss Frontier Mail*, 1936). But in the '70s, the dramatic element around a train was reinforced. Films like *The Train* (1970), *Parwana* (1971),

---

[8]M.K. Raghavendra, 'The 1950s and 1960s', *Seduced by the Familiar: Narration and Meaning in Indian Popular Cinema*, Oxford University Press, 2008, p. 147.

Shor (1972), *Pakeezah* (1972) and *Do Anjaane* (1976) actually portrayed the train as an ominous presence capable of generating mystery, crime, anxiety and causing upheaval in human life. The haunting nature of R.D. Burman's composition for '*Dhanno ki aankhon mein*' (*Kitaab*, 1977) emphasized this shifting view of the train.

Contributing to this changed depiction of the train were Salim–Javed. Just like in *Yaadon Ki Baaraat*, where the train has an inherently menacing and circular narrative presence, the duo's epic effort *Sholay* (1975) begins with the shot of a train slowly entering a station and ends with the train moving out of this very station. It is on a train that we are first introduced to the brothers-in-arms, Jai and Veeru, and their fight with Gabbar Singh's men, which showcases their valour, is also part of a longish train sequence that is as dramatic as it is iconic. *Zanjeer*, from the same year as *Yaadon Ki Baaraat*, has Keshto Mukherjee's character pushed off the train. Most importantly, the impact of the iconic line '*Mere paas maa hai*' from *Deewaar* (1975) is underscored almost instantly by the sound of the train in the next scene, one of the trains on which the protagonists' father dies as he crisscrosses the country, rootless and shame-struck.

Kaushik Bhaumik argued that a 'certain leftist cinema tradition' contributed to this changed representation of the train. Bhaumik contended that names like Gulzar (*Kitaab*) and Chetan Anand (*Aakhri Khat*, 1966), who came from this tradition, 'saw the train as an ambiguous thing. It can kill people, it can run over people, it can be used for smuggling things, villainy can happen within it. It can separate people in as much as it can bring people together. It becomes multidimensional whereas earlier it was unidimensional.'

In Husain's *Baharon Ke Sapne*, a film which is certainly left of centre, the train is used very much as a device to create tension in keeping with Bhaumik's remarks. While Ram journeys to and returns from Bombay in a train, he is also shown walking on the railway tracks as if in a trance early in the film. Fearing that he is out to commit suicide, Geeta lunges and saves him at the last moment just as a train screams by. A similar dramatic moment, when Ram's mother learns that her husband (Nana Palsikar) has lost his job at the mill over a month ago, is enhanced by the sight and sound of a moving train.

Returning to *Yaadon Ki Baaraat*, however, Husain (along with cinematographer Munir Khan) executed a complex, intricate sequence to depict Shankar's traumatic relationship with the train. The young Shankar, having just committed a petty crime, comes to the bridge where he had seen his younger brother Vijay for the last time. As the young Shankar, wearing shorts, leans against the bridge, we hear the sound of an approaching train. The camera moves down to Shankar's feet, then slowly swivels around in a single 360-degree move, taking in the sight of the train and returns to Shankar's legs, now in trousers. The camera pans up to reveal the grave, grown-up Shankar (now Dharmendra). The shot ends only when Shankar moves away from the bridge. This single, uninterrupted shot, which depicts the passage of fifteen years, is as dramatic as it is impressive since it goes against the conventional norms of depicting passage of time.

Jai Arjun Singh explained the novel nature of the sequence lucidly on his blog. 'Actually, as Bollywood representations of children morphing into adults go, this is quite a complex and artistic sequence – better crafted than all those standard-issue shots of a boy's running legs dissolving into the man's. One might even call it cinematically ambitious. After all, a dissolve or a cut is the accepted way of marking a shift in time; movies use these

MUSIC MASTI MODERNITY

techniques all the time. For example, a little later in *Yaadon Ki Baaraat*, a scene where another boy [the young Vijay] runs behind a train, losing the race as it enters a tunnel, segues into a shot of the grown-up version of the character riding his bike out of a similar tunnel ... Now that's what I'd call a conventional time-shift scene (by Hindi-movie standards). But when 20 [*sic, 15*] years rush by within the span of a single, unbroken shot, it really makes you sit up and take notice.'[9]

This singular shot is a rare exception in Husain's oeuvre. Husain hardly ever indulged in a cinematic statement such as this outside of his song sequences. What is interesting about the shot is that the 360-degree camera pan is anti-clockwise, which means that it goes against the idea of the forward passage of time. While this may have happened as an offshoot to the direction in which the adolescent Shankar is looking, Bhaumik observed, 'The clockwise pan is always about showing the expanse of the landscape in a "positive" way, its breadth and spread. The counter-clockwise pan scrambles our brain, goes against the grain of the habits of the eye and produces a resistance, a friction within us. We know this is not a smooth romantic passage through time. The hero owns the landscape in his stubborn urge for revenge, this landscape is dominated by his will and does not want anyone else in it. The fact that Dharmendra's stance dominates all space is then made absolutely explicit when he jumps on to the train – there is no place for anyone else in that world. He is the baadshah of the world, absolutely dominating it in his seething rage. This rage is world destroying, far from being hospitable to others sharing space with him.

'This again is a typical Salim–Javed trick – doing things in masala ways but by a spectacular reversal of film rules to show

[9]Jabberwock (Jaiarjun.blogspot.in), 'PoV 6: Memories of Master Mayur' (http://jaiarjun.blogspot.in/2010/07/pov-6-memories-of-mayur.html)

the contrarian nature of the hero, the antihero literally. In fact, if the clockwise pan is shoe-size 8, the counter-clockwise pan is shoe-size 9. You cover the same landscape but there is something excessive about the counter-clockwise pan, something psychotic that Ajit and Dharmendra share in this film. They are both "tedha" to the ways of the world, which both the counter-clockwise pan and the discrepant shoe-size denote.'

The other distinct Salim–Javed influence in *Yaadon Ki Baaraat* is Bombay city. Besides Vijay's and Sunita's romance, the major portion of which plays out in Mahabaleshwar, it is Bombay where all the other protagonists are present and Shankar and Shaakaal play out their game of hide-and-seek. While the city isn't shown in the same way as in films such as *Taxi Driver* (1954) or *Amar Akbar Anthony* (1977), it is referred to in several places: '*Bambai ke Seth Devidayal*', '*Main kal Bambai jaoonga*' (I will go to Bombay tomorrow) and '*Bambai shehar mein railway line ke kareeb kitne telephone booth hain?*' (How many telephone booths in Bombay are situated adjacent to the railway tracks?). The LIC building shown at the end of the film is final proof of the film's narrative unfolding in Bombay.

Yaadon Ki Baaraat is one of the early films of the 1970s that brought the city back into prominence after the 1950s. While film-makers in the 1960s had ignored the city for the hill station, Salim–Javed demonstrated a propensity to base their narratives in the city in films like *Deewaar, Don, Trishul* and *Shakti*. Other film-makers such as Manmohan Desai (*Amar Akbar Anthony*) and Prakash Mehra (*Muqaddar Ka Sikandar*, 1978), too, followed suit. M.K. Raghavendra opined that the films of the 1970s depicted the city 'as an emblem of opportunity. Each of these films celebrates the rise of an individual from deprivation to immense wealth and power and the discourse is partly about the opportunities in the city – both within and outside the law.'[10]

Linked to the presence of the city in the films of the 1970s is the changing figure of the villain as exemplified by Shaakaal. The villain of the 1950s was not an outright villain and maintained a certain façade in society. He was out to destroy it with his greed and evil ways in films like *Baazi, Footpath, Shree 420, Pyaasa* or *Mother India*. His villainy was symptomatic of the problems that plagued the newly independent nation state. On the other hand, the villain of the 1960s (like in Husain's films) was more a 'personal villain' who is interested in the hero or the heroine's property and wealth, and is related to them by way of social ties and family circles. Any number of films right through the 1960s – such as *Junglee, Bluff Master* (1963), *Ganga Ki Lehren* (1964), *Kashmir Ki Kali, Love in Tokyo*, including many of Husain's films right up to *Caravan* – are proof of this.

However, with the coming of the 1970s, a much larger, more diabolical villain came to the fore. Men like Shaakaal, Saamant (Madan Puri, *Deewaar*), Gabbar Singh (Amjad Khan, *Sholay*), 'Loin' (Ajit, *Kalicharan*, 1976) and Vikram (Amjad Khan, *Mr. Natwarlal*, 1979) came on screen to strike terror. This villain was a reaction to Salim–Javed's 'Angry Young Man' character, who operated as an individual, on the margins of society and against established social rules. His persona had to be matched against a much larger villainous figure.

Husain reacted to such larger-than-life villains following *Yaadon Ki Baaraat* with a 'most wanted' figure like Saudagar Singh in *Hum Kisise Kum Naheen*. As a result, his action sequences at

---

[10]M.K. Raghavendra, 'The 1970s', *Seduced by the Familiar: Narration and Meaning in Indian Popular Cinema*, Oxford University Press, 2008, pp. 180-181.

the end of *Yaadon Ki Baaraat* and *Hum Kisise Kum Naheen* also become far grander than in any of his earlier films. 'Because he has to take into account what has happened in between,' commented Bhaumik. '[Amitabh] Bachchan has happened. He has to acknowledge Bachchan's intervention as an action hero and that's why the scale has to go up.' Husain followed Saudagar Singh up with characters like 'Das, smuggler' (Prem Chopra) and Rana (Surendra Pal) in *Manzil Manzil*[11] and Balram Singh (Amrish Puri) in *Zabardast*. Not all of this was necessarily good as the climax in his last few directorial ventures only got longer and more tedious, ultimately bringing about Husain's downfall.

Yaadon Ki Baaraat, though, bears Husain's stamp. It is yet another example of Husain's changed approach to the film's music beginning with *Teesri Manzil*, where Husain had started incorporating music far more interestingly in his screenplays. *Teesri Manzil*, although borrowing from Raja's profession in *Dil Deke Dekho*, had the entire murder mystery play around Rocky, a musician figure, as the prime suspect. With *Pyar Ka Mausam*, Husain had also shown an inclination to use music to bring people together. *Caravan* is about performing, itinerant banjaras and therefore music fits into the film seamlessly. *Hum Kisise Kum Naheen* builds on *Pyar Ka Mausam*'s and *Yaadon Ki Baaraat*'s theme and uses the song '*Kya hua tera waada*' to help Kaajal realize who Sanjay really is. 'Music becomes a very integral part,' said Aamir. 'I would imagine, as he goes along he realizes that music is something that he loves. That it is his strength. So he starts building it more strongly into the writing.'

---

[11]Rana's character in *Manzil Manzil* is introduced by Das as the man who is the kingpin of the illicit arms trade in India.

While the earlier films essentially used songs to build up the romance between the film's protagonists, the songs from *Teesri Manzil* onwards have several other functions. For instance, we get a glimpse of Ruby's exploitative handling of Rocky all through *Teesri Manzil* in '*O haseena zulfon waali*' when she addresses him with the words, '*Qatl karkey chalein, yeh wafaa khoob hai*' (You walk away, having committed murder, what fidelity you display). In the same song, Ruby is also established as someone who emerges furtively, almost from the shadows, in the film:

Main bhi hoon galiyon ki parchhaayee, kabhi yahaan, kabhi wahaan
Shaam hi se kuchh ho jaata hai, mera bhi jaadoo jawaan

(I am a shadow of the street, a flicker here, a flash there
When evening comes, I come into my own)

In *Pyar Ka Mausam*, '*Tum bin jaaoon kahaan*' serves a variety of purposes. While initially it establishes a connect between Sunder and his father, it also brings Jamuna to her senses and forces her to seek out the singer. However, when Sunder first sings it to Seema, the antaras '*Dekho mujhe sar se kadam tak, sirf pyaar hoon main...*' (Look at me, from head to toe, I am all about love) and '*Ab sanam hai har mausam, pyaar ke qaabil...*' (Every season, my dear, is now only for romance) serenade her. But when he sings the same song at Sardar Ranjit Kumar's house, his tone is far more melancholic. He uses the words '*Kabhi mere gham ki kahaani, dil se mat kehna...*' (Don't ever mention my desolate story to your heart) to taunt Seema over a failed romantic episode.

Caravan's rather sensuous '*Ab jo mile hain toh baahon mein*' actually plays out the entire dynamics of the Mohan–Soni–Nisha triangle in one song. Nisha seduces Mohan with the lyrics:

Yoon hi nasha chadhta rahey, ke tera pyaar badhta rahey
Yeh jhoomta saaya tera, tann pe mere padta rahey,
Tu aa gaya jo hosh mein, kya hoga phir yeh bhool ja

(As yours spirits continue to rise, so may your love
Let your inebriated shadow, engulf me entirely
Were you to come to your senses, forget about that for the
    moment)

To this erotic display of love, Soni responds wistfully, giving a
hint of her complex backstory:

Tu hai hawa, shola hoon main, milkey bhi jo mil na sakey
Bujh na sakey tere bina, tere bina jal na sakey
Majboor hoon teri kasam, jhoothi nahin meri wafaa

(You are the breeze, I am like burning embers, we cannot meet
    even though we have
I can't be put out without you, I can't burn without you
I am helpless, but do not doubt my love)

In *Hum Kisise Kum Naheen*, the song '*Humko toh yaara teri yaari*' is
a signifier of Kaajal's presence as a pawn in Manjeet's entire master
plan to get back his diamonds from her father. While the song's
musical arrangement and its picturization give it the deceptive
appearance of a regular, frothy Husain number, Manjeet sings:

Dil ke heerey, moti aaja mere dil mein aa,
Tu hai daulat meri, aa meri manzil mein aa,
Aye meri tamanna ab tu kaheen na ja, hai re hai, kaheen na ja

(You are like diamonds and pearls to me, come stay with me
You are my wealth, the means to my end
Oh what I long for, now don't you wander anywhere, don't go
    away)

In the same film, the medley sequence plays out the entire
dynamics between Manjeet, Sanjay and Kaajal. When Sanjay
sings '*Chaand mera dil*', he warns Kaajal that true love is found
with great difficulty ('*Milega sachcha pyaar mushkil se*') and that
she will have to return to him sooner or later ('*Laut ke aana hai*

yaheen tumko'). Manjeet responds to Sanjay by promising the world to Kaajal ('*Duniya ki bahaarein tere liye, chaand sitaarey tere liye*'). To this, Sanjay plays the class conflict card. It is then left to Kaajal to join Manjeet on stage and declare unanimously, '*Mil gaya humko saathi mil gaya*'. Feeling cheated by Sanjay for having lied to her previously, she even takes a swipe at him with '*Humse agar koi jal gaya, jalney de*'.

In this context, Husain consistently spoke of the song's role in advancing the film's narrative. 'A song has to say something. It should take the film ahead. I would spend a lot of time with Majrooh sa'ab on song situations,' he said.[12]

It is to this end that '*Lekar hum deewaana dil*', *Yaadon Ki Baaraat*'s pièce de résistance works. Although the song can be read as 'just' a romantic duet between Monto (Tariq) and his girlfriend (Neetu Singh), the picturization tells us so much about the film as a whole. The song begins just after Shaakaal has an aide of his garrotted. The audience isn't made witness to the brutality of the crime, but RD's full-throated, manic voiceover for Monto at the beginning of the song, synchronized with the possible screams of a man being suffocated somewhere in the same hotel, is implicit confirmation of the heinous act. The screen too is drenched in red to signify the beastly act as the nubile frame of Neetu Singh[13] appears.

As the song progresses, we see that Vijay is a steward in the same hotel. Meanwhile, the eldest brother, Shankar, is shown committing his 'Natraj murti' heist in the interludes. Shaakaal

[12]Ambarish Mishra, 'I will always be a romantic at heart', *The Times of India*, 7 May 2000,

[13]Apparently, Singh, who had starred as a child artiste in films like *Do Kaliyan* (1968), was only fifteen when *Yaadon Ki Baaraat* released.

enjoys the proceedings from a vantage point while his moll, Bindu's character, sits on his lap and then pours him a drink. His son, Roopesh (Imtiaz Khan), too makes himself comfortable in the company of a young lady. The backdrop on stage also, possibly, establishes this as Shaakaal's lair. It resembles a human eye-like cobweb setting, whose pupil-like, red light-emitting centre signifies Shaakaal's presence in this space. He watches over his world, with the song's picturization reinforcing the fact that the brothers, all employed by him in various ways – as singer, as steward and hired hand – are caught in the sticky web spun by him. The regular appearance of the colour red through the song – be it through Monto's scarf, Neetu Singh's dress, the clothes worn by Roopesh's paramour, the circular red disc on which Neetu Singh writhes and the lampshade beside Shaakaal's bed – confirm the bloodied nature of this world.

The lyrics provide a microcosm of the film's storyline. While Monto and Neetu Singh's character engage in what appears a playful enough duet, words like '*Kaheen toh pyaare, kisi kinaarey, mil jao tum andherey ujaaley*' (Somewhere my dear, in some corner, I shall find you be it night or day) tell us a lot about Monto's determined quest in finding his brothers. The use of the word 'pyaare' itself is a big hint. 'Pyaare' is used to address the male gender, but by placing Neetu Singh in the song, Husain indulges in misdirection. Dressed in red, Neetu Singh turns out to be the proverbial red herring.

The picturization confirms this. During the first antara, Monto sings the rich-with-innuendo, '*Tum yaheen kaheen, hum yaheen kaheen, phir bhi yeh dooriyaan*' (You are here somewhere, I am here too, and yet such a distance separates us) while his brother Vijay waits on the tables in close proximity to him. Neetu Singh responds to Monto by getting off the stage and going amidst the dining patrons to perform, but only ends up bumping into Vijay. Just as she does this, she delivers the rather loaded line, '*Waah ree*

duniya, duniya tere jalwey hai niraaley' (Strange are the ways of
the world) even as the estranged brothers, Monto and Vijay, come
in direct view of each other. In another wink-wink moment soon
after, when Monto begins to sing the refrain '*Kaheen toh pyaare*',
the shot cuts to Vijay abruptly looking up towards Monto while
taking an order. As Monto sings the rest of the line, '*mil jao tum
andherey ujaaley*', the camera cuts interchangeably between Monto
and Vijay, clearly indicating that this is about these *bichhdey huey
bhai* (separated siblings).

Aamir said, 'This is a remarkable song because it starts with
a guy dying, there is a performance happening and Dharam-ji is
committing a robbery. So this is actually a screenplay marvel that
while this celebration is happening, *wahaan pe chori chal rahi hai,
yeh uska bhai bhi hai, he doesn't know yeh mera bhai hai* (there is
a robbery happening somewhere else, this is his brother, they are
unaware that they are siblings) – all this is happening in one song.'

Bhaumik, who once delivered a lecture titled 'Why Ajit had
to die a spectacular death in *Yaadon Ki Baaraat*' at Jadavpur
University, echoed this. 'Why I find *Yaadon Ki Baaraat* absolutely
spectacularly exciting is precisely because it is so visceral.
Everything is falling apart. The mise-en-scène is falling apart.
The montage is out of sync. Zooms, tracks, there are rapid cuts,
transitions between situations are very abrupt – because it's trying
to show action happening in three or four locations. "*Lekar hum
deewaana dil*" is a great example of the marvel that is the screenplay.
You have multiple locations, multiple strands that keep the story
going, like the heist, the brothers. The cuts are so abrupt because
so much information has to be packed into one song. You have
to show what is happening on stage, then you have to show an
entire heist. It's all extremely fragmented, rapid and extremely
dynamic. It adds an energy to it. The music goes so well with it.

'It would have been interesting to ask RD whether they wanted to have that manic-syncopated rhythm, but it does seem that the way in which the music is composed, it is so fantastically synced to that manic cutting. It undoubtedly was shot like a special sequence. I'm sure it was meant to be a pièce de résistance for the audience and even for the technicians. You get that feeling because the sound is also so much more spectacular.'

With *Yaadon Ki Baaraat*, Husain reformulated his own brand of lost-and-found films, providing, in the words of Doraiswamy, 'the third variant of this [lost-and-found] theme: he draws neither on mythic/epic [*Awara*] narratives nor on the ruse of natural calamity [*Waqt*]. He embeds his lost-and-found theme in the representational world of the Western thriller ... but Nasir Husain's foray into the world of the thriller avoids the dark noir-like density characteristic of the films of this genre.'[14]

In her meeting with me, Doraiswamy termed the film a 'game-changer'. She complimented Husain for refashioning the lost-and-found theme based on his realization that more than one hero was required to hold the film together and that each of these heroes would need different energies. 'Because the 1970s are a period of crisis, of social upheaval. The whole vision of India as a country is changing,' said Doraiswamy. 'The post-independence era was a period in which institutions were built by the decolonizing state for ensuring social/economic justice, inclusive democracy and secular polity. This changes in the '70s. This is the time when the belief in the ability of the state to dispense justice is questioned. *Yaadon Ki Baaraat* is one of the new multi-starrer films and

[14]Dr Rashmi Doraiswamy, '"These Days" of Our Modernity: The Cinema of Nasir Husain', Film and Television Institute of India, Pune, 4 September 2004, p. 10.

it brings in three different heroes: the youngest continues the earlier preoccupation with the music performer; the middle is the struggler who tries to get ahead at any cost; the eldest is the one who wants vengeance. So you are creating different energies, characters who are going to hold your narrative together and all multi-starrers after this followed this blueprint. This splitting of the energy of the protagonist into three is very important. So what Nasir Husain is doing is that he is going back to *Waqt*, revisiting several of the lost-and-found narratives of the '50s and '60s and bringing them together in a very modern way.'

Yaadon Ki Baaraat is the archetype of the multi-starrer film that became quite the rage in Hindi cinema, beginning with the 1970s. Its influence can also be seen on Manmohan Desai's *Amar Akbar Anthony*, which released a few years later. In Desai's film, three heroes coming from three separate socio-cultural backgrounds, donating blood to the mother figure, definitively represented the pluralistic idea of India. Together, these three films – *Waqt, Yaadon Ki Baaraat* and *Amar Akbar Anthony* – epitomize the lost-and-found theme in Hindi cinema. There are other similarities, too, between them. One sibling in all three films is shown to be in conflict with the law (Raja in *Waqt*, Shankar in *Yaadon Ki Baaraat* and Anthony in *Amar Akbar Anthony*). Both *Yaadon Ki Baaraat* and *Amar Akbar Anthony* have a musician figure (Monto in *Yaadon Ki Baaraat* and Akbar the qawwal in *Amar Akbar Anthony*). *Waqt* and *Amar Akbar Anthony* also have one sibling each who represents the law (Ravi in *Waqt* and Amar in *Amar Akbar Anthony*). But the differences between the three films, particularly from *Yaadon Ki Baaraat*'s perspective, need to be considered as well.

Waqt is the most maudlin of the three films, particularly in its treatment of the characters essayed by Achala Sachdev and Shashi Kapoor. In contrast, *Amar Akbar Anthony* is undoubtedly the zaniest of the three. Scenes like the three children being orphaned under the statue of Gandhi, the father of the nation, or the film's title track, which gives away the three masquerading protagonists, but still leaves Robert (Jeevan) and his henchmen clueless about their identity, make the film a spectacularly absurdist venture. Moreover, both *Waqt* and *Amar Akbar Anthony* are about family reunion. *Yaadon Ki Baaraat*, in comparison, is purely a tale of sibling reunion.

But perhaps the biggest difference between *Yaadon Ki Baaraat* and the two lost-and-found dramas before and after it is that it isn't anywhere near the level of the 'multi-starrer' that the other two films are. *Waqt* relied on the established star status of Raaj Kumar, Sunil Dutt, Shashi Kapoor, Balraj Sahni, Sharmila Tagore and Sadhana to carry the story. *Amar Akbar Anthony* had Bachchan in his prime, complemented by Vinod Khanna, Rishi Kapoor, Pran, Shabana Azmi, Neetu Singh and Parveen Babi pretty much at the top of their respective careers. *Yaadon Ki Baaraat*, in contrast, only had Dharmendra packing in the star quotient. Ajit was the most seasoned name among the rest of the cast, most of whom were rank newcomers.

Although Zeenat Aman was quite the rage at the time *Yaadon Ki Baaraat* released, thanks to her hippie character, Janice, from *Hare Rama Hare Krishna*, she was barely a few films old in the industry. That Zeenat played the hero's sister rather than his love interest in that film also signalled her fledgling status in the industry. Zeenat was cast in *Yaadon Ki Baaraat* after Husain had seen her at the famous Fredrick Hotel in Mahabaleshwar. When I spoke to Zeenat, she said that although she didn't remember the episode, Husain later told her that he had spotted her at breakfast one morning at the hotel, while she had been happily sipping away at *naariyal paani* (coconut water). 'He said there was such beauty and freshness in the person he saw that it set in his mind that I have to utilize this girl somewhere in one of my projects,' Zeenat said. She also admitted to *Yaadon Ki Baaraat* being the film that catapulted her career into the big league. 'Yes, it propelled my career no end. It established me as a romantic lead.'

Starring opposite Zeenat Aman was Vijay Arora, who had graduated from the Film and Television Institute of India. Arora had done a few films before *Yaadon Ki Baaraat*, such as *Zaroorat* (1972) and *Mere Bhaiyya* (1972), where he had played the lead, but was still looking for the film that would give his career a fillip. Alas, *Yaadon Ki Baaraat* turned out to be his only success in an underwhelming film career. It was only later in Ramanand Sagar's television series *Ramayan*, where he played Meghnath, that Arora came back into public reckoning. Arora died early, in 2007.

Two other actors who made their debuts with *Yaadon Ki Baaraat* were Jayshree Khosla, who was introduced as Anamika, and Tariq Khan. Anamika played Jack's daughter and is the lady who wears the black sari all through the film. Tariq Khan, Husain's nephew, who had earlier worked as an assistant director on *Caravan*, essayed Monto's role. Incidentally, *Caravan* was also the film through which Husain launched his brother Tahir Husain, Aamir's father, as producer. Before *Caravan*, Tahir had played small roles in Husain's *Dil Deke Dekho* (the character Chandra in Neeta's home, who feigns an accident as a way of getting close to her) and *Jab Pyar Kisise Hota Hai* (the secretary character Chintoo alongside Rajendra Nath). Tahir had also worked as production executive on Husain's films beginning with *Jab Pyar Kisise Hota Hai*. *Caravan's* success established Tahir as an independent producer and he went on to produce a few successful films like *Anamika* (1973), *Zakhmee* (1975) and *Hum Hain Rahi Pyar Ke* (1994).

Speaking on how he came to star in *Yaadon Ki Baaraat*, Tariq said that, as someone had told him, Husain offered him the role of the youngest brother after seeing him dance at a party in his own house. Tariq had been interested in joining films after an astrologer, who knew his connection with Husain, told him that he should consider a career in films even though it would be 'short-lived'. According to Tariq, Husain initially turned down the idea, saying, '*Main rishtey-daaron ko kaam nahin deta acting mein* (I don't cast relatives).' Husain was more keen that Tariq take to direction. Since Husain was scripting *Yaadon Ki Baaraat* around this time, Tariq speculated that Husain must have thought that the youngest brother's was the smallest role and the film's fortunes didn't depend on him. '*Itna bada star nahin hai Rajesh Khanna ki tarah ki isi ke naam pe picture chalegi* (He isn't a star like Rajesh Khanna, whose name alone is enough to carry a film).' Consequently, Husain called Tariq to his office. He first warned him about the pitfalls of acting and then talked about the hard work put in by screen legends like Dilip Kumar, Ashok Kumar and Balraj Sahni. It's only after this that Husain offered Tariq Monto's role, saying '"*Yeh hai ek chhota sa role. Dekho kar saktey ho ke nahin* (This is a small role. See if you can do it)." That's how it worked out,' Tariq recollected.

It is with such greenhorns that Husain delivered a film as spectacular and memorable as *Yaadon Ki Baaraat*. Pitted against *Waqt* and *Amar Akbar Anthony*, *Yaadon Ki Baaraat* holds its own despite the presence of just one-and-a-half (Dharmendra and Zeenat Aman) stars. 'For me, the hair-raising moment is when the three brothers unite because of the song. I still get goose bumps when I talk about it. That is something that I would like to take and put in a movie. For me, it is one of the great cinematic Bollywood moments,' remarked film-maker Farah Khan, endorsing the cult status of the film. Jerry Pinto, too, commended the film. '*Yaadon Ki Baaraat* is the one film that really places the song at its heart. Because it's that song which is constantly the MacGuffin, one boy is leaving the room, the other is singing the song. And you're thinking, "Stop! Go back! Meet

your brother." It's wonderful. It's absolutely brilliantly done ...
There is also an impression that there is a lot of cotton candy in
the film, fluff, but there isn't. There is also solid melodrama. It's
very, very important ... this separation, these near-misses, those
orphans looking for the last traces of family.'

Jerry sees *Yaadon Ki Baaraat*'s separated *trois frères* storyline
as a larger allegory of the parallel histories of India, Pakistan and
Bangladesh. 'I think the storyline faded and lost currency as we
began to realize that Partition was a permanent thing and that
we were going to be three countries. But for a long while there
was a hope that we might one day be one nation again, and this
bichhdey huey bhai theme was very popular. And so we constantly
played out this story – three brothers who go their separate ways
and come together in the end, one big happy family. It comes to
its apogee in *Amar Akbar Anthony*. And Manmohan Desai owes
a lot to Nasir Husain, whether he knows it or not. If you look
at *Aa Gale Lag Jaa* [1973], he is finding his feet, but by the time
he has hit *Chacha Bhatija* [1977] and *Amar Akbar Anthony*, he is
firmly in Husain territory.'

Bhaumik concurred. '*Yaadon Ki Baaraat* is absolutely the film
that defines Bollywood. That is the film that makes Bollywood,
Bollywood. There is no doubt about that. It is the spectacular
masala film. In comparison to *Waqt* and *Amar Akbar Anthony*, the
urbanity, the glamorous women, the viscerality, violence, action
in *Yaadon Ki Baaraat* are all magnified manifold. I think between
Caravan and *Yaadon Ki Baaraat*, he works it out completely. It is
precisely through films like *Caravan* and *Yaadon Ki Baaraat* that
the general framework is being put into place, which Manmohan
Desai would perfect. Which is why I say that Nasir Husain is the
important figure, one who defines the masala cinema of the 1970s
in a certain spectacular manner. It is not that he is the father of
the masala film. Even Manoj Kumar is contributing to the logic of

the multi-starrer. But Nasir Husain is just the tighter director. He puts the spectacle together like no one else manages to do. *Caravan* and *Yaadon Ki Baaraat* really set up the frame for the 1970s masala films, which, sadly, are no longer made. It's a tragedy.'

These views only reinforce *Yaadon Ki Baaraat*'s stature as *the* big commercial entertainer of the 1970s and the way people of a certain vintage look back at the film. There are yet other signifiers of the film's enormous success. Zeenat Aman told me that if she was identified as the '*Dum maro dum*' girl before *Yaadon Ki Baaraat*, she came to be known as the '*laal kapdon waali memsa'ab*'[15] (the lady in red) after the film. Tariq Khan became a 'stage' star, performing at a number of musical programmes. 'I did a lot of musical stage shows in my own name,' Tariq remarked. 'I started "Tariq night".' At Chennai's legendary Star Talkies, the film ran for 100 weeks. Tariq recollected, 'We were called for a special ceremony. Dharam-ji, myself, Zeenat Aman, R.D. Burman, we went for the function. The music was like wildfire. People danced in the theatre and threw coins on the stage whenever my song played.'

But perhaps the decisive signpost for any true-blue Hindi masala film is how it comes to be received in popular imagination, of how it becomes some kind of a cultural marker in its time or afterwards even if by way of parody or imitation. To this extent, Madhulika Liddle paid *Yaadon Ki Baaraat* the ultimate accolade when she remembered an episode from the past, choking with laughter all the while. 'Imagine, it was so popular that I remember this one cousin of mine saying years ago, "*You know humaari family ko, hum sabko ek gaana compose karkey seekh lena chaahiye, kaheen hum bichhad na jaaye...* (All of us in our family must compose and learn a song, just in case we get separated some day...)."'

---

[15]The words with which Monto calls Sunita on stage for '*Aap ke kamrey mein koi rehta hai*'.

11

THE OTHER BIG B

'Nasir Husain sa'ab ka bahut bada involvement hota thaa unkey music mein. (Nasir Husain was very involved with his music.) He is the only director I have found in my entire career who used to make his own music in his copybook. He used to have a book. His direction, all the shots used to be written there. He would write all that he wanted in the song, he would take it to Pancham and then Pancham would translate that into music. It was not as if any music director gave him a song and he took it. Nasir sa'ab slept over it, he thought about it, whether it suited his situation, everything. He had great, great knowledge of music.'

– Actor Rishi Kapoor

'For me, his films and music are one. I look at his music as his film-making.'

– Film-maker and producer Aditya Chopra

The 1970s was the decade of Amitabh Bachchan. Having endured a number of flop films and tepid releases, Bachchan finally hit the big league with Prakash Mehra's *Zanjeer* in 1973. There was no stopping him thereafter. Bachchan's success led to Rajesh Khanna's downfall sooner than anticipated. He became Hindi cinema's biggest screen legend for the body of work he put together in the years that followed. Be it as the perfect embodiment of Salim–Javed's 'Angry Young Man' or Yash Chopra's brooding romantic lead in *Kabhi Kabhie* (1976) or Manmohan Desai's hysterically funny Anthony bhai in *Amar Akbar Anthony*, Bachchan did it all. His stature and baritone were enough to carry several run-of-the-mill action potboilers like *Khoon Pasina* (1977), *Mr. Natwarlal* (1979), *Suhaag* (1979) and *Kaalia* (1981). Such was his appeal that the gangster character essayed by him in *Don* (1978) didn't even go by a proper name. The invocation of 'Don' in the film underscored Bachchan's larger-than-life persona. There was nobody through the 1970s and the early 1980s who captured the nation's imagination like him.

Unless you consider Rahul Dev Burman, the undisputed *mausikaar-e-azam* of Bachchan's era. While he may not have matched Bachchan's fan following in sheer numbers, RD's impact on popular culture was second to none. His score for *Teesri Manzil* had already become something of a milestone in Hindi cinema for its nouveau style. Then with *Hare Rama Hare Krishna*'s (1971) '*Dum maro dum*', he once again conjured up a composition that was both epochal and trippy. Then there was *Caravan* (1971) followed by *Amar Prem* (1972) 'which, in later years, was considered Pancham's best work of all time'.[1] In 1972 and 1973, RD scored for about thirty films, with twenty-four of those having 'hit' music, a staggering 80 per cent success rate.[2] By the time he reached the late-1970s, RD had an enviable list of films on his resume, prominent among which were *Kati Patang* (1970), *Jawani Deewani* (1972), *Parichay* (1972), *Aa Gale Lag Jaa* (1973), *Anamika* (1973), *Yaadon Ki Baaraat*, *Aap Ki Kasam* (1974), *Aandhi* (1975), *Khel Khel Mein* (1975),

---

[1]Anirudha Bhattacharjee and Balaji Vittal, 'Dawning of the 1970s', *R.D. Burman: The Man, The Music*, HarperCollins *Publishers* India, 2011, p. 97.

[2]Ibid., 'Inexpensive Grass, Free Love', p. 127.

Ghar (1978) and *Gol Maal* (1979). Like Bachchan, RD was often the distinguishing factor who catapulted a film's fortunes from good to great or rescued them from oblivion. Films like *Shaan* (1980), *Love Story* (1981) and *Rocky* (1981) benefitted immensely from RD's scores. If Bachchan came to be known as the 'Big B' for his action-packed, towering inferno performances in this period, R.D. 'B'urman was the other 'Big B' who left his indelible stamp on this era of Hindi cinema.

Husain, in his prescient fashion, divined that RD could address the demographic he wanted for his films. Songs like '*Aaja aaja*' and '*Dum maro dum*' became anthems for the youth. Sunil Dutt said as much about RD, 'He understood youth like no other music director did.'[3] Equally, Husain may have connected with the younger Burman on account of their shared passion for music beyond the familiar. While RD had been schooled in Indian classical music and had also been exposed to Rabindra Sangeet from an early age, he had shown an affinity for jazz, Cuban Big Band, Latin American, European and Middle-Eastern music.[4] RD's distinctive use of Western rhythms and patterns may have enamoured Husain who, as we know from *Dil Deke Dekho*'s songs, was already looking westwards so far as his own musical tastes were concerned.

'My dad definitely had a strong Western [influence]. He had this Zenith radio and he would tune in and listen. He was an avid listener of world music. He had a great sense of Arabic folk tunes,' said Mansoor. Nuzhat elaborated on her father's music sensibilities: 'He was the one responsible for us listening to so much music as we were growing up. And it was never classical. And it was never Indian. He would buy records every time he went abroad, and at

---

[3]Ibid., 'Old Boys' Alumni', p. 242.
[4]Ibid., 'Musical Legacy and Beyond', pp. 29-31.

that time we had those little records, the short play ones – each one had one song on it. Even before the term "top of the pops" became a thing, they used to be all the latest music.'

Speaking on some of Husain's favourite artistes and songs, Nuzhat said, 'The earliest I remember is *Come September* [1961]. The Beatles always. It was very pop and rock. Rock was great. He was the one, I'm sorry to say, who brought ABBA to India [laughs].[5] Before that it was the Rolling Stones. He would listen to everything new and it was very, very modern … Elvis. "*Sweet Caroline*" I remember. Engelbert Humperdinck. He loved José Feliciano. He would play them and sometimes it wouldn't even fit into a film or a song that he was writing, but he would listen to the music again and again and again, ten times, fifteen times, the same song. And Mansoor has that habit, if he likes a song he will play it fifty times.'

Other clues to Husain's taste in music can be gauged from song references in his films outside of regular song sequences. In *Dil Deke Dekho*, for instance, the first glimpse we get of Asha Parekh is when she is singing and clapping her hands to the Buddy Holly song, '*Baby I don't care*', in the company of her friends. Likewise, in *Hum Kisise Kum Naheen*, Kaajal Kiran is introduced to viewers while dancing to the Tina Charles's 1976 UK chartbuster, '*Dance little lady dance*'. In the same film, the club that Kaajal and Rajesh come to where Sanjay eventually sings '*Kya hua tera waada*', has the ABBA number '*Honey, honey*' being performed by two women.

Manzil Manzil uses the *Chariots of Fire* (1981) theme song and Barbara Streisand's '*Woman in love*' at separate moments. While Mansoor referenced The Champs' rock-'n'-roll instrumental '*Tequila*' for *Jo Jeeta Wohi Sikandar*'s pie fight sequence at Ramlal's Café, Husain had used the same track in *Phir Wohi Dil Laya*

---

[5]This is a reference to *Hum Kisise Kum Naheen*'s '*Mil gaya, humko saathi mil gaya*', which was a copy of the ABBA song, '*Mamma Mia*'.

Hoon. These choices reveal Husain keeping with the times and acknowledging what had gained popular traction even if only in the West. Even Difu (Rajendra Nath) in *Phir Wohi Dil Laya Hoon* appears to be mouthing, although in a heightened, operatic style, Petula Clark's '*With all my heart*', when he is getting ready for the dinner hosted by his parents for Mona and Colonel Mahendranath. The real coup de grâce was Husain getting Tariq Khan in *Zabardast* to dance to the opening notes of Michael Jackson's iconic number '*Billie Jean*' from the legendary pop artiste's album, *Thriller*. In the very next scene, Tariq is going all out on the Beatles' number, '*I wanna hold your hand*'. 'I listen to a lot of Western music when I'm abroad ... But I don't always adapt Western tunes. Sometimes I use them as they are. For the title song of *Dil Deke Dekho*, which was a copy of "*Sugar in the morning*", I paid Columbia a royalty for the tune,' Husain said.[6]

It will be incorrect, however, to label Husain's music sensibilities as solely Western. His first few films, barring *Dil Deke Dekho*, and later films like *Baharon Ke Sapne, Pyar Ka Mausam* and *Caravan* were clearly more rooted in Indian folk and Hindi film music traditions. The more important observation is that Husain had a knack for cherry-picking the right song, the right melody that captured popular imagination.

Aamir observed, 'I think that Pancham uncle came in with a lot of Western influence in his style of composing, so the westernization in Nasir sa'ab's songs was the result of Pancham uncle being the composer. But otherwise Nasir sa'ab was very strong on melody and the tune, which you will see consistently whether it is Pancham uncle or any other music director. I would say Chachajaan was into popular music, not necessarily only Western, but even in Indian music ... I would imagine that he thought of Hindi film music as his kind of music. I don't imagine

[6]Resham Shaam, 'Little Big Man', *Super*, May 1978.

him listening to classical Indian music. That was not the kind of music he was into. Nor was he into Western classical music. He was into popular music, whether it was Western or Indian.'

Mansoor said something similar. 'He had a great sense of tune. He was not a trained musician as such. But he could just put his finger on a tune and say this is great ... I am a music person. I play the piano and all. I may understand harmony and chords and structure, but I can't say that I have the same instinct for a popular tune like my dad had. I may get carried away by something that I like, but it may not be something that may work at a broad level whereas he definitely had that. He was very clear about what would make a hit tune. It needn't be suitable for the situation, which is what I tend to go for.'

Husain's ear for picking a quality tune didn't mean that the music for his films was easily composed. If anything, he put RD through the rigour of playing tune after tune for him, until he finally selected a song. Speaking from his experience of attending a few of the musical sittings for *Caravan*, Jeetendra said, 'Believe me, *jab R.D. Burman gaana banaatey thay, usi waqt naachney ko dil karta thaa.* (You would feel like dancing even as R.D. Burman composed.) Each and every song.' But for Husain, RD would have to play six tunes on an average for each track that was eventually chosen, added Jeetendra. '*Aisey aap sochiye, agar chhey gaaney hain, toh chhattis gaano mein, I used to feel that chhattis ke chhattis super-duper hit hain. Akalmandi ismein thee ki woh nagino mein nagina chunn-na* (So consider, that if there were six songs to be selected, then in thirty-six tunes I felt each was a chartbuster. His [Husain's] skill lay in selecting the best song from the other good ones).'

Husain remarked in this context, 'I sit with Pancham for hours on end to get exactly what I want for my films.'[7] Elsewhere it was reported that, 'It had been a practice with Burman to compose as many as ten or fifteen tunes for the same song, and allow Nasir Husain to choose whatever appealed to him.'[8] Javed Akhtar provided a cheeky corollary to this when he said, 'In fact, I happen to know a couple of producer–directors who, when they used to go to R.D. Burman, would tell him, "The tunes that Nasir sa'ab had shortlisted, he wouldn't have used each one of them. You must have given him twenty to twenty-five tunes which he liked, of which he must have selected five or seven. Give us the rest. We will take them." People trusted his music sensibilities to this extent.'

These song selections were preceded by detailed interactions between film-maker and composer. In September 2014, I met Homi Mullan, who had been a part of RD's team since *Baharon Ke Sapne*, in his Chuim Village house in Mumbai's Bandra West area. Homi, who appeared very frail at the age of seventy-four, told me that Husain would be accompanied by one or two assistants, Sachin Bhowmick on occasion and 'Majrooh uncle' for his sessions with RD. 'He [Husain] would tell the whole story first. He would ask where all we could have songs. Pancham would then give his views. Everyone would discuss. Finally, the approval would come from Nasir sa'ab.' Husain would also give RD examples of the kind of songs he wanted in these sittings, which lasted from 'morning to night'. According to Homi, Husain's only expectation from RD was, '*Pancham tere ko jo karna hai kar, mere ko bas ek heera de de* (Pancham, do what you have to, just give me a gem of a song).'

Expanding on her father's interactions with RD, Nuzhat said that the film-maker often referred to a song and enacted it, to convey the feel of what he wanted to portray. 'He would say,

---

[7]Ibid.

[8]Hanif Shakoor, 'The Dilemma of a Commercial Film Maker', *Poona Herald*, 1977.

"Look, heroine enters, the music is playing..." and he would enact the song. "She comes in, she sits down. He is sitting over there." He listened to so much music, so he would try and find a piece of music that conveyed as closely as possible the mood or rhythm or something similar.' As an example, Nuzhat recalled Husain enacting '*Come down Jesus*' by José Feliciano. 'I remember it so well because he dramatized it for us ... And he's imagining it as a blind man, who has composed this song. He would talk about it, enact it and bring it alive as if he was shooting it...'

Credit for a good composition often goes to the composer alone. If that is the case, why is it that the same composer isn't able to create the same magic consistently with other film-makers? Conversely, some relationships between film-maker and technician – like the lyricist Sahir Ludhianvi's work for Yash Chopra or composer S.D. Burman's work for Navketan – are far more productive than when the same talents work elsewhere. Husain's inputs, owing to his musical taste and sensibilities, therefore, were integral to his successful collaboration with RD.

Aditya Chopra was adulatory of Husain in this regard. 'With directors like Raj Kapoor or Nasir Husain, who had a musical sense, the music was driven completely by them. I don't think R.D. Burman composed "*Aaja piya*" as just a tune. No. I'm quite sure that Nasir sa'ab explained to him that he was looking for a song, which has a certain floaty vibe in a film, which is black and white. I'm not sure if he composed or even hummed himself although I won't be surprised. I know Raj Kapoor did. But definitely with minds like Nasir sa'ab it's not possible that he did not drive the music, by either giving a reference or humming or saying *mujhe na guitar aisey chaahiye yahaan par, mujhe aisa chaahiye* (I would like a guitar refrain like this here).' Karan Johar endorsed Aditya's views: 'The music that they created together was unique to just Nasir sa'ab.'

Aamir, who worked as an assistant director with Husain on *Manzil Manzil* and *Zabardast*, actually demonstrated how Husain would eventually select RD's tunes based on his inputs. Husain would enter 'Pancham uncle's' sitting room, sit cross-legged, put his head down and light himself a cigarette as RD started playing a tune. He wouldn't look up until RD finished playing. Taking regular drags of his cigarette, Husain would be in yogi-like trance in these few minutes as his mind worked like a sieve, separating the extraordinary compositions from the rest. 'If he didn't like it, he would say it then and there. He would not mince his words. He was not rude, but he didn't need to pussyfoot around because they were too close. And typically, Pancham uncle had run through five to six tunes before he selected one.'

Bhanu Gupta had been a part of RD's team even before Homi Mullan. He met me in his Kandivali home in Mumbai in July 2014. According to Bhanu-da, it was the 'complete freedom' that Husain allowed RD that led to the terrific numbers. 'Nasir sa'ab knew he would get more than what he wanted,' the eighty-two-year-old Bhanu-da, who was RD's chief rhythm guitarist, told me. The other reason that Bhanu-da suggested for the string of musical successes that the Husain–RD combine delivered was the presence of the musical hero in Husain's films. 'That was Pancham's subject actually. He knew how to make the most of it, how to exploit it. He got very involved in it,' Bhanu-da said.

Hum Kisise Kum Naheen, Husain's next film after *Yaadon Ki Baaraat*, once again foregrounded this musical hero. Both the lead characters Rajesh/Manjeet (Rishi Kapoor) and Sanjay (Tariq Khan) are shown being adept at music. While Rishi Kapoor's character sings and performs at hotels and clubs, Sanjay plays the iktara and the guitar in the film. The film is yet another true-blue musical where songs are used to advance and resolve the narrative.

Husain approached Rishi Kapoor on the back of the actor's successful films since *Bobby* (1973). 'I became a star after *Bobby*,' Rishi told me in his office at R.K. Studios in Chembur one September afternoon in 2014. 'Perhaps Nasir sa'ab felt that he needed someone more youthful in his film and that's why he approached me for *Hum Kisise Kum Naheen*. I was only too happy to work with him.' There was also a comfort factor at play between Husain and Rishi in that Husain had worked with nearly every member of the Kapoor khaandaan. 'Apart from my grandfather and father, all the Kapoors have worked with him. Shammi, Shashi, Daboo [Randhir Kapoor later in *Zamaane Ko Dikhana Hai*], myself and Chimpu [Rajiv Kapoor in *Zabardast*]. And don't forget that in those movies apart from my paternal uncles, my maternal uncle was also there, Rajendra Nath [as also Prem Nath]. He was my mother's brother and they were my father's brothers. So I always had two uncles in his films.'

According to Mansoor, if Husain found the same energy, the flamboyance in any of his heroes after Shammi Kapoor it was in Rishi Kapoor. Rishi's films just before *Hum Kisise Kum Naheen*, like *Rafoo Chakkar* (1975), *Khel Khel Mein* (1975) and *Kabhi Kabhie* (1976), where he mostly played effervescent, youthful characters, reflected this. 'Despite the disparity in age, he was much my senior mind you, he used to behave as if he was my pal. That was his way, thinking young and making youthful films. His thinking, his writing, his music, his songs – everything was very youthful,' Rishi remarked.

The emphasis on youth is most visible in *Hum Kisise Kum Naheen* in the opening song of the film, '*Bachna ae haseeno*', and in the song and dance competition at the Nainital Club. Rishi's sheer madness through the former as he blows the trumpet and ends it on a completely hysterical routine (*'Talk to me, talk to me'*) is vintage Husain. The only difference is that the song, with Rishi's shimmering silver-white outfit, and its exaggerated, almost psychedelic stage lighting, now articulated the aspirations of a newer, more 'disco'-oriented generation.

Bhaumik agreed. 'Disco has happened in the middle. Rishi Kapoor has emerged as a star, which actually allows him to invert the *Yaadon Ki Baaraat* focus. *Yaadon Ki Baaraat* is all melodrama, gangsters and song in the background from the point of the view of the youngest son. He inverts it in *Hum Kisise Kum Naheen*. That is interesting. He is prescient. He is already announcing in *Yaadon Ki Baaraat* that a new generation, with new values, is at the edge of this world. It's new. It's happening in the cities. And now that world takes over. The gangster bit has become secondary. There is an updating of genre rules.'

The other song which highlights this youthfulness, and which is perhaps the most significant sequence in *Hum Kisise Kum Naheen*'s screenplay, is the medley, an offshoot of the 'All India Pop competition' held at the Nainital Club. The sequence begins with Manjeet (or Rajesh) on the cusp of winning the competition, having beaten five opponents. He is about to celebrate his victory by blowing his trumpet (quite literally) when Sanjay emerges with his guitar, singing the wonderful ballad *'Chaand mera dil'* to challenge Manjeet. What follows over the next nine-and-a-half minutes is a singular musical extravaganza where one song leads into another without a break in between.

Husain had got the idea for the sequence while on a visit to Tiffany's discotheque in London. In a *Sangeet Sitarey* episode broadcast on Doordarshan in the early 1990s, Husain had said, 'The younger generation used to come there. I went there to listen to what was new, what were they listening to. What I saw was that people were dancing on the stage and when one song gets over, there is no gap between this and the next song. And those who were dancing, continue to dance.' This is the idea that Husain gave RD: There would be a mukhda which will have its own melody, but which will change to another piece of music with a distinct rhythm. RD said, 'Yes, disco was very much the flavour then, but this was the first time I was given such a situation [by Husain] that "look Pancham, four or five songs have to be played together, one after the other."' Husain clarified further, '*Chaar gaaney, chaar mukhdey, chaar antarey bilkul hi alag hain* (Four songs, four choruses, four stanzas entirely different)', admitting, 'It was quite a job.'[9] Bhanu-da remains convinced that Husain only thought of the idea 'because he knew RD's capability'. He recalled Husain telling RD, '"If you can do it well, *tumhaarey saamne koi nahin hoga.* (You will have no competition.) Maintaining the same scale, same colour, there should be no jerks. It has to change over smoothly. The transition has to be seamless…" We did a lot of sittings for that song.'

Seen in totality, the sequence actually has six distinct sections.[10] The first is the longish prelude, which begins with the high-pitched trumpet, picturized on Manjeet playing the instrument, and heads into its climax with the '*Wakao*' cry. Then, after the declaration made by the judges that any new opponent has only fifteen seconds to challenge Manjeet, there are the four distinct melodies, with their different antaras and mukhdas. The sixth and final bit is the instrumental section, with Sanjay and his partner trying to match

---

[9]Husain's and R.D. Burman's comments on the genesis of the *Hum Kisise Kum Naheen* medley can be viewed at https://www.youtube.com/watch?v=yteVAXqZhkk

[10]Anirudha Bhattacharjee and Balaji Vittal, 'Packing a Musical Wallop', *Gaata Rahe Mera Dil: 50 Classic Hindi Film Songs*, HarperCollins *Publishers* India, 2015, pp. 236-239.

pace with Manjeet and Kaajal step-for-step, the former pair led by Sanjay's guitar, the latter with Manjeet's trumpet. As this bit nears its end, the pace picks up. Husain resorted to Dutch angles to signify the shift in pace. It is only when Kaajal puts her fingers to Manjeet's lips, in a rather public display of affection, does Sanjay put down his guitar (his weapon) in this contest of love (and war) and walk off the stage, signalling Manjeet's victory.

Musically, the six distinct sections once again highlight a seamless bridging of cultures. According to Sadanand Warrier, while the prelude reminds us of a musician like Herb Alpert (in the use of the trumpet) and has a strong Latin influence (the Cuban bongo drums), 'Chaand mera dil' is more like a love ballad. 'Aa dil kya' has a 'disco/rock' feel while 'Tum kya jaano', which clearly doffs its hat to RD's 'Mehbooba mehbooba' from Sholay (even in the manner Sanjay ties the headband), 'has a very Mediterranean, North African voice'. 'Mil gaya humko saathi mil gaya' appears to be a direct copy of ABBA's 'Mamma Mia', but as Sadanand pointed out, it does not have the 'I've been waiting for you' bit with which the ABBA song begins. Also the metre of the 'Tere liye' refrain is different from the 'Mamma Mia' refrain. The coda or the end section is again very Latin influenced. 'It ends with some really high trumpet notes. I suppose Rishi Kapoor having won being the rooster,' concluded Sadanand.

Extended preludes, seamless shifts between musical genres and frenetic finishes were standard Husain fare. Refer, for example, 'Megha re bole' which turns into 'Bade hain dil ke kaaley'. The club song in Jab Pyar Kisise Hota Hai has Miss Pony swinging to some boogie-woogie rhythms before Nisha takes over the stage with 'Tum jaise bigde babu'. The one in Pyar Ka Mausam begins with the cabaret artiste dancing to some Latino tune and then changes into 'Aap chaahein mujhko'. Teesri Manzil's 'Aaja aaja' has a seventy-two-second prelude and a fifty-second-long wild climax. A ninety-second prelude and a frenzied finish also bookend *'Chunari sambhaal gori'* in *Baharon Ke Sapne*.

Doraiswamy remarked, 'For Husain, music was never enough, unless it was in excess! In *Dil Deke Dekho, Jab Pyar Kisise…*, *Yaadon Ki Baaraat* and *Hum Kisise Kum Naheen*, he revels in presenting one song after another.'[11] Articulating the key reason for Husain's medley-like sequences, Doraiswamy had this to say: 'He has a fondness presenting song sequences in the performative mode, which is also a reason why many of his heroes are singers by profession. The performative mode provided Husain the opportunity to mount the multiple song sequences … Husain uses this sequence playfully to foreground the performative and spectative aspects of the song-and-dance sequence.'[12]

Yaadon Ki Baaraat, too, has a longish, multiple song sequence early in the film. Monto (Ratan) is introduced in the film as part of the band 'Prince Monto and The Avengers', where he renders surf music-sounding guitaring, with RD's crazy voiceovers. After this initial bit, Monto sings the film's title track, when Vijay goes out to attend a telephone call. *'Aap ke kamrey mein'* follows next, after which comes *'Dil mil gaye'* and then finally, *'Dum maro dum'*. The sequence comes to an end only after the audience has joined in and reached a state of frenzy with *'Dum maro dum'*. This nearly eleven-minute sequence, as Doraiswamy observed, served several key functions. 'It creates the ambience of a real band; the brother and his group are called "Monto and The Avengers" and even have a poster out on the show; it also creates the feel of the real duration of a band performing one song after the other at a hotel. It functions as a narrative device for it postpones the

---

[11]Dr Rashmi Doraiswamy, '"These Days" of Our Modernity: The Cinema of Nasir Husain', Film and Television Institute of India, Pune, 4 September 2004, p. 13.

[12]Ibid. pp. 13-14.

moment of recognition when the elder brother misses the other's "song signal". The savvy girl in a red dress, who dances and sings with élan on the stage, Zeenat Aman, quotes her own self in the "*Dum maro dum*" song, and alludes to an image of a modern westernized woman within the domain of the Hindi cinema of the seventies.'[13]

But the *Yaadon Ki Baaraat* sequence is, strictly speaking, not a medley. It is punctuated by dialogue on more than a few occasions. During these moments, the music comes to a halt, with the dialogue serving, possibly, as a breather for the next bit of music. In *Hum Kisise Kum Naheen*, the music never stops. Even when the judge announces the fifteen-second time limit for anyone to challenge Manjeet, the trumpet can be heard in the background. This is, therefore, a unique sequence, even taking into account similar depictions in films such as *Awara*,[14] where multiple song sequences are used to '"externalize" internal conflict'.[15] The *Hum Kisise Kum Naheen* medley, conversely, is a pure celebration of music and by extension, a celebration of Husain's cinema.

Seen together, the recourse to the multiple song exercise in *Yaadon Ki Baaraat* and *Hum Kisise Kum Naheen* went against the rules of Hindi cinema, where songs are spaced out over the narrative. Both films had fewer music sequences than Husain's previous film *Caravan*, but the medleys allowed for longer musical indulgences than in *Caravan*. Jerry Pinto said as much. 'There is

[13]Ibid. p. 14.

[14]In *Awara*, the multiple song sequence occurs as a dream sequence in which the songs '*Tu aa aa ja*' and '*Ghar aaya mera pardesi*' come one after the other to give a glimpse of Raj's (Raj Kapoor) traumatic state of mind.

[15]Dr Rashmi Doraiswamy, '"These Days" of Our Modernity: The Cinema of Nasir Husain', Film and Television Institute of India, Pune, 4 September 2004, p. 14.

a complete breakdown of Bollywood logic, which is, pace your songs. Song, then give us some narrative, then song to heighten the narrative, then song to reflect the narrative. But here he is breaking this rule magnificently.' Husain, too, admitted to being warned against doing the sequence in *Hum Kisise Kum Naheen*. 'Just when people start enjoying one song, you leave it and go to the next song and then to the third song. It shouldn't happen that people get irritated with this,' Husain recalled someone telling him in a Doordarshan programme aired on RD's death. But Husain acknowledged RD encouraging him to go ahead with the idea, saying, 'There may be some risk, but Nasir sa'ab, if you don't undertake such a bold experiment, who will?'

Lending further dynamism to the song is the way it is shot. Using crane shots, dolly tracks, zooms, swish pans, low angles, Dutch angles, wide shots, sometimes even a combination of these in the same shot, interspersing these with shots of the audience and resorting to quick cuts between Manjeet, Sanjay and Kaajal, Husain added to the vibrancy of the entire sequence. Cinematographer Munir Khan's son, Shamir Khan, affirmed this in an interview with me. 'The pace of the entire sequence had to match the shot-taking. The shot-taking had to be with a lot of movement. If you watch every frame, you will notice there isn't a static shot. There is movement in every shot. There is a fluidity that was very unique for a dance sequence. A lot of films are shot with static shots where the characters are moving around. Here the camera is in motion throughout the song. That is the beauty of this song sequence.'

Karan Johar lauded Husain's vision in the song. 'Who would have thought of a dance sequence that was fourteen or fifteen minutes long? It just went on where each melody is a victory. From "*Chaand mera dil*", going into the change in beat and melody, to hold that situation and to hold it musically? Who had ever thought of something like this? It was pure genius. And it is so cool. And he had a non-dancer in the frame – Tariq, who was not a dancer, and to hold it with him. And with a new girl...' Including this sequence in their book *50 Classic Hindi Film Songs*, Anirudha Bhattacharjee and Balaji Vittal wrote, 'Medleys had been made earlier and were made later too; but the character of the medley in *HKKN* has never been replicated in Hindi film music.'[16]

Husain also used music as a means to avoid melodrama. '*Bachna ae haseeno*' happens just after Rajesh is driven to tears over the dramatic change in his fortunes because of his father's death and the disappearance of the diamonds. Ramu dada (S.N. Banerjee) even regrets Rajesh having to perform in hotels because of this. While Rajesh laughs off Ramu dada's lament, the next thing we hear and see is the packed auditorium in which Rajesh's performance begins with the vibrant notes of the trumpet.

In *Jab Pyar Kisise Hota Hai*, when Nisha hears Sunder telling his mother that he has fallen out of love with Nisha, Nisha is heartbroken. But instead of making up with Sunder with a longish, maudlin tirade, Nisha harks back to the film's title track. And so even as Nisha remains weepy through the song, the happy, frothy nature of '*Jiya ho*'s' arrangement, absolutely identical to the time it is sung in Rafi's voice, works as a balm. At the end of the song, Sunder and Nisha are together.

Something similar happens in *Pyar Ka Mausam*'s '*Che khush nazaare*'. The song occurs only a few scenes after Sunder becomes aware that the people who raised him aren't his true parents. But

---

[16]Anirudha Bhattacharjee and Balaji Vittal, 'Packing a Musical Wallop', *Gaata Rahe Mera Dil: 50 Classic Hindi Film Songs*, HarperCollins *Publishers* India, 2015, p. 240.

instead of wallowing in self-pity, Sunder heads out for Nandipur gaon.[17] After making a few preliminary enquiries, he is shown, guitar in hand, singing with the feisty khaanaabadosh. Sunder's mien changes from desolate to upbeat in a few scenes because of this.

But it is in *Yaadon Ki Baaraat* and *Hum Kisise Kum Naheen* that Husain perfected this technique. In *Yaadon Ki Baaraat*, the reunion between Vijay and Monto happens during the rendition of the title track at the end. Even Shankar is made aware of who his brothers are during the song. The brothers get misty-eyed, shed tears and Vijay and Monto fall in each other's arms all during the song. There is no dialogue acknowledging the teary-eyed reunion after the song gets ever. This is yet another distinguishing factor between *Yaadon Ki Baaraat* and films like *Waqt* and *Amar Akbar Anthony*. In the latter films, family members engage in dialogue, give backstories, proof of filial ties, shed *khushi ke aansoon* and only then can they unite. In *Yaadon Ki Baaraat*, the emotional moment passes with the end of the song. As a friend observed of Husain's cinema, 'It wasn't important that characters cried in the film, but that the audience watching the film cried.'

If it was possible to better this episode, Husain did so in *Hum Kisise Kum Naheen*. Here Kaajal is made aware that Sanjay is her long-lost companion from childhood when Sanjay sings '*Kya hua tera waada*'. The song, like the *Yaadon Ki Baaraat* song, helps in recognition and reunion. The lyrics are cathartic but scathing. Sanjay says so, too, that his song is not about happy reunions, '*Balki unn badnaseebon ka hai jinhe thukraaya gaya hai* (but about those unfortunate who have been spurned)'. When Kaajal hears

---

[17]In *Waqt* (1965), for example, Ravi (Sunil Dutt) goes into a shell and leaves home after his sister tells him that he is nothing but an orphan from the streets.

the song, she weeps copiously, right through its rendition. Even Rajesh is so moved that he extends his hand of friendship to Sanjay at the end of the song. All this is because of the lyrics. But what about RD's composition for the song?

It sounds almost rock-'n'-roll[18] in the manner in which Sanjay hits the strings of his electric guitar to begin the song. Other than for the first time that Mohammed Rafi sings the initial line of the mukhda, '*Kya hua tera waada, woh kasam, woh iraada?*', the arrangement, with the percussion beats, the electric guitar and Rafi's full-throated rendition of the initial halves of both antaras, is remarkably upbeat and buoyant. Mansoor observed, 'Dad knew the milieu because he is performing on stage. I'm sure they would have consciously agreed to make it peppy and up-tempo because when the kids sing it, it's more mellow, but when he sings it, the tempo is up and more popular-sounding, with the electric guitar and all.'

When I asked Tariq about the cheery nature of the composition, he replied, 'My character was that of a stage pop singer. I can't stand like Bharat Bhushan. I have to do something which suits my character.' But something else that Tariq told me in the context of '*Lekar hum deewaana dil*' appears to be Husain's guiding philosophy even for '*Kya hua tera waada*'. 'His songs were always very vibrant. He said that they must be catchy so that the audience, who are watching, should feel a part of the film. He used to say that if a person sings a song after seeing your movie and sings the same song even six months later, it means you are a hit.'

Bhaumik made a more elaborate reading of Husain's use of music in such situations. 'I think he doesn't allow melodrama

---

[18]This is also another example of Husain's ready cosmopolitanism and secularism. Before the song, the hotel/club's compere asks if someone has a 'geet' or a 'ghazal' to celebrate 'Mr and Mrs Saleem's' first wedding anniversary. What they get instead is a vibrant, up-tempo number.

to come in because he is so focused on the youth as his main reference point ... Music is his way out of melodrama. It seems almost like an article of faith for him that music will get you out of any sort of trouble. That I think is one of the really important distinctions from other directors. For Nasir Husain music is organic. It's not just a plot device. Like for Vijay Anand it's a sheer technical exercise, how you give a musical basis to the entire film is a technical exercise for him – how you integrate music and action and diegesis and so on. For Nasir Husain, the music is far more than that. It is an antidote for melodrama. For the characters in Nasir Husain's films, music is therapeutic. *Yaadon Ki Baaraat* makes it very clear that music will resolve your internal problems and your trauma will be healed.'

A point needs to be made here about Majrooh Sultanpuri. There is no denying that Husain and he shared a great affinity. Mansoor said as much, 'Majrooh uncle enjoyed working with my dad immensely because my dad would give him examples with a sher or a phrase or some anecdote from a literary point of view.' And in every one of these songs, Majrooh was able to give the right expression to Husain's narrative requirements through song. He enjoyed his working relationship with Husain. 'While working with Guru Dutt, I used to feel that I was working with a colleague. I've had the same feeling when working with one other director, Nasir Husain. The feeling is that you're working with an equal, that we were both on the same level. With other people I felt employed by a producer/director and that I am his songwriter. There is a feeling of distance, which was there with everyone, but not with Guru Dutt. With him there prevailed an atmosphere of friendship. And because he was a decent man there was no cheap humour, forced laughter, the kind of thing one got used to later. He was not that kind of man. Like my friend Nasir Husain, I mentioned his name because as I talk of working with Guru Dutt, Nasir also comes to mind.'[19]

There is another interesting aspect at work in the Husain–Majrooh collaboration. Majrooh often took grammatical liberties to cater to the demands of song-writing. For instance, for *Aar Paar*'s title track, he wrote, '*Kabhi aar, kabhi paar, laga teer-e-nazar*'. The words '*aar-paar*', like the film's title, are always used in tandem, but Majrooh conveniently used them separately to come up with a very popular song. In the same film, he also wrote, '*Sunn sunn sunn sunn zaalima, pyaar humko tumse ho gaya*'. This is incorrect because as Javed Akhtar explained to me,[20] 'When you are saying "sunn", you can't say "tum". It should have been "tujh" or it could have been "suno". But he [Sultanpuri] felt that "tujh" would not sound correct musically. He took liberties with grammar for the sake of better phonetics.'

Majrooh's liberties for the sake of phonetics or for narrative purposes are visible right through his work with Husain. In *Yaadon Ki Baaraat*'s '*Chura liya hai tumne jo dil ko*', he writes the line '*Sajaoonga lutkar bhi tere badan ki daali ko*' for Vijay's entry into the song. The hummable nature of the melody allows us to waft past this line, but a more careful examination reveals Majrooh's comparison of a woman's beauty, more specifically her body, with the branch of a tree (*badan ki daali*). In the very next line Majrooh writes, '*lahu jigar ka doonga haseen labon ki laali ko*', meaning 'I will douse your beautiful lips with the blood from

---

[19]Nasreen Munni Kabir interviewed Majrooh on 18 November 1986 in the context of Guru Dutt. Nasreen sent me the relevant transcribed bites via email in July 2015.

[20]When I interviewed him for my earlier book, *Sahir Ludhianvi: The People's Poet*, HarperCollins *Publishers* India, 2013.

my heart'.[21] It's a very graphic description, one that Majrooh gets away with given the lilting nature of the song. The only reason one can guess Majrooh used these words – 'daali' and 'laali' – or such imagery – 'badan ki daali' and 'lahu jigar ka doonga' – is to get the meter right. He was too much of a thoroughbred for such lyrical 'adventurism' to be assigned to his naiveté.

There are more such instances. In the *Yaadon Ki Baaraat* title song, the opening lines are 'Yaadon ki baaraat nikli hai aaj dil ke dwaarey…' The use of 'dwaarey', a rather non-poetic word, in an isolated manner sounds funny. It, however, makes perfect phonetic sense when used in the context of the lyrical meter of the song, which has words like 'pukaarey', 'pyaarey pyaarey' and 'sang humaaraey'. For *Caravan*'s 'Piya tu', Monica sings, 'Tann ki jwaala thandi ho jaaye, aisey galey laga ja'. What is to be debated is whether 'tann ki jwaala', a rather crude expression, remains true to the idiom used by Monica in the film. The scene which introduces Monica in the film has her use lines like 'Stay there, you blooming rascal!' and 'tum mere jism[22] se khele ho'. The only reason for her to use 'tann ki jwaala' then is that the carnality of the song is perhaps best expressed with those three words. Also, as music expert Manohar Iyer explained to me, Majrooh's lyrics 'tann ki jwaala thandi ho jaaye aisey galey laga ja' are not very different from Sahir's 'Aaj sajan mohey ang laga lo… hriday ki peeda, deh ki agni, sab sheetal ho jaaye' for *Pyaasa*. But while Sahir's song is for a baul singer in *Pyaasa*, it is Majrooh's vocabulary that makes it perfect for the cabaret in *Caravan*.

Raza Mir laughed when I discussed Majrooh's inventiveness in these songs and said, 'True, true. But *kya karein*? (What to do?) This is Majrooh.' Raza then drew me back to the same comment

---

[21]The precise literal translation for 'jigar' is actually 'liver'. In the world of Urdu poetry the liver is seen as the repository of passion.

[22]'Jism', meaning body, is a synonym for 'tann' but she says 'jism' specifically.

about the playful nature of Husain's cinema and added, 'That is why Majrooh's lyrics are a little more playful than normal. I guess there is a little bit of instruction and a little bit of freedom.'

Freedom or instruction, music was at the core of Husain's film universe. Majrooh probably understood this given how his heart-breaking words are trumped by RD's bubbly composition in *'Kya hua tera waada'*. Or that in the *'Aa dil kya'* segment of the medley, the mukhda plays out almost disjointedly – *'Aa – dil kya – mehfil hai tere – kadmon mein aa'* – alongside RD's changing musical notes. The last bit, *'kadmon mein aa'*, is even sacrificed each time the song heads into its antara, *'Duniya ki bahaare tere liye'*, leaving the mukhda somewhat incomplete the second time round. But Majrooh's ability to match this buoyancy, this peppiness, while playing an active part in furthering Husain's screenplays and taking his cue from the music is what perhaps made him special to Husain. He may not have written a *'Hum bekhudi mein tumko pukaarey chale gaye'* (*Kala Pani*, 1958) or *'Jaltey hain jiske liye'* (*Sujata*, 1959) for Husain, but his willingness to bend the odd grammatical rule, use unconventional words ('chulbula', 'qibla'), be innovative, funny and also make compromises in terms of imagery and metaphors, show a pliant but master technician at work.

But to return to RD, the composer certainly enjoyed pre-eminence among Husain's technicians. 'He fell in love with Pancham,' Bhanu-da told me. 'They were indeed very close. Like family. For no rhyme or reason he would come and sit in Pancham's house. Anything Nasir sa'ab would do, any occasion, Pancham had to be there.' Homi Mullan spoke of Pancham's fondness for Husain, 'He had a special affinity for Nasir sa'ab. He used to work very hard for him.' Both Bhanu-da and Homi also confirmed both men's shared love for food, be it biryani or Bengali cuisine.

At the premiere of *Caravan* (1971).
Courtesy: NH Films/Nuzhat Khan

At the premiere of *Yaadon Ki Baaraat* (1973).
Courtesy: NH Films/Nuzhat Khan

With good friend
Raj Kapoor and brother
Tahir Husain, whom
Nasir Husain launched
as a producer with
Caravan. *Courtesy:
NH Films/Nuzhat Khan*

With
Rajesh Khanna,
R.D. Burman
and
Tahir Husain
at the premier
of *Caravan*.
*Courtesy: NH
Films/Nuzhat
Khan*

With Dharmendra
and Tariq Khan on
the sets of
Yaadon Ki Baaraat.
Courtesy: Tariq Khan

With Zeenat Aman,
who acknowledged
Yaadon Ki Baaraat
as the film that
established her as
a romantic lead.
Courtesy: NH Films/
Nuzhat Khan

From L to R:
Vijay Anand,
Nasir Husain,
Dharmendra and
Anand Bakshi.
Courtesy: NH Films/
Nuzhat Khan

From L to R: Imtiaz,
Tariq Khan, R.D.
Burman, Dharmendra,
Nasir Husain and
Vijay Arora. *Courtesy:*
NH Films/Nuzhat Khan

Teesri Manzil was a fine meeting of minds between Vijay Anand and Nasir Husain. *Courtesy: NH Films/Nuzhat Khan*

From L to R: Jeetendra, dance master Suresh, Ravinder Kapoor, Dharmendra, Husain and Salim Khan. *Courtesy: NH Films/Nuzhat Khan*

From L to R: Jalal Agha, Asha Parekh, Vijay Arora, Zeenat Aman, R.D. Burman, Salim Khan, Nasir Husain and Javed Akhtar. *Courtesy: Shamir Khan*

Having a blast during the outdoor schedule of *Hum Kisise Kum Naheen*.
Courtesy: Shamir Khan

The stylish, suave villain in Husain's films: Pran and Asha Parekh in *Phir Wohi Dil Laya Hoon*. *Courtesy: NH Films/Nuzhat Khan*

The original ending for *Baharon Ke Sapne* had Ram and Geeta dying; Husain reshot the climax when the film opened to a sub-par audience response. *Courtesy: NH Films/ Nuzhat Khan*

R.D. Burman and Rajendra Nath's rather animated routines in *Pyar Ka Mausam* were in keeping with the physicality of Husain's cinema. *Courtesy: NH Films/ Nuzhat Khan*

With Shaakaal (Ajit) in *Yaadon Ki Baaraat* (1973), Husain, in tandem with scriptwriters Salim–Javed, ushered in a new diabolical villain in Hindi cinema, one who was different from the cinematic villains of the 1960s. *Courtesy: NH Films/Nuzhat Khan*

The shelving of his intended magnum opus, *Zabardast*, starring Dilip Kumar (seen here with Raj Kiran and Kaajal Kiran), Dharmendra and Rishi Kapoor, dented Husain's confidence. *Courtesy: NH Films/ Nuzhat Khan*

Husain's dialogues in *Jo Jeeta Wohi Sikandar* (1992) articulated the voice of a generation much younger than his own. *Courtesy: NH Films/Nuzhat Khan*

In keeping with the hit medleys in *Yaadon Ki Baaraat* and *Hum Kisise Kum Naheen*, Husain incorporated one in *Zamaane Ko Dikhana Hai* too. However, it lacked the chutzpah and novelty of the ones in the earlier films. According to Mansoor Khan, it appeared too early in the film. *Courtesy: NH Films/Nuzhat Khan*

By the 1980s, Nasir Husain and his team seemed to have lost their touch. The garish, tacky sets and the somewhat crude aesthetics of *Manzil Manzil* were at complete odds with the usual fun, stylized fare offered by a Nasir Husain film. *Courtesy: NH Films/ Nuzhat Khan*

Husain, possibly, even exploited their relationship to his advantage when he cast RD in *Pyar Ka Mausam*. RD plays Jhatpat Singh's (Rajendra Nath) secretary, who regularly uses the phrase, 'Very true', sounding cuckoo-clock like, to humorous effect. RD had acted only once before in Hindi cinema, in Mehmood's *Bhoot Bangla* (1965). There, too, he had a regular taqia-kalaam, *'Main khaa raha hoon* (I am eating)'. Husain had seen RD and was, probably, convinced of his composer's comic timing. But RD was apprehensive. *'Kahaan phansa raha hai? Yeh gadbad cheez hai* (Where are you involving me? This is fraught with trouble),' Bhanu-da recalled Pancham telling Husain. Homi Mullan confirmed RD's trepidations, remarking, 'He said, "Am I a music director or an actor?" But he couldn't say no to Nasir sa'ab. It worked well.'

Aamir detailed Husain's relationship with RD vis-à-vis the film-maker's association with Majrooh. 'With Majrooh sa'ab, Nasir sa'ab's relationship was more of an equal, age or seniority wise. Majrooh sa'ab was someone he would call "Majrooh sa'ab". And if I am not mistaken, Majrooh sa'ab would call him "Nasir". I never heard Nasir sa'ab calling him Majrooh. With Pancham uncle, who was younger than him, Chachajaan would call him "Pancham". He never said Pancham-ji or Pancham-da. And Pancham used to call him Nasir sa'ab. With Pancham uncle it was more playful. Pancham uncle used to look up to him because he was part of the initial stage of his career. Between Pancham uncle and Chachajaan, it was like Pancham uncle was his younger brother. And they have created mad stuff. If you look at *Caravan*,' Aamir paused, took a deep breath and then started singing *'Daiyya yeh main kahaan aa phansi'*. 'I mean what a song!'

And madness incarnate 'Daiyya yeh main kahaan aa phansi'
truly is. The sequence is pure Nasir Husain. Subodh Mukerji
'theatrewallah' has engaged the banjaras to perform. Nisha
(Aruna Irani) is supposed to be the marquee attraction of this
performance. But Nisha refuses to take part, saying that she will
not get onto the stage unless Soni (Parekh) is ostracized by the
banjaras. Determined to put Nisha in her place, Mohan decides
to perform with Soni instead, even though he knows she cannot
dance. But Mohan is dealing with a hostile audience, who have
only come to see the sizzling Nisha perform. To make matters
worse, Ratna kaki (Manorama) sabotages Soni's costume. Soni
comes out on stage wearing a green witch hat and an oversized
clown dress that seem to have been stitched together from assorted
bed linen. 'It was a fun song. The whole concept was given to
the dress designer, how it was going to be done. No, it wasn't a
traditional costume at all. It was made out of stitching two or
three clothes together,' Parekh told me.

Then as bagpipes start playing, Mohan, who is in the middle
of his own dysfunctional, animated routine, urges Soni to do
something to keep the audience from lynching them. Soni
responds with a couple of remarkably off-key renditions of 'Holi
aayee re'[23] and 'Ghar ghar mein Diwali hai mere',[24] but Mohan
shuts her up. He asks her to sing some 'chaaloo cheez' (something
catchy) instead. With Soni struggling to find her voice, and the
performance threatening to come apart, Mohan thrusts her centre
stage. Just as he does this, Soni finds her voice and begins singing,
'Daiyya yeh main kahaan aa phansi'.

The genesis of the song can perhaps be traced back to I.S. Johar's
directorial debut, Shrimati Ji where Shrimati Indra (Shyama) and

---

[23]Song from Mother India (1957).
[24]Song from Kismet (1943).

her friends step in for Mr Rajesh (Nasir Khan) and party after
the latter group has a tiff with the theatre owner over terms. But
the audience at the theatre has turned up to see Rajesh and crew,
the star attraction of the show. Even as Indra's friends bumble in
their attempts to please this antagonistic gathering, Indra is thrust
into the limelight in a last-ditch effort to salvage the situation.
Just as everything seems lost, Indra bursts into the breezy, '*Eh
babu oh babuji, main na karoon teri naukri*'. Through the song,
Indra makes fun of the 'buddhey', 'jawaaan' and 'gentleman', all
very much a part of her audience. By the end of her performance,
which relies entirely on Indra's theatrics, her expressions and her
mannerisms, she has the audience singing and clapping with her.
They show their approval by showering Rajesh and his team with
eggs and tomatoes.

'*Daiyya yeh main kahaan aa phansi*' is on an altogether different
level. It is a crazy, crazy song. Unlike the *Shrimati Ji* track, which
lampoons the audience to create comedy, '*Daiyya yeh main...*'
has Soni fretting over the situation she has landed in. There is
definite doublespeak involved here, as Soni is not just referring
to her immediate circumstances in the context of the song, but
also her larger situation, which is that she is on the run. This is
much like '*Lekar hum deewaana dil*' or *Hum Kisise Kum Naheen*'s
medley and '*Humko toh yaara teri yaari*'. We think of these songs
in the context of the moment they occur in, but they actually go
back to the basic storyline of Husain's narratives.

With chairs falling around, chickens appearing out of a barn, an
egg materializing from within someone's collar, the zestful banjaras
joining in and Soni swinging from a rope all the way up to the
audience, Husain created an iconic sequence that embodied the
hystérique, the masti in his cinema. There is also the narrative of
Soni eluding Rajan's henchmen intertwined in the song, beginning
with the antara '*kaise hai Rama yeh milan ki ghadi*', but which

is cleverly passed off as Mohan thinking that Soni is referring to him. By the end of the song, the once lascivious, loutish audience is transformed. They are on their feet, dancing and singing, with a general feeling of delirium and joy having filled the entire room.

'I asked Nasir sa'ab this question,' recollected Aamir. 'I said did you create those situations first and then get the song written and composed because the song is referring to so many things that are also happening visually. So did you all plan *"Ki yeh gaana aisey shoot hoga? Ya aap logon ne ek mad gaana banaaya aur phir usko mad shoot kiya?* (That the song would be shot this way? Or did you all come up with a mad song and then shoot it like a mad sequence?)" He said, *"Humney mad gaana banaaya aur usko mad shoot kiya* (We came up with a mad song and then shot it with a certain madness)."'

Asha Parekh and Jeetendra confirmed the spontaneity in picturizing the song. 'He [Husain] had given us the whole concept. So we worked on it. Then there was Suresh master, directing the song. Little, little things came out *ki nahin abhi aise kartey hain, aisey kartey hain.* That's how it was picturized,' remembered Parekh. 'That shot of me swinging on the rope, it was after going on set that he thought of it,' she added. Jeetendra said something similar. 'The whole song was fun. *Ek toh Suresh dance master unkey favourite, aur movement kartey kartey kuchh improvise ho jaata toh Nasir sa'ab would say, "Aap yahi karo, bas yeh karo."* (Firstly, Suresh dance master was his favourite, and if we improvised while dancing, he would say "Keep going. Keep going.") He [Husain] gave you that latitude. And then you enjoyed freaking out with him because he would appreciate. He would not make fun.'

Javed Akhtar was effusive in his praise for the song. 'It is difficult to write a good song, but to write an absurd song, consciously … It is a different matter that in the pursuit of writing a good song, some people create absurd stuff. But if you really want absurdity and you write a song like "*Daiyya yeh main kahaan aa phansi*" – what a song! What a composition! And how well has Majrooh Sultanpuri, a literary poet, written such a song, with such competence. And how well was it picturized by Nasir Husain.'[25] Anuradha Warrier, too, was bowled over by the sequence. She called it 'One of the most fascinating dance sequences ever filmed' and wrote, 'It is sheer cacophony, sheer mayhem. But oh, how controlled! ... Asha [Parekh] is a fantastic dancer – see, it is easy enough to do traditional steps in a regular dance. To wear a costume that is beyond hysterical, to be graceful when you are asked to swing and stand on a chair and jump and lord knows what else. She did a smack-up job and it is a sequence I watch again and again. In awe.'

But why this song absolutely epitomizes the Husain–RD association is because the music director keeps pace with Husain's madness. By composing a number which sees Asha Bhonsle sing several short, fast, high-pitched notes and a higher scale each time the mukhda[26] is repeated, RD is able to translate Husain's hyper excessiveness. Even Majrooh is forced to match up by writing lines like '*Paappey bacha lo tussi*' (Boss, save me) and '*de ke andaa kahaan ja basi*' (look where it rests after laying an egg). The personalities, the creative energies of both Husain and RD can be seen in perfect sync with each other in the song. Aamir agreed with this assessment, saying, 'It's the one song which really illustrates their genius as music people and in the visual arts as well. See where the song starts from and see the kind of instrumentation. The song also shifts octaves at one point.' And so, if 'half an octave higher' is how Raza Mir sees Husain's films as distinct from everyone else's,

---

[25]Zee Classic's *Classic Legends: Season II*, featuring Nasir Husain.

[26]Based on Sadanand Warrier's explanation of the song to me.

'*Daiyya yeh main kahaan aa phansi*' is at least two octaves higher, both, literally and figuratively.

Perhaps, it is this chemistry that led R.D. Burman to say, 'Nasir Husain had to only narrate the screenplay for me to get charged. I used to get the sort of vibrations that made me compose songs immediately. That's how he inspired me to compose songs for *Caravan* – extempore – when actually I was in no mood to compose.'[27] Balaji Vittal opined, 'Nasir Husain knew his music very, very well. He also knew how to get the best out of his composers. And on his part, Pancham would try and squeeze out everything that was needed as an input from the director about the scene – the minutest of details. This was the chemistry. Both were willing to experiment.'

Together, Husain and RD were able to create a brand of music that was distinct from RD's successful collaborations with other directors such as Shakti Samanta or Gulzar. Karan Johar agreed, saying, 'I have always believed that the best musical combination that existed was Nasir Husain and R.D. Burman. The music that they created was way ahead of their times ... Both enjoyed the world of Western music. Their music had a different melody, a different spark, a different orchestra, a different arrangement.' At the same time, the music in Husain's films, too, with the coming of RD is distinct from his collaborations with composers who worked on his earlier films. Aditya Chopra, who suggested that Husain couldn't have been 'assertive enough' with the more senior O.P. Nayyar, opined in RD's context, 'I think with R.D. Burman, his [Husain's] celebration of music and his flamboyance came out more because by then he was also very successful. Now he was the bigger star, giving a break to a younger musician. That is when he took full charge on how his music should be.'

And so it is that the music was the biggest star element in Husain's film-making enterprise. Karan endorsed this view. 'His music is super iconic. Whether it is *Yaadon Ki Baaraat* or *Hum Kisise Kum Naheen* – these are legendary movies but that has a lot to do with the music. Like "*Yaadon ki baaraat*" – if you hear that particular song even today, it strikes a chord. It has nostalgia in it. Whichever zone of life you are in, it takes you back to a certain nostalgic feeling. Some of those songs are just forever. They have survived decade after decade after decade.'

The question, however, remains: for what specific purpose did Husain use this music? Bhaumik put forth one view. 'The physicality in a Nasir Husain film is far, far more palpable than in Dev Anand's films and that is what makes him an auteur for me. To express that physicality, music is the best medium.' That a lot of Husain's song sequences emphasize the performative nature and the physical aspect of his characters bears this out.

But perhaps the larger purpose of Husain's reliance on music was to negate the 'star effect' so far as his hero was concerned. That is why Husain's cinema isn't synonymous with any one star actor. Shammi Kapoor, who did three films with Husain (and Husain directed only two of them), had six films with Shakti Samanta.[28] Moreover, Shammi's first film with Husain was while the actor's career was in free-fall. Husain directed Dev Anand, Joy Mukerji, Rajesh Khanna, Shashi Kapoor, Jeetendra, Dharmendra in one film each. Of these men, Joy and Shashi hardly ever hit the really big league in terms of true stardom. Khanna was at the beginning

---

[28] *Singapore* (1960), *China Town, Kashmir Ki Kali, An Evening in Paris, Pagla Kahin Ka* (1970) and *Jane Anjane* (1971).

of his career when Husain signed him. Even the association with Rishi Kapoor was for two films only. In this sense, Husain was unlike many great film-makers, whose cinema was often defined by their associations with great actors or star personalities as Manmohan Desai's was with Amitabh Bachchan.

Husain understood that music is the only real alternative to the 'star system' in Hindi cinema. Quality music can make a good film great and even save the most ordinary of films. So while Husain didn't collaborate with any one actor to the extent that other film-makers did, he put maximum emphasis on his music. This is probably why in a film like *Yaadon Ki Baaraat*, the Salim–Javed track, which is represented by Dharmendra's character, has no songs. But Husain propped up his own contribution in the romantic and musical characters of newcomers Vijay and Monto through great music. To this extent, if *Yaadon Ki Baaraat* stands its ground against films like *Waqt* and *Amar Akbar Anthony* despite lacking in relative star power, it is because of RD's scintillating soundtrack.

Continuing with this logic, it is with RD by his side that Husain stood up to the Bachchan–Salim–Javed combine that saw the Hindi film hero in a towering rage. But at the same time, none of the Salim–Javed films are particularly remembered for their music be it *Zanjeer, Sholay*,[29] *Deewaar, Don, Trishul, Kaala Patthar, Shakti*. This is why much of *Yaadon Ki Baaraat*'s success owes to Husain, because even the presence of R.D. Burman in films like *Sholay, Deewaar* or *Shakti* didn't result in the kind of spectacular music that *Yaadon Ki Baaraat* has.[30] *Yaadon Ki Baaraat* is the only

---

[29]Anirudha Bhattacharjee and Balaji Vittal remark in their book *R.D. Burman: The Man, The Music* that the music album sales for *Sholay* only took off when the dialogue long-play records hit the market.

[30]*Shaan* (1980) is a possible exception, but one would have to take into account Ramesh Sippy's contribution on the film since Sippy's films, as

(Contd...)

Salim–Javed film whose music can be safely termed evergreen. This is why even with the dominant Salim–Javed vendetta narrative, it is Husain who leaves his stamp, with his choice of music, on the film. This is why *Yaadon Ki Baaraat* is certainly Husain's best work. Bachchan's other films, too, which rode on his superstardom in the late 1970s aren't about music, but looked to exploit the raging persona of the man. Jerry Pinto commented, 'The Bachchan wave was erasing heroines. And erasing songs. And erasing romance. The Bachchan oeuvre has very few really good songs in it. Most people cannot remember two songs out of *Zanjeer*. And Nasir Husain was only focused on the song, the romance and the heroine. I mean the biggest memory today we have of Zeenat Aman is not Raj Kapoor's *Satyam Shivam Sundaram* [1978]. It's her in *"Chura liya hai tumne jo dil ko"*. And she's looking gorgeous. She's dressed in Western clothes. It suited her perfectly. She's strumming a guitar and she's in the middle of a party. She's central. And look at who the hero is.'[31]

It is also worth noting that at Bachchan's peak, most film-makers, who debuted around the time that Husain made *Tumsa Nahin Dekha*, be it Vijay Anand or Hrishikesh Mukherjee or Yash Chopra or Raj Khosla or Shakti Samanta or Manmohan Desai or Pramod Chakravorty, turned to Bachchan. These men either

---

(…contd.)

established by *Andaz* (1971), *Seeta Aur Geeta* and *Saagar* (1985), generally had good music. Also, *Shaan* didn't do well at the box office, which is why its music didn't enjoy as much appeal as *Yaadon Ki Baaraat*'s.

[31]Not coincidentally, in *Trishul*, where Bachchan's and Shashi Kapoor's characters face-off for most of the film, Shashi (a former Husain hero) stands for love and romance (*'Mohabbat badey kaam ki cheez hai'*) while Bachchan, dour and grim, considers love a waste of time (*'Zamaane ke bazaar mein yeh woh shay hai ki jiski kisiko zaroota nahin hai'*). This song, although from a Yash Chopra film, is a perfect juxtapositioning of Husain's cinema and Bachchan's 'Angry Young Man' avatar.

gave Bachchan some of his best films or went to Bachchan to rescue their sagging careers. Husain was the only one who made it huge without Bachchan. With *Caravan, Yaadon Ki Baaraat* and *Hum Kisise Kum Naheen*, Husain more than stood his ground in the 1970s, Bachchan's decade, with three immensely successful commercial films. With RD by his side, Husain defied the Bachchan wave. Karan Johar agreed. 'Nasir Husain didn't need Bachchan. He had a separate story happening. He was a "*hatke dukaan*" (something else) as they say. His music was just on another level.'

It is not surprising then that with RD's decline in the mid-1980s Husain, too, went through his worst phase, with films like *Manzil Manzil* and *Zabardast*. Their enviable jodi that endured over twenty years and resulted in many fine films came to an end after *Zabardast*, with Husain's son, Mansoor Khan, selecting Anand–Milind to helm the score for *Qayamat Se Qayamat Tak*.

'The memories of men are too frail a thread to hang history from,' wrote the English author John Still. But the apocryphal tales of octogenarian men make for enchanting kaleidoscopes to look back at great artistic collaborations. Bhanu Gupta mentioned an episode about a Pakistani producer who once came to meet Husain and exhorted him to make a film specifically for the Pakistani audience. Apparently, Husain's 'musical comedies' had a great audience and fan base across the border. Husain heard the man out patiently, but ultimately said no. His logic was clear. 'Even if everything else fell in place,' said Husain, '*magar mujhe R.D. Burman kahaan milega wahaan*? (Where will I get an R.D. Burman in Pakistan?)'

12

STYLE, SPECTACLE AND
A STRING OF FLOPS

'I don't know what Nasir sa'ab was like as a person but his aesthetics and his projections were uber cool and chic. Even today I find myself referencing some of the clothes from his films. Shammi Kapoor's blazer [in '*O haseena zulfon waali*'] in *Teesri Manzil* is just iconic. I mean today everyone's done it on a million stages. Who knew that what was just a costume in *Teesri Manzil* would attain that kind of stature and memory. I mean even Helen's clothes. They are just genius.'

– Film-maker and producer Karan Johar

'In many ways, at that point, song was also spectacle. And Husain was master of this spectacle ... With Husain you were very clear – a song is an extravaganza. You look at "*Chhaiyyan chhaiyyan*" [*Dil Se*, 1998], but "*Hoga tumse pyaara kaun*" has already happened on top of a train way before.'

– Author Jerry Pinto

Among Javed Akhtar's observations on Husain's music sensibilities was the poet–writer's affirmation of Husain's innate sense of style and sophistication. 'Even when you look at his films, they were Indian films which had westernized norms to a certain extent,' Akhtar said. 'This was his whole persona. He was deeply rooted in Urdu, but at the same time he had a certain Western aspiration and sophistication. That is why his Urdu was sophisticated Urdu. That is true of his music also. There is a certain kind of music that he would never take, which was "small town" music.' Akhtar even qualified this remark when he hummed and sang '*Oh phirkiwaali tu kal phir aana*' (*Raja Aur Rank*, 1968) to me. '*Iss tarah ke gaaney nahin ho saktey thay. Woh jo unki music bhi thee woh Hindustani hi hogi, lekin usmein bhi ek Western polish honi chaahiye. Woh unki music mein aapko dikhaayee dega* (He would never have such songs. Even if his songs were Hindustani they had a Western polish in them. That is what you will see in his music).'

This refinement that Akhtar spoke of is evident pretty much all through Husain's cinema. Not only were his characters urbane and exuded a certain comfort with modernity, they also reflected this demeanour in their attire. The men wore tuxes, bow ties, cravats, dinner jackets, three-piece suits, tweed coats, bold printed shirts, waistcoats; they sported aviators, panama hats, trilbies and smoked cigars – to either reflect the latest fashion trends or to mark their Western influences. Shammi Kapoor was certainly modelled on Elvis's image for much of *Dil Deke Dekho*. Joy Mukerji's wife, Neelam Mukerji, told me that Mohan's look in *Phir Wohi Dil Laya Hoon*, particularly when he wanders about in a black suit while Mona shows the villainous Ramesh around, earned Joy Mukerji the moniker 'the Indian Rock Hudson'. The elegance extended to the villains as well. 'A lot of films in which my father acted were stylish films like Nasir Hussain [sic] Saab's earlier films and the ones with Shammi Kapoor. When you saw the film you felt that here was a villain with whom the girl also could run off,' Sunil Sikand, the actor Pran's son, remarked in his father's biography.[1]

---

[1] Bunny Reuben, 'Pran: The Gentleman Villain', *...and Pran: A Biography*, HarperCollins *Publishers* India, 2005, p. 345.

The women, too, were well turned out. Parekh invariably made a style statement with figure-hugging churidar kurtas, printed blouses, winged eyeliners, puffy bouffants, high ponytails, bling accessories and chandelier earrings. Zeenat Aman was all style and oomph in her flared high waist pants, her miniskirt, red boots, her one-piece swimsuit, large hoops, bling belts and waistcoats. Even Neetu Singh, who is there only for a brief while in *Yaadon Ki Baaraat*, became quite the rage with her red miniskirt and open tresses in '*Lekar hum deewaana dil*'. Clearly, Husain's sartorial choices were rather fashionable and the characters dressed correspondingly.

The costumes for many Husain films – *Dil Deke Dekho, Jab Pyar Kisise Hota Hai, Teesri Manzil* and *Hum Kisise Kum Naheen* – were helmed by eminent costume designer and Oscar winner, Bhanu Athaiya. 'Now you are looking at the best of the best,' Sidharth Bhatia told me in reference to Athaiya working on Husain's films. 'Nasir Husain was sophisticated in terms of storytelling, in terms of production value. *Jab Pyar Kisise Hota Hai* is a very well-produced movie. Look at the clothes people are wearing. For example, in "*Yeh aankhein, uff yumma*", he is wearing gloves ... it's all very sophisticated. *Teesri Manzil*, let's assume that the production value, the look and the feel are Goldie's [Vijay Anand], but *producer ka paisa toh lag raha hai na*. (It is the producer putting in the money.) Costume design is critical to *Yaadon Ki Baaraat*. The club set is fantastic. There's the whole feel of it being a well-mounted film.'

One of the songs that exemplifies Husain's sense of style is '*Chura liya hai tumne jo dil ko*' from *Yaadon Ki Baaraat*. With Zeenat dressed in a white jumpsuit palazzo, a black choker around her neck and disco hoops falling from her ears, the actor is elegance personified. Vijay Arora is able foil, wearing a ruffle-front tuxedo shirt, skinny bow tie and black tux. RD's melody, inspired by *'If it's Tuesday, it must be Belgium'*, enhanced the mood with its gentle strains and smooth, silken rendition by Asha Bhonsle and Mohammed Rafi.

Zeenat Aman detailed the interesting backstory to her lovely outfit in the song. In the scene leading into the song, Husain had dressed her in a traditional, Indian way. 'I was wearing this pink shalwar kameez, with a little waistcoat, with my hair tied up. I was a slim tall girl and somehow it looked very gawky. It just didn't work.' Both Husain and Zeenat concurred that her look wasn't working. At that point, Zeenat suggested to Husain that she should try on something that suited her, something Western and a little contemporary. 'I suggested the palazzo, the one-piece suit and leaving my hair open. He loved it. He said, "Okay. Let's go with this."' That's how Sunita transformed for *'Chura liya'*, with the makeover happening in the time that Sunita excuses herself to respond to Kunwar Vijay Kumar's shaayari. Sidharth Bhatia complimented the style statement of the film, saying, 'My memory of that film is the gloss. See the clothes Vijay Arora is wearing. See the clothes Zeenat is wearing. Everyone is so smart. Everyone is so nice looking ... Barring the fact that he had this one story idea, what else did he bring in to say that this is a Nasir Husain film – great music, good-looking people, a certain kind of gloss.'

'Chura liya', perhaps, has another significance too. Hindi cinema for the longest time has generally been averse to the idea of alcohol. The villains committed their acts of villainy, having had their fill of liquor, but when our heroes or heroines took to the bottle, it was either to signal their moral decline or to drown their sorrows as a result of unrequited love. Songs in popular Hindi

cinema have also mirrored this. One can think of any number of film songs which show the hero, glass (or bottle) in hand, grieving aloud after his lady love has spurned him. On the odd occasion that there was mirth associated with drinking, it came from a defensive/apologetic standpoint like in *'Thodi si jo pee lee hai, chori toh nahi kee hai'* (*Namak Halaal,* 1982). Alternately, the consumption of liquor even offered our heroes a rare clarity, which allowed them to comment on social evils or take a harsh, incisive look at society while they could hardly stand on their feet. One of *Pyaasa's* defining songs, *'Jinhe naaz hai Hind par woh kahaan hain'*, comes after the poet Vijay (Guru Dutt) has been on a drinking binge.

In the last couple of decades, Hindi cinema has gone to the other extreme, where there is a completely hedonistic view of consuming alcohol. A number of recent film songs will validate this. However, forty-odd years ago, *'Chura liya'* appeared to accept, if unwittingly, the consumption of liquor among the youth without suggesting anything devious about their characters. Although Sunita and Vijay Kumar clearly mention to each other that they don't drink, the fact that liquor is being served at this 'house-warming' party suggests there is nothing wrong about its consumption. In an earlier scene, Sunita has already asked Vijay's father (the man who raised him) to organize liquor for her friends. This, in tandem with drinks being served at the party, the clinking of the 'wine' glasses to begin *'Chura liya'* and Sunita's movements choreographed around the bar, replete with its White Horse, Vat 69 and Haig whisky bottles, in the initial half of the song, is quite remarkable for the time.

The other memorable song that Zeenat was a part of alongside Rishi Kapoor is the qawwali from *Hum Kisise Kum Naheen*, '*Hai agar dushmann, dushmann*'. This is yet another instance of Husain's remarkable cultural inclusiveness where a qawwali, a style of Sufi devotional singing, is being rendered by Rajesh, a pop-disco artiste, to celebrate India's Independence Day among the NRI community in cosmopolitan London. A cursory look at the audience suggests resident Londoners, Sikh gentlemen and other Indians of various descent in attendance for the occasion. But Rajesh also uses the song as a means to brazen out his romance with Sunita before her father, Mr Kewalchand. He is convinced that Sunita will take his cue and boldly stand up and respond to his overtures, which she ultimately does.

Qawwalis have featured in Hindi cinema ever since the advent of the talkies. Sanjit Narwekar recorded that the 1935 film *Barrister's Wife* had the qawwali, '*Nazariya taane hai teer kamaan*,' which 'would become the first ever qawwali to be shown in Indian cinema'.[2] Another film in the same year, *Talaash-e-Haque*, reportedly, had a qawwali sung by Jaddan Bai, the actress Nargis's mother.[3] Although devotional in its roots, and meant to address Allah and the Prophet, the qawwali in Hindi cinema underwent a metamorphosis. It has essentially been used as a face-off between two parties or to underscore the idea of romance between the protagonists. Husain, who often resorted to music for competitive purposes, used the qawwali in *Hum Kisise Kum Naheen* to celebrate Rajesh and Sunita's love. Rajesh begins the song challenging his beloved to join him to complete the qawwali; otherwise, he says,

[2]Sanjit Narwekar, 'The Indian Charlie', *Eena Meena Deeka: Story of Hindi Film Comedy*, Rupa & Co., 2005, p. 23.
[3]Anna Morcom, 'The Musical Style of Hindi Film Songs', *Hindi Film Songs and the Cinema*, Ashgate Publishing Ltd, 2007, p. 73.

he will not live to see the rising sun the next day. Sunita does not disappoint Rajesh, much to her father's chagrin. In an excellent track composed by RD, boasting an arrangement that brings out the rhythm and the vibe of the qawwali perfectly, it is Majrooh who takes centre stage, with his remarkable, feisty lyrics:

Daal kar aankhon ko tere rukhsaaron pe
Roz hi chaltey hain hum toh angaaron pe
(Having cast my eyes on your beautiful cheeks
I walk every day on burning coal)

and

Bhes Majnu ka liya maine jo Laila hokar
Rang laaya hai dupatta mera maila hokar
(The beloved's guise that I wear, having become Laila
My scarf has been coloured by this stain)

In *Hum Kisise Kum Naheen*, the qawwali becomes a convenient mechanism for Husain to do away with any confrontation between father and daughter. Sunita openly defies Kewalchand in the presence of her to-be fiancé and his father.[4] Nothing has to be said via dialogue because the song says it all.

Zeenat recalled her role in the film and the song. 'I knew he was making *Hum Kisise Kum Naheen*. He approached me to do a small role. Of course I had enjoyed working so much with Nasir sa'ab. He told me, "You will not be disappointed. I will not waste you. You will be cast opposite the main leading man and I will give you a tremendous song." And true to his word, I was cast opposite the main hero. And then he gave me this brilliant qawwali. But I told him, "Nasir sa'ab, I'm sort of this westernized girl, I am not very good with qawwalis." He said, "It doesn't matter. You go and

---

[4]This is yet another instance of the woman exercising her choice in Husain's films.

rehearse." And I did. I rehearsed for a whole week so that I could get all the adaas, all the andaaz and I could perform with great confidence. I don't remember how many days it took to shoot, but he was very pleased with my performance by the end of it.'

The song is another example of Husain's aesthetic sensibilities, leaning towards a certain spectacle. This can be seen in the rather Western-looking, pink, ruffle-front tuxedo shirts and red vests worn by Rishi Kapoor and the junior artistes. Their performance takes place on a large stage lit by several chandeliers, with a kaleidoscopic-patterned ceiling. All this made the *Hum Kisise Kum Naheen* qawwali, also the film's title song, a statement in grandeur and plush production qualities. Aditya Chopra said as much. 'There is now a very clear-cut Nasir Husain song as a reference. If someone tomorrow needs to design a really big qawwali you can't escape what you have from *Hum Kisise Kum Naheen*.'

The song is also a ready pointer to the difference between Husain's and Manmohan Desai's cinematic sensibilities. *Hum Kisise Kum Naheen* released in the same year as Desai's *Amar Akbar Anthony*. Desai's film had Rishi Kapoor featuring in two popular qawwalis, 'Shirdi waale Sai Baba' and 'Purdah hai purdah'. In Desai's film, Rishi Kapoor as Akbar and his accompanying crew are dressed as more traditional qawwals in both songs. More specifically, the stage for 'Purdah hai purdah' is nowhere near the spectacle that Husain's is. Desai's audience, too, in this song is far from the landed gentry that make up Husain's. Although the subtext of Desai's qawwali is partly comic, it has the somewhat similar thread of the female character rebelling against her father's wishes, going up on stage and acknowledging her fondness for the qawwal. Neetu Singh as Salma does this while dressed in a traditional burqa. In contrast, Sunita is all style and glitz, with her chic choker, bling earrings and the rings on her fingers. She exudes a certain modernity in her maxi. Laxmikant–Pyarelal's score is also far more earthy compared to RD's music for the Husain sequence.

Come to think of it, every song in *Hum Kisise Kum Naheen* is a spectacle. In '*Bachna ae haseeno*' and the medley sequence, Husain created a visual extravaganza with the lighting, the clothes worn by the protagonist/s and, in the case of the medley, the competitive element of the sequence. The scale of the medley also appears huge, with Husain cleverly incorporating a couple of separate shots of the audience against a mirrored background. The reflective image of the audience in the mirrors gives the impression of a much larger audience than in reality. This mirrored backdrop on either side is clearly established in the pan shot of the audience from left to right, when the judge begins to say, 'Ladies and gentlemen, *naach gaaney ke iss muqaabley mein…*' Just a few shots before this, the true breadth of the set (and the audience size) is presented in a wide shot when the camera works from behind Rishi Kapoor and his denim-jacket-clad opponent dancing on the two circular discs.

Munir Khan's son, Shamir Khan, told me in the context of the song, 'He was very passionate about the *Hum Kisise Kum Naheen* medley sequence. It was cutting edge because there had not been a song sequence that long and at that pace, at that tempo, ever before. The kind of techniques he used to light it up, it was a beautiful sequence. There were a whole lot of challenges in that – they had this huge set, which was completely mirrored at the back and to get all the reflections in there – he [Munir Khan] got the Filmfare Award[5] for that.' Husain's intelligence comes through in the fact that while '*Bachna ae haseeno*' is only about a singer

---

[5]Filmfare Award for Best Cinematographer. This was Munir Khan's only Filmfare Award.

performing in a hotel, the medley is an 'All India' competition. The spectacle of the medley sequence reflects the grandness of the competition.

If the medley is a good example of RD living up to Husain's expectations, there are other instances where Husain's inventive picturization matched RD's peppy compositions. Homi Mullan confirmed this, adding that there was 'healthy competition' between Husain and RD. '*Pancham ne music achha diya hai, mere ko achha picturization karna hai* (Pancham has given good music, I have to complement it with good picturization).' A good illustration of this is '*Yeh ladka, haaye Allah*'. While it wasn't unusual by this time for Hindi film protagonists to sing romantic songs from the skies,[6] Husain cleverly created the illusion of Kaajal soaring high above courtesy some hot-air balloons midway through the song.

Shamir Khan gave the backstory to how the episode was executed. 'While Nasir uncle briefed Dad about this shot, where Kaajal is taken away by the balloons, Dad suggested shooting this entire scene with Kaajal on a crane. She was placed on a crane and then the movements were matched to that of a balloon being taken up.' Mansoor detailed the sequence. 'This was like a little gimmick that she flies off holding on to balloons. She's on the end of the crane. The camera is below her and the crane is just turning around,' which gives the impression that Kaajal is in full flight. For the interlude before the second antara, which has a couple of wide shots to suggest that Kaajal is indeed suspended mid-air (perhaps a 'head-in-the-clouds' moment), before Sanjay shoots a few of the balloons to bring Kaajal down (and therefore down to earth), Husain used a dummy. 'This was just for madness and for fun,' said Mansoor, chuckling at his father's picturization ideas.

---

[6]The beginning of '*Aasmaan se aaya farishta*' in *An Evening in Paris* (1967) has Shammi Kapoor serenade Sharmila Tagore from a helicopter.

It is clear that both the medley and '*Yeh ladka, haaye Allah*' were complicated song sequences to execute. 'You had to work on it,' Mansoor said. And Husain used to put much thought into each of these moments before attempting them. 'I used to watch him working. He would sit and conceive each episode, what happens in each antara. He would discuss it with Suresh uncle,[7] it was like adding episodes in the song.'

Aditya Chopra remarked, 'In a Nasir Husain film, each song is celebrated. You can make out that probably the screenplay moved towards a particular song because he wanted that song in this way. And that's what these masters did so well. They were not apologetic. They embraced the song and said my songs are the lifeblood of my film. So I am going to mount them. At least with Nasir sa'ab, I'm hundred per cent sure he believed that. I don't think he would have thought that *Shammi Kapoor mera star hai or Dev Anand mera star hai* (Shammi Kapoor is my star or Dev Anand is my star). He said, "*Mere gaaney mere star hain* (My songs are my stars) and my songs will be bigger than anything else in the film because that is what will give the greatest joy to my audience." *Agar ek kahaani hoti hai, woh kahaani aap ek hi baar sunn saktey ho na. Aap phirse woh same kahaani kaise sunogey? Par aap gaaney dekhney dus baar aa saktey ho* (You can't hear a story more than once. But you can revisit the same song again and again) ... So here's a man who loves music, who recognizes the power of songs commercially, who now puts all his craft and his head into celebrating each song so they become huge assets for him. Of course he also has a blast while doing it.'

Those writing on Husain's cinema in his time echoed Aditya Chopra's views. One journalist, who did a piece on Husain just before the release of *Hum Kisise Kum Naheen*, wrote, 'He [Husain]

[7]The choreographer Suresh Bhatt, who was a regular crew member in Nasir Husain Films, beginning *Baharon Ke Sapne*.

decided to put in all the money he saved on the galaxy of stars into production costs and give his film a plush treatment that would turn out to be a point in its favour. He made costly sets, made them glitter and appear gorgeous. He clad his stars in the costliest of costumes and gave the entire film a look of grandeur and extravagance that is usually reserved only for the historical films.'[8]

It isn't with *Hum Kisise Kum Naheen* that Husain moved towards spectacle or creating a stimulating visual experience. It had been part of his oeuvre right from the start. *Jab Pyar Kisise Hota Hai*'s title track, with Dev Anand singing atop a jeep to Asha Parekh within the train, is an exercise in spectacle. The many colourful songs of *Phir Wohi Dil Laya Hoon* are similarly oriented. In the same film, Husain built a rather opulent, extremely well-lit set, which had a giant Natraja figure, other ornate sculptures, and mirrored walls for the song '*Dekho bijli dole bin baadal ke*'. '*Goriya kahaan tera des re*' from *Caravan* is also a scenic extravaganza with wide shots of the gypsies travelling in their colourful bullock carts against the green landscape. 'He [Husain] wanted a lot of grandeur in his shots, that is what Dad used to tell me,' recalled Shamir Khan. 'He did something that was really grand and vast in canvas.' Editor Zafar Sultan, likewise, observed, 'He was a lavish film-maker. *Woh ek, ek shot ke liye set lagaate thay* (He would prepare his set for each shot).'

This spectacle extends to nearly all of *Zamaane Ko Dikhana Hai*'s songs. '*Hoga tumse pyaara kaun*' is a good example. Husain had already shown his fascination for the train as representative of

---

[8]Hanif Shakoor, 'The Dilemma of a Commercial Film Maker', *Poona Herald*, 4 February 1977.

modernity and a meeting place for strangers in his early films. With *'Hoga tumse pyaara kaun…'* Husain returned to the train as a place where romance could play out between his protagonists, or more specifically, where the hero could serenade his beloved on top of the train.

One of the earliest Hindi film songs to show the hero singing on the roof of a train was *'Mujhe apna yaar bana lo'* from *Boy Friend* (1961), starring Shammi Kapoor. But Shammi is on top of the train for only half the song, up to the point that the first antara comes to an end. With *'Jiya ho'*s novel picturization behind him, Husain already had a template for the song in *Zamaane Ko Dikhana Hai*. Mansoor advanced a more general explanation for Husain's reasoning to shoot this song on a moving train. 'Every film-maker tries to go one better on his earlier work. So you see a new thing that you haven't tried, for instance the medley of songs. He wanted the songs to be dynamic. *Taangey mein gaana ho gaya, yeh ho gaya, woh ho gaya* (a tonga song has been done, this has been done, that has been done), now you have to move beyond that.'

While a lot of *'Hoga tumse pyaara kaun'* relies on back projection, Husain brought in spectacle by taking a number of aerial shots of a moving train. The natives in their colourful scarves hark back to the *Tumsa Nahin Dekha* title song and *'Banda parvar'*. Lending further spectacle to the entire sequence are some actual shots of the wheels of the train in motion and an aerial shot of Ravi (possibly a stuntman) jumping from one compartment to another. Rishi Kapoor recalled, 'Train songs had been used earlier. Nasir sa'ab himself had done it in *Jab Pyar Kisise Hota Hai*, but this we wanted to shoot live. But having come on the sets, we realized it was not possible because the train was moving a lot, there was a helicopter, so we did get a few live shots and then we shot it indoor. It was between Coonoor and Ooty, in that area.

It was not practical to shoot because the camera, the artistes, the rattling of the train, you know people could fall off. It was not very safe.'

Irrespective of the back projection, Farah Khan, who choreographed '*Chhaiyyan chhaiyyan*' (*Dil Se*) with Shah Rukh Khan, Malaika Arora and several junior artistes actually on a moving train, was effusive in her praise for '*Hoga tumse pyaara kaun*'. 'At that time to think of a song on top of a moving train, like in *Zamaane Ko Dikhana Hai...*' When I asked Farah if Husain's song influenced her own picturization in any way, even if subconsciously so, Farah replied, 'I don't know. Maybe. Actually we put "*Chhaiyyan chhaiyyan*" [on the train] because we didn't get permission to shoot at the station. But to have someone who had already done it earlier...' The choreographer–film-maker's open-ended statement is perhaps validation of Husain's pioneering vision once again.

What the train does for Husain in the open landscape, the lighting does for *Zamaane Ko Dikhana Hai*'s indoor, set-based songs. From *Yaadon Ki Baaraat* onwards, Husain had turned to the stage for showcasing most of his musician protagonists' songs. He stuck to that even in *Zamaane Ko Dikhana Hai*, where Ravi isn't a musician but an industrialist's son. The very first sequence, which starts off with '*Main hoon woh albela*', followed by '*Bolo, bolo, kuchh toh bolo*' and finally '*Poochho na yaar kya hua*', is an offshoot of the informal face-off between Vijay Arora's character and Ravi and Kanchan at Honeymoon Hotel. Inspired by John Travolta's *Saturday Night Fever* (1977), Husain used synchronized floor lighting in the sequence to match the choreographed steps. Mansoor, who is credited with 'Electronics and Light Effects' for the film, can actually be seen next to Vijay Arora's friends in the song, manually operating the lighting. Mansoor recollected, 'At that time, *Saturday Night Fever* had released. Dad used to watch all this. He said we want something like this. He was very impressed with the synchronization of the lights, which is what I helped him with ... He wanted the lighting to be in sync with the beat of the music. Now it may sound very simple these days, but in those days it was ... [laughs wryly]. We had all those disco lights, but they were on top. He wanted a floor where the individual squares light up because that was how it was in *Saturday Night Fever*. He was very taken up with that. He was a showman in his own way. He wanted it to look modern.'

This play with lighting can be seen in the *Zamaane Ko Dikhana Hai* qawwali title track as well. Aditya Chopra observed, 'Who could have thought *qawwali ke saath disco hai*. (That there will be a qawwali-cum-disco.) The beauty is that he makes something as traditional as qawwali, and obviously a part of his tradition as a Muslim, he makes that also [look and sound] young. By the time *Zamaane Ko Dikhana Hai* came, he must have realized that if I just do a qawwali, I am not sure I will be able to pull it off like *Hum Kisise Kum Naheen*. *Mujhe ismein beats dene padengey youngsters ke liye* (I will need to embellish it with beats for the youth).' Farah agreed, saying, 'To have a qawwali shot like a disco song, the vision was remarkable.'

'*Dil lena khel hai dildaar ka*' and '*Poochho na yaar kya hua*' further reflect this obsession with lighting pyrotechnics. '*Dil lena khel hai dildaar ka*' also has a rather longish prelude, with gimmicky thunder and lightning special effects, and a commentary about doomed lovers such as Laila–Majnu, Shirin–Farhad running alongside before the song begins. The 'I Luv Kanchan' stunt by the audience at the beginning, with the song ending with them waving sparklers and chanting '*Yaar ka, yaar ka*' is vintage Husain spectacle. '*Poochho na yaar kya hua*' lapses into dream sequences in the antaras, where the lighting and set design (the mammoth butterfly behind the shaadi mandap) are geared to inspire awe.

Zamaane Ko Dikhana Hai has its moments. RD's music, while not exceptional, is certainly better than some of his efforts later in the decade. The comic sequences, such as when Kanchan disguises herself as the Nepali caddy and creates several misunderstandings between Ravi and Colonel Tipsee, or the interactions between Ravi and Bahadur Singh, are genuinely funny. But the film fared miserably and was Husain's first real taste of failure. 'I did a bit of soul-searching and realized that the film lacked pizzazz. *Rooh nikal gayee thee* (Its soul was missing),' Husain explained.[9] But Husain's remarks don't explain what he meant. There is much more to the film's debacle than his one-line summary.

The original premise of *Zamaane Ko Dikhana Hai* has Ravi (Rishi Kapoor) setting out to find his brother Ramesh (Randhir Kapoor) and his wife (Kanchan's sister). But once he reaches Darjeeling, he seems to be more interested in courting Kanchan (Padmini Kolhapure) than pursuing his original agenda. There is also Sharif mian's (Amjad Khan) backstory with his wife Razia (Yogeeta Bali) that gets entwined with Ravi and Kanchan. While Husain had previously shown a knack for weaving elaborate plot structures and then disentangling them deftly, things just fell apart in *Zamaane Ko Dikhana Hai*.

'I told him that you forgot your original premise,' explained Mansoor. 'Basically he [Rishi Kapoor's character] gets floored with Padmini. Now in four songs he keeps wooing her. And each time

---

[9]Ambarish Mishra, 'I Will Always Be a Romantic at Heart', *The Times of India*, 7 May 2000.

it goes in a loop that he is trying to woo her and she gets wooed. *Pehley waaley mein bhi aisa hua, doosrey mein bhi, teesrey mein bhi* ... (It happened in the first song, then in the second and in the third as well). And so the story didn't progress. The audience will go with you [initially]. They will say *haan mazaa aa raha hai, mazaa aa raha hai* (yes, we are enjoying this). But when you re-enter the plot, the audience is rudely reminded, *ki achha kahaani woh thee* (Oh, that was the storyline).'

Mansoor's explanation is fundamental to understanding Husain's cinema and the failure of *Zamaane Ko Dikhana Hai*. Unlike his earlier films, where the songs move the story forward, the *Zamaane Ko Dikhana Hai* songs, barring '*Hoga tumse pyaara kaun*' possibly, don't do that. Unlike the *Hum Kisise Kum Naheen* medley, which combines spectacle with storytelling, the *Zamaane Ko Dikhana Hai* medley seems to exist purely for the purpose of reminding the audience of the earlier film's multiple song sequence. It has no narrative objective. Mansoor admitted as much when he told me, 'It was too early to do a medley in the film.'

Moreover, while the *Hum Kisise Kum Naheen* medley and the qawwali have a certain sophistication about them, the lighting and sets in each of the *Zamaane Ko Dikhana Hai* songs come across as garish and self-indulgent. 'He got carried away with trying to do sensational songs,' said Mansoor. 'Each song had to be a huge thing by itself. So again, you are losing track of what the purpose of the song is within your film. The integrity of your screenplay cannot be a showcase for songs.' Speaking specifically on the *Zamaane Ko Dikhana Hai* medley, Mansoor observed, 'If you go back and look at that set, it was lit so much that when we used to shoot on the sets it was boiling. There were so many lights. We went berserk. He wanted "*Yahaan pe bhi light laga do, wahaan pe bhi* (Put a light here, there too)." It was a miracle that the fuse didn't blow in Filmistan studio and everything didn't burn down. The lighting dominated everything. It didn't look like anything on earth.' Taking a larger view of the similar nature of the lighting in the other songs in the film, Mansoor concluded, 'It looked repetitive also because it was always these dazzling lights. Whether we realize it or not, the audience notices these things. And then it starts dulling down. So you can do it very grand, but it is not the grandeur that the audience is necessarily interested in.'

Aamir saw the *Hum Kisise Kum Naheen* effect on the *Zamaane Ko Dikhana Hai* songs. 'I would suspect that was a bit of a hangover from *Hum Kisise Kum Naheen*. In *Hum Kisise Kum Naheen* these things were happing more naturally. Yes there was scale, but it was in sync with the script. By the time he went into *Zamaane Ko Dikhana Hai*, he was a little overexcited about this, using technology in songs, the lighting, floor patterns.'

Another disconcerting element about *Zamaane Ko Dikhana Hai* was Husain's attempt at, possibly, reviving sinking careers. Vijay Arora, who hadn't made much of a splash post *Yaadon Ki Baaraat*, is seen as the bearded, misbehaving character whom Ravi takes on in the dance medley face-off. That Arora's character does not even have a name (Kanchan refers to him as '*woh daadi waala*') and has no other connection to the narrative render the entire sequence somewhat arbitrary.

Tariq Khan makes an even more disjointed appearance in the last half hour of the film. Following *Yaadon Ki Baaraat*, Husain had given Tariq a meatier role in *Hum Kisise Kum Naheen*. Tariq had some of the best numbers of the film, '*Chaand mera dil*', '*Tum kya jaano*' and '*Kya hua tera waada*' shot on him. He had found fame for a brief period, but couldn't sustain the success. Husain incorporated Tariq in *Zamaane Ko Dikhana Hai*, as the quirky, hippie-like character Robin who appears out of the blue, claiming to be Shekhar's (Kader Khan) long-lost son from an earlier affair. Although shorter in length than *Hum Kisise Kum Naheen*'s climax, *Zamaane Ko Dikhana Hai*'s ending appears to be a never-ending one as Husain clearly made a concerted effort to outdo the spectacle of his previous film. Here we have vans chasing each other, Shekhar making repeated appearances in a chopper, Sharif mian playing a friend in need who puts his life on the line to save the Nanda family, machine guns firing, with Robin ultimately revealing his real intentions and turning rogue on Shekhar. Husain's dialogues for Robin, in an attempt to create some pathos for the character, end up caricaturing Robin even further as he repeatedly refers to Shekhar as '*mere baap*' in anger. Robin's extended tirade against Shekhar for all the wrongs done to him make *Zamaane Ko Dikhana Hai*'s climax a heavy-handed one, killing whatever prospects the film might have had.

Tariq agreed. 'He went off-track totally. When we saw the trial preview, everyone was asking, "*Kaisi hai picture, kaisi hai* (How is the movie? How is it?)" I didn't know what to say. I felt *lafda hai. Bahut gadbad hai* (Something is wrong. There is a serious problem here).' According to Tariq, Husain should have incorporated his character from the beginning. 'If you had taken him from the start, from his childhood … without that, you weren't able to create any pathos for him with the audience. If a Hindi film is a tear jerker, where you show some incident from a character's childhood, the audience feels that the poor chap has been wronged. The audience has to see that and cry with you. *Aap roye, woh bhi roye.* (You cry and they do, too.) The audience has to feel what the character goes through.' Rishi Kapoor, too, blamed the off-course ending for the film's failure. 'We digressed at the end. We lost the film there.'

What Rishi may have also added is that Subhash Ghai's *Karz*, which released a year before *Zamaane Ko Dikhana Hai*, and presented Rishi as a pop superstar, had a certain punch in its score. At least two of its songs, '*Om shanti om*' and '*Ik haseena thee*', not only enjoyed immense popularity but had also been picturized with a certain style, a much more contemporary disco feel and drama than any of *Zamaane Ko Dikhana Hai*'s songs. Ravi, the businessman character from Husain's film, paled in front of Monty, the pop superstar from Ghai's film. In a sense, Ghai beat Husain at his own game.

Zamaane Ko Dikhana Hai's poor showing devastated Husain, as more than one family member confirmed to me. Mansoor said, '*Zamaane Ko Dikhana Hai* affected him negatively. He never recovered from that ... I found that very strange for a person who had made so many films. I mean, other film-makers have had ups-and-downs. Maybe it just took him by surprise, the extent to which the audience didn't like the film ... That definitely shattered him.'

But there is another episode that played its part in wrecking Husain's confidence. Just before Husain started making *Zamaane Ko Dikhana Hai*, he had announced an epic multi-starrer called *Zabardast*. It was to be produced and directed by Husain himself and starred Dilip Kumar, Dharmendra, Rishi Kapoor and Raj Kiran. The women paired opposite Dilip Kumar were Asha Parekh and Sharda, one of the top actresses from the south. Zeenat Aman was to star opposite Dharmendra, Tina Munim was paired with Rishi Kapoor and Kaajal Kiran with Raj Kiran. Amjad Khan was to play the villain in the film. 'When *Zabardast* was announced, it was the biggest film of the time,' recalled Aamir in awe. 'I remember all the territories were closed at seventy-five lakh rupees per territory minimum guarantee [MG], which was a very high figure for that time. And overseas was closed at 1.25 crore rupees

MG. All territories sold, overseas sold on announcement. No film had ever got this kind of price.'

Husain, however, had to abandon the film after shooting a few reels with Dilip Kumar. Apparently, the thespian wanted changes made in the script, in the scenes and in the dialogues. Husain didn't like that. Though he had the option to replace Kumar with another actor, he shelved the film instead. 'Nasir sa'ab came from the old school,' Aamir explained. 'He had a lot of respect for Yusuf sa'ab. He would never drop Yusuf sa'ab and take another actor. These are old-fashioned, emotional people. He would rather shelve the film and say, "I'm not making it." Today they would replace the actor, which is the more practical thing to do.'

According to Mansoor, Husain and Dilip Kumar should have never worked together. 'They were totally different personalities and represented two totally different styles of film-making. I am not blaming anyone but they were not compatible. My dad liked to shoot scenes his way and I think Dilip sa'ab wanted scenes his way. So after some time Dad felt he was not in control. He felt it's better to shut down the thing than to shoot the whole thing where he is not in control … I don't think Dilip sa'ab and he even met and resolved it. It just shut down.'

This *Zabardast* setback was a huge shocker for Husain. Nuzhat elaborated, 'Imagine how much money he would have put into it, shooting that schedule, and in those days producers used to put in their own money, and then sell it to distributors. And also the shock of having written a whole film, starting it and then not being able to make it. It had never happened to him.'

Aamir used the *Zabardast* fiasco to explain Husain's film titles. According to the actor–producer, Husain's film titles – be it *Tumsa Nahin Dekha*, *Dil Deke Dekho* or *Pyar Ka Mausam* – were not necessarily connected to the story. 'It could apply to any romantic film. It was Nasir sa'ab telling the audience *Dil Deke Dekho*. Then he was telling the audience *Phir Wohi Dil Laya Hoon*. These were phrases. He is saying *Jab Pyar Kisise Hota Hai toh mazaa aata hai life mein* (life becomes enjoyable when one falls in love).' Aamir agreed that while *Teesri Manzil, Baharon Ke Sapne, Caravan* and *Yaadon Ki Baaraat* were very much about those specific films, 'What is *Hum Kisise Kum Naheen*? What did it have to do with the film?' Aamir answered his own rhetorical question. 'It's his arrogance. "*Hum kisise kum naheen* (We are second to none)." In a flamboyant way, in a nice way. *Zabardast* also had that quality. Then he makes *Zamaane Ko Dikhana Hai*? What's *Zamaane Ko Dikhana Hai* got to do with the story?' According to Aamir, the fact that *Zabardast* had been shelved following *Hum Kisise Kum Naheen*, Husain chose *Zamaane Ko Dikhana Hai* to make a statement: he wanted to show the world that he still counted. 'His personality reflected in the titles of his films.'

Despite the double whammy, Husain went ahead and made *Manzil Manzil* in 1984. He had wanted to continue with Rishi Kapoor as his lead hero, but the actor didn't show up. 'I don't know why, I had this big guilt within me that I was probably responsible for the film [*Zamaane Ko Dikhana Hai*] not doing well, I don't know why,' Rishi told me. 'I started avoiding meeting him. He wanted to meet me all the time because he wanted me for his next film, *Manzil Manzil*. Aamir Khan tells me that he was waiting for me because he had written the film for me. Mansoor tells me the same. But I thought I was responsible for *Zamaane Ko Dikhana Hai* not being a success.' Aamir confirmed Rishi's version of events and said, 'I think there was some lack of communication between Rishi uncle and Nasir sa'ab. And because Nasir sa'ab was also close to Dharam-ji, he said let us take Sunny [Sunny Deol].'

Sunny Deol thus became the central male protagonist of Husain's last two directorial ventures, *Manzil Manzil* and *Zabardast*. This *Zabardast*, which Husain made following *Manzil Manzil*, was based on an entirely different script from the one that had been shelved. Sanjeev Kumar, Sunny Deol and Rajiv Kapoor constituted the male star cast while Jaya Prada and Rati Agnihotri played the lead heroines. The film was produced by Mushir–Riaz.

Sunny Deol had become a star with his debut film *Betaab* (1983). At that stage, Sunny was far away from being boxed into the raging, action star that would become his persona by the turn of the 1990s with films like *Tridev* (1989), *Ghayal* (1990) and *Damini* (1993). In fact, his first few films were essentially love stories. Yet, Sunny couldn't measure up to Husain's earlier heroes, Shammi Kapoor, Rishi Kapoor or even Jeetendra. There was a certain stiffness about him that was far removed from Husain's effervescent, animated heroes. Husain further constrained Sunny by limiting him to playing the mouthorgan in *Manzil Manzil*, instead of the guitar, an instrument that allowed Joy Mukerji and Shashi Kapoor greater physical freedom. Sunny's problems were compounded in *Zabardast* where his character was solely limited to seeking revenge, a la Shankar from *Yaadon Ki Baaraat*. The few comic moments given to him hardly tickled the audiences' funny bone.

But it will be grossly unfair to apportion all the blame on Sunny. There was a general decline in the creative talents around Husain as is particularly evident in the set design and the music in these films. If R.D. Burman had been Husain's hero through the entire 1970s, his low patch in the mid-1980s certainly contributed to Husain's downfall. It is hard to term any of RD's compositions for *Manzil Manzil* or *Zabardast* anywhere close to memorable. And with his best technician hitting rough weather, the spirit of a Husain film seemed to have been sucked out. This reflected in his cinema – in the tasteless set design for '*Hey baba*' (*Manzil Manzil*), with the large demon-like face (so-not-a-Husain-prop) forming the backdrop for the stage on which the song takes place. Aamir observed, 'It happens to the best of directors and actors. Because, remember, the people working with him were the same. The music was not a patch on the earlier films, the lyrics were nothing to crow about, the choreography was going down. The entire team was ageing. Nasir sa'ab, Majrooh sa'ab, Pancham uncle, Suresh Bhatt, Munir Khan. All of them were responsible for what we were seeing and hearing. Creatively they were in decline. It's not just the song – the entire film was not good.'

In sharp contrast to any song in Husain's earlier films, '*Hey baba*' is marked by rather crude, inelegant dance steps.[10] Actually, glimpses of coarseness had already appeared in *Zamaane Ko Dikhana Hai* where Rajendra Nath's character offers Kanchan a lift with a definite, devious agenda. Pappu's (Master Ravi) '*su-su*' jokes and the half-clad men and women rushing out of Honeymoon Hotel in the midst of their coital acts were also pointers to an element of uncouthness previously unseen in Husain's cinema. *Manzil Manzil* and *Zabardast* had a lot of their humour centred on a female protagonist getting pregnant (Seema in *Manzil Manzil*; Mala in *Zabardast*) or other double entendre. Husain, who had previously never relied on such tropes, definitely distanced cine-goers with such attempts at humour. 'I found it very disconcerting. It was getting desperate. It was not needed,' admitted Mansoor.

This was also a reflection of the cinema of the mid-to-late 1980s. The 1970s and 1980s saw another wave of migration from villages and small towns into cities, creating new ghettoes and

---

[10]This song is yet another rare instance of Husain ceding the song space to someone other than a key protagonist in his films. The male hero, Sunny Deol, is seen attending the performance passively and in morose spirits, so very unlike a Husain hero.

STYLE, SPECTACLE AND A STRING OF FLOPS   333

slums. With the coming of home video (which resulted in the middle class preferring to watch films on the video instead of going to the theatre) and underworld money into Hindi cinema, there was a new urgency to pander to the lowest common denominator. Action, vendetta films proliferated, music and lyrics were severely compromised and most A-list film-makers went through the worst phase of their respective careers. Names like Manmohan Desai, Prakash Mehra and Yash Chopra all suffered in this period.[11] That Bachchan's and R.D. Burman's decline happened in this time also is no mere coincidence. Husain's fate was no different. Sidharth Bhatia commented, 'All I know is that whenever I look back on the '80s in terms of what was going on creatively, in movies, music, I can't remember anything.'

Further, Husain introduced the element of maudlin melodrama, a genre he had consciously stayed away from, in *Manzil Manzil*. Seema's (Dimple Kapadia) amnesia and her weeping her way through it is most unlike Husain's upbeat characters. The temple scenes from *Yaadon Ki Baaraat* to *Zamaane Ko Dikhana Hai* to *Manzil Manzil* reflect Husain's shifting stance in this context. While in *Yaadon Ki Baaraat*, Sunita (Zeenat Aman) visits the temple and makes her pleas to the almighty in a rather comic way, in the latter two films the female protagonists wail and rant in the temple. In *Manzil Manzil*, Husain actually ventures into Manmohan Desai territory as the temple, with the bhajan

---

[11]While Manmohan Desai had duds like *Gangaa Jamunaa Saraswathi* (1988) and *Toofan* (1989), Prakash Mehra delivered the biggest flop of Bachchan's career with *Jaadugar* (1989). Yash Chopra had the ignominy of three flops in *Silsila* (1981), *Faasle* (1985) and *Vijay* (1988) in this decade. Even Ramesh Sippy's much-awaited *Saagar* (1985), despite bringing together Rishi Kapoor and Dimple Kapadia and boasting a superlative R.D. Burman score, came a cropper. It was as if an entire generation of film-makers who ruled the 1970s could do nothing right.

playing in the background, becomes the place for miracle and
Seema recovers her memory. While Desai generally pulled off
such moments with aplomb, inducing in the audience a willing
suspension of disbelief, Husain's picturization is completely bereft
of zing.

There is also the matter of Husain abandoning his musical hero
in these last three films. The hero doesn't take recourse to shaayari
to turn on the charm. While Rajiv Kapoor plays a musician figure,
Tony, in *Zabardast*, much of the film is about Sunder/Shyam
(Sunny Deol) looking to have his revenge against Ratan Kumar
(Sanjeev Kumar). Unlike *Yaadon Ki Baaraat*, however, *Zabardast*
doesn't have Vijay's enchanting romantic track with Sunita or
Monto's enthralling musical numbers.

Upward social mobility, so typical of the hero in most Husain
films, also goes missing in *Zamaane Ko Dikhana Hai*, *Manzil
Manzil* and *Zabardast*. Kanchan's rant at Ravi in *Zamaane Ko
Dikhana Hai*, 'Bye, you rich, filthy lover boy,' could have distanced
Husain's audience from the very world that he had created in his
earlier films. The world of clubs and hotels, of estate managers
and of fashionable couture are all conspicuous by their absence,
particularly, in Husain's last two films. The insipid music, the
action-oriented nature of *Manzil Manzil* and *Zabardast*, the
melodrama and tacky art direction resulted in a concoction that
just didn't have Husain's frothiness or flamboyance. 'I honestly
feel it's tragic, my father actually tripped,' said Mansoor. 'He lost
his self-confidence with *Zamaane Ko Dikhana Hai*. With *Manzil
Manzil* and *Zabardast* he was trying too hard to regain his, (a),
self-confidence and, (b), reputation. They were not inspired films
at all.'

Sometime after *Zabardast*, Husain started work on his next film, which too he would direct. However, while writing this film, the film-maker had to have bypass surgery. This led to Mansoor and Nuzhat convincing Husain to stop directing because of how it could impact his health. 'We would tell him, "You should not make films,"' admitted Mansoor. 'We were concerned about the kind of stress he went through as a producer, as a director and as a writer. But we didn't tell him not to write.' Nuzhat added, 'I got more and more anxious about him directing another film. I just didn't want him to have another flop. There were three films [the three flops]. But I couldn't tell him that – I couldn't say, "I don't think you can make another film," but that's what I thought then and I think I am right. Call it whatever you want, I wanted to preserve his legacy, I didn't want him to go through this. So we made the bypass the excuse.'

Zabardast, then, turned out to be Husain's last directorial venture. Its failure at the box office following the cancellation of the original *Zabardast*, the disappointing fortunes of *Zamaane Ko Dikhana Hai* and *Manzil Manzil*, took its toll on Husain. He appeared to have lost the pulse of the audience he had entertained ever since making his debut with *Tumsa Nahin Dekha*. This ending to his directorial career didn't mirror the happy endings so intrinsic to his cinema. Husain seemed to be headed into the sunset, with his craft, his creativity having deserted him entirely. Just over sixty at the time of his bypass, his detractors thought he was finished. A *Star & Style* article published in the 16 September 1983 edition, even before the release of *Manzil Manzil* and *Zabardast*, had asked: 'Has the hit-maker lost his touch?'

Husain would prove them wrong. And how.

13

BURNING BRIGHT, FADING AWAY

Rashmi: *Pata nahin humaari shakal kaisi lag rahi hai.* (I don't know how my face looks.)

Raj [smiling gently]: *Lekin yeh sab hua kaisey?* (But how did this happen?)

Rashmi: *Hum Sitanagar ja rahey thay aur humaari bus kharaab ho gayee. Hum jungle mein kuchh tasveerey leney lagey aur phir na jaaney kahaan se ek ladka aur uskey dost wahaan aa gaye aur humaarey saath budtameezi karney lagey. Humney bhi usey ek aisi laat maari ki yaad rakhega.* (We were going to Sitanagar and our bus broke down. I was taking some pictures in the jungle, when a boy and his friends appeared from nowhere and started misbehaving with me. I also kicked him in such a way that he won't forget.)

Raj: *Aur kahin chot lagi hai?* (Any other injuries?)

Rashmi: *Nahin. Dettol waali koi chot nahin.* (No. None that can be treated with Dettol.)

– Rashmi (Juhi Chawla) and Raj (Aamir Khan)
in *Qayamat Se Qayamat Tak*

Ratan: *Yeh le, Sanju! Bank mein paisey jama kar de. Double roti main bana deta hoon.* (Sanju, go and deposit the money in the bank. I will make the bread.)

Sanjay Lal: *Ah! Bank tum chale jao! Kalpana ke liye double-roti main bana leta hoon, Tunna!* (No. You go to the bank. I will have the bread organized for Kalpana, Tunna.)

Ratan: *Dekh, zyaada hoshiyaari mat dikha, haan!* (Listen, don't act smart.)

Sanjay Lal: *Theek hai, theek hai ja! Lekin sunn, yeh mauka haath se mat jaaney dena. Jhappi maar ke pappi le lena.* [Sanju's friends laugh] *Chal be Ghanshu, Ghodey, yahaan bahut garmi ho gayee hai, yaar.* [Starts singing] *Aankhon hi aankhon mein ishaara ho gaya, baithey, baithey jeene ka sahaara ho gaya...* (It's ok, it's ok! But listen, don't let this chance go. Take her in your arms and kiss her. Ghanshu, Ghodey, come, let's go. Things are heating up here...)

– Ratan (Mamik) and Sanjay Lal Sharma (Aamir Khan)
in *Jo Jeeta Wohi Sikandar*

Among the more endearing moments from *Yaadon Ki Baaraat* is when the title track is rendered by the mother at the beginning of the film. While the mukhda of the song is being repeated, the youngest of the three children, dressed identically to his elder siblings, signals his intention to go to the toilet. He reappears, buttoning up his shorts, as the first antara is being sung ('*Badley na apna yeh...*'). The mother takes this boy, with his bow tie, his toothy smile and his neatly combed hair with a sharp left-parting, on her lap. The older two siblings gather around the mother and she extends her right arm to offer them similar love, but her youngest son, still seated comfortably on her lap, enjoys pride of place in her affections.

Aamir Khan, who played this youngest child, was only eight years old when *Yaadon Ki Baaraat* released in 1973. Husain had earlier cast Mansoor and Nuzhat as the young Mohan and Mona in *Phir Wohi Dil Laya Hoon*. The pair are also seen in the song '*Aaja piya tohe pyaar doon*' in *Baharon Ke Sapne* where they play the young Ram and Geeta. Continuing with this trend, Aamir was actually supposed to play the young Sunder in *Pyar Ka Mausam*. But that role eventually went to Aamir's younger sibling, Faisal Khan. Apparently, Aamir threw a fit on the day of the *Pyar Ka Mausam* shoot. 'On the day of the shooting I was crying my head off and they could not calm me down,' recalled Aamir. 'They were shooting at Mehboob [Studios]. After attempts were made to calm me down, Nasir sa'ab said, "*Arrey yaar abhi chhodo isko. Faisal ko le aao* (Forget him. Get Faisal)." So Faisal was brought in and he calmly gave all the shots,' said Aamir, chuckling. Consequently, Aamir's film debut happened only four years later in *Yaadon Ki Baaraat*. Aamir didn't remember how exactly his uncle roped him in for the film but said that it was while he was 'playing carrom one day at my uncle's [Husain] house'.

But this didn't mean that Husain was waiting to launch Aamir. On the contrary, Husain had discouraged his nephew from turning actor. Aamir remembered that while in his early teens, at a party at Aamir's house, when someone suggested that Husain should cast his nephew sometime in the future, Husain said, 'No, he can never be an actor. I am a director. I have a director's eyes. Aamir can never be an actor.' Aamir's explanation for Husain's reaction was, 'He was saying that to protect me. Plus I was a very shy kid, very shy. I hardly spoke. I was an introvert. It was very unlikely for anyone to be able to read that this guy is going to be a good actor.'

By the time Aamir had completed his twelfth standard, he was clear that he wanted a career in films. 'I didn't have a clear thought whether I wanted to be an actor or a director. I wanted to do both, but didn't know which would come first. I wanted to learn as much about acting and film-making. That is why I became an AD [assistant director].' Aamir told Husain that he wanted to work in his films. 'I told him, "I want to work as an assistant. If you take me, great. If you don't take me, I will go and meet some other directors and I will find some work somewhere.'" This is how Aamir came to be an assistant director on *Manzil Manzil* and *Zabardast*. As an AD, Aamir impressed Husain with his work ethic. He introduced Husain to the concept of action continuity, which basically helped the film-maker establish where exactly to pick up a scene in terms of its little nuances (what are the background artistes doing, etc.) after the previous shot. 'He was the best AD ever,' admitted Nuzhat. Aamir is also seen in passing in a couple of sequences in *Manzil Manzil*.

However, before he worked as an AD, Aamir had already acted in a short film called *Paranoia*, followed by a couple of student diploma films called *Subah Subah* and *Young Törless*. He also worked backstage in Gujarati theatre with Mahendra Joshi for a year and a half. While Aamir was working as an AD with Husain, he got a call to act in Ketan Mehta's *Holi* (1984), which was under production. 'I told Chachajaan, "*Chachajaan, mujhe woh film karni hai.* (Uncle, I want to do that film.) You need to give me forty days' holiday from work.'" Husain agreed and Aamir went to Pune, shot for *Holi* and returned. Up to this point, Aamir hadn't mentioned the 'acting' word to Husain, 'but he [Husain] knew that I had been acting – diploma films, theatre, the movie with Babla [Aditya Bhattacharya's pet name, who made *Paranoia*].'

Later, towards the end of *Zabardast*'s shooting, which was under production in Khandala, Javed Akhtar happened to visit Husain at Farias Hotel. During their chat in Husain's room, in which Aamir was also present in 'one corner, far away', Akhtar asked Husain, "'*Woh ladka kaun hai?* (Who is that boy?)" He said, "*Woh Tahir ka beta hai.* (He is Tahir's son)."' Akhtar then asked Husain what he did to which Husain replied, '*Yeh mera assistant hai* (He is my assistant).' It was at this point, as Aamir clearly recalled, Akhtar told Husain, '*Yeh aapka assistant kyun hai? Isko toh aapka star hona chaahiye* (Why is he your assistant? He should be your star).'

Akhtar's remark may have been the tipping point in Husain making up his mind on casting his nephew since the film-maker had been aware of Aamir's acting pursuits. 'It must have had some impact,' Aamir told me. 'Over time, when he saw that I was serious about it [acting], and I wanted to do it, when they [Husain and Mansoor] saw *Holi*, it gave them confidence. I'm assuming that the kind of person he was, he wouldn't have taken me unless he felt that I could deliver.' Nuzhat endorsed this sentiment. She said that while her father always had a 'huge sense of family responsibility', which led to Tahir Husain being launched as an independent producer in *Caravan*, Tariq being given a break in *Yaadon Ki Baaraat*, 'he must have seen more in Aamir because Aamir AD'ed with him. He saw that the man was willing to put in the labour.'

But Aamir didn't bring up Akhtar's comment with Husain. However, a few days later at Farias Hotel again, Husain met with an old friend. Husain introduced Aamir to him as, 'This is Aamir, the star of my next film.' The introduction surprised Aamir completely. '*Toing karkey main ruk gaya*. (I was dumbstruck.) Where did that come from?' recalled Aamir of that pleasant moment. But even after this Aamir didn't follow up the matter with Husain. He thought Husain was 'joking'. Meanwhile, *Zabardast* released and didn't do well. It was after this that Husain called Aamir one day and said, '"I'm writing something, which I want you to act in." That film was *Qayamat Se Qayamat Tak*.'

Husain had started writing *Qayamat Se Qayamat Tak* with Sachin Bhowmick. But because Bhowmick and Husain appeared to have run out of ideas, Husain replaced Bhowmick and involved Aamir and Nuzhat to write the script along with him. The broad idea that Husain had was that he was writing a film for Aamir, which was a pure love story, but with a doomed ending. 'We were clear that it was going to be *Romeo and Juliet*,' Nuzhat confirmed to me. Husain was clearly going against the norm since action, vendetta films, with an overall coarseness in language, music and lyrics dominated the Hindi cinema landscape in the late 1980s.

Meanwhile, Husain's illness forced him to turn to Mansoor to direct the film. Mansoor at this time was struggling with his own career. He had dropped out of engineering, having spent eighteen months at IIT Bombay, a couple of years at Cornell and another eighteen months at MIT, 'all of which adds up to five years without getting a degree,' Mansoor told me self-deprecatingly. Having returned to India from the US in 1980, Mansoor assisted his dad on *Zamaane Ko Dikhana Hai* with the lighting, and then 'pretended' to assist him in *Manzil Manzil*. 'I was a useless assistant. I should have been thrown out actually. I was reading Ayn Rand on the sets.'

The one good thing that Mansoor did in this period was that he made a short film called *Umberto*. The film's central character is a 'bum', not unlike Sanjay Lal Sharma in *Jo Jeeta Wohi Sikandar*. When Husain saw *Umberto*, he liked it. 'I liked his picturization of songs,' Husain told Nasreen Munni Kabir. 'He felt that I had some control over the storytelling medium,' Mansoor added. That's when Husain asked Mansoor to direct *Qayamat Se Qayamat Tak*. But Mansoor was uncertain. He was focused on making *Jo Jeeta Wohi Sikandar*, but was stuck with its writing. Additionally, for Mansoor, Husain's film was 'like looking through the same lens – *pehley yeh ho jaata hai, phir woh ho jaata hai …* (full of coincidences)'. Even when Husain told Mansoor that his film was a good love story, and that the time was right for such a story, Mansoor dismissed the idea saying, 'All stories are love stories. What's new about this?' Husain, though, convinced Mansoor to listen to the screenplay. 'When he narrated *QSQT* to us, I quite

liked the film's premise. And that remained just the way he had
written it, which was the first eleven scenes, up to the titles. I
really liked the set-up. I found it interesting, detailed. And then
I said I was willing to do it. We started working together on the
screenplay.'

Mansoor's entry considerably changed the approach to
Qayamat Se Qayamat Tak. Husain was now dealing with Nuzhat,
Aamir and Mansoor, whose sensibilities were very much attuned
to the voice of a younger generation. 'When Mansoor came in,
the slant of every scene changed. It became much more fresh,'
said Aamir. 'Nasir sa'ab had his own flavour as a director. He used
to write the scenes in a particular way and he wanted us, Nuzhat
and me, to write the scenes in a particular way. But once Mansoor
came in, Nasir sa'ab used to be very unhappy with the three of us.'
Husain frequently sparred with the three of them while writing
QSQT's screenplay. 'He was like a tiger with us when he was
arguing about the scenes,' recalled Aamir. But Mansoor admitted
that Husain was collaborative at the same time. 'He was willing
to see reason. We would have disagreements, arguments, fights
also, but somewhere we knew that we had to meet. And Aamir
and Nuzhat were the mediators.'

One of the major sources of these creative conflicts between
Husain and the next generation pertained to *Qayamat Se Qayamat
Tak*'s climax. Midway through the scripting, Husain wanted to
change the climax to a happy ending. He thought that would be
more palatable to the audiences. Husain was also probably haunted
by *Baharon Ke Sapne*'s tragic ending and that he had to change
that in the wake of the film's underwhelming opening. His fears
about the tragic ending found support amongst his friends, who
belonged to his peer group. 'He panicked,' said Nuzhat. Mansoor
explained that Husain used to tell him, 'You cannot make it a sad
ending because in India people have too much tragedy in their
lives anyway.' Although Husain rarely came on the sets of *Qayamat*

Se Qayamat Tak, he would call up and say, '*Mansoor woh happy ending zaroor shoot karna* (Mansoor, shoot the happy ending).' But Mansoor, Aamir and Nuzhat stood their ground.

When Husain saw the final cut of the film, with Raj and Rashmi dying, he was convinced he had a 'hit' in his hands. He told Nasreen, 'Mansoor did the right thing by changing the ending. I had not seen the film but when I went for the first trial I said, "It is a hit picture." The moment I saw it, I said that. Even my wife asked and I said it is "super hit".' When Nasreen asked him how he knew that, Husain replied, 'It's a gut feeling. Every evening we used to have a drink and whosoever came, I used to tell them it is a "hit". Mansoor used to think I was talking about the drink.'

Qayamat Se Qayamat Tak is vintage Husain. While ostensibly a story about enmity between two thakur families, the focus on Raj and Rashmi's romance, the movement from Dhanakpur gaon to Delhi to Mount Abu to Sitanagar to Delhi, the young people wanting to go on a holiday, for shikaar, and Raj impersonating Roop Singh are all quintessential Husain tropes. 'His whole conception of the characters, and those hilarious scenes, "*fataafat*" *waala scene ya shaadi mein ghus jaata hai* (the "fataafat" scene or when he gate-crashes the wedding),[1] that is classical my dad's stuff,' confessed Mansoor. Aamir said, 'Dialogues and story are all him. Screenplay, we all wrote together.'

It is not easy to write about *Qayamat Se Qayamat Tak*'s impact. It was certainly one of the biggest hits of the year. At the 1989 Filmfare Awards, it swept nearly every honour that mattered,

---

[1] The 'fataafat' scene featured Ajit Vachhani, playing the lawyer character who uses fataafat as his catchphrase. The 'shaadi' episode is when Raj lands up at Rashmi's birthday in Dhanakpur gaon and is mistaken for Roop Singh.

ranging from Best Film to Best Director, Best Male and Female Debut awards, Best Music and Best Screenplay. But its bigger success lay in the fact that the film had a certain sophistication, a certain tehzeeb about it that had gone missing in Hindi cinema. Mansoor's tragic climax gave Hindi cinema perhaps its finest adaptation of *Romeo and Juliet*, but without a particularly overwrought ending. There was a distinct freshness about the film, which came across principally in the lead pair's casting, the film's soundtrack and in its dialogues.

The exchanges between Raj and Rashmi as they get to know each other and their romance builds up are marked by some of the most charming dialogues. Take, for instance, the scene where Rashmi is photographing Raj against the sunset and Raj startles her from behind. The camera drops from Rashmi's hand, which leads Raj to tender an apology:

Raj: *Oh I'm sorry! Toota toh nahin?* (Oh I'm sorry. I hope it didn't break?)

Rashmi: *Nahin, it's all right. Waise sooraj ke saath humney aapki bhi tasveerey le li. Aapney bura toh nahin maana?* (No, it's all right. By the way, I took some pictures of you against the sun. I hope you didn't mind?)

Raj: *Nahin, agar tasveerey achhee aayengi, toh bura bilkul nahin maanengey.* (No, if the photographs come out well, I won't mind at all.)

Rashmi: *Photography ke baarey mein hum zyaada toh nahin jaantey, bas kismet aazmaatey rehtey hain.* (I don't know too much about photography, I just keep trying my luck.)

Raj: *Ji haan! Har nayee cheez ke liye kismet ko aazmaana bahut zaroori hota hai.* (That's correct. It's important to test one's luck with anything new.)

Rashmi: *Aah! Ji.* (Yes. Correct.)

Raj: *Waise aapney ek cheez bahut sahi ki.* (By the way, you did one very good thing.)

Rashmi: *Woh kya?* (What is that?)

Raj: *Aap sahi waqt pe sahi jagah pahunch gayee.* (You reached the right place at the right time.)

Rashmi: *Achha?* (Is that so?)

Raj: *Mera matlab hai, jagah toh aapney achhee chuni hi hai, lekin doobtey huey sooraj ki kirnon mein har khoobsurat cheez aur bhi khoobsurat lagne lagti hai.* (What I mean is, you had already selected the right place, but in the evening sun's light, the attractiveness of every beautiful thing gets enhanced.)

The inherent tenderness of these lines, the use of 'hum' by Rashmi's character to address herself, lends a distinct nazaaqat to Raj and Rashmi's romance. As Jerry pointed out, '*QSQT* is an anachronism. No girl of the 1980s would call herself "hum" and refer to a boy of her age as "aap". It's as if *Chaudhvin Ka Chand* [1960] had moved into the 1980s.' Be that as it may, to a milieu accustomed to bombastic dialogues and starved for gentility, *QSQT* must have been like a breath of fresh air. But Husain had shown his talent for writing enchanting, romantic sequences from much before *QSQT*. Take, for instance, the scene in *Teesri Manzil*, when Sunita leads Anil away from the car in which they are making their way to Madanpur. Here, Husain gave us a moment of pure romance between the two, but with the dialogues also leading so wonderfully into the song, '*Deewaana mujhsa nahin*':

Anil: *Mud mud kar dekh rahi hain. Koi khaas baat hai peechhey?* (You keep looking back. Is there someone special behind you?)

Sunita: *Peechhey aap hain. Khaas baat nahin?* (You follow behind me. Isn't that special?)

Anil: *Yoonhi dekhti rahi aap, toh yoonhi chaltey rahengey hum, peechhey peechhey.* (If you keep looking at me like this, I will keep walking this way, behind you.)

Sunita: *Yoonhi chaltey rahey hum, toh raasta kaun dekhega?* (But if we keep walking like this, who will keep sight of the path?)

Anil: *Raasta dekhne waala jo hai, peechhey peechhey.* (The person who keeps track of the path is walking behind.)

Sunita: *Aur agar thokar lag gayee, toh girega kaun?* (And if we stumble, who will fall?)

Anil: *Girney ki baat kaisi? Thaamney waala bhi toh hai, peechhey peechhey.* (How can one fall? The person who walks behind is there to lend a hand.)

Sunita: *Achha ab aaee-yay, saath saath chalein.* (Ok, come now, let's walk together.)

Anil: *Ji nahin humaari yahi jagah hai, peechhey peechhey.* (No, thank you, this is my place, behind you.)

Sunita: *Peechhey peechhey, peechhey peechhey. Deewaane toh nahin ho gaye aap?* (What's with this *peechhey peechhey*? Have you lost it?)

Anil [starts singing]: *Deewaana mujhsa nahin…* (There isn't a romantic like me)

It is this exchange between Anil and Sunita, with its genteel syntax and the use of 'aap' (you) and 'hum' (me), that Husain expanded upon and used for Raj and Rashmi in *Qayamat Se Qayamat Tak*. Husain's emphasis on romance and his ability to write these simple but exquisite romantic lines marked him out as one of the fine romanticists in Hindi cinema alongside names like Yash Chopra, Sahir Ludhianvi and Shakeel Badayuni. Husain said as much, 'I am an incorrigible romantic and though I no longer make films, I will always remain a romantic at heart.'[2]

[2]Ambarish Mishra, 'I will always be a romantic at heart', *The Times of India*, 7 May 2000.

But it isn't just in the romantic dialogues that Husain's craft shone. In a film that deals with the animosity between two thakur families, Husain never let the language degenerate into the kind of '*kuttey, kaminey, main tera khoon pee jaaoonga*' variety that had become so typical of Hindi films in this period. Despite the ominous, violent undertone of the film, the dialogues between Randhir Singh (Goga Kapoor), Dhanraj (Dalip Tahil) and Jaswant Singh (Alok Nath) remain menacing without deteriorating into anything crude. As an example, when Dhanraj learns of the advertisement put out by Randhir Singh, which offers a reward of one lakh rupees for any information on Raj's whereabouts, Dhanraj calls up Randhir Singh. He threatens him in the most ominous way: '*Tumney mere bete ki tasveer akhbar mein toh de di hai magar ek baat yaad rakhna, agar mere bete Raj par aanch aayee, toh main aaj bhi wohi Dhanraj hoon, jo chaudha saal pehley hua karta thaa* (You have advertised my son's photograph in the newspapers, but remember one thing, should anything happen to my son Raj, I am still the same Dhanraj I was fourteen years ago).'

Mansoor pointed to the confrontation between Rashmi and Randhir Singh, when the latter puts an end to his daughter's going to college, as another example of Husain's deft dialogue-writing. 'There is tension between father and daughter, but no rudeness. It reaches a slightly tense moment but it doesn't get ugly.'

This all-round sophistication in dialogues drew Javed Akhtar's compliments in no uncertain terms. 'When I saw *QSQT*, I cried. I honestly cried. Not because there was some great heart-wrenching, emotional scene. What made me cry was the level of decency of the film. I was so deeply touched because those were the times when crudity was at its peak. And here I was watching a film where there are two big families, who would like to see each other dead, but at the same time when there is any confrontation, there is any interaction, there is any dispute, the language is civilized.

The anger is the anger of decent people. It touched me so deeply because that was something which was lacking so very badly in those times. I called him and I told him your film has made me cry because after a long time I am hearing decent words.'

In his book on *Dilwale Dulhania Le Jayenge*, Aditya Chopra said about *QSQT*, 'Mansoor Khan has a slightly westernised approach. It was Nasir Husain sa'ab's dialogue that gave *Qayamat* the Hindi film touch.'[3] When I met Aditya, he explained this in greater detail. 'If you see *QSQT*, it's actually a Nasir Husain film. But Mansoor brought his own cinematic language to a story which is according to me completely Nasir Husain – thakurs, Romeo and Juliet, journey – *sab kuchh same hai* (It's all the same). The only thing I don't think Nasir Husain would have wanted is to kill them. I'm assuming that's Mansoor. It's beautiful: a Nasir Husain fan could see Nasir sa'ab but could also see the baton being passed over to somebody, to a voice that obviously has issues with a lot of what Nasir Husain brings. And it is that sangam which made *QSQT* so memorable. But yes if Nasir Husain hadn't written the dialogues, or if Nasir sa'ab's words were not in *QSQT*, I think Mansoor would have made a slightly elitist film. So it's the balance between Nasir sa'ab's old-world sense of drama and words, with Mansoor's new-age view of the same things.'

One of the major contributions of *QSQT* is that it gave Hindi cinema a new pin-up star, Aamir Khan, who continues to rule the box office almost thirty years later. I asked Aamir to reflect on the success of the film and the impact it had on his career. 'It was my first step,' he said. 'It's why I'm here. And the fact that Nasir sa'ab had that faith and confidence in not only me, but also Mansoor, because both of us were taking our first steps. And mind you he was not doing well in life at that time. As a production house and

---

[3] *Aditya Chopra Relives Dilwale Dulhania Le Jayenge: As told to Nasreen Munni Kabir*, Yash Raj Films Pvt. Ltd, 2014, p. 117.

as a creative person, he was at his lowest. So at that time, to have faith and trust in two newcomers, to deliver and to back them financially was not easy. But he took that chance for which I will always be very grateful.'

If *Qayamat Se Qayamat Tak* is all about nazaaqat and tehzeeb, *Jo Jeeta Wohi Sikandar* has sharaarat ingrained in its idiom. This film was scripted and directed by Mansoor, but the dialogues were written by Husain. There is a distinct impishness visible in Sanjay Lal Sharma's (Aamir Khan) character that is a throwback to Husain's earlier heroes. At the same time, Husain's dialogues for Sanjay and his friends, Ghanshu and Maqsood Ghoda, reflect a small-town sensibility very distinct from Raj and Rashmi's genteel grammar. Sample this attempt by Ghanshu (Deven Bhojani) in making an impression when the girls from Queen's College, from a more aristocratic background, visit Mall road:

> Ghanshu: *Hi, Reena! Kaisi ho tum?* (Hi, Reena! How are you?)
>
> Queens' College student: *Kaun hai tum?* (Who are you?)
>
> Ghanshu: *Arrey main Ghanshu! Bhool gayee? Apun Delhi mein miley thay, Bengali Market mein. Tum bhelpuri khaa rahi thee, main panipuri khaa raha thaa. Yaad hai, Reena?* (I am Ghanshu. You forgot? We met in Delhi, at Bengali Market. You were eating bhelpuri and I, panipuri. Don't you remember, Reena?)
>
> Student: *Mera naam Reena nahin hai, Tina[4] hai.* (My name isn't Reena. It's Tina.)
>
> Ghanshu: *Oh Tina, Tina! Achha Tina, kya logi tum? Chocolate, vanilla, strawberry, pista, badaam, mango ya chiku? Chiku khaaogi tum? Chiku solid hai...* (Oh Tina, Tina. Ok Tina, what will you

---

[4]This girl is actually Mansoor's wife, Tina Khan.

have? Chocolate, vanilla, strawberry, pista, badaam, mango or
chiku? Will you have chiku? Chiku is really good…)

[At this point, a nun from Queen's College approaches Ghanshu
and Maqsood Ghoda[5] from behind and canes them, leading the
duo to beat a hasty retreat]

Ghanshu [runs with Maqsood to where Sanjay and Anjali are
sitting]: *Buddhi ka haath bahut zordaar hai yaar. Patloon ke neechey
khaal nikaal di meri poori!* (The old lady has an iron hand. She
almost skinned me alive.)

There are other examples of Husain's comfort with two very
distinct idioms in these two films. In *Qayamat Se Qayamat Tak*,
when Jaswant Singh confronts Ratan Singh (Feroze) about his
relationship with his sister Madhumati and that he is going to be
the father of her child, he asks Ratan: '*Toh kya yeh sach nahin ki
Madhumati haamila hai?*' Jaswant Singh uses the word 'haamila',
an Arabic word, meaning 'pregnant'. The use of 'haamila' instead
of more clichéd terms like '*garbhvati*' or '*tumhaarey bachchey ki
maa banney waali hai*' in no way dilutes the seriousness of the
moment in the film's screenplay. Contrastingly, in *Jo Jeeta Wohi
Sikandar*, when Sanjay Lal tells Devika (Pooja Bedi) of Shekhar's
(Deepak Tijori) past misdemeanours with women, such as Kamla
and Bimla, he says:

Sanjay Lal: *Bada dhokha hua bechaariyon ke saath.* (The poor
souls were taken for a ride.)

Devika: *Kya hua?* (What happened?)

Sanjay Lal: *Kaise bataaoon?* (How do I say it?)

Devika: *Bataao na.* (Tell me.)

---

[5]Maqsood Ghoda's character was played by Aditya Lakhia. As Mansoor
told me, the character was named after a character in a Shafiq-ur-
Rahman story, surely Nasir Husain's hand at work.

Sanjay Lal: *Dono* [points to his own tummy as if he was pregnant] *aisi ho gayee.* (They both became like this.)

Devika: Huhhh … I don't believe it. You mean pregnant?

Sanjay Lal: *Uhhh ab, jab yoon hoga* [again gesticulates at his own tummy], *toh wohi hoga na.* (When this happens, it can only mean that.)

This exchange between Devika and Sanjay not only reflects a very different sensibility from the one used by *QSQT*'s characters, but does so with humour. That Devika also switches to English, underscores her Queen's College pedigree, while Ghanshu's reference to 'Bengali Market' for panipuri and bhelpuri indicates an altogether different world the Model College boys belong to. This also reinforces the class divide between the Queen's College girls and the '*pyjama chhaap*' Model College boys, such an important element of *Jo Jeeta Wohi Sikandar*'s story.

While Mansoor had a 'bigger role' to play in the dialogues for *Jo Jeeta…*, in that he would often write the scenes in English, it was Husain who adapted the scenes and gave them his own flavour. This is true of the film's title as well. Mansoor gave Husain 'Winner takes all' as the film's title, which Husain correctly interpreted as *Jo Jeeta Wohi Sikandar*. 'It was his title in that sense,' said Mansoor. 'But there were lots of scenes like, "*Uss Thaapar ka paapad bana ke aaoonga*" where it was his flair.'

While on the subject of titles, Mansoor also told me that *QSQT* was initially titled or had the working title, '*Nafrat Ke Waaris*'. This was an offshoot from one of the dialogues in the film when Raj has a confrontation with Randhir Singh. In the heat of the moment, Raj tells Randhir Singh, '*Main aur Rashmi aap dono ke nafrat ke waaris banney ko taiyaar nahin* (Rashmi and I don't wish to inherit the hatred between you and my father).' Consequently, Aamir, Nuzhat and Mansoor would suggest titles like, '*Daraar*' and '*Nafrat Ke Waaris*'.

'Dad had a great flair for titles. One day he came home, fixed his whiskey and then he got it, "bingo". So he called us and said, "Achha, listen with an open mind. Just listen to it, don't react. I've thought of a title." We were all very excited. I remember Aamir, Nuzhat and I were there. He said, "*Qayamat Se Qayamat Tak*",[6] and all three of us went, "We don't know why, but we like it." See, we were looking for a rationale for *Nafrat Ke Waaris* and literally trying to tell the story [with the film's title].' Mansoor admitted that this was yet another good example of Husain's literary bent. Husain even vetted the title with Majrooh Sultanpuri. 'I remember he spoke to Majrooh sa'ab on the phone. And Majrooh sa'ab said it's very good.'

While Husain's literary and old-world sensibilities shone with *QSQT*, his ability to enunciate the grammar of a generation entirely different from his own (he was over sixty-five when he wrote the dialogues of *JJWS*) is what added to the overall appeal of *JJWS*. Javed Akhtar said as much. '*Jo Jeeta Wohi Sikandar* was about the youth of that time ... If you listen to the film's dialogues, you will feel that it is written by someone who is twenty or twenty-two years old. That is because that youngster always remained within Nasir Husain, in his personality and in his writing.'[7] Mansoor agreed. 'Addressing the youth, or having that flair, was always the top thing in his mind. He had the knack of writing young dialogues, which would appeal to a new generation.'

Karan Johar offered a more perceptive explanation for Husain's skill in writing such dialogues. 'I think that dialogue is a reflection

---

[6]The literal meaning of 'qayamat' is the day of reckoning or great catastrophe. Since the film begins with Ratan Singh's murder and ends with the death of Raj and Rashmi, *Qayamat Se Qayamat Tak* translates to 'from one great catastrophe to another', an excellent summary of the film's plot in its title.

[7]Zee Classic's *Classic Legends: Season II*, featuring Nasir Husain.

of your awareness of the times. He was constantly evolving. The fact that he had a lot of young people around him helped. I feel that about Yash Chopra also because he had two young boys, he kept himself alive and young. Nasir sa'ab had Aamir and Mansoor and the girls, Nuzhat and Nikhat [Aamir's sister]. Some were esoteric, some were evolved, some were internationally informed. Aamir was a little more filmy. Mansoor was a little more evolved in a different way. I think he surrounded himself with such a blend of energies even in their growing-up years; that definitely helped him. I also think he was an observer. The fact that his costumes were such, his music is contemporary, that means his awareness factor was huge. I've always felt that Nasir Husain was a very aware man. He was aware of his surroundings. He was aware of what was happening in the world, not just his country and city.'

What the dialogues of *JJWS* also established is that Husain, who first started writing for films in 1949, remained relevant for close to forty-five years. He had kept himself updated to the changed idiom of every passing decade. His dialogues for Amar/ Raj in *Munimji* or Ramesh in *Paying Guest* in the mid-1950s were as true to the syntax of those times as Sanjay Lal Sharma's were to the early 1990s. Aamir spoke at length to explain the significance of Husain's talent in dialogue-writing: 'I think he wrote characters very well, which also come out through dialogues ... Dialogues are the main source from which you come to know what a person is like. What are the words that a person uses? This tells you a lot about the character. So dialogues are very, very important in building a character. Dialogues also carry your scenes. So while I may have a story in the broad sense, the screenplay is one step deeper, the dialogues at the deepest level, which actually then incorporates all the things that the story and the screenplay originally intended. Now if the dialogues don't ring true, no matter what I'm imagining the scene is, it won't turn out that way unless the dialogues actually carry that feeling. So that's the final step in writing – the dialogues.

'And what is amazing about Nasir sa'ab is that he remained relevant creatively for a very long time. From 1949 to *Akele Hum Akele Tum* [Husain wrote the dialogues], which is 1995, is forty-six years. There are a handful of names that cross five decades and remain relevant creatively over such a long period. Now Nasir sa'ab may not have remained relevant as a director, but he began as a writer. So as a writer he remained relevant over five decades. It is a very remarkable thing, to be able to write for an audience in the 1940s and then to be able to write for an audience in each successive decade all the way through to the '90s. To remain relevant for different audiences of different decades really speaks about your longevity as a creative person.'

This adaptability across decades made Husain the Majrooh Sultanpuri of dialogue-writers. Majrooh, who debuted as a lyricist with *Shahjehan* (1946), kept his lyrics relevant and updated to reflect the voice of every successive generation right up to the new millennium, writing for films such as *Akele Hum Akele Tum*, *Khamoshi* (1996) and *Pukar* (2000).

Jo Jeeta Wohi Sikandar, however, is a film that almost didn't get made. Mansoor, who directed the film, had severe problems with the original cast of the film. The actress Nagma had been taken on to play Devika's role, but she bowed out just a few days before shooting commenced for the film in Ooty. Another lady, Karishma Pahuja, was then taken to play Devika's role, with south Indian actress Girija Shettar playing Anjali's character and the model Milind Soman playing Shekhar Malhotra. But for various reasons, this cast didn't work. Mansoor had to sacrifice an entire schedule of the film before he replaced this cast with the cast that is now seen in the film.

'About thirty to forty days of work was reshot,' confessed

Mansoor. While Mansoor complimented Aamir for keeping faith in the script and boosting Mansoor's morale for reshooting, he also recognized Husain's role in backing the film despite the financial setback that a reshoot involved. 'He never let me feel that I had failed in any way despite the fact that he was totally confused about what we were shooting. He knew that he had written good scenes, but at the same time it was not his genre. So for him it was still an experiment, but he fully supported the experiment.' Aamir, too, acknowledged Husain's belief in *JJWS*. He disagreed that it was an emotional decision for Husain to back Mansoor. 'No, he loved the script. Otherwise, he wouldn't have backed it. He thought it was a great script and he wanted to produce it.' For all the obstacles that came the film's way, *Jo Jeeta Wohi Sikandar* picked up Best Film at the 1993 Filmfare Awards.

Jo Jeeta Wohi Sikandar was the last film under the Nasir Husain banner. After this, Husain wrote the dialogues of *Akele Hum Akele Tum* (1995), an adaptation of Sidney Pollack's *Kramer vs. Kramer* (1979). The film was directed by Mansoor, but was produced by Ratan Jain (Venus). *Akele Hum Akele Tum* turned out to be the last film Husain worked on. I asked Mansoor whether Husain had any reservations about him working as a director on *Akele Hum Akele Tum* outside the home banner, a film with a far more serious thread than Husain's cinema. 'No, he didn't,' Mansoor said. 'He felt *Akele Hum Akele Tum* was an emotional subject so it doesn't necessarily have to be his style, but he felt that the story had enough appeal and it was worth making.'

In the years following *Akele Hum Akele Tum*, Husain went into a shell. 'He wouldn't talk or participate in public gatherings,' said Mansoor. 'He would want to quietly leave the party.' Nuzhat, likewise, observed, 'He had become so self-deprecating, which was in contrast to how he used to be earlier, when he used to be all cocky and corny.' Nuzhat found Husain's behaviour hard to understand. 'He was never a depressed person. All his life he was always extremely energetic, lively, with a lot of passion and someone who enjoyed life to the fullest. He was never the kind of guy who would drink at home and be depressed.'

Mansoor rationalized this as a reaction of someone who had always been active as a film-maker having to let go. 'Maybe because he wasn't making films. It was a kind of depression … I think it is the result of somebody who has been very active having nothing to do. This happens to a lot of achievers who retire.' Nuzhat opined on a more regretful note, 'I feel guilty about stopping him from directing although I know that it was the right thing to do for the film [QSQT]. That finally took away from him who he was. And although we entirely valued his writing capabilities and he was the one who wrote those lovely dialogues in QSQT and in Jo Jeeta, Akele Hum Akele Tum also, but by then you can already see it's kind of fading. He, I think, became depressed because when a man is forcefully retired like that, you know…'

According to Aamir, Husain's state was an outcome of more than one factor. 'I have a feeling, it's probably a combination of a few things. That his last three films as a director didn't work caused him to go into depression. The impact of that takes time to set in. He was still a fighting force in QSQT and in Jo Jeeta, but the fact is that he was also getting older. Physically, a person is getting slower. Plus he was not directing. As director you are in command. Now he had to listen to Mansoor and to me – not that I was the director but I was hiding behind Mansoor's shoulder and fighting with him.'

Aamir continued. 'He felt that he was getting less relevant. While I believe that he remained relevant as a writer and as a dialogue-writer, but if you look at it from his point of view, he saw himself as a film-maker. So he felt that he was no longer relevant as a film-maker. "*Haan main Mansoor ke liye dialogue likh deta hoon* (Ok, I'll write dialogues for Mansoor)", but that was not that important to him. So internally he felt that, "*Jo filmein main banaoonga woh aaj ki audience shaayad samjhegi nahin. Mera rishta unke saath shaayad toot gaya hai* (Today's audience may not understand the films I make. I have, perhaps, lost my connect with them)." I think that is what got him down.'

Nuzhat concurred with Aamir's remarks. 'It was the loss of his identity, I feel. The three flops would have hurt him tremendously because he had such a soaring record before that. For a film to flop, it's like a cold, sinking stone in the pit of your stomach, you cannot imagine it. He continued to be very happy with family but he didn't want the outside world anymore. He cut himself off. He didn't want to be seen anymore. He felt ashamed of his fall. He must have felt it keenly. He never spoke about it.'

The final blow for Husain was the sudden death of his wife, Ayesha Khan, in June 2000. 'The thing which hit him the most is when my mum passed away,' recalled Mansoor. 'Then he just shut down.' Less than two years later, on 13 March 2002, a day before Aamir celebrated his thirty-seventh birthday, Husain passed on. He died of a stroke.

Mansoor remembered that the last time he saw his father happy was following *QSQT*'s release. 'His real happy, high moment was when *QSQT* was a success because he had bounced back. And then with *Jo Jeeta* also he was happy, but *Jo Jeeta* was not a financial success.' Some years later, when Husain was very much in the midst of his reclusive state, when 'he didn't want to revisit the past,' Mansoor found him watching television. 'I remember him watching one of his films and he was crying,' recollected Mansoor. 'He was saying, "I can't believe that I have done all this…"'

14

A 'FROTHY', 'FORMULAIC' FILM-MAKER'S LEGACY

'The unmistakable razzle-dazzle in Husain's films is definitive of what the great Indian celluloid dream is all about – vibrant spectacle of matinee idols, unflinching showmanship, charismatic melodies, frothy romance, fanciful but persuasive narrative and incredibly sleek technique.'

– Film critic Sukanya Verma[1]

'It just seems that the word "formulaic", meant always as a pejorative, just tends to very lazily get used only in the mainstream context. It always seems to be really mainstream directors, mainstream films that get accused of being formulaic. Nobody would ever use the word "formulaic" for Ingmar Bergman, even though he spent his entire career making films about man's crisis of faith, with one film after the other being a retread of the issues that haunted him … It's the same film being made over and over and over again, over a thirty-to-forty-year career. Nobody would ever call Bergman formulaic. He is the guru of highbrow cinema.'

– Film critic and author Jai Arjun Singh

[1]Sukanya Verma, '*Teesri Manzil*: Style, Substance, Suspense and Shammi!' (http://www.rediff.com/movies/slide-show/slide-show-1-teesri-manzil-style-substance-suspense-and-shammi/20130411.htm#9), *Rediff.com*, 11 April 2013.

Although *Jo Jeeta Wohi Sikandar* was fleshed out of Mansoor's short film, *Umberto*, it has all of Husain's classic elements. The impish Sanjay Lal Sharma, the hero masquerading as a rich man's son, the apparent class conflict between Sanjay and Devika, between the Model College boys and the Rajput College students, the intercollege music competition and the overall emphasis on youth are very much part of Nasir Husain territory. Even the melee that breaks out at Ramlal's Café as a result of Sanju's shenanigans, can be construed as a reference to the pie fights in *Jab Pyar Kisise Hota Hai* and *Pyar Ka Mausam*. Mansoor's adaptation of *Kramer vs. Kramer* to the story of a musician couple in *Akele Hum Akele Tum* is also a subtle Husain influence. When I asked Mansoor, if these moments, these various ideas for both films were given by Husain, he denied it, but also admitted, 'There is a hangover from all our films, my dad's films.'

Javed Akhtar was candid in admitting Husain's influence. 'I have no hesitation in saying that Nasir sa'ab was one of the people who influenced me. I used to watch his films when I was in school and college ... You go and see *Betaab* [1983] – the first romantic film I ever wrote, you will see Nasir Husain influences so very clearly. For example, the father comes, he tells him [Sunny Deol's character] I will give you money, you forget my daughter. This is right from Nasir Husain's films.' Nasreen Munni Kabir said that she sees more Nasir Husain in commercial mainstream Hindi cinema today than Mehboob Khan, Guru Dutt or Raj Kapoor. 'Nasir sa'ab's legacy is that the heroes have become very important ... You have romance, good music, entertainment, have a good time and go home.'

Rauf Ahmed echoed Nasreen's views. 'The Nasir Husain concept had not changed until the '80s and even till the mid-'90s. All these youngsters grew up on the Nasir Husain formula. Aamir, Shah Rukh and Salman. But the enduring thing was the song and dance. Even today, films are promoted on song and dance.' Nasreen concluded, 'Today's heroes are the grandsons of Shammi Kapoor and Nasir Husain.'

Madhulika Liddle sees Husain's influence right through the films of the 1960s and beyond. 'Husain had a very major influence on films from the late 1950s well into the '70s. Not only did he make these hugely entertaining films that endured (and which are still revered – look at *Yaadon Ki Baaraat*, for instance), he also proved an inspiration for several other film-makers … I would go so far as to say that a lot of the most popular films of the '60s owe something or the other to Nasir Husain, if not directly, in an indirect way. That *roothna-manaana*, the prolonged stalking-disguised-as-courtship, the crime angle, the comic side plot, the club song, the lost-and-found tropes of films like *Mere Sanam, The Train, Love in Tokyo, An Evening in Paris, China Town, Sharmeelee* [1971], *Humsaya* [1968], and so many others—that's all very Husain. He did it better than nearly all his contemporaries, but just the fact that they followed in his footsteps goes to show. Even though his style may not be in vogue in current cinema, it cannot be denied that he was one of the major film-makers of Hindi cinema: he introduced a certain style, a flamboyance and modernity, a slick yet not completely alien escapism that resonated with audiences – and continues to do so.'

Kaushik Bhaumik, who credits Husain with providing the framework for the 1970s 'masala' film, saw Husain's impact extending to one of Hindi cinema's most successful films from the mid-1990s. 'That is something that really stunned me … I remember watching *Dilwale Dulhania Le Jayenge* the first time. After the first half had ended, I turned around and said, "How did this strange '60s genre come back?" By that time Mansoor Khan had already made his version of the redux of these films. But actually it's *DDLJ*, which completely pays homage to that.'

Aditya Chopra validated Bhaumik's remarks, admitting that *DDLJ* was a combination of the influence of three film-makers. 'Raj Kapoor for his intensity of romance. Manoj Kumar for the patriotism that comes through the song "*Ghar aaja pardesi*" and Nasir Husain for the sheer fun and exuberance of life. The road trip through Europe is Nasir Husain for me. In his films the boy and girl are nearly always finding themselves on a journey together, and on their travels they fall in love.'[2] In his conversation with me, Aditya admitted to having watched Husain's films, *Hum Kisise Kum Naheen* and *Zamaane Ko Dikhana Hai*, as a child. The whole imagery of the 'hero with a guitar' left a strong impression on Aditya. 'The sheer joy, songs, I just remember loving the songs. And the music spoke to me very, very strongly. It used to seem that the music of these two films was very different from the rest.' Consequently, when Aditya grew up and realized that he wanted to make Hindi films, he watched Husain's cinema as part of his 'conscious effort to go back and study the masters ... I think I pretty much saw everything – *Baharon Ke Sapne*, *Jab Pyar Kisise Hota Hai*.'

Raj and Simran's initial interaction in *DDLJ* owes itself to Husain's cinema, acknowledged Aditya. 'The boy–girl banter' is how Aditya termed it. 'One of my favourite all-time English films is *When Harry Met Sally* [1989]. I find a lot of *When Harry Met Sally* [to be] a derivative of Nasir Husain films. For me, a Nasir Husain film is a boy and girl on a journey. So when Raj and Simran meet, they are now in a Nasir Husain film. His films make me feel very young. It reminds me constantly that be young, stay young and stay musical.'

Aditya further elaborated on how Husain's music spoke to him and influenced his own sensibilities. 'There were two very strong

---

[2]*Aditya Chopra Relives Dilwale Dulhania Le Jayenge: As told to Nasreen Munni Kabir*, Yash Raj Films Pvt. Ltd 2014, p. 115.

influences musically. One was the Raj Kapoor–Shankar–Jaikishan combination and the other was the Nasir Husain–R.D. Burman combination. And whenever I sit to do music, subconsciously, I think my music is a sangam of these two. It's something I aspire towards.'

Husain's inspiration is visibly seen in *DDLJ*'s '*Ruk ja o dil deewaane*'. The zest, the mood of the song, the trumpets and the audience joining Raj by the end of the song are all classic Husain. Even Raj's series of false piano notes to begin the song appear to be a reference to Soni's off-key beginning in '*Daiyya yeh main kahaan aa phansi*'. Aditya confirmed this. 'The full song is Nasir Husain.' Aditya said that it was a 'very conscious' decision on his part to emulate Husain. '"*Ruk ja*" is very "*Bachna ae haseeno*" in tune. It was my Nasir Husain sequence.'

Karan Johar who termed Husain an 'underrated genius', too, has his Nasir Husain song. 'I come from the school of cinema that Husain belongs to. In my first film, *Kuch Kuch Hota Hai* (1998), the song "*Koi mil gaya*" was my ode to the memory of Nasir Husain. If you remember what Rani Mukerji wore, the colour in that song, the beats of that song. My entire briefing to Jatin–Lalit was that I wanted a Nasir Husain melody. Even the choreography. Farah is a big fan [of Husain] herself. My first film was a combination of the works of many film-makers that I have loved and adored – be it Yash Chopra, Nasir Husain or Raj Kapoor.'

Farah confessed to being a fan girl. 'I have watched all his movies, even the bad ones, *Zamaane Ko Dikhana Hai* and *Manzil Manzil*. There was a breeziness to his movies. There was something very modern about his technique, about his moviemaking. Even now when you see a *Hum Kisise Kum Naheen*, it looks fresher than some of the movies being made today. I don't find his movies judgemental or preachy. It is all very youthful. It is like you are in college again.' Farah singled out *Hum Kisise Kum Naheen*'s medley sequence for high praise. 'It's a very underrated song in Indian cinema. It was the first time ever somebody did that, made four small, small songs. I still try to recreate it every time. I tried it in *Happy New Year* [2014] also, on a bigger scale, but the germ always comes from there.'

Farah also conceded that the frenetic finish in Husain's songs is something that she looks to emulate. 'I think it's very interactive. I do a lot of that in my songs. There will always be a crescendo. By the end it should be like a rock concert where you force the audience to get up and participate.' When I asked Farah which of her films is closest to Husain's film universe, she replied, '*Main Hoon Na* [2004]. The freshness, the girl–boy equation, the college, the Darjeeling setting. I used a lot of his songs as background music.[3] The prom song, yes. *Main Hoon Na* was most Nasir Husain.'

Husain's legacy includes the music from his films, too. The songs from his early films be it *Tumsa Nahin Dekha* or *Phir Wohi Dil Laya Hoon* continue to be popular to this day. Any retrospective on Dev Anand or Joy Mukerji or Shammi Kapoor will reference the music from Husain's films. *Teesri Manzil*'s score is at an altogether different level. The long drumming prelude in '*O haseena*' has possibly inspired the beginning of *Hasee Toh Phasee*'s (2014) song '*Shake it like Shammi*'. '*Bachna ae haseeno*' was remixed and presented with Ranbir Kapoor in a film by the same title in 2008.

Karan, consequently, termed the music in Husain's films as being ahead of its time. 'It definitely was. A lot of the remix culture comes from the Nasir Husain–R.D. Burman combine.

---

[3]Watch Shah Rukh Khan's character burst into '*Chaand mera dil*' each time he sees the chemistry teacher Miss Chandni (Sushmita Sen) in the film. This is just one of the songs from *Hum Kisise Kum Naheen* referred to by Farah in *Main Hoon Na*.

The younger kids walking into the remix path understood the value of Nasir Husain and R.D. Burman's music. Understood that the beats were actually quite cool ... their music set the base for modernity. It already had that in its DNA whether you hear *"Yeh ladka, haaye Allah"* or you hear all the music of *Hum Kisise Kum Naheen*. His failure films also had strong music, because his sense of music was exemplary. When I am listening to Hindi film music, in my playlist of my top forty Hindi film songs, twenty will be Nasir sa'ab–R.D. Burman's. And in 2015 to still have that musical impact is nothing short of genius.'

A number of films from the recent past embody Husain's narratives. The boy and girl meeting on a train and falling in love while on a journey in films like *Yeh Jawaani Hai Deewani* (2013) and *Chennai Express* (2013) is a revival of Husain's signature trope. Going back to the 1980s, films like *Karz*, with its musician character and which forayed into the countryside, to underscore the romance between Tina Munim's and Rishi Kapoor's characters, appear to be a hat-tip to Husain. Mansoor, subsequently, posited that Husain's influence extends to 'the style of romance, the style of humour. It has been embedded in people's minds. Whenever I meet younger directors they tell me how much they are influenced by my father's films. I never bothered to analyse and see exactly in what way.'

The moot point to consider is if Husain's legacy extends in such a big way, why is he not given his due? Why is he not considered at par with film-makers like Raj Kapoor, Guru Dutt or Yash Chopra, who are regarded as greats? Or even with Manmohan Desai and Subhash Ghai, who are feted for their big-budget escapist cinema? As Sidharth Bhatia remarked with great consternation, 'Husain is not scoffed at, *he is not even looked at.*' This is quite disappointing because as Bhatia, Javed Akhtar or Asha Parekh repeatedly told me that in his time, a Husain film was given great importance by the trade, producers and distributors alike. The announcement of a Nasir Husain film was also looked upon with great excitement and anticipation by the movie-going audience.

There are several reasons for Husain's diminished status. Foremost among them, as Nuzhat stated, is 'because he is not seen as anything other than froth'. This is probably true because all the 'big' ideas in Husain's cinema – his secularism, his cosmopolitanism, his romance (unlike Yash Chopra's idea of romance) – were couched in fun. Husain stayed away from sermonizing and making intense declarations. Karan weighed in on Husain's place being relegated behind the likes of Mehboob Khan, Raj Kapoor and Bimal Roy because of this, saying, 'Anything that's lofty, heavy, making strong social statements or dealing with intense tragedy is always placed on a pedestal. It's always given much more love and respect. Fun, frolic, music, melody, good times are always considered frivolous. The party finishes and you are back to work. And back to work is serious.'

Javed Akhtar opined that a large part of Husain's insignificance stems from rigid definitions about art, literature and cinema in our society. 'I think we as a society are incapable, and have always been incapable, of creating a Charlie Chaplin. We have no serious respect for lighter literature, anything which has humour. We'll enjoy it, not that we have contempt for it, but it doesn't have that kind of gravitas for us. We can't remember it for a long time or give it status.' Akhtar cited the example of the British National Museum, which has a large hall, 'almost as big as a football ground', which features some of the greatest English literary writers and poets like William Shakespeare, William Blake, George Bernard Shaw and Alfred Tennyson. In the same hall, said Akhtar, 'they have "*Yesterday*" in Paul McCartney's handwriting. This shows the self-assurance of a nation that they are confident enough to give respect to Paul McCartney's "*Yesterday*", a popular song. And they have put it in the same hall as Shakespeare.' Akhtar wondered, 'if we have the courage to put an Anand Bakshi song like that'.

There is a larger point about Filmistan's film legacy here. Hindi cinema of the 1950s has only been looked at and written about for its nation-building and Nehruvian socialism agendas. Anything outside Mehboob Khan, Raj Kapoor, Guru Dutt or Bimal Roy has largely been sidelined. The films made by Filmistan, although big money spinners, didn't make any obvious attempts to address these themes. Consequently, there has been little attempt to document the creative energies and film narratives taking shape at the studio. Names like Bibhuti Mitra, Nandlal Jashwantlal, Subodh Mukerji or P.L. Santoshi were big in their time, but haven't been written about. The disdain for Husain's cinema is an offshoot of Filmistan's and its patron-in-chief S. Mukerji's forgotten legacy.

The same apathy extends to Hindi cinema of the 1960s, which is narrowly summarized as colour, couture and countryside, and nothing else. Film-makers such as Shakti Samanta, Raj Khosla and Pramod Chakravorty, too, who did some of their best work in this decade, have gone unrecognized. Husain's fate is no different.

Husain compounded matters by often only emphasizing the entertainment aspect of his cinema. Statements like, 'A film is born with a taqdeer of its own'[4] or reducing his own cinema to the formula of 'the chase [the boy winning over the girl] … good music and lot of humour',[5] belittled the effort he put into his craft. At the Zee Cine Awards, where he was honoured with the Lifetime Achievement Award, but by which time he had turned considerably reticent, he reflected upon a long, sparkling career with the rather terse, '*Picturein banaayee nahin jaateen, aap hi*

---

[4]Ambarish Mishra, 'I will always be a romantic at heart', *The Times of India*, 7 May 2000.

[5]Deepa Gahlot, 'It's the chase that is exciting', *Filmfare*, 1 November 1984, p. 75.

bann jaati hain.' He was also reluctant to talk to Nasreen Munni Kabir[6] about his film career, but was ultimately prevailed upon to do so by Aamir.

Karan sees Husain's modest attitude as a positive. 'He never came across as taking himself seriously. There is brilliance in that. When you are making a serious film, there is huge self-worth that is being projected. I don't think Nasir Husain did that. He moved from one film to another and I respect that ethos very strongly. Guru Dutt took himself more seriously. Nasir Husain didn't. He achieved and he moved on. He fumbled, he fell, he rose and he moved on. And that is something every film-maker should emulate because sometimes you get very caught up.'

Husain's admission of following a formula did him the maximum wrong. It allowed him to be dismissed as of little consequence by audiences and lazy film critics alike without either group examining his hold over his craft in any serious way. This needs to be put in proper perspective. Here, there are two aspects at play. Firstly, even if a film-maker, and there have been several great film-makers who repeated themselves in some way, incorporates elements from his earlier works, the only real way of critiquing a particular film is to see a consistency in the elements that make the film. A present-day film-maker whose films could be seen as 'formulaic' is Imtiaz Ali. His films are essentially about the journey that his protagonists set out on, their falling in love during the course of the journey and good music. [7]

Jai Arjun Singh, who has authored a book on Hrishikesh Mukherjee's cinema,[8] offered an incisive viewpoint here.

---

[6]This is about the 2001 interview, which has contributed most of Husain's quotes in this book.

[7]Although in Imtiaz's films, the journey is for far more existential purposes than romance.

[8]Jai Arjun Singh, *The World of Hrishikesh Mukherjee: The Filmmaker Everyone Loves*, Penguin/Viking, 2015.

'Formulaic is a pejorative word generally used to denote laziness. But say you set the word aside and instead think of someone, who uses a particular formula, and sticks to that formula over a period of time, now that should not be a pejorative at all. What you have then is the question of how good or how bad the execution is. Hrishikesh Mukherjee has done formula as well. Now very few people describe Hrishikesh Mukherjee as formulaic. His better work is more self-consciously serious and grounded. But with someone like Nasir Husain or Subhash Ghai, a more commercial sort of director – it becomes very easy to use the word formulaic for their work and to use it as a put-down. The better option might just be to say, these guys, in much of their best work, they used formulas, but it's for us to assess how well they did it and what they did with those formulas. The very definition of the auteur theory, and I am not saying that everyone has to respect it, is that great artists, maybe not all of them, but a majority of them, tend to rework things that are very important to them. They just sort of examine the same themes over and over again, play with them, approach them with different perspectives once in a while.'

There is a second side to the formula straightjacketing. While this is true of Husain's early films up to *Phir Wohi Dil Laya Hoon*, it certainly isn't the case if one were to view his films in reverse chronology. Skipping the three duds in between, at the broad story level *Qayamat Se Qayamat Tak* has very little in common with *Hum Kisise Kum Naheen*, which is very different from *Yaadon Ki Baaraat*, which is as different from *Caravan* as chalk from cheese. The banjara road film is a world apart from *Pyar Ka Mausam*, which, in turn, is far removed from *Baharon Ke Sapne*, which is distinct from *Teesri Manzil*, which has little in common with Husain's first four films. Seen this way, it is hard to categorize Husain as the formula man.

Aamir remarked tongue-in-cheek, 'Perhaps, also what happens in our industry, or in life, is that we like labels. So we label a person. I'm labelled a perfectionist. Now I maybe the most imperfect person, but I have been labelled a perfectionist. *Khatam ho gayee baat* (The matter rests). Now everyone uses that. So if he got a label of "Oh he has one story to sell", which was a joke he himself had cracked – *"ki main ek kahaani lekar aaya hoon aur main wohi banaata hoon,"* toh ab logon ne usko zyaada seriously le liya ... Phir woh label atak jaata hai unpe* ("That I have got one story and I will base everything on that," so people took him seriously ... Then that label stuck to him).'

To contextualize Husain as one of the important film-makers of mainstream Hindi cinema, one also needs to view his legacy as the sum of many parts. Besides the films that he directed, Husain had an important role to play in several seminal films like *Paying Guest*, *Teesri Manzil* and *Jo Jeeta Wohi Sikandar*. If we don't reflect on his contribution as a writer, it would be difficult to assess his legacy on a film like *Qayamat Se Qayamat Tak*. Cinema is also a collective enterprise. The lionizing of film personalities by their fans, be it Vijay Anand or R.D. Burman or Shammi Kapoor, does Husain's work a disservice. Likewise, to merely reduce *Yaadon Ki Baaraat* as a Salim–Javed film is to disregard Husain's individual stamp on the film.

Ultimately, the narrow, reductive view taken of the Hindi film song in recent times hurts Husain's legacy. In his essay, 'One Hundred Years of Bollytude', the writer and historian Mukul Kesavan quotes Salman Rushdie thus, 'Most Hindi movies were then and are now what can only be called trashy. The pleasure to be had from such films (and some of them are extremely enjoyable) is something like the fun of eating junk food. The classic Bombay talkie uses scripts of dreadful corniness, looks tawdry and garish, and relies on the mass appeal of its star performers and musical numbers to provide a little zing.'[9] While Kesavan mounts a passionate defence against this, Rushdie's views are symptomatic of the contempt with which a certain Anglophone audience receives song and dance in our cinema. And to be dismissive of song and dance is to ignore Husain.

A number of film-makers today, focusing on a certain element of 'realism', are also contemptuous of song and dance. As Aditya Chopra remarked, 'The new-age film-makers find that a hindrance rather than an asset ... Today's younger film-makers shy away from flamboyance.' The question that these film-makers, as Aditya believes, grapple with is, 'Will reality come in the way of celebrating songs?'

Karan Johar agreed, saying, 'We have lost the sparkle in our cinema. We are trying to be too clever now. We are trying to make too much sense. We don't break into song and dance as easily as we used to. The brain has superseded the heart. Logic has taken over abandon. And it's unfortunate because everything that we stood for in Bollywood films, in Hindi films, which was so abandon based ... breaking into songs, of course is completely free of any logic. But it was what came organically to film-makers then. It wasn't even questioned. Not by the intellectuals, nor the critics or the cynics. Today, you have the social media police on your head. You have the early morning critic who can lambast you. You have your own surrounding that will judge you. You are so aware. You've let go of having fun at the movies. You are apologetic about song today. Yet, we all love music and music is a big part of our commerce. But now we want to do non-lip sync songs. Because the characters are real, their syntax is so real, they suddenly can't start singing a song. So there is no scope for the Nasir Husain abandon anymore in our films unfortunately.'

---

[9]Mukul Kesavan, '"Bombay's Talkies", One Hundred Years of Bollytude', *Homeless on Google Earth*, Permanent Black, 2014, p. 53.

But Husain cannot be ignored. To do so is to overlook one of the high auteurs of Hindi cinema who championed the musical like few others before or after him. His work impacted several aspects of Hindi cinema across forty-five years, be it the spectacle he put together in his song sequences or the Western-style musician character that he introduced in *Dil Deke Dekho* or through his collaboration with R.D. Burman beginning with *Teesri Manzil* or in giving Aamir *Qayamat Se Qayamat Tak*. His cinema was naturally youthful. His romances were flirtatious but never indecent. He drew from a variety of cultural influences be it P.G. Wodehouse, Shafiq-ur-Rahman, Urdu poetry or the world of Western pop and rock-'n'-roll music, to present his own unique brand of cinema. Amidst all this, he also made a film like *Baharon Ke Sapne*, which made explicit his politics.

Javed Akhtar was lavish in his praise of Nasir Husain. 'There are so many people who we don't know about, but their work is invaluable to us. In the same way, it is a real tragedy that nobody knows who started this rom-com tradition; this tradition of light-hearted romantic comedy, beautiful songs, beautiful picturization, everything being presented with a certain aesthetic sense, which makes life pleasurable and beautiful, and which suggests that the world is not such a bad place to live, and which you call escapist cinema. These very strong hero images of Dev Anand or Shammi Kapoor, hardly anybody knows whose pen shaped their personas. The cinema which Nasir sa'ab made has crept slowly into several of today's films. Even today when films are made, some parts of them, unconsciously, originate from the same tradition that Nasir Husain started. But the people making these films seldom realize who the original master of this genre was, who started this tradition. This also happens in life, but it would be good if we remember what our great actors, film-makers and writers have given us. And Nasir Husain's contribution in mainstream commercial cinema is definitely very important.'[10]

To conclude, the biryani that Husain had referenced to defend himself against Randhir Kapoor's jocular remark comes to mind. It is in Hindustan that the biryani, entirely distinct from the Turkish and Arab versions of pulao, came into existence. Although consisting of largely the same broad ingredients – rice, all kinds of garam masala and meat – the biryani varies from region to region in our country depending on the finer nuances of its preparation. For instance, the Hyderabadi biryani is very different from the Lucknawi biryani which is distinct from the Bengali biryani which is entirely dissimilar to the biryani made by the Gujarati Bohri Muslim community, which has little in common with the Bhopal biryani. Yet, all of them taste fabulous and are a delight to the gastronomic senses.

Husain's cinema is a bit like the biryani. It may consist of the same broad elements, the same tropes and the same plotline. But in his execution, Husain gave audiences something new, delightful and appetizing every time. He was one of a kind. A cinematic master chef!

---

[10]Zee Classic's *Classic Legends: Season II*, featuring Nasir Husain.

EPILOGUE

Towards the end of my many conversations with Mansoor about his father's cinema, I asked him whether they didn't appreciate Husain's films enough during his lifetime. Mansoor replied, 'Yes, I feel so. Actually, I did not watch his films. I saw *Teesri Manzil* much later. Also, we used to criticize his films like hell, my sister and I. In the sense that, *arrey, phir woh coincidence ho gaya, phir woh usi ka baap nikla* (Oh yet another coincidence, he turned out to be his father), all that stuff.'

Husain would indulge them, accepting their criticism, saying, '*Ki haan*, correct, correct,' but also ask, '*Lekin mazaa aaya ki nahin* (But didn't you have fun)?'

FILMOGRAPHY

Anarkali (1953)
Story: Nasir Husain | Screenplay & Dialogues: Ramesh Saigal | Associate dialogue writer & dialogue director: Hamid Butt | Director: Nandlal Jashwantlal | Producer: Filmistan

Key Characters and Cast: Anarkali (Bina Rai), Saleem (Pradeep Kumar), Shahenshah Akbar (Mubarak), Raja Maan Singh (S.L. Puri), Gulnar (Kuldip Kaur), Rani Joda Bai (Sulochana)
    The film that got Husain noticed. Based on Imtiaz Ali Taj's play of 1922, *Anarkali* is the story of the doomed romance between Anarkali and Saleem.

Munimji (1955)
Story idea: Ranjan | Screenplay: Nasir Husain | Dialogues: Nasir Husain and Qamar Jalalabadi | Scenario and Direction: Subodh Mukerji | Producer: Filmistan

Key Characters and Cast: Amar/Munimji/Raj (Dev Anand), Roopa (Nalini Jaywant), Ratan/Kala Ghoda (Pran), Malti (Nirupa Roy)
    The first Dev Anand film which gave him a sophisticated, flamboyant makeover. Malti has a son, Ratan, out of a relationship with Ramlal. But Ramlal refuses to acknowledge Ratan since he is already married and has a son, Amar. But Ramlal dies. Malti then exchanges Ratan's place with Amar's. The two children grow up with Amar taking on the guise of a munim. He shows Ratan up for his deviant ways with his alter ego, Raj.

Paying Guest (1957)
Screenplay and dialogues: Nasir Husain | Story, scenario and direction: Subodh Mukerji | Producer: Filmistan

Key Characters and Cast: Ramesh (Dev Anand), Shanti (Nutan), Babu Digambernath (Gyani), Chanchal (Shubha Khote), Chanchal's husband Dayal (Gajanan Jagirdar), Prakash babu (Yakub)

A charming, delightful film that has Dev Anand playing an upbeat, urban character. Ramesh is a struggling lawyer. He has to frequently change his paying guest accommodations because of his errant behaviour. In one such accommodation, he meets Shanti. After a series of shenanigans, Ramesh manages to woo Shanti. But Shanti finds herself on the wrong side of the law because of her deviant brother-in-law, Prakash babu and her friend, Chanchal. Ramesh eventually saves Shanti from the gallows.

Tumsa Nahin Dekha (1957)

Director of Photography: Marshall Braganza | Editing: Babu Lavande | Art: H.R. Saple | Dances: Parvati Kumar, Sudarshan Dheer | Music: O.P. Nayyar | Lyrics: Majrooh Sultanpuri & Sahir Ludhianvi | Story, Screenplay, Dialogues & Directed by: Nasir Husain | Produced by: Filmistan

Key Characters and Cast: Shankar (Shammi Kapoor), Meena (Ameeta), Sohan (Pran), Vishnu (Raj Mehra), Sardar Rajpal/Gopal (B.M. Vyas), Seema (Sheila Vaz), Bhola (Kanu Roy), Johnny (Ram Avtar)

Husain's first film as director, which gave Shammi Kapoor's career a dramatic makeover. Shankar and Sohan both land up at Sardar Rajpal's estate presenting themselves as his long lost son. As Sardar Rajpal grapples with who among the two is stating the truth, Shankar and Meena fall in love after initially getting on each other's nerves. Eventually, Sardar Rajpal gets to know who his son is and the impostor is revealed.

Songs: *Jawaaniya yeh mast mast bin peeye* – Mohammed Rafi (Majrooh Sultanpuri); *Tumsa nahin dekha* – Mohammed Rafi (Sahir Ludhianvi); *Tumsa nahin dekha* – Asha Bhonsle (Sahir Ludhianvi); *Aaye hain door se* – Asha Bhonsle, Mohammed Rafi (Majrooh Sultanpuri); *Chhupnewaale saamne aa* – Mohammed Rafi (Majrooh Sultanpuri); *Dekho kasam se* – Asha Bhonsle, Mohammed Rafi (Majrooh Sultanpuri); *Sar par topi* – Asha Bhonsle, Mohammed Rafi (Majrooh Sultanpuri)

Dil Deke Dekho (1959)

Music: Usha Khanna | Lyrics: Majrooh Sultanpuri | Dances: Parbati Kumar, Morey, Sachin Shankar, Herman | Costumes Designed by: Bhanu Athaiya, Madam Pompadour, Satyavan | Art Direction: Shanti Das | Editing In Charge: J.S. Diwadkar | Editor: S.E. Chandiwale | Director of Photography: Dilip Gupta | Written & Directed by: Nasir Husain | Producer: S. Mukerji (Filmalaya)

Key Characters and Cast: Roop/Raja (Shammi Kapoor), Neeta (Asha Parekh), Harichand (Wasti), Jamuna Devi (Sulochana Latkar), Rana

Raghuvir (Surendra), Nagina (Indira Billi), Jagat Narayan (Raj Mehra), Sohan (Siddhu), Kailash (Rajendra Nath)

The film in which Husain introduced the Western-style musician character. Rana Raghuvir walks out on his wife Jamuna Devi with his son, Roop, because of Harichand's crafty ways. Years later, Roop (or Raja) comes to be in Jamuna Devi's employment but the two are not aware of their relationship. Raja is also in love with Neeta, but Jamuna Devi wants Neeta to marry the boy who is posing as her son, but is actually Harichand's son, Sohan. Things turn nasty before the truth is established.

Songs: *Dil deke dekho* – Mohammed Rafi; *Megha re bole* – Mohammed Rafi | *Bade hain dil ke kaaley* – Asha Bhonsle, Mohammed Rafi; *Do ekum do* – Mohammed Rafi, Asha Bhonsle; *Pyaar ho toh keh do yes, pyaar nahin toh keh do no* – Mohammed Rafi; *Raahi mil gaye raahon mein, baatein huyee nigaahon mein* – Mohammed Rafi; *Hum aur tum aur yeh samaa* – Mohammed Rafi; *Pyaar ki kasam hai* – Mohammed Rafi, Asha Bhonsle; *Dilruba meri Neeta* – Mohammed Rafi, Usha Khanna; *Yaar chulbula hai* – Mohammed Rafi, Asha Bhonsle

Jab Pyar Kisise Hota Hai (1961)

Art: S.S. Samel | Story Idea: Anis Khan | Editing: Babu Rao | Director of Photography: Dilip Gupta | Dances by: Gopi Kishan | Costumes: Bhanu Athaiya, Madam Pompadour, Bilquis Khan, Mrs. Parekh | Fights composition by: Shetty | Production Executive: Tahir Husain | Chief Production Secretary: Yash Johar | Lyrics: Hasrat Jaipuri, Shailendra | Music: Shankar–Jaikishan | Written, Produced & Directed by: Nasir Husain

Key Characters and Cast: Sunder/Monto (Dev Anand), Malti (Sulochana Latkar), Nisha (Asha Parekh), Sardar Roop Singh (Mubarak), Popat Lal (Rajendra Nath), Sohan (Pran), Khanna (Raj Mehra)

Husain's first home production. Sardar Roop Singh reneges on his late wife's promise of their daughter, Nisha, marrying her best friend Malti's son, Sunder. But Sunder gets to know Nisha and the two fall in love. However, Sardar Roop Singh wants Nisha to marry Sohan, his estate manager and friend's son. But Sohan has a past for which he is being blackmailed by Khanna. Sohan thinks his marriage to Nisha will solve his problems, but a determined Sunder ultimately triumphs over both Sohan and Khanna.

Songs: *Nazar mere dil ke paar huyee* – Lata Mangeshkar (Shailendra); *Tum jaise bigde babu se main ankhiyaan bachaaoon* – Lata Mangeshkar (Hasrat Jaipuri); *Yeh aankhein, uff yumma* – Mohammed Rafi, Lata Mangeshkar (Hasrat Jaipuri); *Jiya ho, jiya o jiya* – Mohammed Rafi (Hasrat

Jaipuri); *Sau saal pehle* – Mohammed Rafi, Lata Mangeshkar (Hasrat Jaipuri); *Seeto peeto reeto seeto reeto peeto re pa pa ja* – Lata Mangeshkar; *Teri zulfon se judaayee toh nahin maangee thee* – Mohammed Rafi (Hasrat Jaipuri); *Jiya ho, jiya o jiya* – Lata Mangeshkar (Hasrat Jaipuri); *Bin dekhe aur bin pehchaane* – Mohammed Rafi (Shailendra)

Phir Wohi Dil Laya Hoon (1963)

Art: S.S. Samel | Director of Photography: Marshall Braganza | Dances composed by: Gopi Krishna | Fights: Shetty | Production Executive: Tahir Husain | Lyrics: Majrooh Sultanpuri | Music: O.P. Nayyar | Written, Produced & Directed by: Nasir Husain

Key Characters and Cast: Mohan (Joy Mukerji), Mona (Asha Parekh), Colonel Mahendranath (Wasti), Jamuna (Veena), Difu (Rajendra Nath), Mr. Kapoor (Krishan Dhawan), Ramesh (Pran), Kamala (Ram Avtar), Mona's friend (Tabassum)

Husain's first colour production. Jamuna walks out on her husband, Colonel Mahendranath, after a tiff with him. She also has her son, Mohan, abducted from her husband's house and goes and lives in Kashmir. Years later, Mohan is reacquainted with his father, but Mahendranath does not know who Mohan is. Mona, who is raised by Mahendranath, falls in love with Mohan. But their romance is interrupted by the appearance of Ramesh, who is presented as Mahendranath's long-lost son.

Songs: *Dekho bijli dole bin baadal ke* – Asha Bhonsle, Usha Mangeshkar; *Laakhon hai nigaah mein* – Mohammed Rafi; *Aji qibla, mohatarma, kabhi shola* – Mohammed Rafi; *Aanchal mein saja lena kaliyaan, zulfon mein sitaarey bhar lena* – Mohammed Rafi; *Aankhon se jo utri hai dil mein* – Asha Bhonsle; *Banda parvar thaam lo jigar, bann ke pyaar phir aaya hoon* – Mohammed Rafi; *Humdum mere khel na jaano* – Mohammed Rafi, Asha Bhonsle; *Meri berukhi tumne dekhi hai lekin* – Asha Bhonsle; *Zulf ki chhaaon mein chehrey ka ujaala* – Asha Bhonsle, Mohammed Rafi

Teesri Manzil (1966)

Story, Screenplay & Dialogue: Nasir Husain | Edited by: Vijay Anand | Production Executive: Tahir Husain | Choreography: P.L. Raj, Aysha Khan, Harman | Fights: Shetty | Costume Designers: Mrs Parekh, Bhanu Athaiya, Leena Shah & Bilquis Khan | Art Direction: Shanti Das | Director of Photography: N.V. Srinivas | Operative Cameraman: Munir Khan | Lyrics: Majrooh Sultanpuri | Music: Rahul Dev Burman | Produced by: Nasir Husain | Directed by: Vijay Anand

Key Characters and Cast: Rocky/Anil Kumar Sona (Shammi Kapoor), Sunita (Asha Parekh), Ruby (Helen), Kunwar Mahinder Singh (Prem Nath), Ramesh (Prem Chopra), CID Inspector Das (Iftekhar), Rocky's friend (Salim Khan), Roopa (Sabina)

A meeting of minds between Vijay Anand and Nasir Husain. Sunita believes Rocky to be responsible for her sister, Roopa's death. She intends to teach him a lesson. Rocky, however, comes to know of Sunita's plans and pretends to be Anil Kumar Sona. The two fall in love with each other. It's only later that Sunita gets to know that Anil is Rocky. But unknown to both Sunita and Anil, Roopa's real murderer is someone close to them. This man will go to any lengths to keep his secret.

Songs: *O haseena zulfon waali jaan-e-jahaan* – Mohammed Rafi, Asha Bhonsle; *Aaja aaja main hoon pyaar tera* – Mohammed Rafi, Asha Bhonsle; *Deewaana mujhsa nahin* – Mohammed Rafi; *O mere sona re* – Mohammed Rafi, Asha Bhonsle; *Dekhiye sahibo* – Mohammed Rafi, Asha Bhonsle; *Tumne mujhe dekha* – Mohammed Rafi

Baharon Ke Sapne (1967)

Dialogues: Rajinder Singh Bedi | Director of Photography: Jal Mistry | Production Executive: Tahir Husain | Art Direction: Shanti Das | Editing: Baburao, Guru Dutt | Dances: Suresh, Aysha Khan | Lyrics: Majrooh Sultanpuri | Music: Rahul Dev Burman| Story, Screenplay, Produced & Directed by: Nasir Husain

Key Characters and Cast: Ram (Rajesh Khanna), Geeta (Asha Parekh), Das (Jairaj), Bhola Nath (Nana Palsikar), Ram's mother (Sulochana Latkar), Mr. Kapoor (Prem Nath)

The film with which Husain broke the mould. *Baharon Ke Sapne* is about an ordinary mill-worker Bhola Nath's dreams of having his BA educated son, Ram, landing a big job. But to Bhola Nath's disappointment, Ram struggles to find employment. Ram ultimately has to work in his father's mill as a daily wage labourer. Circumstances lead Ram into becoming the workers' leader. This is where *Baharon Ke Sapne* articulates a non-violent mode of struggle as against militant trade unionism.

Songs: *Aaja piya tohe pyaar doon* – Lata Mangeshkar; *Chunari sambhaal gori* – Lata Mangeshkar, Manna Dey; *Kya jaanu sajan hoti hai kya gham ki shaam* – Lata Mangeshkar; *Do pal jo teri aankhon se peene ko mile* – Asha Bhonsle, Usha Mangeshkar; *Zamaane ne maare jawaan kaise kaise* – Mohammed Rafi; *O more sajna, o more balma* – Lata Mangeshkar

Pyar Ka Mausam (1969)

Art: T.K. Desai | Editing: Babu Rao Lavande, Guru Dutt | Dances: Suresh | Fights: Shetty | Associate Producer: Tahir Husain | Cinematography: Munir Khan | Lyrics: Majrooh Sultanpuri | Music: Rahul Dev Burman | Written, Produced & Directed by: Nasir Husain

Key Characters and Cast: Sunder/Sunil (Shashi Kapoor), Seema (Asha Parekh), Sardar Ranjit Kumar (Wasti), Ramesh (Krishen Mehta), Hamid (Ram Avtar), Gopal (Bharat Bhushan), Jamuna (Nirupa Roy), Jhatpat Singh (Rajendra Nath), Shankar (Madan Puri), Jhatpat Singh's friend (R.D. Burman)

Sunder is separated from his parents, Gopal and Jamuna, as a child. He is raised as Sunil by a childless couple and grows up to romance Seema, who has been raised by Sardar Ranjit Kumar. But Sunil is Sardar Ranjit Kumar's long-lost grandson. Ranjit Kumar does not know this and instead takes Ramesh to be his grandson. But Jamuna, who had lost her senses at the time of the tragedy that separated her from her husband and son, recovers in time to correct all misunderstandings.

Songs: *Tum bin jaaoon kahaan* – Kishore Kumar (two versions); *Ni sultana re, pyaar ka mausam aaya* – Mohammed Rafi, Lata Mangeshkar; *Aap se miliye, pyaar thaa inko* – Lata Mangeshkar; *Aap chaahein mujhko* – Lata Mangeshkar; *Main na miloongi* – Lata Mangeshkar; *Tum bin jaaoon kahaan* – Mohammed Rafi (two versions); *Che khush nazaare* – Mohammed Rafi; *Na ja mere humdum* – Lata Mangeshkar

Caravan (1971)

Screenplay: Sachin Bhowmick | Dances: Suresh Bhatt | Art: Shanti Das | Fights Composer: Shetty | Editing: Babu Lavande, Guru Dutt | Cinematography: Munir Khan | Lyrics: Majrooh Sultanpuri | Music: R.D. Burman | Produced by: Tahir Husain | Written & Directed by: Nasir Husain

Key Characters and Cast: Sunita/Soni (Asha Parekh), Mohan (Jeetendra), Rajan (Krishen Mehta), Johnny (Ravinder Kapoor), Meetha Lal Tota (Madan Puri), Nisha (Aruna Irani), Monica (Helen), Mohandas (Murad), Karamchand (Shivraj)

The quintessential road film. Sunita runs away from her husband, Rajan, once she learns that it is he who killed her father. She changes into a village belle, Soni, and takes refuge with Mohan, who performs with a group of banjaras. Soni evades Rajan's henchmen through the film, until Mohan helps Soni and brings Rajan to book.

Songs: *Hum toh hain raahi dil ke* – Kishore Kumar; *Piya tu ab toh aa ja* – Asha Bhonsle; *Dilbar, dil se pyaare* – Lata Mangeshkar; *Chadhti jawaani meri chaal mastaani* – Lata Mangeshkar, Mohammed Rafi; *Arrey ho goriya kahaan tera des re* – Mohammed Rafi, Asha Bhonsle; *Daiyya yeh main kahaan aa phansi* – Asha Bhonsle; *Ab jo mile hain toh* – Asha Bhonsle; *Kitna pyaara waada* – Lata Mangeshkar, Mohammed Rafi

Yaadon Ki Baaraat (1973)

Story & Screenplay: Salim & Javed | Choreography: Suresh Bhatt | Art Direction: Shanti Das | Fights: Shetty | Editing: Babu Lavande, Guru Dutt | Cinematography: Munir Khan | Lyrics: Majrooh Sultanpuri | Music: R.D. Burman | Dialogues, Produced & Directed by: Nasir Husain

Key Characters and Cast: Shankar (Dharmendra), Vijay (Vijay Arora), Sunita (Zeenat Aman), Monto/Ratan (Tariq Khan), Shaakaal (Ajit), Gulzar artist (Nasir Khan), Seth Devidayal (Murad), Jack (Satyen Kappu), Roopesh (Imtiaz Khan), Verma ji (Shivraj), Monto's girlfriend (Neetu Singh)

Arguably, Husain's best film. Shankar, Vijay and Monto, three brothers, are separated in their childhood after Shaakaal murders their parents. They grow up to lead distinct lives. Ultimately, the song that they learnt from their mother reunites them and Shankar has his revenge against Shaakaal.

Songs: *Yaadon ki baaraat* – Lata Mangeshkar, Padmini Kolhapure, Shivangi; *Yaadon ki baaraat* – Kishore Kumar | *Aap ke kamrey mein koi rehta hai* – Kishore Kumar, Asha Bhonsle | *Dil mil gaye* – Kishore Kumar, Asha Bhonsle, R.D. Burman | *Dum maro dum* – Asha Bhonsle; *Chura liya hai tumne jo dil ko* – Asha Bhonsle, Mohammed Rafi; *O meri soni* – Kishore Kumar, Asha Bhonsle; *Lekar hum deewaana dil* – Kishore Kumar, Asha Bhonsle; *Yaadon ki baaraat* – Kishore Kumar, Mohammed Rafi

Hum Kisise Kum Naheen (1977)

Costumes: Bhanu Athaiya, Mani Rabadi, Bilquis Khan, Satywan | Story & Screenplay: Sachin Bhowmick | Choreography: Suresh Bhatt | Art: Shanti Das | Fights: Fazal Khan | Editing: Babu Lavande | Cinematography: Munir Khan | Lyrics: Majrooh Sultanpuri | Music: R.D. Burman | Dialogue, Produced & Directed by: Nasir Husain

Key Characters and Cast: Rajesh/Manjeet (Rishi Kapoor), Sanjay (Tariq Khan), Kaajal (Kaajal Kiran), Sunita (Zeenat Aman), Saudagar Singh (Amjad Khan), Kewalchand (Ajit), Ram Kumar (Om Shivpuri), Seth Kishori Lal (Kamal Kapoor)

Rajesh's father had handed over a belt of diamonds to a stranger while dying at Beirut airport. A man presents himself as Saudagar Singh to Rajesh and tells him that Kishori Lal has taken the diamonds from Rajesh's father. While Rajesh looks to get his diamonds back, Kishori Lal's daughter, Kaajal falls in love with Manjeet. But Manjeet is actually Sanjay, Kaajal's childhood sweetheart. By the time Kaajal gets to know of this, Rajesh, Sanjay and Kaajal find themselves entwined in the dangerous Saudagar Singh's plans.

Songs: *Bachna ae haseeno* – Kishore Kumar; *Yeh ladka haaye Allah* – Asha Bhonsle, Mohammed Rafi; *Chaand mera dil* – Mohammed Rafi | *Aa dil kya mehfil hai tere* – Kishore Kumar | *Tum kya jaano* – R.D. Burman | *Mil gaya humko saathi mil gaya* – Asha Bhonsle, Kishore Kumar; *Hai agar dushmann, dushmann* – Mohammed Rafi, Asha Bhonsle; *Humko toh yaara teri yaari* – Kishore Kumar, Asha Bhonsle; *Kya hua tera waada* – Sushma; *Kya hua tera waada* – Mohammed Rafi, Sushma

Zamaane Ko Dikhana Hai (1981)

Electronics & Light Effects: Mansoor Khan, Anil Pal, Arvind Rao, Nitin Borwankar | Art Director: Shanti Das | Fights: Surendra-Kasim | Dances: Suresh Bhatt | Editor: Zafar Sultan | Photography: Munir Khan | Story & Screenplay: Sachin Bhowmick | Lyrics: Majrooh Sultanpuri | Music: R.D. Burman| Dialogue, Produced and Directed by: Nasir Husain

Key Characters and Cast: Ravi (Rishi Kapoor), Kanchan (Padmini Kolhapure), Ramesh (Randhir Kapoor), Sharif mian (Amjad Khan), Shekhar (Kader Khan), Robin (Tariq Khan), Colonel Tipsee (Om Shivpuri), Mr. S.K. Nanda (Shriram Lagoo), Razia (Yogeeta Bali), Pappu (Master Ravi)
Ravi sets off for Darjeeling to look for his brother Ramesh and his wife. Unknown to Ravi, Ramesh and his wife have died, but their son, Pappu, is in the care of Ramesh's sister-in-law, Kanchan. Ravi meets Kanchan and woos her, but she resists his advances for the longest time. Shekhar is keen on usurping Nanda's wealth and property, since he is Nanda's stepbrother. When Ravi presents Kanchan and Pappu to his father, Shekhar is exposed.

Songs: *Main hoon woh albela* – Manna Dey, Asha Bhonsle | *Bolo bolo kuchh toh bolo* – Asha Bhonsle | *Poochho na yaar kya hua* – Mohammed Rafi; *Mohabbat kaise kartey hain, zamaane ko dikhaana hai* – Shailendra Singh, Asha Bhonsle; *Dil lena khel hai dildaar ka* – R.D. Burman; *Poochho na yaar kya hua* – Asha Bhonsle, Mohammed Rafi; *Hoga tumse pyaara kaun* – Shailendra Singh

Manzil Manzil (1984)

Assistant Director: Saleem Agha Rizvi (Chief AD), Shanawaz, Aamir Khan | Art: Shibu | Action: Azim Bhai | Dances: Suresh Bhatt | Editing: Zafar

Sultan | Director of Photography: Munir Khan | Story & Screenplay: Sachin Bhowmick | Associate Director: Mansoor Khan | Lyrics: Majrooh Sultanpuri | Music: R.D. Burman | Dialogue, Produced and Directed by: Nasir Husain

Key Characters and Cast: Sonu/Vijay (Sunny Deol), Seema (Dimple Kapadia), Malhotra (Kulbhushan Kharbanda), Meera (Asha Parekh), Gautam (Danny Denzongpa), Vijay/Roopesh (Feroze), Das (Prem Chopra)
Malhotra is searching for his friend Gautam, whose magnanimity many years ago helped Malhotra set up his business empire. He also wishes his daughter Seema to marry Gautam's son Vijay based on a promise made by him from that time. Das takes advantage and presents Roopesh as Vijay. Meanwhile, Seema meets the real Vijay in Shimla. Then unfold a series of circumstances that finally has Das exposed and Vijay and his mother reunite with Gautam.

Songs: *Jhalak dikha ke kar gayee deewaana* – Shailendra Singh; *Mitwa* – Asha Bhonsle; *Lut gaye hum toh raahon mein* – Asha Bhonsle, Shailendra Singh; *Oh meri jaan, ab nahin rehna tere bina* – Asha Bhonsle, Shailendra Singh; *Hey baba* – Asha Bhonsle; *Yeh naina yaad hai piya ke bhool gaye* – Asha Bhonsle; *Mann re pyaar Hari ke* – Chandrashekhar Gadgil; *Oh meri jaan ab nahin rehna tere bina* – Shailendra Singh

Zabardast (1985)
Assistant Director: Aamir Khan | Art: Sudhendu Roy | Fights: Azim Bhai, Ahmed Bhai | Dances: Suresh Bhatt | Editing: Dilip Kotalgi, Zafar Sultan | Cinematography: Munir Khan | Story & Screenplay: Sachin Bhowmick | Associate Director: Mansoor Khan | Lyrics: Majrooh Sultanpuri | Music: R.D. Burman | Produced by: Mushir–Riaz | Dialogue and Directed by: Nasir Husain

Key Characters and Cast: Sunder/Shyam (Sunny Deol), Ratan Kumar (Sanjeev Kumar), Ravi/Tony (Rajiv Kapoor), Anwar (Tariq Khan), Mala (Jaya Prada), Sunita (Rati Agnihotri), Balram Singh (Amrish Puri), Maharani Maanwati (Tanuja), Bikram (Feroze), Dr Saigal (Kulbhushan Kharbanda)
The last film directed by Husain. Ratan Kumar's life is thrown in disarray because of Balram Singh. He is a man on the run. Circumstances separate Ratan from his wife and two sons. His eldest son grows up to be Shyam, who because of a misunderstanding wants to kill Ratan Kumar. But Ratan Kumar and Shyam get acquainted with each other in later life. Eventually all misunderstanding are resolved and Ratan reunites with his wife and his two sons, including the younger one, Ravi.

Songs: *Dekho idhar janaab-e-mann* – Kishore Kumar; *Karega zamaana kya* – Kishore Kumar, Asha Bhonsle; *Jab chaaha yaara tumne* – Kishore Kumar; *Bhool ho gayee jaane de sajna* – Kishore Kumar, Asha Bhonsle; *Aise na thukrao* – Asha Bhonsle; *Suno sitamgar mere* – Asha Bhonsle, R.D. Burman

Qayamat Se Qayamat Tak (1988)

Story, Screenplay & Dialogue: Nasir Husain, Assisted by: Nuzhat Khan, Aamir Khan | Lyrics: Majrooh Sultanpuri | Music: Anand–Milind | Directed by: Mansoor Khan | Produced by: Nasir Husain

Key Characters and Cast: Raj (Aamir Khan), Rashmi (Juhi Chawla), Randhir Singh (Goga Kapoor), Dhanraj Singh (Dalip Tahil), Jaswant Singh (Alok Nath), Shyam (Raj Zutshi), Ratan Singh (Feroze)

The film that had a distinct freshness to it amidst the violent, garish films of the 1980s. In this Romeo and Juliet version, Raj and Rashmi fall in love with each other despite the history of enmity between their families.

Jo Jeeta Wohi Sikandar (1992)

Dialogues: Nasir Husain | Lyrics: Majrooh Sultanpuri | Music: Jatin–Lalit | Story, Screenplay & Directed by: Mansoor Khan | Produced by: Nasir Husain

Key Characters and Cast: Sanjay Lal Sharma (Aamir Khan), Anjali (Ayesha Jhulka), Ratan (Mamik), Ramlal (Kulbhushan Kharbanda), Shekhar Malhotra (Deepak Tijori), Devika (Pooja Bedi), Ghanshu (Deven Bhojani), Maqsood Ghoda (Aditya Lakhia)

The last film Husain produced. *Jo Jeeta Wohi Sikandar* is the story of the annual inter-college cycle race between the various schools and colleges in Dehradun. Sanjay Lal Sharma, who is Ratan's younger brother, has never shown any seriousness in life. But when Ratan gets badly hurt as a result of his enmity with Shekhar Malhotra, Sanjay has a makeover.

Other films Husain Was Associated With

Shabnam (1949)

Story: Helen Devi | Screenplay: B. Mitra | Lyrics & Dialogues: Qamar Jalalabadi, Associate: Nasir Husain | Director: Bibhuti Mitra | Producer: Filmistan

Shart (1954)

Written by: I.S. Johar, Nasir Husain & Qamar Jalalabadi | Director: B. Mitra | Producer: Filmistan

Love Marriage (1959)
Story & Screenplay: Subodh Mukerji | Dialogues: Nasir Husain | Produced
& Directed by: Subodh Mukerji

Akele Hum Akele Tum (1995)
Dialogue: Nasir Husain | Producer: Ratan Jain | Writer & Director:
Mansoor Khan

Notes

1. *Chandni Raat* (1949) was Nasir Husain's first uncredited film where he
   worked as a dialogue writer. It was directed by M. Ehsan.

2. *Shabistan* (1951) was directed by Bibhuti Mitra and produced by
   Filmistan. Although a copy of the film is unavailable, it is certain that
   Husain worked as an associate writer with Qamar Jalalabadi on this film.

INDEX

SELECT BIBLIOGRAPHY

Books

Aditya Chopra relives Dilwale Dulhania Le Jayenge: As told to Nasreen Munni Kabir, Yash Raj Films Pvt. Ltd, 2014

Anirudha Bhattacharjee and Balaji Vittal, *R.D. Burman: The Man, The Music*, HarperCollins *Publishers* India, 2011

Anirudha Bhattacharjee and Balaji Vittal, *Gaata Rahe Mera Dil: 50 Classic Hindi Film Songs*, HarperCollins *Publishers* India, 2015

Anil Zankar, *Mughal-E-Azam: Legend as Epic*, HarperCollins *Publishers* India, 2013

Bhaichand Patel (edited by), *Bollywood's Top 20 Superstars of Indian Cinema*, Penguin Books India, 2012

Bunny Reuben, *…and Pran: A Biography*, HarperCollins *Publishers* India, 2005

Deepa Gahlot, *Shammi Kapoor: The Legends of Indian Cinema*, Series Editor: Shefali Vasudev, Wisdom Tree, 2008

Dilip Kumar, *The Substance and The Shadow: An Autobiography*, as narrated to Udayatara Nayar, Hay House Publishers (India) Pvt. Ltd, 2014

Dinesh Raheja and Jitendara Kothari, *The Hundred Luminaries of Hindi Cinema*, India Book House Publishers, 1996

Diptakirti Chaudhuri, *Written By Salim–Javed: The Story of Hindi Cinema's Greatest Screenwriters*, Penguin Books India, 2015

Ganesh Anantharaman, *Bollywood Melodies: A History of the Hindi Film Song*, Penguin Books India, 2008

Gautam Chintamani, *Dark Star: The Loneliness of Being Rajesh Khanna*, HarperCollins *Publishers* India, 2014

Har Mandir Singh Hamraaz, *Hindi Film Geet Kosh*, Volumes 2, 3 & 4

Jai Arjun Singh, *The World of Hrishikesh Mukherjee: The Filmmaker Everyone Loves*, Viking / Penguin Books India, 2015

Jai Arjun Singh (edited by), *The Popcorn Essayists: What Movies Do to Writers*, Tranquebar, 2011

Jerry Pinto, *Helen: The Life and Times of an H-Bomb*, Penguin Books India, 2006

M.K. Raghavendra, *Seduced by the Familiar: Narration and Meaning in Indian Popular Cinema*, Oxford University Press, 2008

Mukul Kesavan, *Homeless on Google Earth*, Permanent Black, 2014

Rauf Ahmed, *Shammi Kapoor: The Game Changer*, Om Books International, 2016

Sanjit Narwekar, *Eena Meena Deeka: The Story of Hindi Film Comedy*, Rupa & Co., 2005

Sidharth Bhatia, *Amar Akbar Anthony: Masala, Madness and Manmohan Desai*, HarperCollins *Publishers* India, 2013

Magazines/Newspapers

Filmfare, 'Behind the screen: Producer-director Nasir Husain', 01 May 1964 (Author not mentioned)

Filmfare, Deepa Gahlot, 'It's the Chase That Is Exciting', 01-15 November 1984

Filmfare, Nasir Husain, 'My First Take', 6 December 1968

Filmfare, Nasir Husain, 'What the People Want', 04 August 1967

Filmfare, Nasir Husain, 'Thanking my Stars', 25 November 1966

Filmfare, Reviews, '*Baharon Ke Sapne*', 04 August 1967

Filmfare, Reviews, '*Munimji*', 16 September 1955

Filmfare, Reviews, '*Tumsa Nahin Dekha*', 31 January 1958

Hindustan Times, Imran Khan, 'To Shammi Uncle, with love', 15 August 2011

Poona Herald, Hanif Shakoor, 'The Dilemma of a Commercial Film Maker', 04 February 1977

The Times of India, Ambarish Mishra, 'I Will Always Be a Romantic at Heart', 07 May 2000

Super, Resham Shaam, 'Little Big Man', May 1978

Screen, Rajiv Vijayakar, 'Adieu Nasir Husain', 22 March 2002

Screen, Roshmila Bhattacharya, 'Murder and Melody', 12 April 2002

Star & Style, Harish Kumar Mehra, 'The Story of Movie Moghul S. Mukerji', 28 June 1968

Star & Style, Rajinder Singh Bedi, 'Nasir Husain and I', 1 August 1967

Star & Style, Sushama, 'Has the hit-maker lost his touch?', 16 September 1983

Star & Style, Tahir Husain, 'My Brother Nasir', 01 October 1971

The Indian Quarterly, Nasreen Munni Kabir, 'The Goldie Standard', Volume 4, Issue 1, October–December, 2015

'Nasir Husain's Fake Workers', A review of *Baharon Ke Sapne* sourced from the National Film Archive of India

Blogs
Dusted Off (madhulikaliddle.com) by Madhulika Liddle
Jabberwock (jaiarjun.blogspot.in) by Jai Arjun Singh
Conversations Over Chai (anuradhawarrier.blogspot.in) by Anuradha
Warrier

Other Sources
Rediff.com, Sukanya Verma, '*Teesri Manzil*: Style, Substance, Suspense and
Shammi!', 11 April 2013 (http://www.rediff.com/movies/report/slide-
show-1-teesri-manzil-style-substance-suspense-and-shammi/
20130411.htm)
Alain Désoulières, 'Historical Fiction and Style: The Case of *Anarkali*'
(http://www.urdustudies.com/pdf/22/08DesoulieresAnarkali.pdf)
Brian Shoesmith, 'From Monopoly to Commodity: The Bombay Studio
in the 1930s', (http://wwwmcc.murdoch.edu.au/ReadingRoom/hfilm/
BOMBAY.html)
Dr Rashmi Doraiswamy, '"These Days" of Our Modernity: The Cinema of
Nasir Husain', Film and Television Institute of India in Pune, 4
September 2004
Martin Scorsese, The Musical – A Personal Journey Through American
Movies (1995) –(https://www.youtube.com/watch?v=N028ZvX8bdM)
Zee Classic's *Classic Legends: Season II*, featuring Nasir Husain

ACKNOWLEDGEMENTS

I would like to sincerely thank the following people for giving me their time through interviews: Aditya Chopra, Anees Bano, Anil Zankar, Asha Parekh, Ashim Samanta, Bhanu Gupta, Deb Mukerji, Farah Khan, Faroukh Mistry, Gauhar Raza, Homi Mullan, Jai Arjun Singh, Javed Akhtar, Jeetendra, Karan Johar, Kersi Lord, Lekh Tandon, M.K. Raghavendra, Neelam Mukerji, Rauf Ahmed, Raza Mir, Rishi Kapoor, Salim Khan, Sanjit Narwekar, Shamir Khan, Subhash Mukerji, Sulochana Latkar, Tabassum, Tariq Khan, Zafar Sultan and Zeenat Aman.

I would also like to thank the following people, who helped me in various ways with the research for this book: Ameet Mallapur, Ashish Singh, Balaji Vittal, Devdutt Pattanaik, Gautam Chintamani, Namit Sharma, K. Vijayakrishnan, Mahesh Ambekar, Manohar Iyer, Naresh Fernandes, Pavan Jha, Rajesh Nagul, Rudradeep Bhattacharjee, Saif Mahmood, Sayyed Mumtaz, Sidharth Bhatia, Sumant Batra, Trinetra Bajpai and the good people at the National Film Archive of India.

I would like to acknowledge my friends Aabhas Sharma and Arvind Sivakumaran for indulging me and serving as perfect sounding boards for my views on Husain's cinema and yesteryear Hindi films. I would like to thank two of my closest friends Aniruddh Kaushal and Rehana Munir, both of who made their own significant contributions in helping me realize this book.

I would also like to thank the many people at HarperCollins *Publishers* India involved with the designing and marketing of this book.

I extend my sincere gratitude to the following people without whose help and inputs this book would never have been possible:

My friend (and guardian angel) Kausar Munir, who introduced me to Nasir Husain's family and provided encouragement at various points. To the Warriers – Anuradha and Sadanand – who live many, many miles away in the United States but were always an email away from answering my queries be it about Husain's films or the music in them. To Madhulika Liddle, who helped me in so many ways – from serving as a guiding light with her knowledge and understanding of Hindi films of the 1950s through to the 1970s, to introducing me to the Warriers, to helping me understand the finer nuances of transliteration and so much more. To Nasreen Munni Kabir, for allowing me access to her interview with Husain, for giving her own views on Husain's films, for offering all kinds of ideas, suggestions, encouragement and opening many doors without which I would have been searching in the dark. To Kaushik Bhaumik and Rashmi Doraiswamy, who with their terrific academic insights, helped me properly contextualize the importance of Husain's films. Meeting the two of them in Delhi in October 2014 was one of the biggest turning points in my research effort. To Jerry Pinto, for taking a keen interest in my work, for his sharp insights, for reading one of the later drafts of this book, and offering crucial suggestions to improve it, but above all for his help with a lot of the translations. To Shantanu Ray Chaudhuri, who edited this book and made it so much better, but who also calmed my nerves and offered emotional support. To Nuzhat Khan, Mansoor Khan and Aamir Khan, who readily accommodated my several meeting requests, always replied to my whatsapp messages and emails and were very magnanimous with their time, hospitality and patience. It was truly a humbling experience interacting with each one of you. To Vidya, my best friend, my fiercest critic, my *shareek-e-hayaat*, who sacrifices so many of her own dreams so that I may realize my own. I can never thank her enough for what she does for me and our family.

Writing a book offers many different experiences, but none more enriching than the various friendships and like-minded acquaintances you develop along the way. I feel truly privileged and special in having the support and good-wishes of several such people. I offer my gratitude to each one of them.

Ingram Content Group UK Ltd.
Milton Keynes UK
UKHW040846190623
423681UK00004B/296

9 789352 640966